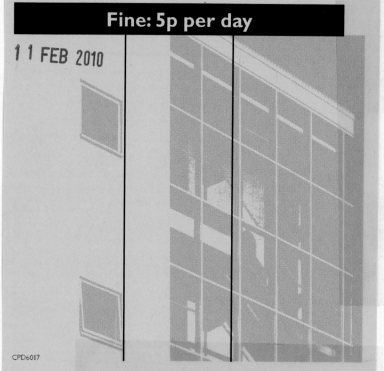

University in Montreal, Quebec. He is the founding editor of *Topia.*
A Canadian Journal of Cultural Studies. Dr Straw is co-investigator in
a Social Sciences and Humanities Research Council of Canada Major
Collaborative Research Project on 'Cultures of the City'.

JOHN STREET is Reader in Politics in the School of Economic and
Social Studies, University of East Anglia. He is the author of *Rebel
Rock: The Politics of Popular Music* (1986), *Politics and Technology*
(1992), and *Politics and Popular Culture* (1997), and co-author of
Deciding Factors in British Politics (1992).

Cambridge Companions to Music

Instruments

The Cambridge Companion to Brass Instruments
Edited by Trevor Herbert and John Wallace

The Cambridge Companion to the Cello
Edited by Robin Stowell

The Cambridge Companion to the Clarinet
Edited by Colin Lawson

The Cambridge Companion to the Organ
Edited by Nicholas Thistlethwaite and Geoffrey Webber

The Cambridge Companion to the Piano
Edited by David Rowland

The Cambridge Companion to the Recorder
Edited by John Mansfield Thomson

The Cambridge Companion to the Saxophone
Edited by Richard Ingham

The Cambridge Companion to the Violin
Edited by Robin Stowell

Composers

The Cambridge Companion to Bach
Edited by John Butt

The Cambridge Companion to Bartók
Edited by Amanda Bayley

The Cambridge Companion to Beethoven
Edited by Glenn Stanley

The Cambridge Companion to Berg
Edited by Anthony Pople

The Cambridge Companion to Berlioz
Edited by Peter Bloom

The Cambridge Companion to Brahms
Edited by Michael Musgrave

The Cambridge Companion to Benjamin Britten
Edited by Mervyn Cooke

The Cambridge Companion to Chopin
Edited by Jim Samson

The Cambridge Companion to Handel
Edited by Donald Burrows

The Cambridge Companion to Ravel
Edited by Deborah Mawer

The Cambridge Companion to Schubert
Edited by Christopher Gibbs

Topics

The Cambridge Companion to Pop and Rock
Edited by Simon Frith, Will Straw and John Street

The Cambridge Companion to

POP AND ROCK

....

EDITED BY
Simon Frith
Will Straw and
John Street

CAMBRIDGE
UNIVERSITY PRESS

PUBLISHED BY THE PRESS SYNDICATE OF THE UNIVERSITY OF CAMBRIDGE
The Pitt Building, Trumpington Street, Cambridge, United Kingdom

CAMBRIDGE UNIVERSITY PRESS
The Edinburgh Building, Cambridge CB2 2RU, UK
40 West 20th Street, New York, NY 10011-4211, USA
477 Williamstown Road, port Melbourne, VIC 207, Australia
Ruiz de Alarcón 13, 28014 Madrid, Spain
Dock House, The Waterfront, Cape Town 8001, South Africa

http://www.cambridge.org

First published 2001
Reprinted 2004

Printed in the United Kingdom at the University Press, Cambridge

Typeface Minion 10.75/14 pt   *System* QuarkXPress™   [SE]

A catalogue record for this book is available from the British Library

Library of Congress Cataloguing in Publication data

Cambridge companion to pop and rock / edited by Simon Frith, Will Straw, and John Street.
    p.   cm. – (Cambridge companions to music)
Includes bibliographical references and index.
ISBN 0 521 55369 5 (hardback) – ISBN 0 521 55660 0 (paperback)
1. Popular music – History and criticism.   2. Rock music – History and criticism.   I. Frith,
Simon.   II. Straw, Will, 1954– .   III. Street, John, 1952– .   IV. Series.
ML3470.C36   2001   781.64–dc21   00–068908

ISBN 0 521 55369 5 hardback
ISBN 0 521 55660 0 paperback

Contents

Notes on contributors

Sara Cohen gained a DPhil in Social Anthropology from Oxford University in 1987, and is currently lecturing at Liverpool University's Institute of Popular Music. She is the author of *Rock Culture in Liverpool: Popular Music in the Making*, and she has published numerous articles based on ethnographic research into popular music. Her most recent work has focused on popular music, place and local identity. She is a member of the editorial group of the journal *Popular Music*.

Jan Fairley has a BA in Comparative Literature, an MPhil (Oxford) in Latin American Studies and a PhD in Ethnomusicology (Edinburgh). She works as a freelance journalist and broadcaster specialising in world music, regularly interviewing musicians and reviewing music. She pioneered world music on BBC Radio Scotland, compiling and presenting a weekly one-hour pro-gramme, *Earthbeat*, for four years in the 1990s. She is a Fellow of the Institute of Popular Music at Liverpool University. Her current research is on singer–songwriters in Latin America and Spain, and Cuban music.

Simon Frith is Professor of Film and Media at Stirling University, Scotland. He has been a rock critic for publications ranging from *Creem* and the *Village Voice* to *The Sunday Times* and the *Scotsman*. His last book was *Performing Rites: On the Value of Popular Music*, and he chairs the judges of the Mercury Music Prize.

Jocelyne Guilbault, Professor of Ethnomusicology at the Music Department of the University of California at Berkeley, specialises in Caribbean studies. Since 1980, Guilbault has done extensive fieldwork in the Creole-speaking islands and the English Caribbean on both traditional and popular music. Her most recent publications include *Zouk: World Music in the West Indies*. She is currently working on two book projects, one on musical bonds, boun-daries and borders in the Caribbean experience both in the islands and abroad (*Traditions and Challenges of a World Music: The Music Industry of Calypso*) and the other on a selected number of superstars of the English Caribbean (*Superstars of the English Caribbean: The Politics of Difference in World Music*).

Keir Keightley did his MA at McGill University, and his PhD at Concordia University, Montreal. He was a SSHRC Post-Doctoral Research Fellow at the John Logie Baird Centre, Glasgow, and is currently an Assistant Professor in the Faculty of Information and Media Studies at the University of Western Ontario in London, Ontario. His book, *Sinatra's Capitol: Celebrity, Masculinity, and Taste, 1953–62*, will be published by Duke University Press.

Richard Middleton is Professor of Music at the University of Newcastle-upon-Tyne. Previously he taught for twenty-five years at the Open University. He is the author of *Pop Music and the Blues*, *Studying Popular Music*, *Reading Pop* and numerous articles on popular music topics. He is also a founding editor of the journal *Popular Music*.

Russell A. Potter is Associate Professor of English at Rhode Island College. He is the author of *Spectacular Vernaculars: Hip-Hop and the Politics of Postmodernism*, and a contributor to several books on popular music and culture, including *Unspun: Key Concepts for Understanding the World Wide Web*; *Key Terms in Popular Music and Culture*; and *Mapping the Beat: Popular Music and Contemporary Theory*.

Barry Shank teaches American studies and cultural studies in the Division of Comparative Studies at the Ohio State University. His first book, *Dissonant Identities: The Rock'n'Roll Scene in Austin, Texas*, was published by Wesleyan University Press. He has published essays on the performance of identity in popular music, the role of theory in historical investigation, the history of American studies, and the convergence of art and commerce in Christmas cards. He is currently working on a book-length study of the intersection of class and love in American greetings cards.

Will Straw teaches communications and cultural studies within the Department of Art History and Communications Studies at McGill University in Montreal, Canada. From 1984–93, he taught Film Studies at Carleton University in Ottawa, Canada. He is the author of numerous articles on music, film and popular culture, and a co-editor of *Theory Rules: Art as Theory, Theory and Art*. He is a former president of the Canadian Communications Association, and on the editorial boards of *Screen*, *Cultural Studies* and many other journals.

John Street is a Reader in Politics at the University of East Anglia, where he also convenes the MA in Cultural Politics. He is the author of *Rebel Rock: The Politics of Popular Music* and *Politics and Popular Culture*. He is a member of the editorial group of the journal *Popular Music* and is an occasional reviewer of pop and rock for *The Times*.

Paul Théberge is Associate Professor in the Faculty of Information and Media Studies at the University of Western Ontario, where he teaches courses in Popular Music, Music and Globalisation, and Sound in Film. As a composer, he has created sound works for various media, including radio and film, and has received awards from the Canada Council and, in the USA, from the National Endowment for the Arts. He has published articles on music, technology and culture, and is author of *Any Sound You Can Imagine: Making Music/Consuming Technology*, recipient of the 1998 Book Award from the International Association for the Study of Popular Music (US Branch).

Acknowledgements

We would like to thank Penny Souster and her colleagues at Cambridge University Press for steering this book through its long gestation period; Susan Beer for her assiduous copy-editing; and Stella Hart for helping to produce the final manuscript.

Introduction and chronology of pop and rock

The chronology of pop and rock which appears at the end of this introduction (see pages xi–xvii) might, at first glance, seem to detail the banal and the trivial, to mark out mundane moments in a period which saw two world wars, the assassination of presidents and civil rights leaders, coups and famines, the dropping of the atomic bomb and the discovery of the structure of DNA. In such a history, what place is there even for a few sad deaths (Brian Jones, Janis Joplin, Jimi Hendrix, Ian Curtis and Kurt Cobain), let alone Gerry and the Pacemakers' 'How Do You Do It?' or Hanson's 'MMMBop'? And yet, of course, those deaths and those songs do matter. They are part of an industry that in 1999 had a worldwide turnover of $38 billion. The United States industry alone was worth $15 billion. Across the globe some 3.8 billion CDs, cassettes and minidiscs were sold. But these figures do not just describe a major industry, a source of revenue and of trade links, they also describe a source of meaning and pleasure. The songs and sounds being manufactured and bought have become part of the memories of people who use them to mark the passage of time; they have become the object of censors who fear for their effects and of propagandists who want to exploit those effects; they have helped to constitute national and ethnic and sexual identities; and they have been used to raise money and awareness of poverty and starvation, of oppression and environmental degradation. This book is about how this has happened (and about the arguments about how it happened). It traces the history of the musical forms that compose pop and rock; it looks at the industries, technologies and performers that gave them their particular character. It explores the ways in which musical pleasure was organised and enjoyed, and looks at the ways these pleasures linked to identities and locations across the world. And most importantly, this book documents the arguments and disputes that animate discussion of popular music: about the power of the industry that produces it, about the figures who have shaped it, about how and when it gives pleasure.

There was a time when pop and rock had no literature of its own, or what it had was neglected and patronised. These days the shelves are well stocked – with biographies and autobiographies, not just of rock stars, but even of rock journalists too. There is also a burgeoning academic market, serving the increasing number of university courses on popular music. And most recently, there have been the rock and pop guides, the most extensive collection of which are the *Rough Guides* – to world music, to dance and techno, to rock and classical. From the people who gave you the *Rough Guide to Spain* and *Mexico* come books that point out the best sites for flamenco and salsa, for ambient house and garage. These guides exist as authoritative maps for the novice traveller, giving crucial tips on bargains and must-sees. This book is not a guide; it is a companion.

A companion is different. Where guides lead, companions accompany; where guides dictate, companions argue and share. This companion does not pretend to offer definitive accounts of the musical forms which it covers, rather it is presenting novel and provocative interpretations of those histories. It recognises that there is no settled history, no definitive canon. The contributors, all experts in their various fields, were briefed to survey their area and to review the ideas and arguments that mark the territory. They were not, however, asked to write dry, formal, cautious histories and surveys. They were asked to provoke, to raise questions about conventional wisdom and settled myths. Each chapter is meant to stimulate discussion, to feed back into the everyday arguments and responses which pop and rock themselves elicit.

The book is broken into three major sections. The first provides the context. Pop and rock were not the simple result of a youthful creative flowering. They were the result of shifts in demography, patterns of cultural production and developments in technology. The first three chapters, therefore, trace the emergence of the recording industry and the practices associated with it.

The words 'pop' and 'rock' do not refer to well-established traditions with clearly demarcated boundaries. From the beginning, there were strands and genres, each with their own histories and conditions of production. The second part of the book reflects upon some of those divergent forms. In particular, chapters are devoted to pop and rock, to rap and dance. These are, of course, not discrete forms, and each incorporates elements of the other. What is important, though, is to note the different ways in which musical forms are created and enjoyed, the way their histories coincide and diverge.

The final section reflects the issues and arguments that mark current concern about popular music – the political, academic and theoretical (and there is no neat distinction to be drawn here either) debates that run through understandings of popular music. It begins with a topic that links all those in the book: the way we make sense of music, whether we understand it musicologically or sociologically, as sounds or social experience. Overlaying this fundamental question, and the way it is answered through the institutionalisation of academic knowledge, are the ways in which society's forms and interests are inscribed in music. This includes music's intimate connection with sexual and ethnic identity, with racism and sexism, and with state and oppositional politics, and with the effects of globalisation.

Interleaved with these chapters are a series of profiles of pop stars. As with the rest of the companion, these do not pretend to be entries in a pop encyclopaedia. They too give a perspective on the figures who have contributed most to pop and rock. Those profiled are not necessarily the artists who have sold most records or survived longest, nor necessarily those who appear in those numerous lists of the one hundred greatest or whatever. They have been selected because of the stories they tell about the history and character of pop and rock. So Jimi Hendrix's career, for example, represents the links with jazz, just as Elvis Presley's represents those with country music. They have been chosen for their centrality, too, within musical genres – James Brown and funk, Abba and Eurodisco, Public Enemy and rap, Derrick May and techno; and for the part they played in introducing new ideas and practices: David Bowie and art, Bob Dylan and bohemia, Madonna and video. Again, they may not have been the first or the most commercially successful, but they form key figures in popular music's serpentine history.

The sections of this companion do not divide neatly between the historical and factual and the polemical and the argumentative, between those chapters that provide data and those that take sides. They all do both. Drawing on recent research into the past and present of popular music, they offer novel perspectives on an apparently familiar landscape. Throughout the companion particular themes appear and reappear: the way in which ideas of 'race' and the practice of racism are part of the music industry's organisation and the musical forms; the way changing technologies alter what is made and heard; and how the 'globalisation' of popular music's political economy is a core component of how it is experienced and used.

Accompanying and linked to these themes is also a sense of the music's power to move and to shock, to cause delight and despair. This companion aims both to reflect on these features of pop and rock, and to deepen our understanding of them: to help explain why the seemingly trite moments in the brief chronology that follows matter so much.

A brief chronology of pop and rock

1877   Thomas Edison demonstrates the first phonograph
1889   Louis Glass of Pacific Phonograph Company creates the first version of the juke box
1896   Emile Berliner patents the flat recording disc

1909 US Copyright Act is amended to establish the basis for royalty payments for recorded music, and not just live performance

1914 American Society of Composers, Authors and Publishers (ASCAP) is formed to enable songwriters to claim the income due under the amended Copyright Act

1920 The first news-and-music US radio station, Westinghouse's KDKA, begins broadcasting

1926 BBC is created as a public corporation; its Music Department is set up the following year

1939 Broadcast Music Incorporated (BMI) is formed as a competitor to ASCAP and to represent the blues and country music ignored by its rival

1947 Wynonie 'Blues' Harris records, according to some commentators, the first rock song 'Good Rockin' Tonight'; Roy Brown releases another version in 1948

1952 The deejay Alan Freed names his radio show 'Moondog's Rock'n'Roll Party'

1953 Bill Haley and the Comets' 'Crazy Man Crazy' is the first rock'n'roll record to make the *Billboard* charts

1954 Elvis Presley releases 'That's All Right Mama' in US; UK release is not until 1956

1955 Little Richard records 'Tutti Frutti'
Bill Haley and the Comets perform 'Rock Around the Clock' in the film *The Blackboard Jungle*

1956 Elvis Presley's 'Heartbreak Hotel' is No. 1 for eight weeks in US; reaches No. 2 in UK
Lonnie Donegan releases 'Rock Island Line' (No. 8 in UK; No. 6 in US)
Tommy Steele's 'Singing the Blues' is No. 1 in UK

1957 *American Bandstand* is broadcast nationally, reaching an audience of 20 million and providing a launchpad for many fifties teen idols

1958 Elvis Presley is drafted into the US Army

1959 Buddy Holly, Richie Valens and the Big Bopper are killed in an air crash
Cliff Richard and the Shadows are No. 1 with 'Living Doll'
Juke Box Jury begins on BBC TV: celebrities vote on whether a single will be a 'hit' or a 'miss'

1960 Congressional investigation into payola begins; it reveals 'pay for play' arrangements between record companies and broadcasters

1962 The Beatles release 'Love Me Do', and later their first LP, *Please Please Me*
Cliff Richard and the Shadows are No. 1 with 'Summer Holiday'

The Rolling Stones begin a Sunday night residency at the Crawdaddy Club, Richmond

Bob Dylan releases his first album, *Bob Dylan*

Gerry and the Pacemakers' 'How Do You Do It?' is No. 1

The Beatles give their last performance at the Cavern Club in Liverpool

First press reports of 'Beatlemania' are published

1963   The Beatles release *With the Beatles*, and appear on *Sunday Night at the London Palladium* and at the *Royal Variety Show*

Ready Steady Go! begins broadcasting on Independent Television (ITV)

1964   The Beatles appear on the *Ed Sullivan Show*; their 'Love Me Do' and 'She Loves You' are No. 1 in the US; John Lennon publishes *In His Own Write*, a collection of his drawings and stories; the Beatles' first film, *A Hard Day's Night*, opens; The Beatles play New York's Shea Stadium (attendance: 55,600, a world record); they receive the MBE from the Queen

The Rolling Stones also appear on the *Ed Sullivan Show*

The pirate stations Radio London and Radio Caroline begin broadcasting

Country singer Jim Reeves dies in a plane crash; soon afterwards eight of his records are in the UK Top 20

The first edition of *Top of the Pops* is broadcast; it is still shown weekly

Robert Moog markets his synthesiser

1965   Otis Redding's *Otis Blue* album is released

Dylan is booed at the Newport Folk Festival and elsewhere for 'going electric'; he gets the same treatment when he tours the UK the following year

1966   The Cavern closes

UK singles rise 7*d* to 7*s* 3*d*

John Lennon says the Beatles are now more famous than Jesus

Pink Floyd take part in 'Spontaneous Underground' at the Marquee Club in London

The Beatles play their last ever tour concert at Candlestick Park, San Francisco

The Jimi Hendrix Experience play their first UK gig and release 'Hey Joe'

1967   'Giant Freakout All Night Rave' (featuring the Who, the Move and Pink Floyd) at the Roundhouse

'Giant Freakout' at Winterland, San Francisco (featuring Jefferson Airplane, Grateful Dead, Quicksilver Messenger Service)

The Monkees first shown on UK TV, a year after the group and the programme debut in the US

The Rolling Stones appear on *Saturday Night at the London Palladium*; Mick Jagger and Keith Richards are sent to prison on drug offences (they are released on appeal)

The Who tour the US for the first time

Elvis Presley marries Priscilla Ann Beaulieu in Las Vegas

The Beatles release *Sgt Pepper Lonely Hearts Club Band*; 'A Day in the Life' is banned by the BBC

Brian Epstein, the Beatles' manager, dies

Monterey International Pop Festival (starring, among others, the Mamas and Papas, Jefferson Airplane, the Grateful Dead, Janis Joplin, Ravi Shankar, Otis Redding, and Jimi Hendrix) is attended by 30,000 fans

Rolling Stone magazine is launched

Cream release *Disraeli Gears*

BBC's Radio 1 begins broadcasting, replacing the now illegal pirate stations

Otis Redding dies in a plane crash

The Beatles' television film *Magical Mystery Tour* is broadcast

1968 The Beatles visit India to learn about meditation

First free Hyde Park Festival (featuring Pink Floyd and Jethro Tull)

1969 Led Zeppelin release their first album *Led Zeppelin*

Paul McCartney marries Linda Eastman; John Lennon marries Yoko Ono and returns his MBE to Buckingham Palace

The Who release their 'rock opera' *Tommy*

Blind Faith, the first 'supergroup' (Eric Clapton, Ginger Baker, Stevie Winwood, Ric Grech), play Hyde Park

Judy Garland dies

The Rolling Stones perform in Hyde Park, following Brian Jones' death

The Woodstock Festival attracts 400,000 fans

The Hell's Angels attack and kill a member of the audience at the Altamont free festival, organised by the Rolling Stones

1970 Jimi Hendrix and Janis Joplin die

The Beatles disband

Soul Train appears on US television; it is influential in reporting new dances, images and fashions to black America (the syndication rights are bought by CBS TV in 1973)

1971 The *Old Grey Whistle Test* starts on BBC2; bands perform live in a bare television studio

The Canadian government implements 'Canadian Content' regulations, which require that radio station playlists contained specified minimum amounts of Canadian music. The Junos, Canada's answer to the Grammy Awards, are named after Pierre Juneau, the civil servant responsible for these regulations

1973   Pink Floyd's *Dark Side of the Moon* enters US charts. It stays there (in the 'Top Pop Catalog' charts) for well over 1,000 weeks

1975   Bruce Springsteen releases *Born to Run*

1976   Sex Pistols release 'Anarchy in the UK'; after swearing on television, the band are dropped by their record company EMI and banned from many UK venues

1977   Elvis Presley dies, aged 42
        Kraftwerk release *Trans Europe Express*, a record that influences hip hop and dance culture

1979   Eleven fans die at Who concert in Cincinnati, Ohio

1980   John Lennon is shot dead in New York

1981   MTV is launched
        Abba's last No. 1: 'Super Trooper'
        The Specials' 'Ghost Town' is No. 1; during the summer, there are a number of urban riots

1982   Michael Jackson's *Thriller* is released (it goes on to sell 45 million copies)

1983   The first CDs go on sale
        The arrival of video is acknowledged with the first American Video Awards
        The Musical Instrument Digital Interface (MIDI) becomes available; it enables synthesisers to be connected to each other, and signals new technical possibilities for music making
        Culture Club are No. 1 with 'Karma Chameleon'

1984   Frankie Goes to Hollywood's 'Relax' is No. 1 and banned by the BBC
        George Michael's first solo single 'Careless Whisper' (No. 1)
        Band Aid release 'Do They Know It's Christmas?'
        Marvin Gaye dies, shot by his father

1985   Live Aid raises £50 million
        Wham! are the first Western group to play in China
        Bruce Springsteen releases *Born in the USA* (which sells 15 million copies in US)
        Parents Music Resource Center (PMRC) gives evidence to Senate committee on the explicit sexual and violent content of records
        Record companies introduce 'Parental Advisory' labelling on records as a way of appeasing PMRC complaints

1986 Paul Simon releases his *Graceland* album; a row erupts over whether it breaches cultural sanctions imposed on apartheid South Africa

Madonna's *True Blue* enters the UK album chart at No. 1, the first US artist to do this

Bob Geldof receives honorary Knighthood for his work for Live Aid

1987 MTV is launched in Europe; MTV globally now reaches 79 countries and 281.7 million households

M/A/R/R/S have a No. 1 with 'Pump Up the Volume', marking the rise of music made with deejay skills and sampler technology

Rhythim is Rhythim (Derrick May) releases 'Strings of Life', a key moment in the emergence of Detroit Techno

1988 Kylie Minogue has No. 1 with 'I Should Be So Lucky'

While still serving a life sentence in South Africa, Nelson Mandela is honoured with a seventieth birthday concert at Wembley; the performers include Whitney Houston and Peter Gabriel

CDs now outsell vinyl records

Dance culture's 'Summer of Love' begins in UK

1989 Public Enemy release *It Takes a Nation of Millions to Hold Us Back*

1991 Bryan Adams' 'Everything I do (I do it for you)' is No. 1 for sixteen weeks in UK, and is No. 1 in seventeen other countries

Nirvana's 'Smells like Teen Spirit' is the most played video on MTV Europe

1992 Garth Brooks' *Ropin' the Wind* is the first Country album to top the US pop charts

CDs now outsell cassettes

1993 Snoop Doggy Dogg's *Dogstyle* is the first debut album to enter *Billboard* charts at No. 1

1994 Kurt Cobain commits suicide

M People release *Bizarre Fruit*; it becomes (and remains) the biggest selling dance album

Julio Iglesias' *Julio* is released and sells 200 million copies worldwide

British government introduces Criminal Justice and Public Order Act which is intended to curb illegal raves (and music that uses 'repetitive beats')

1996 Shania Twain releases *The Woman in Me*, which becomes the biggest selling country album by a female artist (11 million copies in US)

Spice Girls' 'Wannabe' is No. 1 in twenty-two countries

1997 MP3 is introduced: it is a computer digital file format that enables
audio files to be reduced greatly in size; it allows music to be transmitted over the Internet

Oasis's album *Be Here Now* sells 345,000 on day of release

Prodigy's *Fat of the Land* is No. 1 in twenty countries

Garth Brooks has twelve songs in *Billboard* Country Top 75

1998 Madonna wins a record six MTV Music Video awards

B*Witched become first female group to have their debut single
enter the UK chart at No. 1 ('C'est la vie')

Elton John's elegy for Princess Diana, 'Candle in the Wind', sells 1.5
million copies in its first week; US advance orders are 7.8 million

1999 Napster software is introduced; it greatly increases access to music
on the internet

US charts dominated by rap metal acts: Limp Bizkit, Rage Against
the Machine, and by Santana

2000 Napster is sued by Metallica for breach of copyright

Record companies establish copyright deals with Internet music
providers

2001 Hear'Say, a group assembled through a UK televised documentary
series (*Popstars*), become the first band to top the UK album and
singles charts simultaneously with their debut releases

PART I

Context

1 'Plugged in': technology and popular music

PAUL THÉBERGE

Any discussion of the role of technology in popular music should begin with a simple premise: without electronic technology, popular music in the twenty-first century is unthinkable. As a point of departure, however, such a premise demands that one develop an understanding of music technology as more than a random collection of instruments, recording and playback devices. Technology is also an environment in which we experience and think about music; it is a set of practices in which we engage in making and listening to musical sounds; and it is an element in the discourses that we use in sharing and evaluating our experiences, defining, in the process, what music is and can be. In this sense, the ensemble of electronic devices that are used to make, distribute and experience contemporary music are not simply a technical 'means' through which we experience music. Technology has become a 'mode' of music production and consumption: that is, technology has become a precondition for music-making, an important element in the definition of musical sound and style, and a catalyst for musical change (Blacking 1977). However, technology does not simply determine music-making. Pop artists and consumers have often used technology in ways unintended by those who manufacture it. In this way, pop practices constantly redefine music technologies through unexpected or alternative uses.

This chapter presents an overview of several parallel yet interconnected evolutions in music technology: the development and continued importance of electro-magnetic technologies; the evolution of studio recording technologies and techniques; the rise of new musical instrument technologies; and the evolution of consumer audio devices and formats, including recent innovations in digital formats for music distribution on the Internet. The brief survey of musical instruments, reproduction devices and technical formats presented here will be treated as an inquiry into musical concepts, techniques, and social and aesthetic values as much as a history of technology *per se.* In this regard, it is essential to recognise, firstly, that conflicts in musical aesthetics and values have accompanied virtually every development in music technology and, secondly, that the possibilities offered by new musical technologies are never exploited equally, or even accepted, in every sphere of music-making. Indeed, different uses of technology reflect different aesthetic and cultural priorities (Rose 1994).

The specific uses, abuses, or the explicit rejection of various technologies are thus instrumental in defining a particular 'sound' – a pop aesthetic – and contribute to a sense of 'distinction' between popular music genres.

Fundamental technologies

By the second half of the twentieth century, the technologies of sound recording and reproduction, and the industries associated with them, were already firmly established and had become a central component in all of Western musical culture and, increasingly, throughout the world. But the vast array of technical devices that came into use in popular music after the Second World War, and the intensity of the economic and aesthetic debates which often surrounded their introduction, tended to mask the continued importance of a number of other, ancillary technologies developed during the early years of the twentieth century. Specifically, the microphone, electrical amplification and loudspeakers must be considered as absolutely fundamental to contemporary popular music. Their character is underscored, ironically, by the degree to which they have become 'naturalised' and their effects rendered invisible to us. Even in the digital age, however, these technologies remain the beginning and end points of virtually every act of musical production and reproduction, thus giving the lie to the very idea that pop music can be 'unplugged'. The aesthetics of 'high-fidelity' have reinforced the idea that microphones, amplifiers and speakers are *reproductive* technologies, that they are, by design, transparent in their operation. However, such an ideology only serves to efface the impact that these technologies continue to have on our experience of popular music, even in the twenty-first century.

Curiously, these fundamental technologies were developed initially neither within nor for the record industry. Microphones, for example, were first developed by the telephone and broadcast industries and only later adopted for use in music recording and in film production. During the early 1920s, the record industry hesitated in adopting electrical methods of recording in favour of protecting the large investments already made in the production and stockpiling of acoustical recordings. The microphone, in conjunction with electrical amplification, soon proved to be more powerful in its ability to render the subtleties of both the human voice and instrumental sounds than acoustical methods and the industry was forced to convert to electrical technologies in order to compete with the new medium of radio.

The impact of the microphone on musical style was both subtle and profound: for example, the string bass could be heard clearly, for the first time, in jazz recordings and the instrument quickly replaced the tuba which had often been used in earlier recorded jazz. More importantly, a new, intimate style of singing, known as 'crooning', evolved in response to the introduction of the microphone in popular music practice and spurred immediate controversy. As Simon Frith (1986) has pointed out, crooners were regarded by early critics as effeminate and their singing style as both technically and, by extension, emotionally 'dishonest'.

Despite such criticisms, what had become clear for the early crooners was that it was now necessary not only to sing but to develop a technique suited to the microphone. No performer of the period appears to have realised this more than Bing Crosby, who exploited the intimacy offered by the microphone to great effect: his more 'masculine', 'husky' sounding baritone voice not only differed from the style of singing adopted by many of the other early crooners but its low register was also particularly enhanced by the microphone through the physical phenomenon known as the 'proximity effect'.

In this sense, while pop performers sing to an audience, real or imagined, they always sing first and foremost *to* the microphone. In return, the microphone reveals, in intimate detail, every nuance of the performer's vocal style. But it does not do so in a transparent fashion: every microphone has its own characteristics and colours the sound in subtle yet unmistakable ways. Pop performers have become exceptionally sensitive to the manner in which the microphone can flatter the voice and even musicians who publicly denounce the excesses of modern instrument and recording technologies can be found, in interviews, waxing rhapsodically about the ability of a certain microphone to lend 'warmth' to a vocal performance.

As listeners, our experience of the 'grain' (Barthes 1990) of the voice in popular music (not to mention our notions of how an acoustic guitar or other traditional instrument 'should' sound) has been subtly influenced by the intercession of the microphone. The sensuous pleasures that we derive from listening to the sounds produced by pop performers – from the ironic, conversational tones of Brad Roberts (Crash Test Dummies), to the over-the-top ballad styles of Céline Dion or Whitney Houston, to the tortured screams of Axl Rose – are essentially erotic in character (Frith 1981). These pleasures are made all the more powerful by the extraordinary sense of 'presence' (an aesthetic, metaphorical and quasi-technical term used by recording engineers) afforded by the microphone.

In contemporary live performance and recording the microphone is never a singular technology, it is always plural. Indeed, the evolution of multi-microphone techniques have been central to the development of popular music since the advent of rock'n'roll during the 1950s. Prior to this time, it was unusual to find more than a handful of microphones used in live performance contexts or in recording studios. But innovative engineers and producers, in search of a new 'sound' for the emerging music, began to experiment with microphones and their placement: at Atlantic records, for example, 'Tommy [Dowd] did revolutionary things with how he would mike the bass and drums. Nobody used to mike drums in those days [the 1950s] . . . later on he started using multiple miking. We learned all the advantages of remixing and sweetening' (producer Jerry Wexler, quoted in Fox 1986: 146). In this way, engineers gradually took over much of the responsibility for achieving musical balances within the overall sound of first the recording, and later, live performance. Experiments in multi-microphone technique, which involve the selective placement and isolation of instrumental sounds, were among the first steps taken towards the creation of the modern multitrack studio and continue to be an essential factor in the production of the transparent sound and instrumental separation characteristic of most popular music today (Schlemm 1982).

Microphones (and related electro-magnetic technologies such as guitar pickups and the stylus of a turntable), however, would be useless without the ability to amplify electrically the signals they produce. The development of the 'Audion Tube' by Lee DeForest, in 1904, laid the basis for amplification, radio broadcasting, and other electric technologies of the early twentieth century. Since the 1950s, however, amplification has become more than a technical necessity, it has become a crucial element in the evolution of the sound of popular music, particularly rock music. From the outset, rock'n'roll established itself as loud, raucous music by virtue of its emphasis on the sound of amplified electric guitars and, in the decades that followed, rock became synonymous with both volume and distortion. When an amplifier is pushed beyond its normal capacities the electronic components become overdriven, resulting in a brighter sound, rich in harmonic content unrelated to the original sound source. Rob Walser (1993) has argued that the sound of amplified guitar distortion has become a key aural sign of heavy metal and hard rock genres and an important signifier of power and emotional intensity in the music.

Even when tube amplifiers are not overdriven, however, they have a distinct sound, valued by many musicians and engineers, that is difficult to reproduce through other means. In this regard, there is perhaps no more curious an example of the fact that the production of popular music is essentially an aesthetic project, not simply a technical one, than the survival of tube technology. Decades after the introduction of solid state transistors and, more recently, digital circuitry, the vacuum tube remains a viable technology. Throughout the 1990s and into the twenty-first century, equipment manufacturers have done a brisk business in the production of tube-based microphone preamps, guitar amplifiers, compressors and other signal processors. Similarly, as computers became increasingly important in music production, programmers attempted to simulate, in software form, the particular distortion characteristics, buzz and 'warmth' of tube technology in order to cash in on the 'retro' aesthetic prevalent in various genres of pop music.

It is in combination with loudspeakers, however, that amplification makes its most significant contribution to popular music culture. Since its introduction during the 1950s, amplification through transistor circuitry has lent itself to both the economies of power and miniaturisation, thus making it possible to meet the acoustic demands of public venues such as dance clubs and sports stadiums, on the one hand, and the more intimate spaces of automobiles, portable transistor radios and Sony Walkmans, on the other. 'Power' is again in this instance both a description of a physical phenomenon and a cultural value: for it is only through the application of electrical amplification to loudspeakers (or headphones) that we are able to invest both our public and private spaces with a musical intensity unprecedented in cultural history. It could be argued that no other technology affects our subjective experience of popular music more than the amplified loudspeaker: the loudness of rock or the booming bass of hip-hop are sounds that can only be produced and experienced through technological means. Studio engineers recognise the importance of loudspeakers in music consumption and routinely employ two or three different speaker systems in an attempt to approximate the effects of different listening conditions on a given mix.

Loudspeakers were first introduced in radio and public address systems during the 1920s but their most significant development occurred during the early days of sound cinema. Some of the most respected names in the audio industry, such as J. B. Lansing, began their careers developing speaker systems for film theatres during the 1930s and only later oriented their efforts towards meeting the demands of the recording studio, stage performance, and home listening. It was during the 1960s, however, that popular music began to make special demands on speaker technology. As pop bands, such as the Beatles, the Who, and others, turned increasingly to sports stadiums as performance venues, their primitive guitar amplifiers and PA systems proved inadequate. Manufacturers responded to these new demands by creating ever more powerful sound systems and, in the process, created the technical infrastructure of modern live performance. More importantly, amplifiers and loudspeakers became part of a complex social technology: they facilitated the coming together of ever-larger crowds for popular music, thus supporting both the needs of fans and those of the expanding music industry.

As noted above, however, loudness in rock music was only partly dictated by necessity, it was also a fundamental component in an evolving rock aesthetic. And, as in the case of amplifier distortion, rock musicians soon learned that loudspeakers, as the functional source of musical sound, could be employed for musical ends. When a microphone or guitar pickup is placed in close proximity to a highly amplified loudspeaker the phenomenon known as 'feedback' occurs. Rock guitarists, such as Jimi Hendrix, learned to play *to* their amplifier speakers, coaxing novel sounds from them, and making them a true extension of their musical instruments.

Outside guitar-based rock, the loudspeaker must also be considered as central to the experience of a range of pop music genres from reggae to the whole gamut of genres associated with modern dance music. From the early reggae 'sound system' – or mobile discotheque – to the dance club, to the rave party, a premium has been placed on the ability of amplifiers and loudspeakers to produce an artificially loud, or 'heavy' bass sound. Subsonic speaker systems create tones that are felt as much as they are heard, thus supporting the movement of dancers as much as the rhythm of the music itself. Furthermore, the exaggerated emphasis on bass frequencies found in various genres of African–American music, such as hip-hop and rap, has come to be perceived by fans and pop commentators alike as a marker of not only musical genre but cultural identity as well (Rose 1994).

Certainly, microphones, amplifiers and loudspeakers have been important to virtually all recorded music: classical, folk, jazz, or popular. But it is only in popular music and in rock that these technologies can be regarded as truly essential to the processes of both musical expression and experience.

Sound recording

Magnetic recording, in one form or another, has also been a central element in the development of production practices in popular music since the 1950s. While the first magnetic recorder was developed as early as 1898 and wire and steel-band magnetic recorders found limited use in radio broadcasting during the 1930s, it was not until the Second World War that German engineers were able to perfect tape-based recording. In 1948, working from German prototypes, the first commercially successful tape machines were introduced in the United States and were soon put to general use in radio, film and record production. The overall improvement in sound fidelity, duration of recording time and, above all, the ability to edit and splice together different 'takes' of a performance, contributed to a quality and flexibility previously impossible with conventional disk recording methods. Singer Bing Crosby was again one of the first performers to exploit these possibilities: from the late 1940s onward, he insisted that his radio programmes be pre-recorded (first on disk and, later, on tape), thus ensuring 'perfect' performances. The ease and relative low cost of production were also significant factors in the rise of independent, entrepreneurial production (especially in the emerging genres of rhythm and blues and rock'n'roll) during the 1950s and contributed to an overall reorganisation of the recording industry.

From the outset, entrepreneurial producers and engineers experimented with the technical possibilities of tape technology in order to create new sounds. For example, echo, originally produced by the physical gap that exists between the record and playback heads on a tape recorder, was employed as a novelty effect in pop recording from the early 1950s onward (it can be heard prominently, for example, in some of the early rock'n'roll recordings, such as Elvis Presley's version of 'Hound Dog') and later became a standard part of pop recording practice. Similarly, during the late 1960s, an experimental technique known as 'flanging', which can be described as a kind of 'whooshing' effect created by phase cancellations that occur when the speed of two tape recorders is manipulated relative to one another, became a distinctive part of the sound of many psychedelic rock recordings. Audio manufacturers quickly responded by creating electronic devices that could reproduce the effect of such experimental techniques but with greater control and precision; these effects remain part of the standard repertory found in digital effects processors and software today. Thus, in what has become characteristic of the commercial context in which many pop practices originate, what begins as experimentation is soon packaged and sold back to pop practitioners in commodity form.

Beyond such novelties, however, there is perhaps no more salient example of the intimate relationship between popular music and technology than the development of the multitrack tape recorder. Indeed, while the technology of multitrack tape recording was developed in response to the needs of popular music, the evolution of pop and rock from the 1960s onward was, at the same time, predicated on the very existence of the technology and the practices associated with it. Multitrack recording is not simply a technical process of sound production and reproduction; it is also a *compositional* process and is thus central to the creation of popular music at the most fundamental level (Eno 1983).

Multitrack recording techniques were first used in mainstream pop of the 1950s when a third track was added to the stereo pair of tracks found on professional recorders. The extra track was used as a means of isolating and enhancing the vocal sound of pop singers, such as Frank Sinatra and

Nat King Cole, in relation to the backing orchestra. Such applications can be regarded as a simple technical expedient in the service of commercial ends. Overdubbing was put to a much more extensive and creative use, however, in the multiple guitar and voice recordings of Les Paul and Mary Ford during the 1950s (Les Paul is also credited with having created the design for the first 8-track tape recorder; see Sievert 1978). The fusion in timbre created by a single vocalist performing multiple harmony parts, a technique pushed to its limits by artists such as Joni Mitchell during the late 1960s and early 1970s, can only be achieved through overdubbing. By the time that four-track recorders became available during the early 1960s, producers such as Phil Spector were using the technology as an integral component in an overall strategy for the creation of a new pop sound. During the late 1960s and early 1970s, track capacity expanded rapidly from 4-, to 8-, to 16- and 24-track recording, offering greater possibilities for the control and layering of sounds; performers such as Stevie Wonder made use of these enhanced capabilities and released recordings in which they played and sang all the musical parts.

The multitrack tape recorder is one of the principal technical devices within an overall technical environment – the multitrack studio – that needs to be understood as a 'technology' in larger terms. The studio is an environment made up of a specifically designed set of acoustic spaces within which one finds a wide range of technical devices: microphones, tape recorders, mixing console, signal processors, monitors, headphones and, more recently, digital samplers, synthesisers and computers. Furthermore, the multitrack studio comprises a flexible, though well-defined organisation of musical labour and a rational division of specific technical practices: the use of multiple microphones, overdubbing and other techniques to maximise separation, signal processing, and mixing (Théberge 1989). Mixing has become such a complex and specialised task that different engineers (and different studios) are often employed at this stage of the recording process. The work of creative engineers and producers, from the disco producers of the 1970s (such as Freddie Perren and Giorgio Moroder) to the dance remixers of the1980s and 1990s (such as Shep Pettibone), has highlighted the capacity of the studio to act as a tool in reworking pre-existing material in order to meet the needs of different consumer contexts. Such practices also clearly fit within the economic imperatives of the record industry as they allow for the profit potential of every song to be exploited to its fullest (Tankel 1990). Not surprisingly, prominent remix engineers, based on their ability to deliver marketable hits, have been signed to long-term contracts with major labels.

Taken together, the ensemble of technical spaces, devices and practices that constitutes the process of multitrack recording has become the primary mode of production in popular music. It has resulted in both a particular 'sound' – dynamically compressed and spatially separated (Schlemm 1982) – that is characteristic of most contemporary recording, and a new approach to the creative process. Whereas, in the early 1960s, a band would not ordinarily enter a studio without having a selection of material rehearsed and ready to record, less than a decade later it was normal for bands to compose in the studio, spending weeks and months experimenting with the various creative possibilities inherent in the multitrack process. In this regard, 'overdubbing', an essentially additive process in which the various instrumental sounds are layered in temporal succession and then later combined (or stripped away) at the time of mixdown, is a central technique of the studio when used as a compositional tool (Eno 1983). As a compositional tool, the multitrack studio has perhaps been most fully exploited in various genres of dance music, where the contributions of musicians have become little more than raw material which is manipulated, transformed and re-composed in the studio itself.

Initially, the prerogative of 'composing' with the new medium was not given equally to all who participated in the multitrack enterprise: it was the producer, more than anyone else, whose judgement prevailed within the studio environment (on the role of the producer, see Hennion 1989). And, indeed, it is the status of the producer that is valorised in modern copyright law: as far as mechanical rights to the recording are concerned, it is the producer (or the record company) who holds all rights of reproduction. Increasingly, however, popular musicians insisted on having greater control over the multitrack recording process and, ultimately, the sound of their music. Edward R. Kealy (1979) has described in detail the changing patterns of collaboration that came about in the recording of rock music during the period between 1965 and 1975. According to Kealy, an 'art mode' of production evolved during this period where the recording artists themselves were responsible for aesthetic decision-making in the studio. In this, pop musicians have come to rely heavily on the technical expertise and growing artistic contributions of recording engineers with whom they have developed creative relationships. Such relationships often allow musicians to experiment with the technology in unorthodox ways: for example, Tricia Rose (1994) has described how rap musicians and producers (not unlike rock guitarists of the sixties) often work 'in the red', pushing the capacity of tape recorders in order to create a more distorted sound.

From the 1970s onward, many successful artists invested tens of thousands of dollars in constructing their own studios, where they could experiment freely without the pressures of paying for commercial studio time at hourly rates. As an understanding of the basic technologies, routines and practices of studio recording has gradually become an essential part of every musician's store of knowledge and skill – as essential as knowing how to tune a guitar – semi-professional and amateur musicians also began setting up their own studios using low-cost equipment specifically designed by manufacturers for the 'home studio' market. In an effort to simplify the design of multitrack equipment for amateur recordists, manufacturers such as Tascam created the consumer-oriented 'Portastudio', which integrated tape recorder and mixer functions in a single device. Aspiring young musicians now regularly produce demo tapes even before they have learned to play before an audience; as Steve Jones (1992) has pointed out, 'paying your dues' in the music business is no longer simply a matter of playing night after night in bars, it also means working in (and making payments on) your home studio. The sound quality of home equipment has improved to the point where it can often rival that found in commercial studios: by the mid-1990s, digital multitrack recorders, in both tape and hard disk/computer software formats, had become available at modest prices.

This continuous 'democratisation' of the audio marketplace is significant in that it allows for a level of do-it-yourself recording activity (and an associated aesthetic) that is unusual in contemporary cultural production. Punk musicians of the 1970s and 'alternative' bands of the 1980s developed an aggressive, 'lo-fi' approach to the recording medium that both rejected the dominant practices and aesthetics of the record industry and played a role in defining these genres, in ideological terms, as more 'authentic' than other forms of mainstream pop and rock . This type of low-cost, independent production that co-exists with more commercial recording practices is characteristic of the music industry and is significantly different from the type of 'independent' production that takes place in other cultural sectors, such as the film and television industries.

At a very different level, the significance of multitrack recording has also become evident as the next generation of technology – digital technology – has entered into studio practice. MIDI (Musical Instrument Digital Interface) is a hardware/software protocol, introduced into the synthesiser market in 1983, that allows digital synthesisers, samplers, drum machines and computers to be networked together. Sequencers, software programs that allow MIDI data to be recorded, have adopted the multitrack tape recorder as a metaphor for the user interface even though MIDI does not carry sound data, only data related to performance gestures. In this way, software manufacturers have built upon, and thus reproduced, an already existing base of technical knowledge and practice

(Théberge 1997). Similarly, as high-fidelity, digital audio recording has become viable on home computers, the entire multitrack studio has become the object of software simulation: including simulations of multi-track tape recorder functions, mixing consoles and signal processors.

This technical reproduction is not without its social consequences. The technologies of rock and pop music production have long been a male-dominated terrain, and this has been as true for the most basic of rock technologies, the electric guitar, as it is for the wider range of electronic technologies associated with stage and studio (see Bayton 1990). Recent studies conducted by the music instrument industry have suggested that even among women with computer and music instrument skills, the use of music software is extremely limited. In reproducing the multitrack studio in software form, programmers implicitly assume that users *already* have the knowledge required for its use, thus reproducing, perhaps, the social inequalities associated with access to the earlier technology as well.

Musical instruments

Musical instruments are often the centre of controversy in pop and rock because their use is so intimately tied with musicians' notions of personal expression, on the one hand, and audience concerns for the 'authenticity' of music, on the other. Even Bob Dylan's adoption of the electric guitar in folk music of the 1960s was looked upon with derision by his fans. Historically however, rock music has been inextricably associated with the electric guitar in terms of its sound, performance gestures (fans often mimic, on 'air guitar', the exaggerated gestures of rock performers) and iconography. Because of the way in which specific sounds (and images) are linked to musical genres and the way in which nostalgia works in both pop and rock music, guitars of a certain type or vintage – the Gibson Les Paul or the Fender Stratocaster and Telecaster models, for example – have attained a special status among guitarists. The Stratocaster in particular, first introduced in 1954, has been copied by many manufacturers and its distinctive form has become, through commercial advertising and other avenues, one of the musical icons most commonly associated with rock.

But perhaps most important for rock and popular music are the wide variations in sound that can be produced by the electric guitar. In addition to the distortion and feedback techniques described above, the sound of the electric guitar has become increasingly integrated with electronic tech-nologies: from the 'wah-wah' pedals of the 1960s to the elaborate, multiple digital effects employed in the 1990s, our notions of what the guitar is, and can be, have been transformed. It could be argued that the guitar is no longer simply 'electric' – that is, an instrument that has been amplified – but that its sound has become truly 'electronic' in nature.

Similarly, our experience of even the most 'primitive' of musical instrument technologies – the drums – has been altered by the processes of sound recording and electronic manipulation. The multitrack recording process allows for the sound of the drums and cymbals to be spatially separated in the stereo mix, thus creating an artificially enhanced, spatialisation of the rhythmic structure of the music itself (Théberge 1989). The sound of the voice and other instruments and, ultimately, the listener are placed *within* this spatial/rhythmic field. Furthermore, the drums are usually subjected to high levels of dynamic compression and other signal processing which serve to increase the overall impact of the sound of the beat in the final mix. Phil Collins' trademark snare sound – a sound that dominated many pop recordings of the 1980s – was created through a combination of microphone placement and signal processing: including compression, artificial reverberation and noise gating. Despite the controversy created by the introduction of drum machines during the late 1970s and instruments such as the Simmons Electronic Drums during the early eighties, the difference between the sound of processed acoustic drums and their sampled and electronic counterparts can be quite negligible.

Filling the same role as the guitar in rock music, the drum machine has become perhaps one of the most important instruments in the production of a wide variety of pop and dance music genres. The drum machine has its origins in the rhythm accompaniment boxes associated with home organs of the 1950s and 1960s, thus demonstrating that musical innovations do not always flow from the top down (that is from professional to consumer markets); but rather, significant innovations can originate in almost any market sector. These humble origins extend to even some of the manufacturers of drum machines: Ikutaro Kakehashi, founder of Japan's Roland Corporation, which is today one of the major suppliers of electronic musical instruments in the world, began his career in the music instrument industry designing home organs and rhythm boxes.

Both the sounds and the characteristic ways in which rhythm patterns are constructed on drum machines have been important elements in defining pop aesthetics. The Roland TR-808 drum machine (introduced in 1980), for example, became the instrument of choice among many hip-hop, rap and house music producers. Both the ability to detune the bass drum, creating a sound akin to a low-frequency hum, and the necessity of building rhythm patterns in a precise grid-like framework, have been cited as influences on the musical style of these genres. The instrument has achieved its own 'vintage' status: it continues to fetch a high price on the used instrument market, its sounds have often been sampled by producers of dance music, and it has even been reincarnated in the form of a computer software program (Steinberg's 'ReBirth', released in 1997).

Most audiences, however, have never seen a TR-808, and if there is any instrument that has achieved both the musical and the iconic status of the guitar in dance music, it is the phonograph turntable. Using innovative techniques such as mixing and 'scratching', dance club deejays transformed the turntable, a quintessentially reproductive device, into a *productive* one, a musical instrument of the first order. Similarly, one might consider the art of the deejay as founded, initially, upon a type of consumer knowledge – a knowledge of musical style based in judgement and connoisseurship – which is then combined with a particular set of musical skills: the ability to sequence and mix together a series of songs and rhythmic breaks (Straw 1993). Along with the turntable, the form of the vinyl record was also transformed: the twelve-inch single had been developed specifically for dance use as early as the 1970s and, later, specialised distribution networks evolved to serve the needs of professional deejays (often catering to their penchant for secrecy by distributing the records in unmarked, 'white label' editions). Not unlike the preference among rock guitarists for tube amplification, many deejays continued to champion the turntable and vinyl records over CD technology well into the late 1980s and early 1990s.

The evolution of deejay aesthetics and practices – beginning with the Jamaican-inspired work of deejay Kool Herc in the early 1970s and its influence on the New York hip-hop scene and the later development of house music in Detroit and Chicago – created the conditions in which other, more advanced technologies, such as the digital sampler, could be introduced into dance music production. Arguing against crude technological determinist notions of how technology influences musical style, Ross Harley (1993) has suggested that it was the dance floor context, and the deejay practices associated with it, that led to the adoption of digital sampling technology and the particular manner in which it was put to use in house music of the 1980s.

The digital sampler is a hybrid device – a device for recording sound *and* a musical instrument – that was designed to reproduce the sounds of conventional musical instruments, thereby making studio production more economical by eliminating the need for backing musicians. The Mellotron, an analogue keyboard instrument that used tape loops, was introduced during the 1960s for similar purposes; the sound of its taped string ensembles were popularised by bands such as the Moody Blues and King Crimson during the late 1960s and early 1970s, and used on individual cuts by the Beatles, the Rolling Stones, and many others. In many commercial recordings, the digital sampler is used specifically for the mundane purposes for which is was designed: as an inexpensive replacement for grand piano, drum sounds, string and brass ensembles and, more recently, the sounds of traditional instruments from around the world.

However, in the hands of house music producers and remix engineers, the sampler was used to cut sound fragments and loop together rhythmic grooves from a wide variety of sources: especially commercial recordings of soul, funk and heavy metal music but, also, from an increasingly diverse range of sources including film and television sound tracks. By using samplers to extend the possibilities of isolating break beats and mixing together passages from various recordings, sampling artists created a crisis within the music industry with regards to copyright infringement during the 1980s (Frith 1993). While the perceived threat to copyright law was relatively short-lived – the industry essentially bringing would-be samplers into line primarily through intimidation and the threat of litigation – the influence of this chaotic moment in the history of pop should not be underestimated. By the 1990s, sampling had become a tolerated, if not fully accepted, part of musical practice: for example, in 1993, the acid jazz group US 3 was given extensive sampling access to the back catalogue of Blue Note recordings in order to create their particular mix of jazz and rap styles.

The rise of sampling technology must be considered within the overall development and use of keyboard synthesisers within popular music. Prior to the 1960s, the use of electronically synthesised sound had been largely the province of avant-garde and, to a lesser extent, film music composers. While modular analogue synthesisers were already being used in commercial studios by the late 1960s, it was the introduction of the Minimoog, in 1970, that shifted the emphasis of synthesiser design towards the needs of live performance, thus paving the way for the wider acceptance of synthesiser technology within popular music. Despite the reaction to synthesisers mounted by the musicians' unions (who regarded them as a threat to the livelihood of conventional studio musicians) and opponents of disco music during the late 1970s, the sound of analogue synthesisers became central to a wide range of pop and rock styles throughout the decade: from the funky, soul/rhythm and blues style of Stevie Wonder, to the driving, progressive rock sound of Emerson, Lake and Palmer, and the ironic, electro-pop styles of Kraftwerk and Devo, to name only a few.

A number of significant developments occurred during the early 1980s that changed the nature of the modern synthesiser. Manufacturers began to make use of digital circuitry in order to make synthesiser technology more stable, economic, and easier to use. They pursued an aggressive economic and technological strategy that saw the lowering of the cost of synthesisers and samplers, the expansion of synthesiser capabilities, and an ever-increasing capacity to store and reproduce pre-fabricated sound programs. The development of this latter capacity coincided with a subtle shift in the way in which musicians were regarded by manufacturers: no longer thought of as programmers of original sounds, musicians were increasingly viewed as consumers of prefabricated sounds and a small cottage industry developed to meet the supposed 'needs' of this new market. By the 1990s, synthesiser users had become largely dependent upon pre-fabricated synthesiser programs and prerecorded, CD libraries of digitally sampled sounds, thus placing them in a new relationship to instrument and software manufacturers (Théberge 1997).

With the introduction of MIDI (Musical Instrument Digital Interface) in 1983, the ability to use multiple synthesisers, drum machines and samplers in conjunction with one another and with personal computers was greatly enhanced, thus stabilising the synthesiser marketplace and offering greater creative possibilities to musicians. More important, it allowed electronically generated music to become part of a complete production *system*, modelled (as mentioned above) on the multitrack studio, and to become more fully integrated with conventional sound recording than ever before. While electronic pop music was still regarded by many, particularly the rock press, as 'cold' and 'inhuman', the sound of digital synthesisers began to appear in a surprising number of genres: for example, the eighties folk-derived style of Suzanne Vega's music was defined by a combination of acoustic guitar and synthesisers – a combination that would have been unheard of a decade earlier.

At the same time that these developments were taking place in the field of pop production, large music and consumer electronics corporations, such as Yamaha and Casio, were introducing portable electronic keyboards into the consumer marketplace. While regarded by many as mere toys, the impact of these instruments on the musical tastes of an entire generation of musical consumers should not be underestimated. Furthermore, as digital sampling methods became more commonplace, the market for home organs and upright pianos has gradually been displaced by electronic keyboards and digital pianos. In this way, not only has popular music become increasingly electronic in nature, but so too has much of amateur music culture in the West.

Consumer audio

As the above comments suggest, the relationship between the professional and semi-professional worlds of popular music-making and the world of consumer electronics is extremely intimate and complex. Indeed, the economics of technological innovation are such that even the professional world of music production has become dependent, in part, upon the success of home computers and the consumer audio industry to ensure the availability of affordable digital components. At the same time, the record industry has become increasingly hostile towards audio manufacturers (which, in many cases, are only partly independent of the record industry) and, more recently, the computer industry because they supply consumers with the tools with which they can violate copyright in recorded music, thus challenging the record industry's power to control patterns of distribution and consumption.

Quite apart from issues of copyright, however, consumer technologies and audio formats must be understood as being intricately interwoven with the structures of music marketing and distribution. In this regard, historical conflicts between the record and audio industries have often been accompanied by larger, structural changes within the music industry and changes in the character of music consumption. For example, shortly after Columbia Records launched the 12-inch, 33⅓-rpm, long-playing record in 1948, RCA countered with its own 7-inch, 45-rpm format, with the hope of ensuring consumer loyalty by making its own technology incompatible with the LP. A number of reasons contributed to the premature end of the so-called 'Battle of the Speeds' that ensued, not least among them the fact that small, independent manufacturers of high-fidelity equipment decided to develop turntables that could play not only both of the new formats but the older, 78-rpm records as well, thus undercutting the record companies' strategy of exclusivity. Eventually, the 45-rpm format would have been doomed to failure had RCA not aggressively promoted it as the new standard for popular music singles. The 45-rpm record quickly became the preferred format among young consumers of the 1950s and helped to establish the youth market as a powerful force within the popular music industry (the LP did not become a mainstay of youth consumption until the late 1960s).

A different set of conflicts greeted the arrival of Compact Discs during the 1980s. Launched in 1983 after a lengthy collaboration between Japanese (Sony) and European (Philips) electronics manufacturers, CD technology was still not guaranteed success in the marketplace unless the majority of record companies agreed to make music available in the new format, which they were reluctant to do at first. It was only after audio manufacturers dropped the price of CD players to a fraction of their initial retail value that consumer demand for the new technology began to grow. The loss of profits suffered by the audio industry is often cited as one of the reasons for the acquisition of Columbia Records by Sony: the introduction of future innovations in hardware, it was hoped, would not be hampered by the unavailability of music 'software'. Once the CD format was adopted, the record industry soon halted production of LPs on most new releases and began to capitalise on CDs through reissues of their enormous back catalogues of popular (and other) music. In this way, the loyalty of fans and the nostalgia for pop music of the past can be seen to have strategic value for the record industry. The LP has, nevertheless, survived in a kind of half-life in deejay practice and, curiously, among both hi-fi and lo-fi (alternative music) enthusiasts, as well as in various developing nations where consumers have been less inclined to invest in CD technology.

Perhaps the most significant conflict between the record and audio industries and, indeed, the public in the second half of the twentieth century can be found in the controversies surrounding popular uses of cassette tape. Whether made in the form of attacks on 'home taping' (in the industrialised world) or on 'piracy' (just about everywhere else), the record industry has conducted a long campaign against the unauthorised taping of its copyrighted music. Given the difficulties of gaining direct compensation for such uses, the industry has, in recent decades, managed to persuade many Western governments to impose levies on the sale of cassette recorders and blank tapes. This industry-dominated public discourse concerning the supposed abuses of cassette technology has tended to mask the broader social and cultural significance of the medium; economically too, industry lobbying has largely obscured the fact that pre-recorded cassettes outsold both LPs and CDs throughout the 1980s and were thus one of the pillars of the record industry during this period.

As the first recordable audio medium to have gained widespread acceptance among consumers in nearly a century (since the demise of the early Edison wax cylinder; reel-to-reel tape technology never having taken hold outside of the high-end, audiophile market), cassette tape recording offered a form of potential empowerment to users that was unprecedented. Popular musicians and consumers alike used the cassette as an alternative medium of distribution for forms of music that would not otherwise gain the support of the record or radio industries (see Pareles 1987). Cassette technology spread rapidly in the form of devices designed for use in the home, in automobiles, and in portable applications. Given its durability, ease of use, and the huge base of installed hardware, cassettes have been able to fend off other competing technologies and will likely remain a viable format for consumer audio well into the first decade of the twenty-first century (its possible replacement by Digital Audio Tape was effectively blocked by record industry lobbying during the 1980s and other digital audio formats emerging in the 1990s, such as Sony's MiniDisc, met with limited acceptance by the public; digital file formats, such as MP3, are still confined primarily to computer enthusiasts).

Equally important, the low cost and portability of cassette technology contributed to its diffusion throughout the non-industrialised world during the 1970s where its impact on local music cultures has been as profound as it is widespread (Wallis and Malm 1984). Often contradictory in its effects, the cassette has enabled local popular music cultures to thrive, offering greater diversity of content than is available through industry or state-controlled media, while at the same time, it has contributed to the spread of Western pop music. Nevertheless, many commentators agree that the cassette has been a democratising agent in the popular music of the non-industrialised world and has effectively led to the restructuring of the music industry in many countries (see, for example, Regev 1986 and Manuel 1993). Digital technology notwithstanding, the cassette continues to be, on a global scale, one of the most significant audio technologies of our time.

At the dawn of the twenty-first century, many of the debates concerning piracy and home taping that had appeared decades earlier, with the advent of the cassette, have been revived and given a new sense of urgency within the world of online culture – the world of computers and network communications. While a relatively small number of musicians, independent record labels and fans had, at least since the late 1980s, made use of specialised computer networks for sharing and distributing music and information, their efforts were hampered by the sheer size of digital audio files and the relatively slow speed of data transfer. By the late 1990s, the appearance of various file compression techniques and increases in the overall speed of computer networking allowed the digital distribution of music (both legally and illegally obtained) to become a mass phenomenon. The speed with which music can be copied and distributed among, potentially at least, millions of users on an international scale, has become a pressing concern for the record industry.

In particular, the sudden rise in popularity of the MP3 file format – short for Moving Picture Experts Group (MPEG) 1, Layer 3, a digital file format that reduces audio files to a fraction of their normal size while retaining reasonable audio quality – during the 1990s, is a case study in the complex relationships between audio formats, entrepreneurial capital and consumer interests, on the one hand, and the marketing and distribution structures of the record industry, on the other. From the outset, MP3 was recognised, by individual fans and audio pirates alike, as a viable format for sharing and distributing music over the Internet. While the record industry was able, beginning around 1996, to prosecute some of the larger sites offering pirated music, dealing with individual consumers proved to

be more difficult. The problems associated with policing individual behaviour on the Net became even greater with the appearance, in 1999, of a
software program known as 'Napster'. Based on a decentralised, distributed model that allows users to access sound files located on the computers
of thousands of other individuals, Napster immediately became popular
among students on college campuses in the United States and elsewhere.
While many fans (and even some musicians) regard the sharing of copyrighted songs over the Internet as being relatively harmless – a form of
social interaction that may ultimately act in such a way as to promote and
increase record sales – the record industry regards it as a form of theft and
quickly brought legal proceedings against Napster.

The popularity of the MP3 file format also gave rise to a number of web
sites dedicated to offering alternative forms of music distribution and consumer services. For example, MP3.com was founded in 1997 as a site for
the distribution of independently produced music. Funded essentially by
advertising revenues and, more significantly, large sums of venture capital,
MP3.com expanded quickly and, by the year 2000, represented over 50,000
independent artists. In an attempt to diversify its operations, MP3.com
also began to offer new music services, one of which allowed subscribers to
access thousands of copyrighted music files from a centralised data bank.
Once again, the record industry brought suit against MP3.com on the
grounds that the creation of such a data base was in violation of copyright
laws.

While the outcome of both these legal proceedings is, as of this writing,
yet to be determined, it is important to recognise that what is at stake in the
various controversies surrounding the MP3 file format is not simply the
issue of copyright *per se*. The case of Napster needs to be understood as a
clash between radically different value systems – between a particular
notion of what constitutes a legitimate form of social interaction between
fans, on the one hand, and the commercial needs of the industry, on the
other. For its part, MP3.com represents a new type of business model
based on the possibilities offered by digital technology and computer networks (see National Research Council 2000). In taking legal action against
MP3.com, the record industry is, in part, using copyright law to prevent
entrepreneurial competitors from gaining an upper hand in what is, in
essence, a new marketplace. In the meantime, the industry is attempting to
adapt its own marketing and distribution structures to meet the demands
of online commerce.

Aside from the technical formats that support sound reproduction –
vinyl, cassettes, CDs and MP3 – and the possibilities they offer to consumers and industry alike, the various forms of consumer 'hardware' associated with sound reproduction have also played an increasingly

important role in the experience of popular music since the middle of the twentieth century. Above all, the audio industry's penchant for miniaturisation contributed to the reshaping of pop music sensibilities and the social conditions of listening. During the 1950s, the portable transistor radio was an essential component in the sense of freedom and mobility associated with post-war youth culture. Similarly, the 'ghetto blaster', or 'boom box', of the 1970s and 1980s, while significantly larger than the transistor radio, helped fuel hip-hop street culture. Its territorialising power – its ability to lay sonic claim to the street – has been immortalised in Spike Lee's film, *Do the Right Thing*, where the key dramatic moment is precipitated by a confrontation over the blaster's sonic boom and the clash of cultures that it symbolises.

For the more discreet, the Sony 'Walkman' proposed a new kind of balance in the experience of aural and visual environments in the urban landscape during the 1980s (Hosokawa 1984). More than any other technology, the Walkman seemed to epitomise the sense of mobile, privatised musical experience that had been the promise of sound reproduction technology for a century. With a design philosophy and a marketing campaign that was global in scope and targeted at the youth market, the Sony Walkman rose to popularity during the 1980s and early 1990s, influencing the listening habits of an entire generation (see du Gay et al. 1997). In this context, it is perhaps no accident that when the manufacturers of computer peripherals, such as Diamond Multimedia, and others, introduced audio devices dedicated to the playback of MP3 files during the late 1990s, they concentrated their initial efforts on the creation of Walkman-like portable players. Recognising the potential for the portable players to legitimise MP3 as a mainstream consumer format, thus extending its reach beyond the confines of computer-based communications, the Record Industry Association of America launched a legal battle against Diamond Multimedia – a battle that ultimately failed.

While miniaturisation and mobility has been a significant factor in the design of audio technologies, contributing to a wide range of aesthetic and social practices, so too has the development of an increasingly sophisticated set of technologies designed for domestic music consumption. The rise of the modern audio component system – the 'hi-fi' – took place during the post-war period and, together with television, displaced the role of the parlour piano and radio as the central entertainment technologies of the home. As the primary means of listening to music in the home, the hi-fi needs to be understood in terms of its accommodation within, and its contributions towards the construction of domestic relationships: indeed, the incorporation of the hi-fi system into family life can be regarded as a case study in middle-class culture and gender relations of the

1950s (see Keightley 1996). The discourses surrounding the hi-fi experience emphasised hi-fi reproduction as a means of immersing oneself in music; at the same time, the hi-fi was discursively constructed, in opposition to television, as essentially a male domain.

The aesthetics associated with hi-fidelity reproduction have also contributed to the construction of the perceived opposition (or, as I would argue, a complementarity) between domestic and public forms of entertainment. During the late 1960s and early 1970s, for example, as popular music became increasingly used in film soundtracks, the superior audio quality of domestic hi-fi was cited as one of the forces necessitating increased investments in the improvement of audio in both cinema production and exhibition (similar forces were also at play in the live concert presentation of music, resulting in improvements in PA systems). Coming full circle in the 1990s, the introduction of domestic versions of the Dolby Surround Sound system has given rise to the notion of the 'home theatre' and given a new resonance to the aesthetic (and social) ideal of 'immersion' in the experience of hi-fi reproduction.

While phonograph listening was often regarded by critics of the early twentieth century as a form of 'passive' consumption, it should be clear from the examples cited above that this is no longer the case (if, indeed, it ever was). As a final example, one might also consider the rise of *Karaoke*, a practice originating in Japan but increasingly popular in the West during the late 1980s and early 1990s as well, where consumers were invited not to simply sing along with their favourite songs, but actually to take on the role of lead vocalist performing with pre-recorded arrangements of popular hits. Ethnomusicologist Charles Keil (1984: 94) has suggested that we need to consider this novel form of 'mediated-and-live' performance as a kind of 'humanising or, better still, personalisation of mechanical processes'. Keil's analysis could apply equally well to a number of other technologies cited above and highlights, I think, the importance of understanding consumer audio technology as a significant enabling factor, operating at a number of levels, in a wide range of essentially participatory, social and musical practices.

Conclusion

Technology has been central to the production, distribution and consumption of popular music for over half a century; indeed, it has become a precondition for popular music culture at its broadest and most fundamental levels. The debates that have accompanied the introduction of new technology in popular music have often depended on a rigid set of dichotomies:

for example, the distinction between 'live' and 'recorded' music. However, as I have attempted to demonstrate throughout this essay, such distinctions are often misleading: the live performance of popular music is as dependent upon the technologies of audio production and reproduction (not to mention lighting, video and other technologies) as any studio recording (see Goodwin 1992).

As a precondition for popular music-making, technology must be understood as both an enabling and a constraining factor that acts in complex and contradictory ways in music production, distribution and consumption, blurring, in many cases, the distinctions between these otherwise discreet stages in the circulation of music. While it is in the interests of the record industry to use technology in ways that will enhance, rationalise or control the circulation of music, musicians (in the case of sampling) and consumers (with cassettes and MP3 files) have also used technology to disrupt the operations of the industry, if only temporarily. As outlined briefly above, the Internet is, at the turn of the twentieth century, the ground upon which this play between competing interests is currently being acted out. On the one hand, the Internet is regarded as a potentially lucrative forum for direct marketing strategies, sales and licensing for both the traditional record industry and a new generation of entrepreneurs while, on the other, it has given rise to new consumer formats (such as MP3, among others) and emerged as an alternative distribution network for all forms of independently produced music as well as a potential site of new musical experiences and social interactions among consumers. In the end, the outcome of the exploitation and containment of these various possibilities will depend on the ways in which this technology can be used to mediate the ever-shifting set of power relations that exists between the industry and popular music practices.

Further reading

A comprehensive history of audio technology and its role in the evolution of the sound recording industries can be found in Pekka Gronow and Ilpo Saunio's *An International History of the Recording Industry* (Christopher Moseley, trans., London: Cassell, 1998); less detailed but taking a more polemical stance with regards to the musical and cultural significance of sound recording, including the importance of technologies from the microphone to digital sampling, is Michael Chanan's *Repeated Takes: A Short History of Recording and its Effects on Music* (London: Verso, 1995). William Moylan's *The Art of Recording: The Creative Resources of Music Production and Audio* (New York: Van Nostrand Reinhold, 1992) offers a good overview of the technical and aesthetic practices associated with studio recording.

A stimulating account of the shifting musical and cultural meanings associated with the electric guitar – one of the most significant of all musical instrument technologies of the jazz and pop/rock eras – can be found in *Instruments of Desire: The Electric Guitar and the Shaping of Musical Experience,* by Steve Waksman (Boston: Harvard University Press, 1999). The influence of digital technologies on musical instrument design and musicians' practices, as well as an account of the industries that create and promote these technologies, is the subject of my own book, *Any Sound You Can Imagine: Making Music / Consuming Technology* (Hanover, NH: Wesleyan University Press, 1997). An insightful case study of the uses of technology in the production of rap music can be found in 'Soul sonic forces: technology, orality, and black cultural practice in rap music', by Tricia Rose (in *Black Noise: Rap Music and Black Culture in Contemporary America,* Hanover, NH: Wesleyan University Press, 1994).

A number of important studies documenting the diffusion of cassette technology, especially as it relates to non-Western cultures, have been published. Among the first, and the most broadly based, is Roger Wallis and Krister Malm's study of the music industry in some twelve countries around the world, entitled: *Big Sounds from Small Peoples: The Music Industry in Small Countries* (New York: Pendragon Press, 1984). Focused on the dramatic changes in popular music wrought by the advent of cassettes in India is *Cassette Culture: Popular Music and Technology in North India,* by Peter Manuel (Chicago: University of Chicago Press, 1993). Taking a slightly different tack, in *Doing Cultural Studies: The Story of the Sony Walkman* (London: Sage, 1997), Paul du Gay and his colleagues offer a wide-ranging account of the design and global marketing of the Sony Walkman and its impact on consumption practices.

Much of what has been written about MP3 files and the Internet in the popular press (and throughout the Internet itself) has been largely naive, partisan, or sensational in character. A recent study that examines the underlying industrial and structural issues raised by the new technologies was conducted by the National Research Council in the United States and published under the title: *The Digital Dilemma: Intellectual Property in the Information Age* (Washington, DC: National Academy Press, 2000).

2 The popular music industry

SIMON FRITH

The music industry question is straightforward: how to make money out of music? But the answer is 'with difficulty', and pop music as we know it now has been shaped by the problems of making music a commodity and the challenges of adapting money-making practices to changing technologies.

The underlying issue is metaphysical. Music is, by its nature, non-material. It can be heard but not held. It lasts only as long as it plays. It is not something that can, in any direct way, be owned. How to turn this intangible, time-bound aural experience into something that can be bought and sold is thus the question that has driven popular music history since the first wandering performers sang for their supper, and I will examine the changing solutions to this problem shortly. But there's another issue here that needs noting. Music is a universal human practice, like talking or tool making. All of us can do it; all of us do do it: sing to ourselves or our children, hum and chant, dance and tap out a rhythm. To make money out of music, then, means differentiating one set of musical practices (for which we'll pay) from another (for which we don't). The very ubiquity of music in everyday life means that the line between music we make for ourselves and the music for which we go to market is rather more blurred than the music industry would like.

The starting point for an understanding of the music industry, to put this another way, must be the fact that 'popular music' is not the same thing as the sum of the products of the popular music industry. If popular music is the music of everyday life then it is obvious that our soundscape is not just made up of music on the radio, piped through shopping malls or played on our stereo systems. From stretching songs in the shower to skipping songs in the playground to the slurred sing-a-long in the bar, from the music made in churches and coaches to amateur choirs and choral societies, garage bands, front-room string quartets and bedroom electronic boffins, much everyday music is self-made. It often refers to commercial music, of course – as a source of songs and performing styles; and there is a large sector of what we might call semi-commercial music: the *karaoke* night in the pub, the local ceilidh band playing a wedding, the teenage deejay at a children's party. And what this suggests is that in popular music the distinction between the amateur and the professional is hard to draw and easy to confuse. A local club band or singer can suddenly find themselves signed to a major label, paid well to do pretty much the same things they had done for years as amateurs. A musician can 'make it' with a group, have years of fame and fortune only to end up back on the semi-pro circuit, their real living being made outside music altogether.

My point here is that popular music culture isn't the effect of a popular music industry; rather, the music industry is an aspect of popular music culture. The industry has a significant role to play in that culture, but it doesn't control it and, indeed, has constantly to respond to changes within it. Which is also to say that the music industry cannot be treated as being somehow apart from the sociology of everyday life – its activities are themselves culturally determined. As a social activity popular music culture can be mapped along two axes. On the one hand there are degrees of mediation. All musical experiences may in a sense be the same – the hearing of sounds organised into a communicative pattern – but, none-theless, the way music reaches us can be more or less direct, from the sheer physical pleasure of singing to ourselves in the bath to the alienating expe-rience of hearing the same tune as Muzak while we wait on telephone hold. One way to think about this is in terms of choice: singing in the bath is self-indulgence; we are immediately embarrassed when we realise we've got an audience; Muzak on the phone is a widespread source of irritation, it is music imposed on us by machines. This relates to the second axis: the degree of collectivity. And the paradox here is that the technology which has meant the mediation of music also made possible the apparent privat-isation of the musical experience. We can, for example, write the history of twentieth-century popular music culture in terms of a movement from collective to individual activity. The phonograph meant that public musical performances could now be heard at home; the portable gramo-phone and transistor radio meant that music moved into the bedroom; the Walkman meant that each individual could make a personal listening tape for use even in public places. In general terms, the industrialisation of music, as both a technological and an economic process, describes how music came to be defined as an essentially individual experience, an expe-rience that we choose for ourselves in the marketplace and as a matter of our cultural autonomy in everyday life. This account of music – as some-thing that we can possess – would not have made sense in 1800.

What we are possessing, though, is still an access to a collective world: we buy a record knowing that our taste is shared – and measured by the charts; we listen to a radio station whose appeal is that its deejays can make us feel members of a taste 'community'. Even Walkman listeners, turning in on what they alone can hear in order to block off the noises and people around them are, at the same time, moving outwards, to the material and imagined worlds of the performers, as members of implied audiences and scenes. Popular music culture is, if you like, an immense communication network. Some of these networks involve direct relations with other people (the fellow members of a choir or band or club); others are mediated by record companies, radio stations and tapes made by friends. Such networking is by its nature social, whether we experience such sociability materially, bumping up against people at a concert or dance, or virtually, hearing a singer singing just for us, floating off into an imagined community. If music is a universal human practice, then the experience of music is an essentially humanising experience, a kind of ideal of sociability, a way of making us feel what it is to be engaged with other people. And it is precisely this which gives the music industry its chance to make money out of music: the musical experience is so valuable to us that that value can be realised in commercial terms; but it is also so valuable to us that its meaning can never be constrained or determined by the market, especially given the market's tendency to treat us as atomic individuals. And this is the music industry's problem.

Musical storage

I want to return now to my starting question: how can you turn something fleeting and ethereal like music into something material, to be bought and sold for money? The answer is in terms of storage and retrieval. If you can somehow store music, in such a way that access to that store means retrieving it, re-experiencing the music as music, then people might be willing to pay for that storage device. The changing technological possibilities of musical storage, the possibilities that have shaped the music industry and its practices, are best understood historically.

The first musical stores, if I can put it like this, were musicians and their instruments. Musicians stored music in their memories, not just in the sense of remembering a tune or rhythm in their heads, as it were, but also in the sense of remembering how to reproduce that tune bodily, in a particular movement of muscles and hands and breath. For a musician – this is what defines a musician – music is remembered as much physically as mentally. And making music also involves retrieving the sounds 'stored' in musical instruments, whether simply (banging together two blocks of wood, blowing into a pipe) or with great virtuoso skill (playing a Beethoven piano sonata, an improvisation on an electric guitar).

Here, then, were the first sources of musical money making. A musician would retrieve – perform – music in return for payment, whether from secular or religious patrons, from communities or passing individuals. The more skilled they were perceived to be, the higher returns they could command, and from the very earliest days in all societies one can assume both that there was a push to a kind of craft specialisation (so that for the more skilled musicians music-making became their dominant activity) and that other people could get material rewards off the back of the musician, whether acting as an impresario or agent, selling and negotiating the musical services provided, or as an entourage, keeping the performers sober, making sure they were in the right place at the right time (hence the role to this day of popular musicians' friends and family). At the same time musical instrument makers (sometimes themselves musicians, sometimes not) could command a return for their skills in providing instruments with richer sounds, more robust frames, easier to use. From the very beginning of human music-making there was a necessary relationship between two sorts of skill and activity – making music, making musical instruments. And from the very beginning too the differentiation of specialists from the everyday was not just a matter of skill – everyone could retrieve a song from memory, everyone could make something to bang or blow; but also of social organisation. The development of specialist musicians and musical instrument makers was part of the division of labour that marked the emergence of larger communities and more extended networks of trade and manufacture. In terms of popular music, one aspect of this needs emphasising in particular: musicians' 'value' to communities, audiences or patrons, the skills which enabled them to make a living as musicians, were determined by those communities, audiences and patrons themselves. Whether a musician was thought to be any good or not involved judging them in terms of both their immediate effectiveness but also against listeners' own musical memories, particularly when so much music-making was ritualised, an aspect of social events like harvesting, marriage and death. And even when crafts were organised into guilds, with licences, apprenticeships, etc., music-making was too popular a skill to bureaucratise. A musician was still judged in terms of the music made rather than the apprenticeship served (even if, to this day, classical performers lay out their provenance, as if their playing qualities were guaranteed by their teachers' fame).

The first revolution in musical storage was the combination of notation and printing. Music could now be stored in a score, and that score could be reproduced any number of times. Like most technological revolutions this didn't mean that new ways of doing things replaced old ways (for a score to be realised as music, musicians and musical instruments were still needed) but, rather, that new ways of doing things emerged alongside old ways. In immediate terms scoring meant the emergence of a new music-making figure, the composer (who no longer had to take the stage; composition could now be separated from performance), and a new money-making figure, the publisher: composers needed someone to get their work to market (although, of course, in the earliest days of music publishing, the composer and publisher were often the same person).

Three aspects of this change were particularly significant for the development of a music industry. First, there began to develop a distinction between commercial and non-commercial music. I don't mean the distinction between classical and pop, high and low culture with which we are familiar – so-called classical music is precisely that music produced by the first music publishing industry – but between notated and unnotated music, between commercial music and folk music. The modern music industry, in other words, took shape in ways that excluded the most popular forms of music-making. It depended on ways of composing, arranging and learning music which were not the ways in which music following oral traditions worked. Second, the score put into place a new music-making hierarchy: on the one hand, this led to the nineteenth-century emergence of the virtuoso instrumentalist as star (emerging alongside the newly romanticised composer as genius); on the other hand, it meant that people at home could play composed music too, buying instruments (particularly pianos) and scores for themselves. These processes involved two new music markets: paying customers for live performers (replacing the patron system) and middle-class families for sheet music and instruments and music lessons. Third, the rise of new music businesses and markets meant an increasing concern to protect investments and property from theft and piracy. As music became a publishing industry so it took on the general publisher's concern with the legal protection and regulation of copyrights.

Long before it was a record business, the music industry was a rights business. Its profit making depended on its ownership of copyrights. Once a publisher had established its legal ownership of a musical work (under the terms of its contract with the work's composers) it could both prevent anyone else publishing it and later, under performing rights legislation, license its various uses in public performance. The new music industry was thus as dependent on legal structures as on market demand, and I'll come back to its nature as a rights business later. The final point I want to make here is simply that notational storage was a new way of making money out of musical performance: in the commercial music world a musical event now meant musicians retrieving sounds from scores as well as instruments.

The second major music industry revolution followed the technology of recording: sounds could now be stored and retrieved on discs and cylinders. From one perspective the gramophone was just another musical instrument, a device which 'held' music, music that could be heard once

the instrument was played, and certainly in terms of marketing and manufacture there was a straightforward continuity from piano selling to
player piano selling (the music stored on a roll) to gramophone selling
(the music stored on a disc). As late as the 1960s, in small towns in Britain
at least, it was still normal to buy records in a music shop which also sold
instruments and scores. But the gramophone (and player piano) were
different from other musical instruments in one key respect: music was
now stored on roll or disc (provided for the first time as software), it therefore became possible to 'play' a musical instrument without having any
musical skills. Music could be made at home as a matter of consumption
rather than technique.

The immediate commercial effect was the development of a new industry sector – the manufacture of gramophones and gramophone records.
The music industry became part of the electrical goods industry and had a
hugely expanded potential market: every household. Domestic record
buyers didn't have to be musical, and, at the same time, records hugely
increased the potential public use of music, whether by other new electrical media such as the radio or simply in all sorts of places of public entertainment. Rights holders – who were to be given rights now in recorded
sounds as well as in musical works – had unprecedented new sources of
income. By the end of the twentieth century they were making at least as
much money from such public uses as from the sales of records to private
consumers.

The most important effect of recording technology for popular music,
though, was that it allowed music to be stored and retrieved as it was performed rather than as it was written and thus made possible the commercialisation of folk music. Recording, to put this another way, allowed the
mass distribution for repetitive listening of the particularities of a specific
performance. Musical qualities such as timbre, tone and rhythmic individuality could now be stored as effectively as melodies and harmonies had
been by written notes. A process driven by profit-making thus made commercial popular music out of folk music, out of vernacular improvisation.
The global impact of African–American blues and jazz was dependent on
recordings; these were not musics to be played from scores. And later technological developments in recording – the electrical microphone, tape
recording – had similarly unexpected effects. If record companies began
by recording existing musical stars (using their fame to sell the new
machines), they became themselves the most important star-makers. A
singer like Bing Crosby rose to fame as a radio, record and film performer
rather than as a live act. And, similarly, if initially recordings were just that,
records of really happening studio events, they became sonic compositions, studio-created works that had never actually been performed and

often couldn't be – whether a concoction of doctored noise like the Beatles' *Sgt Pepper* or Glenn Gould's spliced together 'perfect' version of a Goldberg variation. The recording studio became less like a photographer's studio – everything carefully arranged to be captured in a sitting – and more like an artist's studio, the finished product emerging from scraps and daubs and overdubs. To make a record was to make something quite new; no longer to pursue 'fidelity' to an original 'live' event.

I stress this here because the third revolution in musical storage, digital technology, was obviously shaped by analogue practices: it allowed people to do more quickly and easily what they were doing anyway. The CD replaced the vinyl LP, digital editing the tape machine, but the music was much the same.

In the longer term, though, the storage of music as information has had three significant industrial effects. First, it poses in new ways the question of the ownership of music. On the one hand, digital technology extends the definition of what can be owned: from work (the score) to performance (the record) to sounds (digital information); on the other hand, it therefore extends the possibility of theft, whether in terms of sampling (sounds taken from one work and manipulated for use in another) or piracy (digital copies are identical to the original and much easier both to make and to pass off). Second, it changes the nature of musical composition from writing to processing, thus confusing long-established distinctions between music and noise (digital recording has among other things transformed music-making in multimedia such as films and video games). The most obvious aspect of this change (already underway with analogue technology) is that we cannot easily distinguish the roles of musician and sound engineer, and the 1990s rise of the deejay as performer also meant a blurring of the boundary between consumption and production: what kind of musical activity is scratch mixing? But the most interesting is its effect on the meaning of collective music-making. This no longer means getting musicians together physically but virtually, so it is, perhaps, ironic that the most successful post-digital popular music, rap, formally combines digital studio composition, ingenious engineers, with good old-fashioned face-to-face improvisation. Third, digital technology makes possible the process that is described by the ugly word 'disintermediation', whether this means musicians sending their works to listeners directly (thus cutting out music publishers and record companies) or listeners downloading music from record companies directly (thus cutting out retailers).

Within the music industry itself, the effects of digital technology are still described as possibilities, and the immediate policy is to encourage some (making money out of sounds) and discourage others (piracy). I'll return to the future later. The point I want to stress here concerns the past. The contemporary music industry has been shaped by its history. In summary it is:

a rights industry, dependent on the legal regulation of the ownership and licensing of a great variety of uses of musical works

a publishing industry, bringing those works to the public but itself dependent on the creativity of musicians and composers

a talent industry, dependent on the effective management of those composers and musicians, through the use of contracts and the development of a star system

an electronics industry, dependent on the public and domestic use of various kinds of equipment.

The supply side

One way of describing the music industry is as a business in which both the supply side (the musicians) and the demand side (the consumers) are irrational; record companies, which make their money from bringing supply and demand into line, are thus organised around the bureaucratic organisation of chaos. Two consequences of this are striking. First, as in other cultural industries, the vast majority of the music industry's products are, in economic terms, failures – fail to cover their costs. Such losses are more than covered by the size of the returns on successes but an industry in which more than 90 per cent of product is loss-making is obviously organised in a peculiar way: failure is the norm. I'll come back to this. Second, there are running tensions between record companies and their artists, on the one hand, and their consumers, on the other. The record industry is organised around legal contracts, on the assumption that companies will rip off musicians, musicians rip off companies unless restrained by the law, and much of the music industry's lobbying efforts go into trying to stop consumers doing things – home taping, for example – or at least to charge them for doing so.

Both these conflicts reflect the problems of musical ownership; both can only be resolved by the legal regulation of rights. The starting point here is the general legal principle that 'creators' (writers, artists and inventors) must be encouraged both to create and to make their work available for public education and delight. On the one hand, this means that creators should be financially rewarded for their work; their reward should be sufficient to cover their investment in the acquisition of the appropriate skills and resources. On the other hand, to be accessible for public use their work must be available at reasonable prices, so that society as a whole may benefit from it. Hence the copyright system: musicians get their financial return on their work by licensing its use by the public for a fee. The music is publicly available and the more it is used – the more popular it becomes – the greater the returns to its authors, the greater the incentives for other people to create too.

There are two problems involved in turning this ideal into material practice. First, individual artists and performers are rarely in a position themselves to get their work to the public. They need to contract other people – agents, promoters, publishers, record companies – to organise and promote concert tours, to manufacture scores and records and CDs. Even Internet selling is going to need some intermediaries: well-known groups may be able to reach a significant market directly; unknown groups are going to need something – probably a branded music provider, the Net equivalent of a deejay like John Peel – to make themselves known. Second, the sheer cost of policing one's rights in a work is prohibitive. To track down its unlicensed uses, collect fees owed from licensed premises, monitor local radio stations and hairdressers, is likely to cost rather more than the fees so gathered. In economic terms the copyright system therefore depends on collecting societies (like the Performing Rights Society in Britain), set up by publishers and composers as non-profit organisations to administer licences and licence fees on behalf of all music rights holders. Such national societies (most established at the beginning of the twentieth century following international agreements on copyright) also collect the monies due to foreign composers and publishers in a chain of reciprocal agreements (a chain now under threat from the rise of multinational publishers and the direct digital flow of music across national boundaries). For creative artists to benefit from their creative rights, in other words, they have to do deals with publishers, deals which can and usually do mean ceding some of their creative power. Except in the case of well-established stars with a known market, record companies rarely act simply as distributors, a mechanism used by artist A just to reach an audience. Rather, the company will attempt to shape A's music to meet its own understanding of the market, and the power to shape music this way is built into artist/label contracts. While popular music thus depends on the collaboration of creators and bureaucrats, the tension between them, a tension usually read ideologically, as *art vs commerce,* is built into the system.

Until quite recently (and certainly when compared to the film and television industries), the music industry did little formal market research, except in the form of the charts. And even the charts, a measure of what is selling and what, given airplay figures, is likely to sell, are primarily used as a means of stock control: further pressings can be quickly made of records that are showing a sales success; all work on non-selling records can be stopped. The industry's assumption of the essential irrationality of the music market can be seen in the respect paid since the earliest days of Tin Pan Alley century to those people (song writers, talent spotters, deejays, producers) who are thought to have 'good ears', whose understanding of popular taste seems to be 'instinctive'.

If some industry ears are better attuned to popular taste than others, no one gets it right every time, and the music industry has therefore developed two devices through which to keep control of unreliable demand. The first device (familiar in other cultural industries) is a *star system*. Stars can be defined as musicians whose past sales successes are taken to guarantee their future sales successes. By thus countering the usual demand uncertainties stars have been absolutely essential for the record industry, often providing the great majority of a label's profits (Elvis Presley for RCA, the Beatles for Capitol, U2 and Bob Marley for Island). Star-making, rather than record selling, is a record company's core activity; the latter is dependent on the former. This means that the music an act or artist makes has to fit a star image and personality; these days as much money is spent on image making as on music-making and no one gets signed to a record label without a discussion of how they will be marketed.

The other way in which the music industry seeks to bring order to the music market is in the use of *genre labels*. Pop music marketing has always meant marketing different types of music to different types of consumer. This is most obvious in the lay out of record shops: discs are racked as rock, country, dance, rap, reggae, world music, and so on. In broader terms, each genre is a kind of popular music world in miniature, with its own magazines, radio programmes, live venues and specialist shops and web sites. As Keith Negus has shown, far from record companies imposing a single corporate culture on these worlds, they seek, rather, to accommodate the different ways in which different musics are used by different audiences. Each record company division – rock, salsa, country, rap – has its own commercial and cultural character (Negus 1999).

Demand

This is to return to my starting point, that we can only understand the popular music industry in the context of a popular music culture, and I want to turn now to the demand side of the equation, to the question of what people want and get from music. The obvious point here is that one can only make money out of music if people are prepared to pay for it; the less obvious point, perhaps, is that this may be less a matter of how a particular piece of music is valued than of the circumstances in which music of some sort is taken to be necessary. We would find it odd nowadays, for example, to attend a funeral without music, to watch a film without a soundtrack, to walk round a shopping mall without background sound. If the development of a music industry depended on the development of a music market, so that performers and composers had to compete for public attention rather than produce music to order for a patron, the emergence of such a market was itself dependent on changes in the organisation of people's lives and leisure. Entertainment as a social activity – an activity necessarily musical – shaped the music industry as much as it was shaped by it.

I want to discuss this here in terms of three issues. First, *the special vs the everyday*. Historically music has been used to mark out the special event – the religious service, the rituals of death and birth and coming of age, celebrations of life, moments of grief. Music marks out both a space and a time as being different from the everyday. It works both to intensify the appropriate feelings (it's as if music makes possible a particular sort of engagement, an undistracted concentration on the moment) and to collectivise them. We feel the music individually but also as a form of what the ethnomusicologist John Blacking called 'fellow feeling' (this is still obvious in the use of song in the playground or at a football match). There's a common experience of music here (even if it is accounted for differently in different musical ideologies) as something that 'takes us out of ourselves', which transcends the everyday material world. And the point I'm adding is that this sort of musical experience is associated with – made possible by – special occasions.

Nowadays, by contrast, music accompanies all activities. People are woken up by an alarm radio set to a music station; they shower or shave to music, go to work wearing a Walkman or listening to a cassette or CD in the car. People listen to music while they work, shop and hold on the telephone. There is music playing while we eat and drink, wait for a bus to come or a train to start, when we sit at a computer screen or do aerobics in the gym. It is difficult to think of any activity now, except perhaps sleeping, which is not carried out to music, whether music we choose or have imposed on us (and there are by now several collections of bedtime tracks). The twentieth century meant an extraordinary explosion of music. We don't just hear music everywhere and all the time but take it for granted that we can hear music from any place and moment in recording history.

There is no doubt that the ubiquity of records has profoundly affected the relationship between music and noise. Much of the music we hear is now noise, whether as an undifferentiated ambient sound or because of its irritating effects. Partly in consequence, the music we do listen to draws on what once would have been heard as noise, most obviously volume: the sheer loudness of contemporary popular music as it competes for attention with every other noise in our soundscape is perhaps its most striking aesthetic feature. And there are numerous other electronically produced sounds that would have once been heard as 'interference' but which are now composed into the music, as it were. What hasn't changed, though, is the belief that music is or can be a special experience. Under certain circumstances we do still pay special attention to the soundtrack of our lives, and it is these circumstances that the music business has to understand.

The industry itself has a touching faith that it is the songs (and singers) themselves which create the right circumstances. If the marketing teams and radio pluggers and video makers can get people's attention for just a moment then listeners may be 'hooked' by a tune or lyric or tone of voice. But the occasions on which people really listen to music are also institutional and emotional. The rise of dance music as the central pop form in Britain in the 1990s is not so surprising when we consider the importance of the dance floor as a site of serious listening, just as the continued popularity of the big ballad (as sung by Céline Dion, say) testifies to the way in which people's love lives sensitise them to the emotional power of music (as well as vice versa). In short, we could say that the popular music industry depends, first, on the routinisation of leisure, on the regular rhythm of work and play, the weekend and the holiday, on the concept of having fun, and, second, on the ideology of romantic love and its consequent narcissistic narratives of feeling. Music is still about special events, it's just that these events are now either commonplace or personal.

This leads to my second issue: *the public vs the private*. Again, in historical terms, we can describe an obvious shift in the experience of popular music from collective activity to private pleasure. Indeed, what would probably most strike a visitor to the twenty-first century from, say, 1850, would not be the sounds of the streets (Victorian cities like London were already cacophonous) but the amount of music in the home, and the development of domestic space as pleasant and comfortable has clearly meant, in part, making it a space in which music plays. In terms of public/private, though, the domestication of music is not straightforward: if listening has been, in a sense, privatised, what we listen to has not. The radio, record and television industries flourished by bringing public events into the home and so we have a situation in which many people who've never seen an opera or a jazz quartet, a punk band or a drum'n'bass deejay, regularly stage such events, on record, in their living rooms.

In more general terms it can be argued, I think, that the effect of twentieth-century media was less to privatise musical and other cultural experiences than to blur the distinction between the public and private spheres. Is listening to a live Proms concert on the radio or watching Oasis on *Later* on television a public or a private activity? And if concert halls and rock clubs can take shape in the imaginary spaces of the bedroom, so public spaces can become the settings for private events. It has been said that the juke box, at least in the United States, saved the record industry in the late 1930s and early 1940s – more records were then sold to juke box operators than directly to the public, and for United States servicemen and women, moving about the country as they prepared for war, the juke box became a particularly valuable way of establishing familiar space in a strange camp or bar. More recently, one of the earliest uses of digital technology was in the development of *karaoke*. The appeal of *karaoke* seems to be the way it allows private people to become public performers and public performances to become private happenings.

Rather than talking about the privatisation of music we should, perhaps, see music as the medium through which we negotiate the complex relations between our public and our private selves. Music's ability to move from stage to sitting room, from the emotional nuances of a particular love affair to the noisy clamour of barroom sentimentality, is precisely what makes it so important in our lives. This is certainly how the music industry sees it. What has mattered for sheet music sellers and film star makers, for record companies and radio programmers, has not been the privatisation of music but its individualisation. For the industry to flourish it needed to encourage a particular kind of musical consumption: buying things, whether records, tapes or discs, concert tickets or club admission. And this in turn means offering music as something that consumers can possess, can own in the same way as the other goods we buy. This is one reason why the industry's campaign against home-taping was so unconvincing: on the one hand, we were told that to buy music on record was somehow to make that music ours; on the other hand, we were told that we couldn't therefore do just what we liked with it.

The individualism at the centre of commercial popular music accounts for the third issue I want to discuss here: *identity vs difference*. Music seems always to have been important for collective identity – communities know themselves through their musical memories – and it has also always been manipulated by nationalist politicians, whether in the form of national anthems or a contrived folk music which can be used to mark off non-nationals as 'other', outwith 'our' song. What the commercial music industry has done is make the way music can offer a sense of belonging (and exclusion) a part of its sales pitch. Whether through the star system (fans identifying with idols) or, more significantly, through genre marketing (types of music – country, heavy metal – standing for ideological communities), record selling has meant persuading people that their music market choices aren't just a matter of self-indulgence but also link them to communities. Musical tastes matter so much to people because, however vainly, they take them to be a statement of what sort of people they are.

One paradox here is that the most obviously 'commercial' of music industry practices – merchandising, say – are also those most obviously tied into the creation of a fan community (in the construction and marketing of boy bands to young girls, for example). One could perhaps conclude that what seems most glaringly commercial from the outside (the way pop acts are packaged for the teen market) doesn't seem so manipulative from the inside, for the teen consumers who belong to the Westlife or Boyzone fan clubs. Rock fans are certainly notoriously blind to the role of merchandising, packaging and smart promotion in their own investment in Oasis, Beck or Travis. Woe betide the rock critic who suggests, as I once did, that there was not much difference in the selling of Genesis and Bros! Gender ideology is certainly at play here too: the same boys who despise girls for their collection of Boyzone mags and toys will proudly show off their collection of Radiohead b-sides and tour tee-shirts; girls, it seems, are dupes; boys are cognoscenti.

Music media

But there's a broader issue for the industry here. In constructing communities of consumers (and using that sense of community to make a star or record appealing in the first place) record companies depend on media that they don't control. Teenybop culture is shaped by magazines like *Smash Hits* and *Top of the Pops*; indie rock culture by music papers like *Spin* and *New Musical Express*. Every musical genre has its specialist magazine – *Kerrang!* for heavy metal, *Vibe* for rap, *Muzik* for dance music – and record companies reach their markets through such magazines, rather than directly. To put this another way, record companies have rarely constructed a new music market themselves; their sales activities have meant, rather, responding, more or less quickly and efficiently, to musical taste patterns emerging from the market itself, and given meaning by music media (the most obvious example of this is the role of the American magazines, *Crawdaddy* and *Rolling Stone*, in shaping the new rock market in the United States in the late 1960s). What matters for the music industry here is not whether their records get good or bad reviews, but that their acts find a place in the appropriate music world. The first question asked of any demo tape arriving on any record executive's desk is: what sort of music is it? What the question means is: which market is it for?

The print media occupy a particular place in the history of the popular music business: they have probably had the most influence on how people understand and talk about particular genres. But they are only ever read by a very small part of the music market. Their general effect is indirect: the way in which music writers respond to a new act or sound feeds back into the way in which the record company markets them, informs the coverage of non-specialist press, radio and television, influences retail campaigns, stage performances and the broader popular music culture. In this communicative network the original argument is simplified but remains recognisable – the development of punk in the mid-1970s is the most transparent example of how a way of writing about music came to define what performers and audiences thought they were doing and so how punk was marketed. But whatever print journalists' ideological influence, particularly in the marking out of genre boundaries, the most important medium through which record sellers reach record buyers has been and is still radio.

In the early years of the twentieth century the radio and record industries were thought to be competing for consumers: they seemed to be offering alternative ways of enjoying music in the home. Why would someone with a record player and disc collection need to listen to a radio programme of music they had neither chosen nor necessarily liked? Why should someone who could tune into music for free go out and buy records for themselves? These remain valid questions, even if we take it for granted these days that the two kinds of listening go together – it is rare nowadays to find someone who only listens to the radio, or who only listens to records. Ever since the invention of the radiogram it has been assumed that domestic consumers wanted electrical goods that would allow them to choose from a range of listening options, and since the 1920s the radio and record industries have therefore had a symbiotic rather than competitive relationship: radio needed music to attract its audiences, and the cheapest source of music supply was recordings; record companies needed radioplay to reach its markets (and the rights income from radio play was itself substantial).

But while the record and radio industries thus serve each other's interests, it is not the case that their interests are identical. The audience radio stations want (whether to deliver to advertisers or as a matter of public service) is not necessarily the market record companies need, and, on the whole, it has been the record industry which has adapted to radio requirements rather than vice versa, whether we're referring to Top 40 pop formats or FM rock programming. It could be argued, I suppose, that in Britain in the 1960s pirate radio stations were developed under record industry pressure (a pressure which eventually led to the BBC launching Radio 1) but as the pirates developed their own musical ideology, so record companies had to start supplying the appropriate records, and the history of Radio Luxembourg, as a station which British record companies could use as a direct sales outlet, suggests that the more its play policy was dictated by record company sales divisions the worse its listening figures.

The point here is that radio is as concerned as other media to create a community from its listeners and uses music to that end, but it is not necessarily concerned to create a community of record buyers – the development of 'gold' stations in both the United States and the United Kingdom in the 1990s thus posed record companies a problem: gold listeners were listening precisely to hear records they already had; it became increasingly difficult for the industry to launch new acts on the radio except in the particular context of youth programming. Differences between commercial and public service radio have also been significant for music industry practice. Commercial radio is organised around demographics, the targeting of social groups of interest to advertisers, divided according to purchasing habits (by age, income, race, etc.); public service radio is organised to meet the needs of a general public. Commercial radio stations thus tend towards a coherent musical sound (boring or reassuring according to taste); public service radio stations to variety (with specialist programmes defined by reference to musical rather than demographic differences). Persuading commercial or public service radio programmers to take a record involves different kinds of arguments and, in the end, different kinds of record making policy. This is one reason why since the heyday of British rock in the early 1970s, the transatlantic traffic in popular music has been surprisingly light – in 1999 there was no British record among the United States's one hundred best selling singles; the sounds of the two countries' pop radio stations are quite different.

Whatever the broadcasting principle, whatever the musical format, the central figure in music radio is the deejay. It isn't music alone that draws together a listening community, but music plus person presenting that music and so, through a tone of voice and use of language, presenting a sense of belonging. And from a record company perspective deejays are, whatever their style, salesmen. The very fact of playing a record on a show is to endorse it, and most of the time radio deejays do more than just play it – they also are its boosters. It is rare indeed – perhaps only on the BBC chart show when the tracks played are chosen by record buyers rather than programme producers, that a deejay will play a record and deride it on air. And, more generally, the radio deejay's role – as representative cum salesman – can be used to describe the promotional role of club deejays too.

Television works in different ways. Television is the medium with the best musical reach – its audiences are bigger than radio's and were, traditionally, designed to cross a variety of musical tastes – and it has a greater audience impact, partly because television, even more than radio, offers audiences events, the sense of being there while the music happens, partly because star-building needs people to see performers as well as hear them. Television was thus the key to the process in which Elvis Presley became a national American star, the Beatles and the Rolling Stones British cultural phenomena, and even now an appearance on *Top of the Pops* or *The Lottery Show* is probably worth more in promotional terms than rotation on Radio 1's A playlist. Until the 1980s, though, and the development of specialist music channels like MTV, television mostly lacked the radio sense of commitment: on television it certainly is possible to present an act and mock it – this was Elvis Presley's initial treatment on national US television shows.

Television can take on some of radio's clubby role, and ape the radio format of music plus presenter, but only in programmes aimed at a specific audience segment. In British and North American television the only audience segment that has really been significant in these terms has been young people. Children's television has been the key to commercial success in the teenpop market, from the Monkees and Osmonds to Take That and S Club 7, and the television shows that have been most important for the music industry – *Oh Boy!*, *Ready Steady Go*, *Whistle Test* and *The Tube* in Britain, *American Bandstand* and *Soul Train* in the United States – have, in television terms, had small audiences. And even these shows were shaped by television's sense of its audience rather than by record company understanding of its markets. The emphasis was on offering viewers access to a seeming live event, whether in a youth club, dance hall or disco. The stars these shows helped to create were thus as much defined by their ability to stand out in a television studio as by their ability to build a record selling career. It was only with the invention of MTV that a form of music television emerged that could be treated like music radio.

Perhaps surprisingly, the cinema has probably had more effect on the sales of specific records than television. In pop terms, films are primarily significant as star vehicles which can be kept under greater promotional control than television shows and which have a greater global reach – for much of his career Elvis Presley used only films to promote his records. British stars, from Cliff Richard to All Saints, have all felt the need to make a film at some stage in their careers and while most of these have had little cinematic impact, the Beatles' *Hard Day's Night* undoubtedly moved their career up a notch, particularly in international terms. But from the beginning of sound cinema films' most important feature for the industry was their ability to get a song into people's heads, whether in musicals (throughout the mid-sixties the Beatles were competing for the top chart spot with the soundtrack of *The Sound of Music*) or, following the success of Henry Mancini's 'Moon River' (from *Breakfast at Tiffany's*) as a number over the opening or closing credits.

Film soundtracks are still the most significant source of best selling singles in the United States and the film/music industries now have their own symbiotic relationships: films are created and produced as a joint film/record company venture, like *Saturday Night Fever* or *Dirty Dancing*; they feature already existing album cuts chosen following elaborate cross-company negotiations. Either way the film promotes both its soundtrack and individual songs on it; the soundtrack album (which may have only a passing resemblance to what is actually heard in the cinema) promotes the film; and a video clip can be used to promote film and music simultaneously.

Gatekeepers and networks

The music media were once thought of as 'gatekeepers'. The image was of a record being released (an act having already got through the gates of the record company) which then, to be successful, had to be approved by various arbiters: music paper writers, radio programmers, television producers, club deejays, concert promoters, record retailers, etc. Each of these people had the power to stop a release getting to the market place; a record that is neither seen nor heard might as well not have been released in the first place. The question then becomes how the gate keepers can be persuaded to let a record through (one answer has been financial inducement or payola); the problem is that their reason for choosing a track – that it is appropriate for a readership or a playlist or a show – does not necessarily rest on the same sort of market assessments that are made by record companies.

Nowadays, though, this model is misleading. Records do still reach the public by passing through a media network, but there is no longer that constant sense of banging against blockages. Fewer records are released these days without the record company ensuring that the gates are open in advance: marketing and promotional strategy can be decided before an act is even signed; indeed, the ability to formulate such a strategy becomes one reason for making a signing. From this perspective one could say that records are, in effect, made for the media rather than the public or rather, perhaps, that they are made for the public as defined by the media. The model of film promotion – songs composed for a soundtrack; soundtrack compiled for a record – can be applied more extensively. A new boy band is put together as a television show and *Smash Hits* spread before a record is released; an indie band is signed because the company hears it as right for the Steve Lamacq or Jo Whiley shows, can see the band's videos on MTV rotation; a dance record is made to deejay order and a company like Ministry of Sound uses its club to sell its records, its records to sell its club and its magazine to sell both. Branding (and a star name is essentially a brand) is by its nature a multimedia strategy, and this kind of networking, which describes a commercial music culture in which success depends on the coordinated circulation of value, has probably always been a more accurate description of the relationships involved (in terms of trusting other people's judgements, for example) than the conflict implied in the gatekeeper model. The gatekeeper image was itself a sales pitch: it contributed to the rock ideology of triumphant artists and their fans storming through the conservative commercialism of the suits.

That said, it is still true that the music industry is particularly dependent commercially on media it doesn't itself control. Even if it is involved formally (through the corporate ownership of a cable service, for example) there remain differences of economic interest and with the exception of film/music tie-ups there are few examples of record companies successfully exploiting their ownership of a television network or magazine publisher. Corporate control of star-making machinery and the album sales pitch involve different institutions.

First, advertising. By and large record advertising is effective only for established stars. Television adverts are for hit packages and artist 'best of' collections; posters give news of the latest superstar release. New acts can't be sold effectively this way; airplay of a new album is a much better way of exciting listener interest than an advertisement for it, whether on radio or television. This comes back to the point that to sell, an act or record has to take its place in a musical culture and, culturally, the advertising voice just sounds wrong. This situation was changed to some extent by MTV, which can be considered as music radio on television, with playlists, charts, veejays, etc. The video clip itself is hybrid. It only exists to promote a record (and to fill out a star image) but it is not an advert for it. What it offers, rather, is a new kind of experience of a record (videos often work to explain what lyrics mean, for example); the aim is still to persuade people to buy the disc (and not the video itself). The advantage of the video from the record company point of view is that it makes the clips itself and can thus control the ways acts are presented; but to work effectively videos are dependent on MTV's decisions – not just the decision to show or rotate a clip in the first place, but decisions about flow and genre and presentation. Repeated video viewing becomes tedious much more quickly than repeated record listening, and continued interest in a clip depends on its interest as television, in the context of a video flow, as framed in different ways by different veejays.

There is an additional promotional issue here. Video production is very expensive (compared to poster or magazine advertising, for example) and to justify such costs marketing departments need to be sure a clip will be widely shown, either because the record is a guaranteed seller (i.e. made by an established star) or because the clip is likely to cross national boundaries, to do its promotional work on MTV and other music programmes in a variety of countries. In promotional terms, then, the good video is the video that can be fitted into a great variety of television contexts, and this is to bring a new sort of constraint to record selling: the major labels rarely sign acts these days without reference to their potential international appeal.

The other form of promotion over which record companies can exercise some control is live performance. Concert tours are planned (and often funded) by record companies to sell an album; promoters have become, in effect, the fee-paid providers of a professional service. Live tours are important promotionally not just because in concert a group can seal its own image, as it were, but also because the concert (rather than record release) becomes the event which focuses all other promotional activity at a local level – the radio play, retail display, press coverage, merchandising, and so forth. Except for the biggest stars, though, live performance is a loss-making activity and dependent on a ever decreasing network of suitable venues. One consequence in the last decade, at least for rock, has been the rising importance of the annual festival, a two or three-day event at which dozens of bands play. Festivals are a cost effective way of staging live music – promoters and audiences both benefit from the economies of scale; they are equally useful for superstars and new acts; they have become settings for the enactment of genre communities that are the key to the record selling process in the first place. The rise of the festival means a return of the package tour which dominated the British pop scene till the end of the 1960s, but overlaid now with a Woodstock vibe, a rave sensibility, a general New Ageism.

The record industry

The rock festival can be taken to stand symbolically for the state of the contemporary music industry. Here we have a gathering of fans and musicians hoping for the unexpected, and the proximate threat of drugs and drink and anarchy, but all, in fact, tightly controlled. Festivals depend on interminable negotiations as to who will appear where and in what size type on the posters, who will perform when and for how long on which stage; on detailed arrangements with local fire and police services; on carefully calculated logistics of sewage, food and first aid. The only real threat of chaos is the weather. The festival is symbolic, then, because the industry is also essentially concerned with the rational organisation of irrational forces – talent, taste – while celebrating itself as buccaneering.

Mike Jones has suggested that we can understand the music industry better if we regard it as more about the production of failure than success (Jones 1998). He's not only referring here to the statistic I've already mentioned: if ten out of eleven issued records fail to cover their costs then clearly the industry is devoting a lot of its time to fruitless projects, whatever the compensating cash flow from the hits. Jones is also drawing attention to management strategies and to a management culture that reflect a sense of fatalism. To begin with, although the industry presents itself in risk-taking terms, and it's true that every release is a kind of gamble, in day-to-day practice what this means is a strategy of risk avoidance. To be profitable a company has to maximise the returns on a would-be winner, minimise the losses on a likely loser – hence the charts as the central form of market research and the importance of size as the best hedge against misjudgement (small companies can't carry so many losses and so, paradoxically, often find it harder to cut and run from a project that clearly isn't working). One effect of the resulting system of portfolio management (companies put out a range of products to ensure they've always got something that can profit from market trends) is that different acts signed to the same label can be treated in quite different ways, partly because the genre divisions of companies are run and budgeted differently, but partly because a continuous assessment is being made of an act's potential value, and this can change regardless of how they are developing musically. I'll come back to this.

The second point I want to take from industry analysts like Jones and Negus is that built into the record industry is what we might call a culture of blame. To begin with a project's failure can be blamed either on the fickleness of public taste or on the obduracy and/or self-indulgence of the artists, but, as Keith Negus has shown, such blame is also turned inward (Negus 1992). The record industry involves in practice the collaboration of two groups of employees: the A&R (Artists and Repertoire) department, which works with the talent (signing acts up, developing their potential, taking charge of the process in which they produce something for the market) and Marketing, which takes that something and tries to sell it. These departments have equal status both in budgetary terms (promotion and production costs are similar) and as decision makers (marketing executives are centrally involved in the discussions of what acts to sign and what then to do with them). When a project is successful these departments will both take credit (I've always been struck at the Mercury Music Prize awards ceremony by the way in which record company A&R and marketing executives will modestly accept applause for a record's success, as if was all their own work). When a record fails, though, it is routine for one department to blame the other. How can we be expected to sell such crap? asks a marketing team (putting the blame on the musicians and on A&R, the people meant to be looking after them). Why didn't you do a proper sales job? responds A&R (putting the blame on the public and on marketing, the people meant to be looking after it). It's all the fault of the producer, the protagonists then agree – the producer, as the person employed to turn an act's sales potential into a marketable product, is usually not a company employee and so a useful scapegoat.

Negus points out that the tension between A&R and marketing often reflects social differences. When he was doing his British research, in the 1980s, A&R was dominated by male rock fans, committed to a long-term strategy of talent building. Marketing departments were more likely to be staffed by female pop fans interested in image building and with a necessarily shorter term outlook – their job was to sell what was to hand. But I want to emphasise a different point. The underlying assumption here among both groups, is that a record company is indeed pursuing success but is thwarted, either by musicians (and producers) not delivering the right product or by the public not responding, often because of factors beyond a company's control (competition from other records or other media; the unpredictable rise and fall of fads and fashions). But what if the problem is that record companies aren't really pursuing success at all? What if a record's failure reflects not the irrational activities of musicians and consumers but the perfectly rational activities of record companies themselves? These are Mike Jones' questions.

The significant decision here is when record companies decide not to release a record in which they have already invested a considerable sum. This is not an uncommon experience for unknown acts (particularly if you include here the decision to release a record but give it no promotion; it might as well not be released). Why would a company do this? The answer lies less in a changing judgement of potential markets (if this was the issue then at least some sort of market testing would be budgeted) than in broader issues of company policy: the development of the portfolio management structure; the carefully orchestrated programme of global release and promotion; the calculation of what budgets are available for what products when; a sense at any one moment of to which project it makes most sense to devote energy. A would-be new release may arrive in the system and simply have no place for reasons which have nothing to do with its musical or market appeal at all.

Jones, writing from his experience of being a member of a relatively successful rock group, Latin Quarter, suggests that there are a number of reasons why record companies decide to make an act they've signed a failure. As they become increasingly involved in the business of selling music to the media, so shifting media demands change record company assessments of the value of their various acts, and this is tied into the pursuit of global strategies. The policy decisions of national or regional divisions of global record companies (and acts are usually signed through local or regional divisions) are themselves subject to the effects of internal competition between different divisions and to edicts on release policy from on high. There is some evidence, for example, that the accounting structures of large corporate companies like Universal are leading to much shorter-term profit taking than used to be the case for the larger indepen-dent companies like Island, now a part of the Universal portfolio. At the same time the organisation of companies into genre divisions can also mean that acts are marginalised as genres mutate. Record companies have always competed with each other by providing the same sort of product rather than by investing in something completely different; in genre terms, the success of another label's acts (Garth Brooks, Chemical Brothers, Steps) can have an instant effect on the evaluation of a label's existing talent.

One result of this is the shifting role of the artist manager, from impre-sario (hustling and hyping an act come what may) to bureaucrat (taking part in company strategy meetings, keeping the boys in line). Jones recalls that Latin Quarter's manager, who went on to manage Oasis, shifted by default from representing the band's interests to the company to repre-senting the company's views to the band; he became privy to record company thinking that he judged best to keep from the band itself. These days managers provide professional services to record companies and acts alike (a common condition in the signing of new acts is that they get pro-fessional management, as recommended by the record company), and have their own professional association, the International Managers Forum. The surviving mythology of ogres and obsessives like Colonel Parker and Albert Grossman, Brian Epstein and Andrew Loog Oldham is just that, mythology.

Conclusion: the music business in the twenty-first century

Once upon a time (up to the end of the 1970s, anyway), the large record company strategy for dealing with risk was to make sure that whatever money was made out of music, it would have a cut, from the moment a teenager first bought a guitar till the moment he was remembered in a tribute show on television. A company like EMI thus bought its way into the musical instrument business, the publishing business, the concert hall and disco business, the retail business, the magazine business, etc. As for record production itself, as many of the support services as possible were provided in house – the studio and engineers and producer, the packaging and sleeve designer and photographer, the plugging and PR teams. But the down turn in the United States record business at the end of the 1970s and the resulting shake out of staff in all departments led to a rethink, and for the last twenty years the corporate strategy for avoiding risk has been to ensure that the necessary gambles are taken by other people.

Although it's not usually thought of in this way, the biggest financial burden in the development of new talent is carried by the musicians themselves. Most musicians develop their skills for years at their own expense, and even when they first go commercial (playing gigs, recording tracks) it is usually at a loss. And whereas a major record company used then to sign up an act for its first release, these days even this process happens out of house: independent producers and record labels have become, in effect, the major labels' research and development departments, developing new acts and markets until they and/or their artists have had enough sales impact to justify a major company getting involved. At the same time, the riskier bits of the music business (the provision of studio services, for example) are now also mostly run by independents; bespoke services (PR and radio plugging and sleeve design, for example) can be bought release by release, according to ever-changing sales strategies and budgetary constraints.

The result of all this is an industry which has as its core the ownership of rights (the major music corporations thus combine record companies and music publishers) and musical distribution (the major music corporations – Universal, BMG, EMI, Sony, Warner – are part of entertainment super-corporations which are seeking to benefit from all the ways in which music can now be carried globally – sheet music, CDs, cable and satellite television, the cinema, the Internet). Content creation, talent spotting, mapping new markets, are left to independent operators, independent financially but bound to the majors in deep laid networks of trust and reputation. This is the context in which fear of the future because of its threat to the owners of rights is balanced by excitement about the commercial possibilities of the new technologies of digital distribution (as suggested by the merger of Time Warner and AOL). On the one hand, devices like MP3 and software like Napster open up the nightmare vision of a global network of home tapers, able to transmit perfect copies of every CD ever made across telephone lines with no obvious legal or material obstacles;

on the other hand, direct downloading from record company to domestic consumer gives rights holders the opportunity to benefit from every home play of a track, and not just from its initial sales.

It is always rash to predict the future, especially in a music industry in which technology has rarely had its expected effects, but it does seem safe to suggest that digital technology and the convergence of the entertainment, telecommunications and IT sectors won't so much transform one sort of music industry into another as accelerate a process in which different music industries are developing alongside each other, sometimes overlapping in their concerns and personnel; sometimes not. My own prediction is that we will see the development of at least three such parallel music worlds. First, the mainstream pop/rock business, which will continue to market established global stars like Céline Dion and Whitney Houston, to invest in would-be global stars like Robbie Williams and Ricky Martin, using all other music media in their sales campaigns. This sector will still depend on cross-counter mass-market retailers like Woolworths and Walmart even while developing on-line access, and selling music to the public will be increasingly tangled up with processes in which music is used to sell all sorts of other services and entertainment too. Second, an essentially chaotic illegal business, involving at one extreme straightforward crooks ripping off rights holders by bootlegging; at another extreme experimental and political artists, refusing to accept the constraints of copyright law in their use of 'found' sounds and images; and in between the usual variety of pirate broadcasters, illicit club and party organisers, home digital distributors, fast turnover deejay suppliers, and so forth. Third, genre music scenes, local players connected through Web sites and digital radio, but semi-commercial, making enough money to go on making music but not seeking to move up a ladder of ever increasing success.

This description of the future is, of course, simply an extrapolation from the past. From the moment the first music copyright act was passed there was an illegal music sector and, as I suggested at the beginning of this chapter, the commercial music industry has always been underpinned by a rich variety of amateur activity. What I am suggesting now, though, is that in the future the distinctions between these worlds are likely to become firmer, movement from one to another more difficult. Rock, as a particular form of popular music, was marked by the way it occupied all these musical worlds: it achieved new levels of global commercial success while exploiting both ideologically and materially the illegal sector, defining itself unabashedly as an anti-commercial commercial sector. It depended for a flow of musical talent from local music scenes into the professional mainstream and back again. What is not clear now is whether this sort of institutional confusion can survive in the world of digital distribution, digital disintermediation. The question most often asked presently is how will the music industry survive the sales of MP3, Napster, and all the other technological threats to its power and profits? But the more interesting question concerns musical culture itself: what is it going to mean to be a digital musician?

Further reading

Literature on the music business tends to go out of date (and out of print) more quickly than most other academic studies and so the books listed here should be read alongside the latest issues of trade papers like *Music Week* and *Billboard* and the academic journal *Popular Music*. A surprising amount can also be learned about music business practices from pop biographies, particularly if the stars involved (like George Michael or the Stone Roses) have been involved in contractual disputes. The most accessible sources of hard data are the various music industry enquiries carried out by the Monopolies and Mergers Commission. Otherwise, for the history of the music business in the United States see Russell and David Sanjek: *The American Popular Music Business in the 20th Century* (New York: Oxford University Press, 1991). The best account of the British music business is still Keith Negus's *Producing Pop* (London: Edward Arnold, 1992). Negus's *Music Genres and Corporate Cultures* (London: Routledge, 1999) is a good account of the international organisation of record companies, though likely to date quickly. Roger Wallis and Krister Malm's *Big Sounds from Small Peoples* (London: Constable, 1984) remains a remarkably visionary book about globalisation, even sixteen years on. Musical rights are explained in Simon Frith ed., *Music and Copyright* (Edinburgh: Edinburgh University Press, 1993) – the details of legal and technological dispute have changed, but not the underlying moral issues and principles. The most incisive analysis of the impact of technology is Paul Théberge, *Any Sound You Can Imagine. Making Music/Consuming Technology* (Hanover, NH: Wesleyan University Press, 1997). For an influential sociological study of the dance/club scene see Sarah Thornton, *Club Culture. Music, Media and Subcultural Capital* (Cambridge: Polity, 1995). There are no good up-to-date books on either the music press or music radio, although Simon Garfield's *The Nation's Favourite* (London: Faber, 1999) does provide dismaying insight into the peculiarities of Britain's youth pop service, BBC Radio 1. Andrew Goodwin's *Dancing in the Distraction Factory* (London: Routledge, 1993) is an exemplary study of MTV in the United States. For MTV Europe see Lida Hujik's admirable PhD thesis, 'MTV Europe', Department of Media and Communications, Goldsmiths College, 1999. Besides Mike Jones' doctoral dissertation cited above, the best recent studies of the music industry from below, as it were, are Mavis Bayton's *Frock Rock* (Oxford University Press: 1998), Jason Toynbee's *Making Popular Music* (London: Arnold, 2000)and Andrew Bennett's *Popular Music and Youth Culture* (London: Macmillan, 2000). Finally, Simon Frith and Andrew Goodwin eds., *On Record. Rock, Pop and the Written Word* (New York: Pantheon, 1990), a collection of key essays in the development of popular music studies, includes a section on the music industry. These were the articles that influenced my and many other people's approach.

3 Consumption

WILL STRAW

In March of 2000, the head of the United States-based MTV Networks outlined, to a journalist, his techniques for understanding the tastes of teenagers. 'We actually in some cases put people under hypnosis', said 54-year-old Tom Freston, 'and we will videotape their lives.' As he spoke, albums by teen stars Britney Spears and 'N Sync were breaking all-time records for first-week sales of new titles in the United States. While alarmed rock critics bemoaned the predictability of adolescent tastes, Freston saw teenage culture as an elusive, mysterious world. To understand it, he had recourse to the methods of the psychotherapist and anthropologist.

The consumption of popular music has long been seen as chaotic and incomprehensible, even when it seems to confirm the crudest laws of hype and fashion. While trends seem driven by their own, unstoppable momentum, the popularity of any given recording or musical style is notoriously difficult to predict. Long-term prognoses about the music industry's development have regularly proved wrong, and even the rosiest of cyclical booms will often coincide with predictions of that industry's imminent obsolescence. Alongside the image of millions of consumers rushing to shops to purchase Britney Spears' 'Oops! . . . I Did It Again', newspapers offered the spectre of thousands of United States college students in their dormitories, busily (and perhaps illegally) down-loading songs from the Internet. As album sales, in the United States and other countries, continued their upward climb in 2000, Internet industry newsletters spoke of a dying industry, deserted by consumers who now demanded music in cheaper, more convenient forms.

At the same historical moment, millions of other people were acquiring music through means which escaped easy statistical analysis. Many music retail chains now sell used CDs alongside new product, to compete with the hundreds of second-hand stores which have emerged since the 1980s. Teenagers buy vinyl records from thrift stores or specialty dance music shops, spurred to do so by the demands of the sampler or the disc jockey's turntable. Others make copies of CDs in their homes or offices, trading these with fans met on Internet listservers. On Ebay, the on-line auction site, the number of individual recordings made available on a typical day reaches 250,000 or more. These other ways of consuming music are rarely registered within music industry sales figures or popularity charts.

With so much consumption invisible to the industry's statistical eyes, claims about major shifts in consumption patterns invite suspicion. Did female buyers in the United States really, for the first time, buy more music than males, as the recording industry had announced in 1998? Was rock music dead, dying, or temporarily out of fashion, as dozens of press reports in the late 1990s wondered? Had the percentage of music buyers who were over forty-five years of age really doubled in the 1990s? Or did these statistics only measure the consumption habits of those who continued to acquire music through old-fashioned means (by going to a music shop)? Were the hip connoisseurs of emerging trends now so unlikely to patronise traditional music outlets that their tastes did not register within the industry's official measures of success?

Throughout most of its history, the recording industry has invested little in the analysis of consumer behaviour, preferring to release products, promote them and see how the market responds. In contrast, the commercial broadcasting industries are regularly condemned for 'over-researching' their audiences, cautiously designing their programming to reach narrowly defined demographic segments. Strong ties between the broadcasting and advertising industries have produced an abundance of market research on radio listeners' tastes, given shape by each newly fashionable tool of demographic or psychographic analysis. The recording industry, in contrast, has preferred to invest in what the sociologist Paul Hirsch (1972) once called 'the cooptation of media gate-keepers' (winning over the radio or television programmers, critics and other taste-makers who mediate a new record's entry into the public realm). While radio programmers, in the United States and Canada, will slice fine lines between 'Heritage Alternative Rock' and 'Adult Album Alternative' formats, the recording industry's own consumer profiles lump styles together in broadly defined categories (such as the Recording Industry Association of America's 'R&B/Urban', which includes rhythm and blues, blues, dance, disco, funk, fusion, Motown, reggae, and soul).

Two sorts of images compete to capture the consumption of popular music. One conveys the aggregate effect of millions of consumer choices, as stars or fads emerge and cycles of fashion turn. Here, the consumption of music is a public event, the movement of collective energy across the spaces of media and popular obsession. However such events might be judged, in moral or aesthetic terms, their relationship to the market is easy to grasp. In another image, the consumption of music is private, even secret, forever bumping up against the limits of legality. Popular music's associations with alcohol, with a demi-monde of nightclubs and vice, and with the violation of social taboos have long served to paint its consumers as morally suspect. Recent years have brought the repeated charge that music's consumers are engaged in the theft of property belonging to others. Controversies over Internet downloading, court challenges to the second-hand or CD-rental markets, and the widespread claim that compact discs are the most commonly stolen of all household items feed the perception that music circulates recklessly in and out of the legal realm. In no other cultural industry are consumers so regularly marked with the stigma of remorseless criminality, or lectured, like United States consumers recently, on the need to pay for music so as to display 'good citizenship'. Here, arguably, we confront one of the most significant paradoxes surrounding popular music and its consumption. Long derided as among the most slavishly malleable of capitalist consumers, fans of popular music are regularly denounced as irresponsible transgressors of a market economy's social contract.

Forms of consumption

We 'consume' music in a variety of ways, of course, many of which do not involve the direct exchange of money. Differences between these kinds of consumption confound our efforts to describe fully music's place in our lives. Music is, much of the time, among the most ubiquitous, easily ignored and trivialised of all cultural forms. It may unfold just beyond our active attention, in the soundtracks to films or the background noise of pubs and restaurants. As Alan Durant (1984) has noted, music seems to enter our ears uninvited, as 'something literally breathed into the body from the air'. This, too, is a way of 'consuming' music, alongside the more spectacularly obsessive ways which make music the centre of attention.

Nevertheless, the ubiquitousness of music has enhanced its social power, by making it one of the most effective markers of public presence and social difference. While books and television are typically consumed in the privacy of our homes, music regularly intrudes upon the variety of spaces in which our lives unfold. In this intrusion, it may well offend, alienate or entice those who hear it, just as it signals the presence of those who have brought it there. The sense that music easily invades the lives of others has helped to give music its political edge, its place in the conflicts of generation, gender, ethnicity and class. Music is important in such conflicts because it compels us to judge the pleasure of others. The music of these others regularly comes across as excessively repetitive or chaotic, loud or innocuous, boring or disruptive. Either side of these oppositions will fuel the perception that the emotional economy of others is distorted relative to a norm, and such perceptions play a prominent role in the stereotyping of race and age. Adult complaints about the loudness of rock or dance music are, at one level, arguments about the limits of physical tolerance, but they also involve the claim that music has not been kept in its proper place – that a natural hierarchy, in which music would be subservient to conversation, or to the everyday sounds of the street or bar, has been violated. The fanatical devotion to music common among young people is usually seen by their elders as inappropriate, an intensity of attachment to be left behind in the ageing process

We consume music in places of widely varying size and intimacy. Music is heard in mass, large-scale spectacles, like rock concerts, whose enormity is matched only by certain sporting events. In other moments, we listen to music as we read books, in contexts which are solitary and undisturbed. Differences of context are not in themselves sufficient explanations for the different kinds of consumer behaviour, however. In his history of live musical performances in pre- and post-Revolutionary France, James H. Johnson (1995) describes a major transformation in the behaviour of audiences. Prior to the Revolution, a concert was the pretext for conversation, intrigue and sexual play between members of the audience. The performance, much of the time, was simply ignored; audience members arrived late and left when they were so inclined. Fifty years later, audience members were likely to sit silent, transfixed by concerts or operatic performances, respectful of artists and swept up in highly individual, emotional responses. This new politeness, Johnson suggests, was a symptom of the new character of big-city life. With the crumbling of a tightly knit aristocracy, the newly ascendant middle class moved in a world of strangers, seeking out forms of entertainment which nourished their sense of individualistic self-improvement. Insecure about their own capacity to judge, they strained to understand what a composer or singer sought to communicate. Uncertain as to their own status, they clung to the most basic laws of etiquette and restraint.

Similar transformations have marked the history of forms such as jazz, whose passage from night club to concert hall to outdoor festival has followed shifts in that music's status. These movements of venue are marked, as well, by changes in the degree to which the experience of jazz is a celebration of in-group solidarity or personal enlightenment for the individual isolated within a crowd. Audiences at live music performances are regularly caught between two views of music and the proper ways to consume it. One sees music as the most communally festive of cultural forms, the backdrop to social games and rituals. The other casts music as the most pure and abstract of the arts, transcending the social forms of language and narrative to connect with a listener's emotional core. Rock bands or club deejays, whose playing drowns out the conversation which they know, nevertheless, will go on, have negotiated this predicament better than many. In the tension between these ways of conceiving musical consumption, the links between modes and contexts of listening are regularly redrawn. Alongside the familiar contexts of the stadium concert or the club gig, the last few years have brought such new twists as deejay turntable performances in restaurants, for customers who sit passively at their tables. In the United States-based 'home concert movement', artists perform live for several dozen fans, in the living rooms of hosts' homes, during evenings which often include communal meals and discussion (but may exclude tobacco and alcohol).

A quarter of a century ago, tours by rock and pop performers were invariably organised to promote the release of new records. The years since have witnessed an unravelling of this system. Older rock acts, such as David Bowie or Bruce Springsteen, have finally acknowledged that those who purchase expensive concert tickets want to hear older, familiar hits, rather than new material which, for longtime fans, often represents idiosyncratic or unappealing shifts of direction. This transformation of concert tours into blockbuster events is one element among many in the ongoing integration of popular music within the larger tourism and leisure industries. Live performances of jazz, 'world' music, Cajun, reggae and a myriad of other styles are now most easily found in the annual festivals which punctuate the holiday calendars of North American and European cities. In recent years, the same has become true of ska or punk, styles marked increasingly by lengthy festivals offering several bands over many hours or days. Older country music stars, long accustomed to lengthy tours of fairgrounds and concert venues, have established permanent residencies in concert halls which bear their names, attracting fans who travel to hear them perform as part of their vacations. While live performances long served as the contexts for experimentation and the trying-out of new material, they are increasingly among the most conservative of musical events, occasions to revisit music which is familiar and tested.

Music, space and time

The consumption of music has helped to reshape our sense of place. In significant ways, it has helped to draw the cultural maps with which Western consumers understand the world. While the publishing and movie industries enshrined London, Paris, Hollywood and New York as centres of cultural power, music did much to nourish a sense of cultural regionalism. Memphis, Liverpool, Seattle, Manchester, and New Orleans all figure prominently within a widely shared cultural geography because they resonate as the places from which important musical styles have emerged. (Indeed, it is much harder to think of major musical movements which originated in New York City or Los Angeles.) Radio and the phono-graph helped to create national – even global – audiences for regional styles like country music or acid house, drawing them out of the places in which they were born and into a shared popular culture. Technically, these media allowed musicians to remain at home, while their music travelled, but they also encouraged musicians to travel, to perform live for the new, distant audiences created by these new media. In his history of country music, Richard Peterson (1997) notes that the growth of touring circuits for musicians in the 1930s followed the ever-expanding reach of the radio signals, which carried live barn-dance programs featuring these musi-cians. At the present time, mix CDs by prominent club deejays have served to make them internationally known, creating the conditions which result in invitations to top the bills of dance events around the world.

Just as importantly, the consumption of music has shaped our sense of time. The phonograph made older performance styles and musical genres available in the present, for imitation or enjoyment. Indeed, and to borrow a term from media historians, the recording serves as a form of 'extra-somatic memory' (memory stored outside the body), preserving music in material artefacts which outlast the moments in which that music was per-formed. Music history accumulates for us, in the range of reissues available at our local record shop, rather than merely passing us by and disappear-ing in the endless turnover of styles and fashions. More broadly, each new development in music delivery systems has extended the availability of the past, if only because expanded storage capacity has allowed the past to be packaged in more abundant and detailed ways. Obvious cases here include the 33-rpm album (which spurred the gathering together of old 78 singles in album form), the cassette (which allowed for personalised compilations longer than the typical vinyl album), and the compact disc (whose extended recording time has dampened, if only slightly, public opposition to its higher price). While each such innovation has been embraced by pro-ducers of new music, its popular acceptance (particularly with older con-sumers) has much to do with its capacity to keep alive the past. In a sense, the rush of reissues of past materials serves to temper the shock of novelty which each new technology risks producing. This is a familiar pattern from the history of communications media, as Marshall McLuhan (1995) and others have noted. Just as the printing press, in the fifteenth century, sparked the massive publication of texts from classical antiquity, the Internet has led to the wide-spread circulation of old album covers, public domain recordings from decades earlier, and fan sites devoted to the most obscure and faded of musical moments. The musical past now seems more minutely differentiated, richly documented and abundantly accessible than at any other historical moment.

If the past of popular music seems increasingly weighty, its present almost invariably seems fragile. As radio and television pull music from different corners of our culture into our own listening environments, they also organise the music available into a constantly evolving stream of songs. Through a variety of mechanisms (popularity charts and release schedules, for example) we have become used to the idea that music changes every week. As Simon Frith (1981) once noted, there are no logical reasons why millions of teenagers, strangers to each other, should listen to the same records at the same time. Records are not, like television or radio programs, subject to fixed schedules, nor, like the newspaper, do they become obsolete in any obvious sense within short periods of time. Nevertheless, like the newspaper, the turnover of records has come to endow the passage of time with a particular rhythm. To consume music is, much of the time, to be caught up within a distinctive velocity of change, a particular (almost metronomic) way of marking time. Top 40, the format conceived by radio programmers in the 1950s, remains perhaps the purest example of this metronomic impulse. Top 40 was never more than a loose grouping of songs from different traditions, but these were organised to compete directly within a single game of popularity. The simple fact of this competition, rather than any shared properties of the music itself, gave Top 40 its unity. Attempts by the music industries to introduce national sales charts in countries which have hitherto lacked them reveal how culturally specific these ideas about popularity may be. In many such contexts, the idea of different kinds of music being measured against each other, on a scale which changes every week, will seem quite ludicrous.

Philip Ennis (1992) once suggested that the modern music industries were born at that point, after the Second World War, when the various ways of measuring a song's popularity began to be aligned with each other – when radio airplay, the sale of records and sheet music, and jukebox play all became calibrated, in a sense, as part of a single process. These different kinds of success no longer corresponded to different musical worlds with their own audiences and operations – each was now part of a record's overall lifecycle, a step in its passage through the public realm. If popularity on jukeboxes typically followed radio airplay by a predictable amount of time, the industry could plan distribution to jukeboxes accordingly. If fans of slow ballads typically took longer in deciding to buy an album than fans of fast-paced dance music, the release of a slow single to adult radio formats might prolong that album's sales momentum, as these slower fans 'took over' from dance fans in purchasing the album. The slow but phenomenal sales success of Moby's album *Play*, in 1999–2000, came from the alignment of numerous different audiences and markets (dance, music television, clothing store sound systems) into a sequence which saw new fans being introduced to the record just as others had moved on.

Differences in taste between different age-groups are often less striking than the rates at which their favourite styles or genres will change and develop. Fans of underground dance music will learn that records rise and fall in three-week cycles of popularity, and are not surprised when entire styles become obsolete within a year of their emergence. Heavy Metal fans, on the other hand, typically learn the complex genealogy of metal – with its founders and respected heroes – as part of their apprenticeship in one or more Heavy Metal fandoms. The casual, middle-aged music fan, hearing a Céline Dion album in July, may request it as a gift the following Christmas, with no anxieties over its possibly being out of date.

Music, consumption and technology

Our consumption of music is almost always technologically mediated, shaped by the devices which bring music into our lives. One of rock culture's most cherished (and self-important) founding myths was that of the post-war American teenager lying in bed, late at night, listening to black music of the American south from a small, bedside radio. The solitude and secrecy of this act of listening would have been almost unimaginable twenty years earlier, when radios were weighty pieces of furniture in the family parlour and it was assumed that music would appeal across generational lines. In the period following the Second World War, as the number of radios (and record players) in the home multiplied – and as radios themselves became smaller – these devices moved into the private spaces of the bedroom or work space. Individuals could now listen more easily to music which might no longer be acceptable or pleasurable to others. Similarly, while the rise of music television networks in the 1980s was made possible by cable and satellite technologies, it was spurred by the growing tendency for middle-class homes to contain more than one television set. One of these sets, located in the teenager's bedroom or basement recreation room, could be tuned to programming which was unlikely to be enjoyed by the family as a whole.

In a broader sense, we might consider the ways in which technologies for consuming music help to unite people in groups or isolate them as individuals. As David W. Stowe (1994) argues, radio and records have often functioned differently to organise individuals into audiences. Radio served to create mass audiences for musical forms (like swing music in the 1930s), while records allowed people to develop more individual tastes in private. And yet, as Stowe notes, the jazz recording became the focal point for jazz communities, who came together to discuss and trade records, or to analyse the solos those records contained. Martha Bayles (1994) suggests that the famous 'mixing' of black and white styles in the American south – another of rock'n'roll's founding myths – was only possible because radio and records gave whites access to black music while not requiring physical, face-to-face contact between the races. The personal stereo, introduced in the early 1980s, let people take their music into streets and public transportation systems, but it meant that much listening was now secret and solitary. Passengers sitting alongside each other, in aeroplanes or on trains, might now pursue their most idiosyncratic musical interests without fear of offending each other or revealing too much of themselves. In contrast, the boom-box, whose popularity rose during the same period, made music a means for asserting one's presence in public space. More generally, music (in the form of cassettes, compact discs and instruments) serves as a token of connection to other places, carried in the baggage of people as they move or sold and played in the restaurants and retail shops which serve immigrant communities.

Music and the youth market

Since the late 1970s, the music industries have grappled with the fact that people seem to buy music less frequently as they get older. A survey of United States music-buying habits in 1999 was much heralded for revealing a boom in the sales of records to those over forty-five years of age; their share of the total music market rose, in one year, from 18 per cent to 24 per cent. Nevertheless, this same study showed that those in the narrower 15 to 24 age-range spent an equivalent amount of money on recorded music (RIAA 2000). The markets for popular music in Western countries have been skewed towards youth for some thirty years now, with only minor fluctuations. Countless explanations, many of them circular in nature, have been used to explain why this is so. Youth, it is regularly assumed, buys more recorded music because the industry keeps producing the kind of music which young people are likely to buy.

In countries with strong private radio industries, such as the United States and Canada, music's associations with youth have produced major tensions between broadcasters and record companies. Record companies have always wanted radio stations to play new releases, to expose them to potential buyers, and have long embraced the excitement which Top 40 formats, chart countdowns and listener request lines brought to the presentation of music. Radio stations, in contrast, have turned increasingly away from contemporary pop and rock, in an effort to reach those listeners most desired by advertisers. By the 1970s, for example, most radio programmers throughout North America had eliminated listener request lines, on the grounds that those likely to call were probably not representative of their desired audiences. Figuring out the musical tastes of desirable listeners – employed, financially stable adults in their thirties or forties – has been a major challenge for the radio industry.

In an earlier age, one might simply have assumed that these older listeners, having grown up before the emergence of rock music, would stay bound to the music of that earlier period. By the 1980s, demographic shifts had made the question more complex. Having been shaped by rock music, what became of people's tastes as they grew older? Were there other styles or genres to which listeners 'graduated' with age? If listeners remained loyal to rock music, would they continue to follow each new development within it? Or would they, rather, seek out programming which offered the familiar and the nostalgic? As people age, do their criteria as to what is important or pleasurable in music shift as well? Throughout the 1980s and 1990s, these questions fuelled innumerable attempts to develop psychological profiles of the ageing music fan. In the mid-1980s, for example, a leading United States radio format consultant tried to characterise the typical 25 to 40 year-old listener of the then-popular Album-Oriented Rock format. These were conservatives who liked 'to party', he claimed, 'weekend hippies' who had been raised on the television show *Saturday Night Live* and retained a rebellious streak. To reach them, radio broadcasters should program the music of Bruce Springsteen or John Cougar, artists who communicated 'real feelings on an intense level'. The ageing of the rock audience appeared to challenge one of the longstanding prejudices about middle-aged radio listeners – that such listeners would inevitably come to prefer instrumental, background music as they grew older. In the late 1960s, middle-aged adults had been targeted with music bearing such labels as 'Beautiful Music' or 'Middle-of-the-Road' – instrumental versions of popular songs in which vocals were absent or reduced to background choruses. By the early 1980s, conventional wisdom within the music industries claimed that listeners in their thirties and forties were drawn, in fact, to music in which vocals were prominent. Vocals offered a connection to real people and real emotions, features seen to assume greater importance for listeners as they confronted the vulnerabilities of middle age. Similar beliefs have led music industry personnel to see country music as the probable choice of those who grow out of rock. 'The adult music of the seventies is country music', a radio executive told *Billboard* in 1977, in a claim which has been repeated ever since.

The effort to hang on to adult consumers has also meant redesigning the places in which musical recordings are sold. By the late 1970s, record retailers realised that their shops had become unwelcoming places for several categories of consumer. They were alienating to older people (who found nothing familiar in the records displayed or played on in-store sound systems), intimidating to women (who felt excluded from the value systems of a largely male sales force) and seemingly snobbish towards those who plucked up the courage to ask sales clerks for information. The rise of the mammoth music superstore, since the early 1990s, has partially resolved these problems. Located on the high streets of most cities, super-stores cultivate an atmosphere of casual browsing, and minimise exposure to unfriendly styles by segregating different sorts of music (such as jazz or classical music) within sound-insulated boutiques. Like the giant book-stores which now dot the cityscapes of urban centres in the United States, the music superstores encourage potential consumers to linger and explore, in an environment which has been carefully designed to be non-intimidating.

The music industry's preoccupation with keeping and winning older buyers has obscured the rise in importance of another demographic sector, one whose contribution to industry sales has soared. In the late 1990s, the owners of toy store chains (such as the United States-based Toys R Us) noted a shift in the sorts of things which children were requesting as gifts. Toys as such were losing popularity; in their place, boys and girls of pre-teen age were asking for music and clothes. This was both a cause and effect of major changes in the programming strategies of music television networks, which have seen their viewers get ever younger. The unexpected commercial longevity of the Spice Girls, who found new fans among eight and nine-year old girls, offered startling evidence that the lower age-range of music consumers was going down. Amidst anxieties over an increas-ingly sexualised pre-adolescent consumer marketplace, analysts noted that sales of music for children had grown enormously throughout the 1990s. If ten-year-olds are now actively engaged in following and consum-ing music, this is not simply because they strive to emulate their teenage siblings. Since earliest childhood, musical films and so-called 'kid audio' CDs have been central to their leisure, with long-term effects on tastes and consuming habits which have yet to reveal themselves fully.

Music in the lives of youth

The broader question of music's importance in the lives of youth, and of youth in the lives of music, has rarely been satisfactorily addressed. Popular music scholars and industry personnel have long speculated about the declining importance of music in people's lives as they age. In doing so, they are often led to claims about music's place in the psychological states characteristic of youth or adolescence. Richard Dixon (1980), in a study of adolescent musical tastes, saw youth as a 'phase generally characterised by heightened social, emotional, sexual and deviant experimentation'. Later in life, he suggested, 'commitments, obligations, and responsibilities . . . arise to divert attention away from musical involvement'. Here, as in other treatments of the issue, 'involvement' serves to designate a number of things. It may mean a psychological or affective connection to music itself. In this kind of involvement, music's appeal comes from its capacity to express (or even resemble) the emotional energies of youth, during a point in the life cycle at which these are particularly intense or confusing. Versions of this claim are often invoked to explain the rise of rock'n'roll. For some, the dull homogeneity of popular music in the decade following the Second World War created pent-up demand by teenagers for more intense and polemical sorts of music. Rock'n'roll records emerged from the independent sector of the music industry to fulfil this demand.

The claim that youth is more intensely involved with music in emotional terms is both misleading and the symptom of a real problem. It is misleading in that it reduces involvement with music to the purchasing of music in recorded form. In fact, the amount of time spent listening to music is a poor indicator of the frequency with which people purchase musical recordings. The elderly and retired, with an abundance of leisure time and an attachment to radio, rarely buy music in recorded form, but it is often a constant backdrop to their lives. (The same is true of office-workers, those in the hospitality industries, and people who drive vehicles for a living.) Major segments of the broadcasting industry cater to audiences whose attentive devotion to musical programming does not result in their purchasing music in recorded form.

Nevertheless, the consumption of music by older listeners has become a 'problem' in the recent history of popular music. From the 1960s through the 1980s, the musical preferences of the elderly, who rarely bought records, became more and more obviously disengaged from new developments in the world of music. They had little familiarity with the ongoing parade of new record releases, and a diminished sense of historical developments. Increasingly, the image of people withdrawing from music as they aged went hand-in-hand with that of a record industry deserting the musical styles to which these people listened. In this context, the musical tastes of older listeners could only be imagined as inconsequential, leftover residues of their own youth and of a collectively shared historical period. Such tastes were no longer seen as distinct, coherent tastes and prejudices which might be just as intensely felt as those of youth. At regular intervals, music critics and industry personnel claimed that this process was not inevitable – that an industry geared to producing the music which older consumers liked would find an eager and involved new market.

There were many reasons to doubt this claim. If people maintain an emotional connection to music throughout their lives, other sorts of involvement may nevertheless wither. These include an immersion in the information which surrounds music, or a preference for those activities in which music plays a central role. In Western societies, at least, these sorts of involvement in music do seem to unravel as people grow older. The strong association of music and youth within our culture might be shaped by the ways in which music circulates. The portability of recordings, playback devices and radios is such that listening to music may be easily combined with other activities – driving around in cars, for example, or sitting in cafés and bars. Music is central to forms of social interaction which are more common in the lives of youth than in those of middle-aged adults (for whom the contexts of such interaction are usually more formal). To buy records frequently is to be integrated within a very distinct kind of consumer behaviour. It involves choosing from a wide array of available options, guided by a range of influences and sources of information. These forms of guidance – conversation about music, media coverage of new releases, and so on – all weigh more heavily in the lives of youth than in those of adults.

Here, again, the argument may seem circular: music is important in the lives of youth because youth invests it with importance. What seems indisputable is that music offers a domain in which, during their adolescence, people begin to explore (and develop) their tastes and skills as consumers. Musical commodities are among the first that young people buy for themselves; they are relatively inexpensive, easily carried around, and lend themselves to repeated enjoyment. Music becomes one of the key realms in which an individual's criteria of aesthetic judgement take shape and are explored within consumer transactions. In such transactions, it might be argued, people develop many of their earliest understandings of the social and personal meanings of consumer choice. Early on, consumers weigh the commerciality of certain artists against the authenticity of others, the genuine against the poser, the has-been against the still relevant. These choices take place against the backdrop of a constantly changing stream of new styles and titles. Only youth exists within the intense peer cultures which invest this change with significance, or make the taking up an attitude towards that change a fundamental social challenge.

The imperative of choice has made music (along with clothing) a key token in that long process by which individuals learn what it might mean to be young or old, black or white, male or female. In this respect, music offers one of the key tokens with which young people mark their differences from others, in a complicated game of status and identity. We are not surprised when secondary school students form social groups on the basis of shared musical tastes. We would hardly expect the same of middle-aged workers in an insurance company or government department.

Music and generation

The very idea of generations as having distinctive cultures is a rather recent one, the product of two long-term developments. One of these is an ever-increasing sense of generational identification, the belief that one's cultural experiences are shared most intensely with others of one's age. Historians of the family have noted that this is a product of modern life. Two centuries ago, classrooms and households might include people of several different generations, living and learning alongside each other. With time – with the decline of agricultural life and the mass migration of people to cities – schools organised themselves into classrooms filled with people of similar ages. By the twentieth century, it was normal that people passed through youth in lockstep with others of similar age, subject to the same sorts of experience and influence at each rung of the age ladder.

The feeling of intra-generational solidarity would be strengthened, in the twentieth century, by new, mostly electronic media like radio and the cinema. With their turnover of titles and styles, these have helped to mark time as an ongoing succession of novelties and sensations. As we grow up, we emerge into a world of cultural experiences unfolding in sequence. We do so, of course, at the same time as thousands of others of similar age, and our collective movement through the lifecycle is interwoven with the turnover of songs, movies, books and historical events. If songs evoke, for most of us, particular moments in our own lives, those moments are usually those in which these songs were released and found popularity. The memories evoked are, as a result, collectively shared, and shared most profoundly with those of similar age. As we move out of the school system and into the workplace, the range of age-groups with which we are likely to associate will expand. The sense of generational solidarity with those around us – of a common set of cultural reference points and shared experiences – will begin to wither. If youth culture seems more coherent and intense than that of other stages in the life cycle, this has much to do with the intertwining of generational histories and the larger parade of public sensations produced by the cultural industries.

Music and subcultures

The term subculture has settled so comfortably within the analysis of popular music that we may forget its origins elsewhere. For the sociologist Robert Park (1996), writing in the early twentieth century, the concept of 'subculture' invited scholars in Western countries to bring the methods of the anthropologist to bear on their own surroundings – on Greenwich Village, for example, or Chicago's North Side. After the Second World War, sociologists began working steadily with the concept, focusing on the urban underworlds of gamblers, jazz musicians or drug addicts. By the 1960s, subcultural analysis had become an important political tool for radical scholars in the social sciences. They argued forcefully that groups previously seen as deviant and dysfunctional – small-time thieves, for example – should be examined in terms of the values and worldviews which gave meaning to their lives (and not simply with an eye to the prevailing laws and norms which they had violated).

Amidst the proliferating youth cultures of the 1960s and 1970s, 'subculture' captured the ways in which music, and its role in people's lives, had been transformed. 'Subculture' was a useful shorthand for the worlds of style in which young people lived, the coherent clusters of dress, drugs, meeting-places and linguistic idioms which had come together around distinct kinds of music. In their fixation on the most visible of these worlds, journalists and academics typically found subcultures only where gangs of (mostly male) youths congregated in public space. (Earlier sociologists had concentrated on the hidden worlds of small-time gamblers or petty criminals as much as on the more conspicuous teen-age street gangs.) Terms like 'tribe' and 'ritual', common in newspaper articles on the mods or punks, kept alive the sense of subculture analysis as a big-city anthropology, but the issues in play were shifting. Scholars of the 1950s and early 1960s had focused on the ways in which subcultural activity – the funding and maintenance of a drug habit, for example – were like everyday work, subject to routines and insider jargon. In contrast, many of those who came to study musical subcultures were drawn by an interest in the creative, possibly transgressive dimensions of leisure.

Increasingly, the term 'subculture' has been used to describe a particular way of consuming cultural goods. Sociologists' earlier emphasis on illegality has given way to debate over the ways in which a range of activities, most of them legal, challenge or support the existing economic order. In this shift, subcultural analysis became focused on the accoutrements of style or the circulation of cultural artefacts. Well-known subcultures of the 1970s, such as punk, were famous for their public displays of violence, but they were also redefining consumption within new networks of small-scale capitalism and artisanal labour. In so doing, they helped to create micro-economies of a sort, social and entrepreneurial worlds in which the divisions between producers and consumers, or artists and audiences were weakened. Subcultural analysis would come to focus on the artefacts produced within these worlds, on the tokens of stylistic warfare and semiotic reshuffling which resulted. The spectacular quality of a subculture's public gestures has often seemed curiously disproportionate to the obscure, ephemeral commodities which circulate within subcultural worlds.

Like artworlds generally, subcultures often combine the vanguardist commitment to social revolution with the aristocratic dream of a life devoted to artistic experience. Subcultures of the 1970s and 1980s very often joined the snobbish attack on mass taste to the ethical claim that music was degraded outside of a life fully devoted to music. In this sense, even such seemingly innocent subcultures as those surrounding Northern Soul or lounge music might seem oppositional, when the innumerable minor objects and practices on which they were fixated formed worlds in which members might live much of their daily lives.

Arguments about musical subcultures are, much of the time, arguments about work and leisure. One strand in the study of subcultures seeks to recast the activities of punks or hip-hoppers as a kind of work – as the creative transformation of materials from the dominant world. This defines subcultures as spaces of experimentation and innovation, but it also involves an insistence (of almost caricatural influence within cultural studies) on the creative labour inherent in any act of consumption. Recognition of this 'labour' challenges the claim that consumers are passive dupes, but it also acknowledges the important contributions which consumer creativity makes to the leisure and style industries. Subcultures mix and match elements from the larger culture in ways that result in new clusters of meaning – signposts to new possibilities which both challenge the market and inject it with new ideas.

The claim that members of subcultures work creatively to produce new meanings out of the detritus of the dominant world might well betray an unacknowledged work ethic. Few musical subcultures today are willing simply to embrace the hedonistic, decadent ethos of earlier bohemian traditions. Even the New Romantics of the early 1980s felt compelled to theorise their commitment to extravagant dress and glamorous nightlife as a challenge to the Thatcher government's warnings about unrealistic expectations. While the recent house music culture of Ibiza and other clubland vacation spots may come closest to an unembarrassed hedonism, its history is regularly retold from the earnest perspective of revolutions won and betrayed, of ongoing battles waged against commercialisation or stagnation.

In the 1960s and 1970s, subcultures intruded dramatically upon public attention, then seemed to recede. By the year 2000, it seemed clear that subcultures almost never disappeared anymore. Rather, they survived and developed alongside each other, perpetuating a collective devotion to different musical styles and historical moments. Doom Metal, death metal, ska, classic punk, LA hard core, garage psychedelia, 1970s funk, indie pop, rockabilly, swing, 1980s electrobeat, German electronica and dozens of other styles now persist within networks of fans and institutions which ensure their continued existence. If the effect of early musical subcultures was to announce a revolution, the passing of a torch, subcultures now work to ensure the longevity of styles, keeping alive the communities in which those who discover these styles may find a home. This suggests the ambiguous value assigned to change within popular music. If, at certain moments, change is the necessary clearing away of the past through stylistic renewal, at others it stands as the cynical operation of an industry devoted to novelty. Punk took shape against the backdrop of an industry heavily invested in the careers of well-established elites; it offered its own turbulence as an antidote. Today's subcultures assert the proven value of long-established styles in the face of an industry widely seen as embracing manufactured, short-term fashions.

Critics of musical subcultures sometimes argue that their members are simply better, more skilled and devoted consumers of capitalist commodities than the mainstream music fans they so consistently denigrate. A common critique of American alternative rock fans, by the mid-1990s, was that they had embraced obscurity for its own sake, reducing all of punk's politics to the notion that one should buy rare, exquisite seven-inch vinyl singles rather than mass-produced compact discs. At one level, this seems unnecessarily harsh and cynical. (Indeed, it might be argued, the only realistic political programme for the music fan is an ethics of consumption which favours the small-scale entrepreneur.) Nevertheless, this critique captures the ways in which music subcultures, in their drive to find obscure, overlooked or marginal pieces of music, keep alive the sense that the music industries are complex and endlessly inventive. Subcultures of fans and collectors undertook the historical sifting and archival ordering which led to major labels releasing their back catalogues of 1960s garage psychedelia or 1950s instrumental exotica. In so doing, they recast what was, arguably, a history of uninformed exploitation as one of voracious open-mindedness. In a more general sense, the collecting of popular cultural artefacts is almost always a means of rehabilitating a market economy. In the complex gradations of popularity and obscurity which settle around records with time, one finds a satisfying rebuke to images of a calculating, rational capitalism. (Even Céline Dion fans, after all, can spend their money and energies tracking down rare promotional CD singles or foreign pressings.)

The meaning of musical consumption is more elusive when we are dealing with places outside those Anglo-American centres in which historically important trends in pop and rock have been born. In Quebec or Mexico, for example, early rock'n'roll subcultures seemed little more than blatant imitations of their United States or British counterparts, more evidence of subservience to the centres of cultural power. In the early 1960s, in both places, hundreds of musicians started groups and began performing cover versions of Anglo-American hits in their own languages. A decade later, musicians and fans came to see this earlier explosion of musical activity as an embarrassment. At best, it was remembered as a frivolous moment on the road to an indigenous, serious rock tradition; at worst, as one more sign of each country's colonisation and underdevelopment. The recuperation of this music would come only twenty or thirty years later, when, with hindsight, it could be remembered as one moment in a political and social awakening from the sombre moral climate of the 1950s. In both Quebec and Mexico, a style which had seemed to epitomise a nation's underdevelopment was also the vehicle through which fans expressed their opposition to the moralising of the Catholic Church or the official culture propagated by the State and its institutions.

The weakness of subcultural analysis in dealing with these contexts stems from its fixation on the ethical dimensions of consumption. In countries outside the Anglo-American world, consumption is never simply a gesture directed at capitalism; it is bound up with complex, international circuits through which information, influence and commodities themselves circulate. To consume underground musical styles in Canada or Australia, for example, usually meant seeking out information on the latest records and shifts of taste in New York or Manchester, reading imported music magazines and buying foreign pressings from specialty record stores. Each subcultural gesture – dressing up in a particular way or choosing this act over another – signalled, more than anything else, a cosmopolitanism, an attentiveness to what was happening somewhere else. As a result, subcultural styles from elsewhere almost always enter these countries through the mediating influence of cosmopolitan, well-informed middle class consumers. Subcultural activity, in such circumstances, bears an uneasy and uncertain relationship to the 'truth' of experience which it is presumed to express.

Global passages

At the end of the twentieth century, the music industry saw signs that the appeal of music from the United States was declining around the world. Industry analysts noted that Asian and European markets were proving resistant to stars and recordings from the United States. Styles which persistently dominated United States sales charts, such as country music and rap, were much less popular outside that country. The problem, European record company executives complained, was that United States music markets were too subcultural, too insistent that performers perpetuate the purest and most hard-core versions of these musical forms. While other markets embraced performers who crossed over, appealing to a variety of audiences, the United States market seemed to reflected the nation's more profound divisions of race, class and region. The days when U2 or REM could stand as genuinely global rock stars, popular both with casual buyers and connoisseurs, were apparently waning. Sales charts in Britain, Japan and Germany showed lower levels of penetration by United States-based performers than throughout most of the previous quarter century. Artists from outside the Anglo-American world, such as the Italian act Nek, sold millions of records in several countries, while failing to break through in North America.

Shortly thereafter, the global success of United States performers like Britney Spears, Eminem and Bon Jovi suggested a renewal of American music's place within the world. These performers stood as evidence that the United States industry had reoriented itself to the marketing of adolescent pop and hip-hop. Amidst predictions that the next generation of teenagers would be the largest in the nation's history, the five remaining major record companies faced accusations that they were dropping long-term strategies for artist development in order to concentrate on the marketing of globally viable pop stars.

Nevertheless, the means by which consumers are exposed to music have changed, in ways which enhance the autonomy of regional or national markets. In Asia, Quebec, Mexico and several European countries, national musical cultures have been strengthened by new media services, such as music video networks. These have bolstered local recording industries and bound populations together within significant new media markets. In this context, the outlets for local performers and national languages have increased. In a challenge to longstanding notions of the authentic, the most nationally distinctive musical styles and performers are often the most blatantly commercial, if only because they are shaped by local traditions of entertainment and celebrity. The cosmopolitan connoisseurs of British dance music or goth metal, trumpeting the freedom of choice they identify with underground styles, are often those who most slavishly follow the fashions of a few global centres.

Writing in *The New York Observer* in 1999, music critic D. Strauss strained to describe the new sorts of taste patterns observable in hip circles in the West. He spoke of people turning away, in large numbers, from the tradition and canon of Anglo-American rock, seeking inspiration in what he called 'the necessarily misunderstood imagined pasts of others: French pop, German hippies, Brazilian tropicalia, Japanese imitations of all of the above'. Interest in all of these things had, indeed, rippled through Anglo-American musical culture in recent years, shaping the mannerist exercises of so-called 'post-rock' forms, the more large-scale strategic moves of performers like Beck, and the endlessly interesting new syntheses found in French or Japanese club music.

Globalism in the music industries is shaped by evolving industrial structures, but it finds expression, as well, in the sense given by consumers to the endless proliferation of new or rediscovered artefacts. As the range of niche tastes and technologies for delivering music expands, one sees a tendency to perpetuate a centre, to revalorise endlessly an Anglo-American canon. The boxed sets, bootlegged live albums, and innumerable variations of classic albums issued by major labels deepen and solidify the presence of that canon, perpetuating a sense of that canon as monumental. On the other hand, global musical relations have been shaped by centrifugal tendencies which send interest outward, leading to the unexpected global circulation of national styles and artefacts. This centrifugal movement is nourished by the scavenger-like record collecting of dance club disc jockeys, lounge music revivalists, or curator-compilers like David Byrne, and by the activities of marginal reissue labels. These tendencies are dragging back, into the realms of hip credibility, musical currents long dismissed as false imitations or examples of debased exploitation. Italian jazz-funk, Asian girl-group garage psychedelia, or funky crime movie soundtracks from India have all moved, in recent years, into the radar range of Western deejay-remixers or lounge revivalists. Rediscovery of these hybrid forms is nourished partly by the thrill with which they seem scandalously counter-canonical, but to embrace them involves a relationship to other musics which inverses the patterns of respect typical, for example, of 'world music'. (Recent revivals of interest in unabashedly imitative Québécois pop music of the 1960s, for example, are driven by the sense that these adaptations, on the margins of a global industry, offer more interesting cross-fertilisations of influence than the original, canonical versions.)

We consume music as we do films or television programmes, for meaning and satisfaction, but the distinctiveness of music comes from the lines of connection linking our acts of consumption over time. These lines of connection map our evolving relationships to peer group unity and individual exploration. They show our shifting propensities for choices which confirm our social identities and others which (deliberately or not) transgress these. The pleasures of musical consumption, elusive as they may be, are rich in the affinities which they express and the range of contexts which they mark. In their succession, the pop music artefacts we consume, minor and ephemeral as each may be, trace our place within the divisions and solidarities of the social world.

Further reading

The works of my co-editor, Simon Frith, have proved indispensable in linking the social and aesthetic dimensions of music consumption. In particular, *Sound Effects* (London: Constable, 1981) and *Performing Rites* (Oxford: Oxford University Press, 1996) offer richly nuanced analyses of the tastes and pleasures of popular music. *The Subcultures Reader* (London: Routledge, 1997), co-edited by Sarah Thornton and Ken Gelder, is a strong, comprehensive collection of articles on the notion of subculture, with great relevance to the analysis of popular music. Histories of musical consumption in the last hundred years are almost always histories of the music industries themselves, and Philip Ennis' *The Seventh Stream: The Emergence of RocknRoll in American Popular Music* (Hanover, NH: Wesleyan University Press, 1992) remains, for me, a highly useful account. The ongoing anxieties of the music industries, in the face of shifting demographics, new technologies and competing new musical directions, are better documented in the business press than in any scholarly literature. *Billboard* and *The Wall Street Journal*, in particular, have both come to be more probing, in recent years, in their discussion of music and cultural consumption in general.

Star profiles I

ELVIS PRESLEY, THE BEATLES, BOB DYLAN,
JIMI HENDRIX, THE ROLLING STONES, JAMES BROWN,
MARVIN GAYE

The history of popular music is a history of pop stars. The music industry is organised around star-making: stars are the best guarantors of sales to a fickle public. Pop fans are almost always fans of particular musicians who seem to speak specially to them. Dance music remains unusual in not being star-based (and even here the top disc jockeys are at the top because they attract personal followings). Stars embody the shifts of taste, the changing musical alliances, the new ways of doing things that mark pop history. And the paradox here is that much as record companies seek to make and market stars, the biggest pop acts have always been surprising, their success revealing to the money-makers market needs and interests they hadn't previously understood. The biggest pop stars change the way pop works and their careers are worth noting – and celebrating – for that reason.

Few people would dispute the key names in the making of rock'n'roll and then rock as new forms of popular music in the 1950s and 1960s: Elvis Presley still stands best for rock'n'roll itself, a glorious, flawed, youthful hybrid of American sounds – rhythm and blues, country, bluegrass, black and white church music, easy listening ballads, novelty numbers. Between them the Beatles and Bob Dylan (moving from opposite ends of the popular musical spectrum: everyday commercial hits, deep-rooted folk songs) delineated a new kind of pop cultural ambition, while the Rolling Stones best symbolise the resulting marketing of rock as the most successful commercial popular music ever. And even while the new rock stars reached unprecedented levels of wealth, power and hedonistic indulgence, none of these musicians forgot that their music was made in dialogue with ever challenging African–American sounds – with funk (and, especially, James Brown), with the jazz-inflected, improvisational genius of Jimi Hendrix, above all with soul music, with Motown, with a kind of emotive singing which by the 1970s had become a white pop norm. Marvin Gaye's career seems exemplary here, if only because of the drama of his own shifting sense of what black American pop music meant.

Elvis Presley

Elvis Presley was one of the great popular singers of the twentieth century. As a musician he had two particular qualities. First, he sang with a remarkable physicality. His body was in his voice, so to speak, whether in the full voluptuousness of his ballad singing, or in the skittering playfulness of his uptempo tracks. Second, he had a remarkable range of singing styles (to match his unusual tonic range – from bass to falsetto). Rock'n'roll is often characterised as a blend of country music and rhythm and blues, but Elvis threw much more into the mix – religious and secular songs, Tin Pan Alley and Neapolitan pop, novelty numbers and folk tunes. As a young man he had not so much the ambition as the confidence to remake every kind of music to his own ends, and the results in the first three years of his recording life, from 1955–8, as Presley entered his twenties, is an uninhibited showcase of American popular song. Presley sang without the introspection of a Frank Sinatra, but with an equal mastery of a song's rhythmic dynamics and an unprecedented pleasure in the act of singing itself. The result (particularly when he was seen performing too – on stage or television screen) was sexually electric. Presley may not have been the first pop idol, but he was the first singer to embody the appeal of youthfulness for its own sake (at the same time as James Dean was doing the same thing as a film star).

In pop terms, then, Presley very quickly became first a phenomenon (in terms of records sold and fan devotion) and then a myth. The story of talent wasted, innocence perverted, came to be the rock story. Rock musicians (unlike country or rhythm and blues or mainstream pop performers) are expected to do their best work at the start of their careers, to sell out to commerce and to be corrupted by fame, and Presley's career was the archetype: signed up as a young man to a local independent label, Sun Records, which refused the genre and racial musical distinctions which were then the music biz norm; taken over by a shrewd but unimaginative manager, Colonel Tom Parker, who had no interest in music but a sharp eye for a quick buck; sold by Sun to a major label, RCA, which (with the help of the army) curbed Presley's more anarchic musical tendencies and sold him globally as a slick white entertainer, the good natured, unthreatening star of countless bad Hollywood films. And even when Presley did briefly assert his own musical interests, in his famous Television Special in December 1968, these were soon to be corrupted once more, into a bloated self-parodying Las Vegas routine. By the time Presley died there seemed to be something grotesque about him. It's no wonder that 'Dead Elvis' became a pop phenomenon in his own right, an object for tabloid excess and bizarre impersonation.

Figure 1 Elvis Presley
© Redferns. Photo: RB

The truth of this Elvis story is less important than its mythical weight, but there's no doubt too that Presley was treated all his life with a class-based contempt, as obvious in the tone of his television show hosts at the start of his career as in Albert Goldman's posthumous biography. Presley was 'Southern white trash', a 'redneck' and rather than this making his achievements all the more remarkable (not least in his denial of a cultural colour bar) it was taken to mean that everything he did was irredeemably trashy. It also means, though, that Presley's career is better understood in terms of country music than rock. Elvis Presley died, at the age of forty-two, in Memphis, Tennessee, a city to which he had moved at the age of thirteen. He had rarely travelled abroad, and for all his Hollywood and Las Vegas success his friends were old buddies, family, rather than stars or fellow musicians. One reason why Graceland became, after his death, the most visited historic site in the United States was, as Karal Ann Marling has noted, not because it is particularly exotic but because it is precisely the kind of house that Southern working-class Americans would have built if they'd come into a bit of money – it's furnished from catalogues! Presley, to put this another way, was a particular kind of populist. His remarkable self-taught musical skills were put to the end of a sentimentality, a religiosity, a patriotism, but also of a loyalty, a joie de vivre, a tolerance that remain the organising foci of country music. Elvis Presley was a superstar, a media phenomenon who remained, literally, the boy next door. Of all pop stars he was the one who could have had everything but (and this is what rock critics have never understood) didn't really want it.

The Beatles

The Beatles were the most important twentieth-century pop stars not simply because of their legacy of songs nor even because of the scale of their commercial success but because they forever changed pop's social and musical meanings and possibilities. At the heart of their impact on pop history were two qualities that are taken for granted now but were unusual then, in the 1960s. First, autonomy. The Beatles were a remarkably self-contained unit, writing their own songs, determining their own production values, making their own career moves. Contrast Cliff Richard, who was part of the same generation and began by following the same skiffle/rock'n'roll route. Second, ambition. The Beatles were the first pop musicians to challenge the clear distinction between high and low cultural spaces, to treat pop music as an art world. They were thus instrumental in the late sixties emergence of rock music. The Beatles were a phenomenon, in short, not only because of their own musical talents but because of the particular historical and social circumstances in which these talents were developed. In effect, the Beatles had three quite different careers. They were remarkable because of the way in which these careers meshed, but at any one career moment the next stage could not have been predicted. From 1957–62 the Beatles were essentially a cover band. Starting as a

Figure 2 The Beatles
© Redferns. Photo: David Redfern

schoolboy skiffle group, by their late teens they could just about make a living playing the clubs of Liverpool and Hamburg. The skills they learnt were performing skills: developing a sound insistent enough to cut through club conversation, distinct enough to give the Beatles an edge among the competing cover bands, clever enough to reproduce the studio effects of American rock'n'roll and rhythm and blues and Motown with minimal technology and resources. At this stage the Beatles were learning a trade (the Dutch scholar, Lutgart Mutsaers, has argued persuasively they were in fact influenced by the Moluccan bands that dominated the Northern European club circuit at the start of the 1960s) and all that made them unusual was their tinge of bohemia – John Lennon and then guitarist, Stuart Sutcliffe, were art school students who were inspired by the distinct Liverpool and Hamburg nightlife mix of sailors, drinkers, painters and teenagers.

From 1962 to 1966 the Beatles rewrote the rules of British pop. Their local Liverpool popularity was translated into first national and then international stardom; for the first time ever there was a mass United States market for a British act. While the Beatles needed the selling power of Britain's biggest record company, EMI, and the promotional support of a national broadcaster, the BBC, for their commercial success, their career was unusual in several respects. Their manager, Brian Epstein, from a

Liverpool music retail company, was not part of the London showbiz scene; their EMI producer, George Martin, was not a pop hack but a versatile engineer – he had been producing Peter Sellers. The Beatles themselves were not naive teenagers but seasoned musicians who were confident that they could write songs for themselves better than any Denmark Street pro. They also had distinct personalities and an intelligence that made them a joy for journalists and radio programme producers; their success defined a new kind of pop audience. The contrast of old and new is obvious in the covers of the group's first two LPs: from chirpy working-class entertainers in sharp suits to moody students in black polo necks. The quality of their songs and the timing of their rise – coinciding with a Labour government and a new kind of youth-fixated liberal consumerism – obviously underpinned their phenomenal success, but just as important was their ability to use this success rather than be used by it. The Beatles became part of a musicians' community that was more influenced by art school than show biz thinking, by the competition for peer prestige than for chart places.

In 1966 the Beatles played their last concert and became hippies. In retrospect this seems inevitable but at the time it marked a positive and startling decision to trade in their status as pop leaders to become youth cultural followers. Socially this meant public engagement with the trappings of hippie culture, most significantly drugs; musically it meant the final move from crowd-pleasing pop stars to studio-based artists. *Sergeant Pepper's Lonely Hearts Club Band* and *The White Album* pleased the crowds anyway, but these LPs also symbolised the Beatles' commitment to making music that was experimental, eclectic and, in the newly coined late sixties term, 'progressive'. And if the Beatles lacked the instrumental virtuosity and compositional sophistication of the new breed of progressive rockers, they retained their melodic gifts and sense of humour. When the band broke up in 1970 they were still at the forefront of a pop cultural revolution that would have been inconceivable only ten years earlier, when they took to the stage in Hamburg.

Bob Dylan

Bob Dylan was born Robert Allen Zimmerman in Minnesota in 1941, moved to New York City in 1961, and by 1964 had helped revitalise that city's folk scene as the charismatic voice of a new singer–songwriter movement that soon spread across the Atlantic. Dylan then went electric, and in 1965–6 made three albums, *Bringing It All Back Home*, *Highway 61 Revisited*, and *Blonde on Blonde* that can still be claimed as the greatest single body of work in rock's history. They certainly had a profound effect

Figure 3 Bob Dylan
© Redferns. Photo: Val Wilmer (?)

on Dylan's musical peers, and equally inspired a new sort of writing, rock criticism, and a new sort of pop fan, the pursuer of meaning rather than pin ups. In commercial terms, though, Dylan never sold records at the unprecedented rate of the rock superstars, which may account for one of the odder aspects of his later career, an almost obsessive touring life of live performances, performances marked as much by Dylan's unconventional and even contemptuous account of his own songs as by the need to connect with his remarkably faithful fans.

Dylan emerged from the folk world and there can be no doubting his love of and sensitivity to the history of American popular music, whether in his initial admiration of Woody Guthrie, in his impressive repertoire of songs in his first folk club and festival performances, in the exploration of the byways of the American vernacular in the sessions with the Band eventually released as *The Basement Tapes*, or simply in his refusal to take much note of genre distinction – blues, commercial country and pop songs were all grist to his mill. But the folk music scene in which Dylan was first involved was not exactly the traditional and political scene that had been sustained by left-wing ideologues in the 1940s and 1950s (which was one reason why Dylan was greeted with both excitement and hostility, in the pages of *Sing Out!*, for example). The New York club scene which Dylan occupied is better understood as a bohemian than a folk community. On the one hand, it was marked by an anti-establishment politics that had more to do with hedonism than socialism, and which was as sceptical of class solidarity as of any other social convention. Dylan wrote political songs and helped bring the term 'protest' into the pop lexicon, but his politics were not organisational. On the other hand, New York's bohemia was haunted by romantics, by would-be poets and performance artists, and it was with these figures (rather than, say, Pete Seeger) that Dylan most obviously identified. What counted here was an individual sensibility expressed with a personal style, using elliptical imagery, a poetic diction, a degree of mystery.

Bob Dylan's great contribution to rock was to suggest that here was a form of music as adept as any other as such a romantic art form. But in doing this (and here Dylan was himself a sixties figure, a Beatles fan) he also utilised those aspects of the pop process that the folk world had defined itself against in the 1950s – not just the use of amplified instruments, but the trappings of stardom, packaging and promotion. These were an aspect of Dylan's original success just as his refusal even now to fall into rock routines is an aspect of his artistic credibility. It is fitting that the American musician with the best understanding of the traditions of vernacular American song should have the most individual, variable and cussed voice in rock. There's no singer–songwriter in the last thirty-five years who doesn't owe something of their craft to Bob Dylan; nobody else has written such an astonishing variety of songs; and there's no one who has been such a loved star while remaining so true to the bohemian ideal of being beholden to nothing but oneself.

Jimi Hendrix

Jimi Hendrix was born in Seattle in 1942 and played guitar in bands throughout his time at high school and in the United Stares Airborne Division, before making his living as a musician in various rhythm and blues singers' backing groups. He was brought to Britain in 1966 and the Jimi Hendrix Experience, with Noel Redding on bass and Mitch Mitchell on drums, was put together to showcase Hendrix's technical skills. From the start, with the hit singles 'Hey Joe' and 'Purple Haze' in 1966–7, the Jimi Hendrix Experience had a major impact on the British musical scene. On the one hand, the group's success suggested the commercial possibilities of psychedelic pop. The trio was put together if not cynically then at least with an eye to the market (it hardly sprang organically from a musical scene or network); great care was taken with the trio's image – not least by exploiting awed British attitudes towards a real African–American! At a

Figure 4 Jimi Hendrix
© Redferns. Photo: Michael Ochs Archives

pop moment of beat groups, Hendrix offered a new type of individual stardom: applying the lessons he'd learnt on the rhythm and blues circuit he brought a sense of spectacle to the actual act of guitar playing – his first appearance on *Top of the Pops* was a genuinely transforming moment. On the other hand, there could be no doubting Hendrix's musical skills, his versatility and invention as an electric guitarist, his demonstration that the instrument was central for adapting the expressive power of the blues to the vast spaces of the stadium show. Following Hendrix, the electric guitar (rather than the voice) became the key rock instrument, the symbol of the music's sexual power, and live performance (in which records were just the starting point for a show of instrumental aggression) became the key rock ritual. In the the short term this meant the formation of other guitar-focused supergroups like Cream and Led Zeppelin; in the longer term it led to heavy metal and mainstream hard white rock.

Hendrix was a black American musician, though, and in some ways his most significant effects were on his own musical heritage rather than on British or European rock fantasies. For a start his recorded legacy is a reminder that rock was as much a black as a white musical form: Hendrix's influence as a sonic pioneer was carried through funk to rap. But the essence of Hendrix's musical approach – the emphasis on improvisation, the exploration of amplification as itself a source of new sorts of sound and sound effect – was as a jazz man and, in consequence, he was the first rock musician to interest jazz performers like Miles Davis and Herbie Hancock, both in their 1970s pursuit of 'jazz rock' and in their general pursuit of the improvisational possibilities of volume, distortion, noise.

Hendrix died in 1970. For all his acknowledged influence on rock music he was never really happy with the starring role that had been written for him, and for the last couple of years of his life he had, with old airforce friend, Billy Cox, and a new group, the Band of Gypsies, been trying to make a more dense and darker music. Most rock musicians who die young do so with a sense of a career finished – the death (Elvis Presley, Brian Jones, Janis Joplin, even John Lennon and Kurt Cobain) is more regretted for what has been than for what was likely to come. Hendrix's death was different. There is a real sense that in his case his best music was still to come, if only because he'd never really worked with musicians with anything like his own technical or imaginative skills.

The Rolling Stones

The Rolling Stones are the archetypal rock group, not least because of the seemingly effortless way in which they've absorbed the contradictions of rock stardom: art vs commerce, rebellion vs conformity, artifice vs authenticity, etc. Formed in 1962–3 in the London rhythm and blues scene of trad jazz purists and art school stylists, the Stones were very quickly paying equal attention to the credible pop success of the Beatles and, under the canny guidance of their equally young manager, Andrew Loog Oldham, they became the first British blues group to translate the non-conformist values of the blues scene into the terms of youth culture (through the all-purpose notion of rebellion, for example). As live performers they appealed as much for the charisma of singer, Mick Jagger, and guitarists, Keith Richard and Brian Jones, as for their musical commitment, and the key to their rise as number two British group to the Beatles was the unexpectedly crafty songwriting skill of Jagger/Richard. Employing a more sardonic and contemptuous tone of voice than the Beatles, and fusing Jagger's rather camp sexuality with Richard's single-minded sense of rhythm (discarding Jones' prissier, more progressive ambitions on the way), the Stones developed a uniquely threatening pop style that culminated in the United Kingdom and United States success of 'I Can't Get No (Satisfaction)'.

Figure 5 The Rolling Stones
  © Redferns. Photo: S & G Press Agency 641

In the later 1960s, although the Stones made gestures at both the frillier end of psychedelia and mod pop, their music developed in darker and more universal ways, both reflecting Keith Richard's genuine obsession with the odder back alleys of black American (and Caribbean) music, reflected most clearly on *BeggarsBanquet*, but also as a marketing ploy: the Stones as the baddies to the Beatles as goodies (a ploy which had its own personal consequences – the Stones were pursued by police and press in ways the Beatles weren't). The Stones' image as dangerous degenerates was confirmed in 1969 by the murderous violence during their performance at the Altamont Festival in California but, in the end, the association of the

Stones with hedonistic excess cemented their place as a rock legend, a place best mapped out by perhaps their greatest record, *Exile on Main Street*.

Thereafter the Stones' menace became a matter of performing style rather than either musical adventure or abandoned lifestyle. Since 1972 the Stones have made little music that has had either commercial or emotional impact; they have paid scant attention to changes in musical fashion; their various solo projects have been matters of self-interest only. And yet even at the end of the century they remained the biggest grossing act on the live circuit. Every two or three years the Stones release an album simply as a way of promoting a world tour on which they can enact once more 'The Rolling Stones'. At one level the sight is ridiculous – a bunch of ageing millionaires, long part of the showbiz establishment – playing out an unconvincing stage version of rebellion. But even if Mick Jagger's vocals get ever more perfunctory, the band's rhythmic power, driven by stoker extraordinary, Keith Richard, is as insistent as ever, and the Stones' live show remains the first rock concert choice of high and low life alike.

James Brown

James Brown occupies an uneasy place in the pop pantheon. A great entertainer, of course, but one is also reminded, tactfully, that he's been to prison, had woman and money trouble, and musically too his reputation is rough rather than respectable. There's a disruptive force to his act. It makes demands on life – for excitement, pleasure, oblivion – that by their nature can't be satisfied but which, in Brown's case, aren't therefore sublimated as individual songs of love and sex (or God and redemption) but remain urgently social. It's as if Brown gives voice to the groundlings of frustration, to the popular refusal of routine that has always haunted the bourgeoisie. Brown is treated even by rock historians with a certain wariness. In all those Q lists and customer surveys of the greatest records of the twentieth century it's Marvin Gaye and Stevie Wonder and Miles Davis even, who get to be the token black rock names. Not James Brown. Not the Godfather of Soul.

Brown's musical career began in the 1940s, in a musical era when an audience, a following, was still put together by live rather than television appearances, by nonstop touring of the chitling circuit. Success was not a matter of market research and calculated crossovers but depended on a hustler's instinct for popular demand and on a performer's rhetorical power to persuade a crowd that he could meet the demand. It was then that Brown developed his ability to make time stop, to suggest that nothing mattered outside the setting of his show. In fact, his career exemplifies the continuity between jazz and soul: Brown was as much

Figure 6 James Brown
© Redferns. Photo: David Ellis

bandleader/arranger/taskmaster as he was singer/showman, and his concerts were as much focused on ensemble toughness and precision, on the controlled aggression of his instrumental soloists, as on his own showmanship. His Famous Flames became a finishing school for generations of session musicians, and alongside the even more eccentric figures of Sun Ra and George Clinton, James Brown kept going the most important of all African–American musical traditions – collective improvisation – long after it was economically feasible to do so.

Crudely speaking, the history of black American music since 1950s rhythm and blues can be divided between two strands – soul (as developed by Ray Charles) and funk (as developed by James Brown). The same musical elements (jazz, blues, gospel) were developed to different social ends. Soul music is a form of seduction, music as a language of personal persuasion, performance as ingratiation. Funk is in your face, the sound of musicians strutting, challenging you to resist the power of their desires not yours. By and large (because it better suits commercial sales processes) soul is now the dominant mode of contemporary pop; funk remains unsettling. No James Brown track could be classified as easy listening.

James Brown is still the musician most likely to be sampled – his voice (over which he's managed to keep some sort of legal control), his riffs (over which he hasn't). His sampling value isn't so much that his sound is distinctive – the James Brown shriek sending a shiver down the spine even in a snatched moment on the dance floor, but that his music was the percussor of both rap (in its vocal tone) and drum and bass (in its rhythmic form). The characteristic James Brown sound might be labelled drum'n'bass'n'horns: a music constructed from beats rather than melodies, from the emotional effects of small shifts in pulse rather than from balladic changes of chord. Brown (this is his place in twentieth-century pop history) first mapped the funk aesthetic, in which repetition, the changing same, is a source of exhilaration. This is not by any definition primitive art but there is something about Brown's show and his persona that doesn't square with modernism. For all the obvious sophistication, the cosmopolitanism of funk, it retained something of its rural African–American origins, a sense of different, stranger rhythms than those of modern city life.

Marvin Gaye

Marvin Gaye had the classic soul career. He began singing in a church choir (his father was a minister); joined a secular singing group, the Marquees; was recruited into the more successful Moonglows; and followed the Moonglows' leader/producer, Harvey Fuqua, into the new Motown records set-up in Detroit, being employed initially as a session drummer and backing singer. He played drums on Little Stevie Wonder's first records, co-wrote Martha and the Vandella's 'Dancing in the Streets', and was first promoted under his own name as a kind of uptown pop balladeer. In the 1960s he became the epitome of Motown's version of soul, both with his own hits like 'How Sweet It Is To Be Loved by You' (1965) and 'I Heard Through the Grapevine' (Motown's best-ever selling single, first released in 1968) and in his duets, particularly with Tammi Terrell. The late 1960s rise of a new black political consciousness and a new use of soul music was best reflected at Motown by Gaye's album, *What's Going On*, in 1971 and film soundtrack, *Trouble Man*, in 1972. 'Let's Get It On', released in 1973, marked another new era – sexual politics, disco and a new dance floor sensibility. Gaye's personal troubles (and his move from Motown) limited his impact for the rest of the decade but 1982's *Sexual Healing* influenced another generation of producers. In 1984 Gaye died, murdered by his father.

There are many artists who could claim to represent 'the Motown sound' (no other record label has come close to assembling such an astonishing roster of writers, players, producers and singers), not least the label's female stars, like Diana Ross and the Supremes. But Marvin Gaye's

Figure 7 Marvin Gaye
© Redferns. Photo: David Redfern

career (in its sloughs as well as its highs) does touch on all aspects of the
Motown story and, in particular on the tensions of sex and race and commerce. He had, to begin with, the perfect Motown voice, at once light and
intense and with a rhythmic nimbleness which enabled him to cover all
bases of sexual feeling. Like the crooners before them, soul singers were
essentially intimate, taking a particular kind of submissive aggression

from soul music and (following the lead of Sam Cooke) adapting it to the conventions of pop courtship. And, again as with the crooners, the soul voice represented an ambiguous masculinity: soul singers seemed feminised in their vocal delicacy, their offered vulnerability, even as they pulled all the strings of the seduction scene. And it was Gaye (rather than, say, Smokey Robinson or David Ruffin) who put soul music at the heart of the explicit sexual politics of the 1970s and 1980s. The issues here can't be separated from race, on the one hand, and money, on the other. Motown was founded by Berry Gordy precisely as a label which would sell black music to white audiences. Its politics lay in keeping control of the production (and profit-making) process but its economic success depended on giving white listeners what they wanted. In terms of the politics of race – and in the context of the Civil Rights movement and the development of Black American consciousness – this was always a policy which made sense economically (Motown was indeed one of the most successful black enterprises ever and almost unique as a major black-owned record company) but with confusing consequences culturally: who were Motown acts performing for? And in the context of rock and its ideology of anticommercialism (by the end of the 1960s it was Motown records that were most often dismissed by rock fans and critics as 'commercial rubbish') even the label's success in the white market place was a political issue. Gaye, like the label itself, never really solved this problem – how to be a credible commercial success in a rock-dominated market – and he died before the white dance floor reclaimed Motown as one of its inspirations.

Gaye's death itself – its very horror – suggests one final way in which Gaye can stand for Motown: in the role of family in his career. Motown's success depended on the extraordinary web of family and friendship ties which brought its musicians together in the first place and kept them all involved with each other thereafter. Gaye himself was married to Berry Gordy's sister; much of the music he made was an effect of longstanding loyalties and commitments. This sort of networking is important for popular music careers generally, but in Motown and other black music scenes, with long experience of being exploited and well aware that American music business regulation, whether copyright laws or union rules, were racially biased, trust was inevitably based more on personal than contractual ties (which meant in turn that breaches of trust were tangled up with a personal sense of betrayal). For Gaye as for many Motown acts a musical career meant both escaping from the Motown family and the resulting sense of drift. And it remains an indictment of the American music business that for all the magnificent music he made, Marvin Gaye somehow was a musician whose promise was never properly fulfilled.

PART II

Texts, genres, styles

4 Pop music

SIMON FRITH

The biggest selling pop single of all time is the version of 'Candle in the Wind' Elton John recorded as a tribute to Princess Diana, and his Westminster Abbey performance of the song, during Diana's funeral service in September 1997, can be considered as the ultimate British pop moment. It was controversial. Pop music is still regarded as a vernacular form unsuitable for a religious occasion, a vulgar form unfit for royalty; and Elton John was not an obvious representative of the state (though he was soon to be knighted, joining Sir Cliff Richard, Sir Paul McCartney, and Sir Andrew Lloyd Webber in the official pop pantheon). He was chosen to sing because he was an intimate of Diana and, in this respect, simply represented her social circle. But it was precisely because she was an Elton John fan that Princess Diana could be described as 'the people's princess': John was an appropriate singer at her service not just as a personal friend but also as the emotional voice of a generation.

In the 1970s Elton John and his lyricist, Bernie Taupin, perfected the musical form that came to dominate Anglo-American pop music in the last decades of the century: the rock ballad. They took the sentimental song (as commercialised in the late nineteenth century), keeping its easy melodic lines, its use of rising pitch to unleash emotion, its lyrical sense of expansive self-pity, but giving it a new rock-based dynamism (in terms of rhythm and amplification). In particular, Elton John's vocal approach was taken from soul music: he sings with a hesitancy, an introversion, an intimacy which contrasts markedly with the full, extrovert, confident vocal tone of the Victorian ballad singer. And this relates to what was most striking about his Westminster Abbey song: the crowd in Hyde Park, watching the service on television relay screens, clearly saw it as a performance. They applauded, and the applause resonated in the Abbey itself. When Earl Spencer spoke, his speech was also heard as a performance, and the applause rippled around the Abbey audience too.

Now of course everyone at Diana's service was performing one way or another, but Elton John's was a specifically pop performance. He was applauded less for being sincere than for performing sincerity: applause was necessary to confirm the skill – the effect – of the performance. Someone just being sincere – crying, say – is not applauded because this involves neither skill nor calculation; it is not an act designed for an evaluative response. Elton John's performance, by contrast, was precisely a display of what we might call emoting skill. What the audience applauded was not John's actual feeling of grief (his business alone) but his ability to provide a performance of grief in which we, as listeners, could take part. 'Candle in the Wind' was, after all, first written for Marilyn Monroe, and it became popular because its feelings were so easily transferred; it was a song through which every lost love could be remembered. It was Diana's song not because she was now its object but because she had so liked it too.

Here are clues as to the ways in which pop performers can be distinguished from rock musicians, on the one hand, and from classical musicians, on the other. Elton John is a pop not a rock star because his authenticity – the authenticity of his expressed emotions – is not an issue. 'Candle in the Wind' is not a song of self-exposure; it was not written to mark off John's difference, his unique artistic sensibility. It was, rather, a pop song, designed for public use. At the same time its pleasures are neither abstract nor in any musical sense transcendent. It is a song infused with Elton John's personality and, for its emotional effect, infused too with a kind of collective sigh. Compare John Tavener's contribution to the funeral service. This also struck an emotional chord with the public (and duly turned up in Classic FM listeners' list of favourite works); but it was clearly a spiritual piece, lifting listeners out of the mundane. It was not applauded.

Definitions

Pop music is a slippery concept, perhaps because it is so familiar, so easily used. Pop can be differentiated from classical or art music, on the one side, from folk music, on the other, but may otherwise include every sort of style. It is music accessible to a general public (rather than aimed at elites or dependent on any kind of knowledge or listening skill). It is music produced commercially, for profit, as a matter of enterprise not art. Defined in these terms, 'pop music' includes all contemporary popular forms – rock, country, reggae, rap, and so on. But there are problems with such an inclusive definition as has become apparent when states have attempted to define pop in law. When in 1990 British legislators (concerned to regulate the content of music radio) defined 'pop music' as 'all kinds of music characterised by a strong rhythmic element and a reliance on electronic amplification for their performance', this led to strong objections from the music industry that such a musical definition failed to grasp the sociological difference between pop ('instant singles-based music aimed at teenagers') and rock ('album-based music for adults').

Here pop becomes not an inclusive category but a residual one: it is what's left when all the other forms of popular music are stripped away, and it is not only rock ideologues who want to distance their music from pop, for them a term of contempt. Country music performers have objected similarly to 'pop stars' like Olivia Newton-John getting country music awards, and these days rap fans dismiss cross-over stars like Will Smith as just 'pop acts'. From this perspective pop is defined as much by what it isn't as by what it is.

Markets

Pop does not have a specific or subcultural, communal market/culture. It is designed to appeal to everyone. Pop doesn't come from any particular place or mark off any particular taste. The partial exception to this rule is teenpop which does appeal to a specific market segment (young girls) but it is misleading to conclude from this that pop is a female form or has primarily female appeal. Much of pop could be called family music. Europop, for example, has been the sound of the summer holiday since Los Bravos's million selling 'Black is Black' in 1966. Los Bravos were a Spanish group with a German lead singer and a British producer. Their success was a model for both cross-European collaboration and commercial opportunism. The skill of the Europop producer (and this is a producer-led form) is to adapt the latest fashionable sounds to Euroglot lyrics which can be followed by everyone with a high-school foreign language, and to a chorus line which can be collectively sung in every continental disco and holiday resort. Thus Boney M, a foursome from the Caribbean (via Britain and Holland), brought together by German producer Frank Farian, sold fifty million records in 1975–8, while the Swedish group Abba, had eighteen consecutive European top ten hits following their 1974 victory in the Eurovision Song Contest. Both groups appealed (particularly through television) to listeners older and younger than the dedicated holiday disco dancers, combining child friendly chorus lines with slick choreography and a tacky erotic glamour that gave Abba, in particular, a camp appeal that was a major influence on late 1970s gay music culture. The most successful British pop production team of the 1980s, Stock, Aitken, Waterman, were clearly influenced by this pop genre, and by the promotion processes that supported it. A group like Steps, which found fame at the turn of the century under Waterman's guidance, managed to combine an up-to-date sense of the Europop sound with British seaside hoofer values which would have been familiar to musical entertainers at the end of the nineteenth century.

Ideology

Pop is not driven by any significant ambition except profit and commercial reward. Its history is a history of serial or standardised production and, in musical terms, it is essentially conservative. Pop is about giving people what they already know they want rather than pushing up against techno-logical constraints or aesthetic conventions. The new in pop thus tends to be the novelty (an instrumental hit like the Tornados' 'Telstar', an 'exotic' number like Althia and Donna's 'Uptown Top Ranking'), and pop is marked by the continuity of its musical values. Common pop terms – easy listening, light entertainment – and the familiar image of fireside crooners like Bing Crosby and Val Doonican suggest that pop is meant to be unob-trusive: if rock involves a kind of in-your-face presence, pop aims to soothe. The contrast can be heard in, say, James Last's orchestral versions of Sex Pistols songs!

Production

Pop is music provided from on high (by record companies, radio pro-grammers and concert promoters) rather than being made from below. Pop is not a do-it-yourself music but is professionally produced and pack-aged. Hence the pop importance of song writers and record producers, on the one hand, and singing stars, on the other. The singer–songwriter is not a common pop figure (though Barry Manilow has shown what can be done with this role). Rather, the key people are commercial songwriters from Stephen Foster and Irving Berlin to Carole King and Dianne Warren, entrepreneurial producers like Berry Gordy and Mickie Most, and versa-tile performers like Jessie Matthews and the Spice Girls.

Aesthetics

Pop is not an art but a craft. It is not about realising individual visions or making us see the world in new ways but about providing popular tunes and cliches in which to express commonplace feelings – love, loss, jealousy. But to work pop must do this in sufficiently individualised ways to appeal to us as individual listeners. And the secret here lies in the pop singers' ability to appeal to us directly, to lay their personality on a song such that we can make it our song too. This is the paradox of pop that Noel Coward described as the 'potency' of cheap music. We can and do despise pop music in general as bland commercial pap while being moved by it in particular as a source of sounds that chime unexpectedly but deeply in our lives.

History

From a rock perspective pop is seen as a kind of unchanging 'old' music, to be contrasted with 'progressive' rock or dance music. This is partly an effect of the way generations work culturally (though the identification of rock with youth does have the odd effect that thirty-year-old tracks can still be used by advertisers and style consultants to provide a youthful ambience) but it also reflects the underlying nostalgia of pop music culture: pop songs are designed both to sound familiar and, often enough, to make one regret that times and people change. But pop itself is implicated in such change: there can be few people over twenty-five who don't agree that they don't write songs like that anymore.

One reason they don't is technological. Pop was the product of a sheet music and then a record industry; it has been shaped by its use in the cinema, on radio, by television. (The most revolutionary moment in pop's technological history was undoubtedly the development of the electrical microphone, which I discuss further below.) Another is sociological. As a mass market music, pop reflects the changing nature of its audience and, in particular, is a kind of musical measure of migration, demographic change and the breakdown of geographical sound barriers. If American pop thus became dominant globally in the twentieth century, pop in the United States was itself the music of Jewish migrants from eastern Europe and the descendants of slaves from Africa. Pop music may come from no particular place, but it absorbs musical sounds from everywhere. And there is a further point to make here. In their very determination to mark themselves off from pop, fans of focused music genres like rock and country are admitting that the lines of demarcation are blurred. It has often been remarked that anything can be rocked; anything can also be popped. The history of pop is marked by the traces of all sorts of musical form – ragtime and blues, jazz and hillbilly, reggae and disco, rock and soul. Even classical music has been popped, as it were, whether in the marketing of opera singers as stars, from Enrico Caruso through Mario Lanza to Luciano Pavarotti, or in the pilfering of classical scores for good tunes – the Boston Pops Orchestra was formed (as an offshoot of the Boston Symphony Orchestra) early in the twentieth century. The success of Classic FM suggests that in Britain, at least, classical music can provide the basic programming for pop radio.

Pop has a history, then, with key moments of change. Perhaps the most important, as I have already noted, followed the marketing of the electrical microphone in the 1930s. Technically the microphone was a way of amplifying the voice, and its immediate use was to enable singers to make themselves heard above the noise of a jazz band or swing orchestra. The amplification of the voice ran parallel to the amplification of the guitar, wind and brass instruments that transformed rural blues into urban rhythm and blues and Western Swing into honky tonk (out of which came rock'n'roll). But in pop terms the microphone's importance was not that it enabled people to sing loudly but that it let them be soft. The electric mike's immediate impact was in the radio and recording studio rather than on stage. The mike meant new vocal techniques (crooning, torch singing) and new kinds of singer whose skill was microphone technique rather than diaphragm control.

What the best of these singers (notably Frank Sinatra and Billie Holiday) quickly realised was that they could sing with a new expressive intimacy. A tone and pitch that were previously only heard in private conversation could now be reproduced publicly, and, of course, central to such intimate conversations are declarations of love and intimations of desire. Listeners could now pretend that they knew the singer, that the singer understood or, at least, articulated their own feelings. This brought a new kind of emotionalism and eroticism into pop, an eroticism most obvious in the emergence of Frank Sinatra's young female fans (who prefigured teen crushes to come), and thus a new kind of stardom: the pop singer as idol.

By the end of the 1930s pop meant vocal rather than instrumental records, and the singer (rather than band leader) dominated the stage (soon displacing the big band altogether). This process was an effect too of radio and cinema, both of which played a central role in the making of the new sort of singing personality, and by the end of the 1940s its consequences for the music industry had become far reaching. Pop songs were increasingly written to display a singer's personality rather than a composer's skill; they now had to work emotionally through the singer's expressivity (rather than the mood being determined by the score) – it was Sinatra's feelings that were heard in the songs he sang rather than their writers'. The new kind of vocal pop star thus needed simpler, more directly emotional songs than those provided by jazz or theatre-based composers, and singers (and their record companies) began to draw on the folk, country and rhythm and blues repertoires. Witty lyrics and sophisticated melodic lines were replaced by melodramatic narratives and unabashed sentimentality. The rise of television reinforced the importance of pop singers as family entertainers (Dean Martin became the biggest television draw in the United States) but brought a new kind of self-consciousness and irony into pop performance (personified most flamboyantly by Liberace).

In many ways the television version of pop that was established in the United States and (with some different national characteristics) in the United Kingdom in the mid-1950s provided a blueprint of pop performance and stardom with which we are still familiar. But two complicating factors should be noted. First, the 1950s also saw the emergence of a teenage market and a teenage taste and if one aspect of this (youth marking itself off from adult entertainment) was rock'n'roll, another (youth music as a new strand of showbiz) was teen pop. Teen pop idols were manufactured (Pat Boone, Fabian) or evolved from rock'n'rollers to all-round entertainers (Cliff Richard, Tommy Steele; in the end, Elvis Presley). Adult pop conventions were adapted for the teenage market. Television was important: American teen idols appeared on *American Bandstand*, British teen idols on *6–5 Special* and *Oh Boy!* On these shows rock'n'roll songs alternated with ballads, and the most successful young performers were pretty but knowable, like the ideal boy next door. When Billy Fury, say, came on to sing 'Halfway to Paradise' he was in essence just a young and more vulnerable version of David Whitfield. Trouser shapes and hair styles change, but there are obvious musical and ideological continuities between Ricky Nelson and David Cassidy, George Michael and Robbie Williams, Pat Boone and Roland Keating, and there have always been model female teen pop singers too, from Connie Francis and Helen Shapiro to Tiffany and Britney Spears.

In commercial terms, then, the 1950s manufacture and marketing of teen pop stars was not a very different process than the manufacture and marketing of pop stars generally, and by the 1960s the pop market was predominantly the teenage market anyway. But there was significant difference in the detail. The writers and producers of teen pop, for example, tended to be young themselves, with a better grasp of teenage vernacular, a better feel for teenage emotions, a better ear for what was hip than the established Tin Pan Alley hacks. The Brill Building became the Tin Pan Alley port of call for young songwriters pitching teen pop songs, and its associated producers were much more at ease with the new technology of tape recording than the established record company studio teams. The record producer changed from being a skilled arranger like Mitch Miller, getting everything in its right place before the session started, to being an inspired sound engineer like Phil Spector, treating the musical tracks as just raw material. Most importantly of all, though, this new generation of pop song writers and producers blended African–American musical conventions into the mix in new ways. In the 1950s black singers had found a television pop niche, whether as a genius entertainer like Louis Armstrong or in the mellow, sophisticated and sexy stylings of Nat 'King' Cole and Johnny Mathis. But what interested the new class of Jewish writers and producers like Jerry Leiber, Mike Stoller and Phil Spector was not the jazz that had influenced their parents, the generation of the Gershwins, but the music they'd heard directly from their African–American neighbours when growing up: rhythm and blues, doo wop, the sound of vocal groups.

The move from pop singer to pop group (which had its ultimate commercial triumph with the Beatles) partly reflected the increasing use of multi-voices for telling teenage stories: teen emotions were seen to be an aspect of everyday conversation that adult emotions are not, and so Phil Spector and Shadow Morton made their 'little operas for kids' with the Crystals and Ronettes and Shangri-Las. But in the longer run the more important point is that multitrack recording found its aesthetic equivalent in the way in which doo-wop broke up the standard pop song into vocal parts, giving it a new rhythmic and timbrel complexity, and in the call/response structure of gospel music. While there was a white pop tradition of group singing (Barbershop groups, for example), its use of close harmony was only really developed by the Beach Boys. For pop in general the group sound came to mean a seductive lead voice (on the gospel derived model of Sam Cooke and Ben E. King) with a chorus of supporters, the sound perfected in the 1960s (and soon dominating the pop sales charts) by the Motown label and acts like Martha and the Vandellas, Smokey Robinson and the Miracles, the Supremes, Temptations and Four Tops.

These pop sounds were fed into rock by British beat groups and then dismissed as 'commercial' by the newly emergent rock fans, and in the last decades of the twentieth century musical influences worked the other way, less pop developments affecting rock, than rock sounds affecting pop. Two trends in particular should be noted: the rise of the power ballad, and the prominence of the soul diva.

Although rock was a musical form that defined itself against pop, the ballad remained central to its appeal. And if jazz performers had used ballads' melodic familiarity as the basis of improvisation – transforming a standard pop song into something quite different – rock musicians (following the Beatles' lead with 'Yesterday') wrote their own ballads but used them in familiar pop ways to bind their audiences into an emotional community. The original rock'n'rollers like Elvis Presley drew on established ballad traditions, whether Italian ('It's Now Or Never') or American (country rock balladeers like Roy Orbison, Charlie Rich and Willie Nelson gave Tin Pan Alley sentiment a new edge of melancholy). But the rock ballad as such derived from soul music and, in particular, from Ray Charles, whose gospel reading of a country song, 'I Can't Stop Loving You', became its inspiration. Charles' emotional sincerity was marked by a distinct vocal roughness and if his tempo was slow it was also insistent. He had a direct influence on such singers as Eric Burdon (of the Animals), Tom Jones and Joe Cocker who, in turn, established the conventions of the ballad as a rock form, as a vehicle for male vocal virtuosity (emotive singing at high pitch and high volume) and chorus line exhilaration. Foreigner's 'I Want To Know What Love Is' (with choral support from the New Jersey Mass Choir) and Aerosmith's 'I Don't Want To Miss A Thing' (with Steven Tyler's vocals so over-the-top as to be parodic) are the classic power ballads, songs of feeling bottled up and bursting out; musical, emotional and sexual release somehow all equated.

This was balladry in a rock context, but such an amplified approach to wanting-songs soon affected pop singing conventions too, as marked initially, as I have already mentioned, by the 1970s emergence of Elton John and then by the success of Michael Bolton in the United States and Mick Hucknall and Simply Red in Britain. The best selling pop singer of the late 1990s, Céline Dion, started out as a child singing French Canadian folk songs and won the Eurovision Contest for Switzerland, but she became a superstar with a singing style that was clearly drawn from power balladry (even working with Meatloaf's producer, Jim Steinman, on one album), and this brings me to the pop importance of the soul diva. In many ways the history of female pop singing follows along the same lines as the history of male pop singing. In the 1960s the sophisticated night club approach of Dionne Warwick (mostly singing the notably adult songs of Burt Bacharach and Hal David) was overlaid by the gospel soul baring of Aretha Franklin and the more adolescent pop seductiveness of Diana Ross in the development of a new kind of vocal virtuosity (and fame) for Gladys Knight, Tina Turner and then Whitney Houston. But in other respects the role of the female pop singer has been different from that of the male pop star. Just as a matter of a wider gender ideology, women singers are heard to have a pathos or vulnerability that men lack – they can make us feel sorrier for them. And then, by this same token, they are also taken to be more skilled at the nuances of emotional expression, more powerful at emotional warfare, more confident at holding up their emotions for our exploration as it were. It is not surprising that Judy Garland, Shirley Bassey, and Dusty Springfield, for example, have had a certain camp appeal, a gay following precisely interested in the performance of emotional excess, nor that there's an element of kitsch in the sexual appeal of the biggest women pop stars – Dion, Houston, Maria Carey and, of course, Madonna.

Even more importantly, though, the very emotional impact of this singing style, its sense of raw feeling bravely dressed, has enabled its sound to be removed from its context: such strong feeling doesn't need an occasion, it can just be added into the mix. From the moment Giorgio Moroder realised that Donna Summer had the ideal voice to put over his machine music, the poppier end of the dance floor in Europe and North America has been dominated by the sound of (mostly anonymous) soul divas, by a kind of collective gospel choir of women wanting love, losing love, celebrating love, bemoaning love, boasting of love found, contemptuous of love lost. It's as if only such voices can guarantee the humanity of the electronic world.

The sentimental song

Paul McCartney once summed pop up as 'silly love songs', and the earliest content analysis of the American hit parade, carried out by J. G. Peatman (1942–3) in the 1940s duly found that 'all successful pop songs are about romantic love'. Indeed, Peatman claimed that he only needed three descriptive categories to characterise American pop: the happy-in-love song, the frustrated-in-love song, and the novelty song with sex interest. In historical terms, though, the popular song hasn't always been about love, and I think it makes better sense to define pop as the sentimental song and then suggest that in the twentieth century (in the West, at least) sentiment came to be applied almost exclusively to affairs of the heart.

This wasn't the case when the pop industry was first shaped in the nine-teenth century. The first great commercial songwriter of the sheet music era, Stephen Foster, wrote his best-loved songs for minstrel shows. Plantation numbers like 'The Old Folks at Home' were sentimental about family, rural life and the past rather than about particular girls or boys, and the song catalogues and manuals for would-be pop composers in the 1900s suggest a range of possible lyrical topics. The pop repertoire was divided into ballad and novelty songs, and the former included not just love songs but also country or rustic songs, Irish songs, songs about Mother.

The obvious question here is what happened to pop in the first half of the twentieth century: why was it reduced to love songs? I'll come back to this. First, I just want to note that although the 1900s classification of song types is quaint it is not incomprehensible. I know what is meant by an Irish song ('Danny Boy', 'When Irish Eyes Are Smiling') and a rustic song (country songwriters like Dolly Parton were coming up with variations of 'My Old Kentucky Home' well into the 1980s). And even Mother songs or, rather, Absent Mother songs are not completely unfamiliar (in the musical *Annie*, for example), while Clive Dunn's 'Grandad' was a British hit as late as 1970. My point here, then, is that while Peatman's findings might accu-rately reflect the hit parade, by the 1940s the hit parade didn't accurately reflect pop. Certainly by the end of the 1950s, when singles sales charts were primarily a measure of teenage taste, 'chart pop' had become a specific and relatively insignificant strand of the pop music to which most people listened – musicals, film soundtracks, oldies, supper club songs, television variety, jazz and country easy listening standards, and so on. It is, in short, misleading to equate pop with record sales.

One of the implications of Peatman's findings was that music that had once had resonance in a variety of social settings, for a variety of social reasons had become focused on the narcissistic feelings of one individual for another. Such individualisation was obviously tied into a shift in pop music marketing: the move from a sheet music to a record industry was a move from collective to individual consumption. But again the interesting question here is not so much why people buy records but about the occasions for sentiment. Pop's history is obviously marked by moments of collective sentimentality. Twentieth-century wars, for example, were fought to the sound of songs of pathos: 'It's A Long Way To Tipperary' (an Irish song to boot!), 'We'll Meet Again'. Even the Animals' 'We've Gotta Get Out of This Place', an obvious favourite for American soldiers in Vietnam, is essentially sentimental (and a love song only in the vaguest way). Twentieth-century migration also involved the use of sentimental songs to remind people of their homelands and to idealise old ways. The Irish song thus continued to be significant throughout the century, meaning among other things that the Irish folk revival of the 1960s (and the pop success of Tommy Makem and the Clancy Brothers and the Dubliners) originated in the Irish bars of New York and that the Riverdance phenomenon started out as interval entertainment, a tourist package, for the Eurovision Song Contest. At a more mundane level, collective sentimentality remains a feature of sports spectating (whether the old Wembley tradition of 'Abide With Me' or the more recent use of Rodgers and Hammerstein's 'You'll Never Walk Alone' on the terraces at Anfield) and drinking. The *karaoke* phenomenon has certainly given new sentimental life to old sentimental songs, turning 'I Will Survive' and 'My Way' into anthems of feminist, gay and heterosexual cultures.

What's important to note about all these examples is that pop here doesn't just mean buying records but also performing them, and performing them in a particular way. Sentimentality describes not just how we listen but also how we sing, *from the heart*, and however embarrassingly we somehow all seem to know how to do that. One way of putting my argument here is to suggest that it is not strong feelings that determine how we sing, but that how we sing gives us the experience of these sorts of feeling. It's the music not the situation that makes us cry, as Hollywood film scorers have long known. To put this another way, it is the sentimental song, sentimental singing, that has come to be the public sign of sincerity. From the earliest days of the music hall, comic turns would wrap up their act with a sentimental song: forget the cynicism and humiliations of music-hall humour they seemed to say, this is the real me, the real you. This became a feature of television comics too (Ken Dodd singing 'Tears', for example) and even a much more aggressive performer like Millie Jackson brings her show to an end by moving out of her contemptuous man-mocking rap into a sentimental soul ballad .

It is perhaps not surprising then that in the latter half of the twentieth century the sentimental song became the sales focus of the musical, on the one hand, and the film soundtrack, on the other. Rodgers and Hammerstein's 1940s transformation of the musical into a vernacular narrative form (with *Oklahoma, Carousel* and *South Pacific*) also involved a new sort of show stopper, the ballad that could stand free of the story ('If I Loved You', 'Some Enchanted Evening'). Such ballads, marketed as pop songs (*West Side Story*'s 'Somewhere' being the classic example), became, in turn, a way of selling a show. This was the promotional strategy mastered by Andrew Lloyd Webber. Hit songs like 'I Don't Know How to Love Him' (*Jesus Christ Superstar*), 'Don't Cry For Me, Argentina' (*Evita*), and 'Memories' (*Cats*) drew people to his shows (rather that the show producing hits on the back of its success – as had been the case with *The Sound of Music* or *Oliver*). This is the reason, I think, that Webber works seem less like musicals than elaborately staged pop shows (one reason, perhaps, why *Cats* works best).

The big ballad has become equally important for film marketing in the last thirty years. Henry Mancini's 'Moon River', written for the opening credits of *Breakfast at Tiffany's*, is usually taken to mark a new relationship between the film and music industries. It was not just that here a song was used to sell a film (rather than vice versa) but also that the song had an accidental relationship to the plot, as it were. It might have had an obvious musical affinity to the rest of Mancini's score, captured the film's ambience, but lyrically it was quite vague and the film would lose nothing if it were removed or replaced. This use of a pop song as simply a film commercial was exploited brilliantly by the James Bond films and by the 1980s stand alone songs were being used over the closing titles too. Here the purpose wasn't just promotional. Audiences were now being sent out of the cinema uplifted by power ballads which bore little musical or lyrical relationship to the rest of the film's score. This trend gave big-voiced singers like Joe Cocker and Jennifer Warnes new careers and culminated in the simultaneous cinema and pop triumph of *Titanic* the film, James Horner's *Titanic* score, and Céline Dion's 'My Heart Will Go On'. What was most interesting here was not how film and music sold each other, but how the very meaning of the film (as a romance rather than a disaster movie) was determined by its closing sentimental song.

Pop music and society

Pop music could be defined as the music we listen to without meaning to; the songs we know without knowing how we know them. These days we equate pop with pop records. Much of the music we hear despite ourselves is 'canned'. Pop music thus reaches us over the radio, through passing car windows, as sound around a shopping centre. Pop songs lodge themselves maddingly in the mind after holidays, children's parties, visits to the dentist; 'La Paloma Blanca', 'Barbie Girl', anything by Abba or Andy Williams. But to use the term 'pop' to describe all the music that insinuates itself into our lives and commercial music is only part of the story. We all grow up into musical cultures, collections of songs and tunes and styles that become our taken-for-granted musical knowledge. And for at least one hundred and fifty years commercially produced music has been an inescapable part of this. But only part, and with various consequences.

As children, for example, we hear lullabies, learn nursery rhymes, join in family songs. Schools teach us folk songs, children's songs; in the playground we join in skipping and jumping songs, on school outings rude songs. Most of us remember these songs throughout our lives, pass them on to children and grandchildren, and the result is a remarkably rich and jumbled repertoire, from traditional tunes which can be traced back over hundreds of years to recent pop tunes whose immediate provenance is soon forgotten. In their classic studies of the lore and language of school children, the Opies (1985) traced the wondrous 1950s journey of 'The Ballad of Davy Crockett' from American television series across English speaking playgrounds around the world, picking up a myriad of local variations along the way. Any hit pop song, it seems (Queen's 'Bohemian Rhapsody', Spice Girls' 'Wannabe'), can be given the a cappella playground treatment.

What's involved here, though, is not just the makeover of new best sellers, the translation of pop into folk, as it were. 'Children's song' is itself a commercial category. Ever since there has been a music business there has been a children's music business, and such 'children's favourites' are resold to generation after generation. BBC radio may have long since dropped its *Children's Hour* and family record request programmes, but the songs these once featured are now performed on children's television programmes (and videos), by children's entertainers like the Singing Kettle. Children's records and cassettes are still a flourishing (if little discussed) sector of the pop industry. An historian could doubtless trace the various musical origins of 'Nellie the Elephant' and 'Going to the Zoo', 'Puff the Magic Dragon' and 'The Lion Sleeps Tonight', 'The Runaway Train' and 'How Much is that Doggie in the Window?' But these songs have become, in effect, timeless, as freshly enjoyed by four-year-olds today as they were by their parents, grandparents and even great grandparents.

This process of musical absorption doesn't stop with childhood, of course, although that is when we hear the most extraordinary range of musical material, and in adult life I have often been struck by how many songs I seem to know without any idea of how I know them. Music hall songs ('My Old Man Said Follow The Van'); cabaret songs ('Mad Dogs and Englishmen'); Disney songs ('Whistle While You Work'); Gilbert and Sullivan songs ('Three Little Girls From School Are We'); film songs ('White Christmas'); songs which come from I know not where ('I Love To Go A-Wandering, A Knapsack On My Back'). What we know this way is obviously shaped by class and place and family and friends; by ethnicity and nation. Most people in Britain probably know the opening lines of 'Auld Lang Syne'; Scots people are likely to know the next lines too, and one feature of a multicultural society is an expansion of the common pop repertoire, as 'Pass the Dutchie', say, takes its place in the playground. Pop defined this way thus provides a kind of map of a changing society just as it maps our own lives, helping give emotional shape to our memories of childhood, friendship, love affairs, life changes. And pop becomes too a resource, a social storehouse from which musicians of all sorts draw and quote and sample.

Pop is not usually treated so positively, so I should stress the two assumptions I'm making here. First, that a song's origin is really only of academic interest. The commercial intent behind 'How Much Is That Doggie In The Window?' is as irrelevant to a young listener now as the political intent behind nursery rhymes like 'The Grand Old Duke of York' or 'Bobby Shafto's Gone To Sea', while Davy Crockett and Tom Dooley are no more or less folk heroes than John Henry or John Barleycorn. Attempts to draw a clear distinction between authentic and inauthentic popular songs, whether using musicological or sociological criteria, are pointless. It's not where pop songs come from that matters, but where they get to. 'Jingle Bells' and 'White Christmas' are every bit as authentic Christmas songs as 'I Saw Three Ships' or 'Silent Night' simply because they are now part of everyone's musical Christmas portfolio.

My second assumption is that pop describes songs that we can and sometimes do perform as well as listen to. Much of this singing is collective – we sing at school, in the pub, at football matches, during weddings and funerals, at the end of parties. But we sing individually too – to our children, with our best friends, above all to ourselves. Indeed, I would add to the definition of pop as accessible music that it is also singable and performable music; it doesn't need the skills that classical or jazz or even rock musicians must acquire. And this argument about participation leads me to a kind of music which is not usually thought of as pop but which has some claim to have determined what pop music means. I refer, of course, to church music: even in these relatively Godless times most of us have sung hymns and carols at some stage of our lives, have come to associate church music with rituals of grief and celebration.

Tim Fleming (1999) has argued persuasively that the contemporary sentimental song has its roots as firmly in the eighteenth-century sentimental hymns of Isaac Watts and Charles Wesley as in the romantic secular songs which were the source of the first big sheet music sales. It was these hymns that gave popular song emotional tropes that we still recognise: a regret for lost innocence, a yearning for paradise as a rustic idyll, a definition of love as comfort in distress. Robbie Williams' 'Angel', to put this another way, is not so different from Isaac Watts', and the translation of gospel into soul shows how easy it is to love a man or woman musically in the same way that one loves God. It could also be said that the Church has been as significant as the music industry in the process of cultural imperialism, spreading Western musical forms East and South. I've always assumed that one reason for Jim Reeves' remarkable global popularity was because his singing style was familiar from years of American missionary work.

Whatever the reason for Jim Reeves' success, pop certainly doesn't work in the straightforward ways that the simpler accounts of commercialism suggest. Why did King Sunny Adé like Jim Reeves' songs so much? How did Smokie become a talisman for radical students in South Korea? Why do some songs become standards the moment they're first heard ('Yesterday', for example) while others not very different make no public mark at all? What's sure is that pop can't be sensibly analysed just in terms of musicology or aesthetics. Yes, we do respond to the song-in-itself but that song-in-itself is soon encrusted with uses and memories and references. Once a pop song is launched on the world, all sorts of things can happen to it. When Bobby Vinton was in the studio laying down 'Blue Velvet', one of his soppier tracks, could he have foreseen that the song would accompany one of the great homoerotic scenes in Hollywood cinema, in Kenneth Anger's *Scorpio Rising*, or become forever menacing, following its use by David Lynch? When Elton John and Bernie Taupin first crafted 'Candle in the Wind' could they have imagined it becoming an official state mourning song?

And if unexpected things happen to songs, so songs have unexpected effects on us. My favourite Abba song, 'The Day Before You Came', describes the wonder of falling in love by flatly documenting how banal life was before love struck. It could equally be a song about the transforming power of music. And so the irony remains. If pop is precisely the music we would usually include in such banality, it is also pop – more than any other form of music – that changes if not our lives then certainly the ways in which we feel about them.

Further reading

Some of my arguments here are taken from my book *Performing Rites. On the Value of Popular Music* (Cambridge, Massachusetts: Harvard University Press / Oxford: Oxford University Press, 1996) though that deals with popular music rather indiscriminately. The best academic studies are historical. For an overview see Peter Van Der Merwe, *Origins of the Popular Style* (Oxford: Clarendon Press, 1989). Tim Fleming's doctoral thesis, cited above, is the best study I know of the origins and commercial and cultural impact of the sentimental song. For the United States see Nicholas Tawa, *The Way to Tin Pan Alley: American Popular Song 1866–1910* (New York: Schirmer Books, 1990). For the United Kingdom see Dave Russell, *Popular Music in England 1840–1914* (Manchester: Manchester University Press, 1987) and Derek B. Scott, *The Singing Bourgeois. Songs of the Victorian Drawing Room and Parlour* (Milton Keynes and Philadelphia: Open University Press, 1989). I don't know of any good pop histories covering the rest of the twentieth century though most of the biggest stars have useful biographies. From the perspective of academic research, pop seems to be that music that isn't much studied. Most books written in the last twenty years with pop in their titles are really about rock; the most suggestive studies of popular music are focused on genres like rap or country. When pop singers or composers are taken seriously it is usually in order to suggest that they transcend their commercial context, can be treated like classical composers or as jazz singers. With the exception of Henry Pleasants' fine *The Great American Popular Singers* (New York: Simon and Schuster, 1974) the resulting studies are often interesting but not often about pop, and I've yet to see an academic article on, say, Perry Como, Andrew Lloyd Webber or Cher.

For music and everyday life on the ground, as it were, see Ruth Finnegan's richly suggestive ethnography of the musical worlds in Milton Keynes: *The Hidden Musicians. Music Making in an English Town* (Cambridge: Cambridge University Press, 1989) and the engaging interviews about people's musical lives collected by Susan D. Crafts, Daniel Cavicchi and Charles Keil as *My Music* (Hanover and London, Wesleyan University Press, 1993). For illuminating if oblique approaches to pop see Mark W. Booth, *The Experience of Song* (New Haven: Yale University Press, 1981) historically arranged essays on songs from madrigals to advertising jingles, and Michael Billig, *Rock'n'Roll Jews* (Nottingham: Five Leaves, 2000) ostensibly a history of Jews in rock'n'roll, in fact a moving meditation on popular music and cultural identity.

5 Reconsidering rock

KEIR KEIGHTLEY

'L'enfance est plus authentique' 'CYBELE'S REVERIE', STEREOLAB, 1995

'Rock' is a term that is instantly evocative and frustratingly vague. Rock may mean rebellion in musical form, distorted guitars, aggressive drumming, and bad attitude. But rock has also stood for much more than a single style of musical performance. Very diverse sounds and stars, including country blues, early Bob Dylan, Motown, Otis Redding, Kraftwerk, P-Funk, salsa, Run-DMC, Garth Brooks and Squirrel Nut Zippers, have all been called 'rock' at one time or another, even though they are also equally describable as non-rock. If this eclectic set of performers and sounds can be grouped under the heading 'rock', it is not because of some shared, timeless, musical essence; rather, specific historical contexts, audiences, critical discourses, and industrial practices have worked to shape particular perceptions of this or that music or musician as belonging to 'rock'. At the same time, no style or performer is automatically entitled to the 'rock' mantle, since rock culture has also been defined historically by its processes of exclusion. The idea of rock involves a rejection of those aspects of mass-distributed music which are believed to be soft, safe or trivial, those things which may be dismissed as worthless 'pop' – the very opposite of rock. Instead, the styles, genres and performers that are thought to merit the name 'rock' must be seen as serious, significant and legitimate in some way. These various conceptions of rock are made more complicated by the ways in which the meanings of 'rock' have shifted over the past four decades, and by how those meanings have been understood in different contexts or by different communities.

One of the great ironies of the second half of the twentieth century is that while rock has involved millions of people buying a mass-marketed, standardised commodity (CD, cassette, LP) that is available virtually everywhere, these purchases have produced intense feelings of freedom, rebellion, marginality, oppositionality, uniqueness and authenticity. It is precisely this predicament that defines rock, since negotiating the relationship between the 'mass' and the 'art' in mass art has been the distinguishing ideological project of rock culture since the 1960s. Rock involves the making of distinctions within mass culture, rather than the older problem of distinguishing mass from elite or vernacular cultures. Rock's values and judgements produce a highly stratified conception of popular music, in which minute distinctions are seen to take on life and death significance. Taking popular music seriously, as something 'more' than mere entertainment or distraction, has been a crucial feature of rock culture since its emergence.

This article attempts to map out a number of rock music culture's dominant features as they emerge, develop and change over time. I will be interested here in dynamic cultural processes rather than static musical–stylistic features. Although each of us may have ideas of what is, or is not, 'really rock', those ideas are not necessarily congruent with what others in the past may have felt, quite justifiably, was 'really rock'. 'Rock', as a term, has always been the focus of debate, and, as such, has come to be embedded within definitions or positions which may seem contradictory or paradoxical.

While rock is frequently treated as a musical genre, it is more useful to approach it as a larger musical culture. There are, of course, particular sounds and styles that tend to be privileged in certain circumstances as the 'core' or essence of rock. However, as we shall see, rock culture both encompasses and transcends various musical styles and genres; those which have been included under the rubric of 'rock' have changed dramatically in the past few decades. For example, the lounge or easy listening revival of the mid-1990s took what had been the mortal enemy of rock culture in the 1960s and 1970s and turned it into a vehicle for rock avantists. Thus, a form of music which had been the absolute antithesis of rock at one historical conjuncture – adult easy listening – could become the keeper of the rock faith for listeners who felt grunge had become too formulaic, too mainstream.

The first part of this chapter offers a critical survey of the three decades leading into the emergence of rock in the mid-1960s. This reconsideration of the pre-history and birth of rock addresses industrial and cultural developments that play a role in the advent of rock. The second part abandons a more-or-less linear historical narrative in order to focus on some of the key principles underpinning rock culture.

Rock'n'roll and its pre-history

The idea of rock, as I have suggested, involves taking seriously music which may be found within a commercial mainstream. Rock culture presumes that this mainstream is already variegated, containing music and musicians of differing degrees of quality and integrity. Rock culture proceeds to sort out and distinguish the music of value from the music that lacks value. But this is not simply about 'likes' and 'dislikes'. Rather, the preferences of the rock fan will always embody ethical judgements about any particular piece of music – musical beauty and pleasure will be evaluated in relation to ideas about the workings of a capitalist system. Rock offers an elaborated worldview in which musical practices (styles and sounds, images and industrial processes) and musical preferences (tastes, pleasures) become intertwined, in which aesthetic and ethical judgements inform each other. The rock fan's claim to 'superior' musical taste involves making serious judgements about popular music, drawing on an awareness of that music's social contexts. This awareness is seen as lacking in the fans of other mainstream music. Thus the distinctions made by rock culture effectively stratify the mainstream of popular music into 'serious' (rock) and 'trivial' (pop) components.

Although it is within rock culture that this activity is at its most intense, some listeners did take mainstream popular music seriously prior to the advent of rock. We can trace the beginnings of a stratified mainstream back to the big band era of the 1930s and 1940s. From around the mid-1930s onward, audience distinctions between performers and styles within the mainstream of popular music began to take on a significance beyond simple personal choice. Increasingly, popular musical tastes could be embedded in forms of ethical judgement concerning the integrity and authenticity of performer, listeners and the music industry (and about the relationships between them). As the big band era progressed, particular musical preferences and tastes began to take on a polemical dimension. This may be seen in the development of oppositions between big band and non-big band popular music styles, and especially in the distinctions made within big band culture between swing and sweet bands (for example, Benny Goodman vs Guy Lombardo), between soloists and singers, between 'jazz' listeners and jitterbug dancers, and even between black and white bands. The first term of each of these oppositions would usually serve to designate a valued, 'authentic' position, while the second would be rejected by many critics and fans as standing for more commercial (and therefore suspect) tastes. We may witness, during this period, a growing sense that the ethical aspects of aesthetic judgement (did the musician really feel the emotions behind the trumpet solo, or was he or she playing merely for money?) could serve as the basis of popular music's value (this band is real, that one is phoney). This development would have far-reaching consequences.

Prior to the big band or swing era, of course, audience members made taste distinctions among singers, bands and songs. The difference is that, in the emerging cultural politics of the big band era, individual tastes came to be linked to broader criteria of judgement, such as commercialism, seriousness of intention or authenticity. The stratification of big band culture produced tensions between competing conceptions of popular music. On the one hand, popular music was seen as a form of serious art that was an end in itself ('art for art's sake'); on the other, it was regarded as mere entertainment for profit ('crass commercialism'). These tensions led to the emergence in the 1940s of a distinct form of art music called 'jazz'. Whereas, in the 1920s and 1930s, 'jazz' was commonly used to designate any contemporary popular music, jazz now defined itself in opposition to popular music as it moved away from a mass audience.

Big band culture also saw the rise of age-grading (the recognition of distinct sub-audiences, defined on the basis of age). This division of the audience into teen and adult segments would have the most immediate impact on the development of popular music in the post-war period. Up until the mid-1930s, the products of Tin Pan Alley (the core of the United States music industries) tended to be marketed towards an undifferentiated audience, with the same songs aimed at everyone from grandmothers to grandsons. During the big band era, however, critics and the industry began to distinguish, not only between taste publics, but between age groups as well. As early as 1939, critics were complaining that some novelty swing bands could be 'understood' only by teen audiences; simultaneously, certain older, established popular songs, called standards, increasingly came to be associated with adult audiences. Age-grading was new to popular music at this time, and would become the key means of segmenting the white mainstream in the later 1940s and 1950s.

We are accustomed to thinking of the teen/adult split in popular music as exploding with revolutionary force in the 1950s. This revolutionary upheaval is usually associated with the emergence of rock'n'roll, but a more accurate account would suggest that rock'n'roll marked the culmination of a long evolution within popular music culture. From the big band era through the late 1940s, there is a growing sense that the mainstream is being divided by age as well as taste. It is not until the mid-1950s that teen taste is officially institutionalised as a separate segment of the mainstream, with 'rock'n'roll' as the name for that taste. The arrival of Bill Haley and the Comets' 'Rock Around the Clock' at number one on the *Billboard* pop singles chart in the summer of 1955 is generally taken to mark the beginning of the rock'n'roll era. There are any number of rock'n'roll hit records which precede it – including several Top 20 hits by Haley! – but none reach number one. Thus, the main significance of 'Rock Around the Clock' is that it is the first rock'n'roll record to reach the top rung of the Tin Pan Alley hierarchy. Rather than marking the beginning of a revolution, the success of 'Clock' represents the final step in the mainstream recognition of separate, age-graded taste cultures for teens and adults.

Earlier steps that contributed to the institutionalisation of the teen/adult split in the popular audience in the 1950s had included new formats for records and radio. With the introduction of the LP (long-play) album in 1948 and the 45 rpm single in 1949, popular music was no longer embodied exclusively in 78 rpm records that had held one song per side. Soon the two new formats came to be aligned with different segments of the market for popular music: the more expensive LP came to be the format of choice for standards, mood music and theme albums, and the cheaper 45 emerged as the medium of contemporary hits. This alignment between format and material contributed to the growing distinction between adult and teen tastes. As a result, the history of rock'n'roll in the 1950s is etched in singles, not albums. The emergence of a mass market for albums of non-adult popular music does not occur until the mid-1960s and, as we shall see, the development of rock culture (*c.* 1965–7 onward) is crucially tied to a shift from singles to albums and an attendant shift in cultural legitimacy.

At the same time, radio programming in the United States was changing, as the one-size-fits-all family fare of network radio gave way to focused local formats associated with adult or with teen audiences. The most spectacular development was the advent of the Top 40 format, which featured a limited playlist of only the latest and most popular hits and was directed at teen audiences. Unlike the relaxed presentation of established standards on adult radio, the high energy and fast song turnover of Top 40 demanded change and novelty. As a result, styles and musicians previously marginal to the mainstream began to make headway. Rhythm and blues and country songs, styles, and performers offered what Top 40 needed, and the 1950s are marked by the growing diversity of radio playlists. The institutionalisation of teen radio meant a shift in what a 'hit' sounded like.

To this point, I have focused on the white mainstream, in order to highlight the emergence of teen and adult segments within it. Usually, however, the rise of rock'n'roll is said to have been marked by a breaking down of racial barriers in the music industry, an industry whose racial biases were hitherto taken to express those of a predominantly white society. The entry into the popular music mainstream of rhythm and blues songs and styles and, later, of African–American performers, comes with rock'n'roll and marks a crucial moment of 'crossover'. From 1955 onward, the presence of African–American performers on the mainstream pop charts grows, so that by 1963 the trade magazine *Billboard* drops its separate (or, as many would say, segregated) black music chart. (That chart would be revived in 1965 in the wake of the British Invasion and the rise of soul music.)

Billboard had ranked 'race' and then 'rhythm and blues' hits under their own headings since the 1940s, because the separate pop and rhythm and blues charts were understood to describe two racially distinct markets. The 1950s are marked by the entry of ever-increasing numbers of African–American-originated recordings onto the white pop charts, expanding a process that had actually begun earlier, with the successes of black swing bands in the 1930s, and of massively popular small combo performers, like Louis Jordan and Nat King Cole, in the 1940s.

It is important to stress here that it was primarily the institutional demand for new material and novelty sounds that drove these changes in the pop mainstream. To argue, as many historians have done, that white teenagers in the 1950s were free of their parents' racial biases, and there-fore actively sought out African–American performers is clearly a retrospective attempt to politicise popular tastes that at the time were only nascently informed by ethical judgements about popular music. (In fact, these arguments actually tell us more about the politics of the period in which they begin to be put forth, the late 1960s.) It is equally important to recall that throughout the 1950s it is white appropriations and hybridisa-tions of 'black' musical styles that sell the most records overall (and white performers of these styles who tend to have the longest careers, for example Elvis Presley).

Music that sounded quite like uptempo rock'n'roll could be found in the 1940s and earlier, but this music was not generally considered rock'n'roll, since it did not involve a specifically white, mainstream and teen audience. We can trace elements of a broadly conceived uptempo rock'n'roll style back to the urban blues styles of the 1930s, to styles asso-ciated with African–American musicians and audiences. Boogie-woogie pianists, and those small blues combos of the thirties that evolved into the jump blues bands of the 1940s, are the most obvious antecedents of an uptempo fifties rock'n'roll style. We should remember, though, that these were popular, commercially successful, and cosmopolitan styles. Like the big swing bands, they played a crucial – and often overlooked – role in cul-tivating popular taste for uptempo, 4/4 dance music, blues chord progres-sions, and riff-based melodies. The Western swing sound of the thirties and forties was likewise significant for its pre-rock'n'roll synthesis of country, jazz, and blues into a goodtime dance music for a predominantly white, rural audience. While the urban dance bands tended to foreground pianos and saxophones, it was their regional and country counterparts who emphasised the guitar. By the 1950s, white country and western per-formers playing a hybrid of Western swing and rhythm and blues called rockabilly were also crossing over from the separate 'country and western' chart to both the white pop and the rhythm and blues charts.

This account of rock'n'roll's ancestry, however, ignores a major current within this history, one marked by slower, more ballad-oriented material. In fact, the first African–American rock'n'roll group to reach number one on the pop chart, the Platters, derived their style from older, mainstream black entertainers who 'crossed over' in the 1930s and forties, performers such as the Ink Spots and the Mills Brothers. It is significant that, after Elvis Presley, the Platters were probably the most successful rock'n'rollers of the 1950s. The Platters occasionally used elements of the uptempo style described above; more often, though, they worked within the mainstream musical traditions of Tin Pan Alley. Nevertheless, because of their teen, crossover audience, they were always considered rock'n'roll.

This is true as well of another key part of 1950s rock'n'roll, a vocal close harmony style called doo wop, which was probably named after the non-sense syllables in the Turbans' 1955 hit, 'When You Dance'. While the Platters came out of the world of professional showbusiness, doo wop performers tended to be groups of young, inexperienced men from the inner city, who practised a cappella, without instruments, and made a record or two before disappearing. Doo wop was the first rock'n'roll style to undergo a revival (in the early 1960s). More importantly, by the late 1960s doo wop could retrospectively be seen as having epitomised many of the key values of rock'n'roll: an innocence with respect to record industry machinations, the spontaneity of amateur performance, and a host of performers no older than their audiences. (Many doo woppers were in their teens, such as the aptly named Teenagers.) While these groups were not as explicitly rebellious as some of the uptempo rock'n'roll performers, the emotional thrill they produced was just as invigorating. Later, however, these groups would be ignored as attempts were made to define an 'essence' of rock'n'roll. This is largely because the Platters and most doo wop groups, though linked to youth culture and its institutions, worked with musical materials similar to those of the pre-rock'n'roll ballad styles that rock culture came to associate with adult easy listening. These sounds do not easily fit into the hard, masculinist aesthetic privileged in dominant accounts of rock as a musical style.

It should be clear by now that any attempt to isolate a definitive or core style of 1950s rock'n'roll is a highly problematic enterprise. It should also be noted that, during the 1950s, rock'n'roll was regularly viewed as just one in a series of passing dance crazes, giving way to the calypso and the twist. Teen culture had yet to acquire the prestige which would mark it in the 1960s, and even rock'n'roll performers themselves might have scoffed at the idea that they were doing anything more than entertaining their audiences. On the other hand, by the mid-1950s, adult popular music had become the most profitable segment of the music industry, and experienced a concomitant growth in the cultural esteem accorded it. Adult pop performers like Frank Sinatra and Ella Fitzgerald were increasingly received as serious artists, and the vehicle for their artistry was the high-profit, long-play album, where mature and sophisticated themes could be explored in depth. Likewise, while jazz and folk music were less popular, they received even greater respect, and had dedicated audiences of young adults and older listeners who bought albums and approached music as a significant artform rather than a disposable entertainment. Though rock-'n'roll may be said to have given teenagers a voice as a social group, that voice was not explicitly raised in artistic debate or social protest at the time. Rock'n'roll, embodied in ephemeral 45s, was dismissed – and not without reason – as a fad and a novelty by those who took music seriously.

The in-between years and the British Invasion

Following the rock'n'roll era of *c.* 1955–8, but immediately prior to the full flowering of rock in the mid-1960s, there are two important historical moments within what was then called 'teen music'. These moments are of interest in part because of the perspective from which future rock historians would make sense of them. One such moment was 'the in-between years', 1959–63; the other was the British Invasion, *c.* 1964–5. According to many rock historians, rock'n'roll suffered a near-death experience around 1959: Elvis had been drafted, Chuck Berry was on his way to prison, Little Richard had retired, and Buddy Holly, the Big Bopper, and Ritchie Valens had died in a plane crash. Thus the golden age was over, and until the Beatles arrived in the United States to revive the lost spirit of rock'n'roll in 1964, the teen music of the in-between years reverted, it is said, to the bland conformity which had marked it prior to the emergence of rock-'n'roll. As is often the case, rock culture, in offering an understanding of its own history, selected certain performers and ignored others in order to suggest that popular taste, during the in-between years, was not what it should have been. As a result, teen idols like Fabian, Frankie Avalon, and Bobby Vee were made to stand for what was, in fact, a rich and complex period in popular music history. Dismissing the music of the in-between years as a formulaic, shallow, and insignificant interregnum between Elvis and the Beatles allowed the arrival of the British beat bands in 1964 to be seen as a heroic overthrowing of the establishment – like rock'n'roll itself, another radical break with the past. This view reinforced the sense of rock as a revolutionary rupture, by discouraging evolutionary accounts of the movement from rock'n'roll into rock (even as it implied a mythical continuity between the two): Elvis started the fire, the in-between years almost put it out, but the Beatles saved the day, coming out of left field and showing the United States how it should be done.

The music and culture of the in-between years were incredibly important, and may be viewed as a laboratory of sorts in which different elements of what would later become rock culture took shape. The years 1959–63 saw a great deal of experimentation in the recording studio, with producers like Phil Spector, Berry Gordy, and Brian Wilson using available technologies to create exciting new sounds that could only exist on tape. Rhythm and blues musicians developed new arrangements and rhythms that would nourish the creation of soul and funk. These were the years of the Twist, a dance rhythm that widened teen music's appeal to an older audience but, more importantly, hurried the transition from the swung or shuffled rhythms of rock'n'roll to the straight eighth-note rhythm of much rock music. The rise of instrumental and surf bands contributed to the development of an amateur language for the electric guitar. Folk music experienced a phenomenal rise in popularity during this period, and, as we shall see, contributed greatly to the rise of rock. The in-between years also saw increased representation of African–American and female performers in the mainstream. The desegregation of the charts accelerated, as Sam Cooke and Chubby Checker became mainstream superstars. Unlike the rock'n'roll era, which had virtually no female stars, the in-between years were characterised by highly successful women performers, with exciting and energetic 'girl groups' like the Shirelles and the Crystals, and immensely popular solo artists like Brenda Lee and Connie Francis dominating the charts. Women such as Brill Building songwriters Carole King and Cynthia Weil and record label owner Florence Greenberg also become important industry insiders during this time.

With the arrival of the Beatles in the United States and the start of the British invasion in 1964, female and African–American performers experienced massive career setbacks, as white, male British bands like the Dave Clark Five, the Animals, and the Rolling Stones reduced the presence of girl groups and rhythm and blues singers on the charts. There is no conspiracy here, but it is significant that rock culture celebrates two highly male-dominated periods (fifties rock'n'roll, British Invasion) as its foundational moments. An important part of rock's taste war against the mass mainstream is conducted in gendered terms, so that 'soft', 'sentimental', or 'pretty' become synonyms for insignificance, terms of dismissal, while 'hard', 'tough', or 'muscular' become descriptions of high praise for popular music. Even the increasing acceptance of the term 'rock' rather than 'rock-'n'roll' in the mid-1960s is tied to this opposition; by excising the trivial ''n' roll', and proudly holding up the naturally hard 'rock', rock culture could express its seriousness and its maturity in implicitly masculine language.

The British Invasion is seen to mark a turning point in the movement toward rock culture for a number of reasons. Because the impact of United Kingdom performers on the US charts prior to 1964 had been negligible, the British Invasion was taken to represent a sudden shift in United States popular taste. However, the sound of the British beat bands was not radically different from that of US groups like the Beach Boys, and, of course, many US bands flourished alongside those of the British Invasion. Explanations, in magazines and interviews, of what was special about the British bands provide important clues toward understanding their role in the emergence of rock. There is a recurring sense that the Invasion bands represented a revivalist sensibility, that they were re-presenting a lost musical spirit with a new twist and a new seriousness previously foreign to the Top 40. The fact that the Beatles' recordings of fifties rock'n'roll, rhythm and blues and Motown songs were seen as homages, rather than commercially motivated covers, is evidence of the fact that the tastes of the musicians themselves begin to be taken seriously as signs of artistic ambition. Even more significantly, bands that had begun as part of an early sixties United Kingdom revival of United States blues, such as the Rolling Stones and the Animals, appear almost messianic in their desire to convert mass taste, with their connoisseurist appreciations of overlooked, non-mainstream, African–American musicians.

The British invasion occurred at a moment when a number of trends that had been developing over the previous few years had begun to bear fruit, and it may be the very punctual quality of the British invasion – its clearcut location in time – that has lead to an oversimplified sense of cause and effect in popular memory. For example, teen LP sales, which had hitherto been negligible, began to rise just before the British Invasion, and really took off in 1964. The LP was at this time considered the serious medium for 'respectable' music (whether adult pop, jazz, folk, or 'classical' music), and the emergence of rock is crucially tied to the rise of the non-adult album market. By 1967, 'teen' albums would overtake sales of adult albums on the *Billboard* charts for the first time, marking a milestone in the establishment of rock culture. Rock's commercial success (LPs are more profitable than singles) and its artistic legitimacy (albums can be serious 'statements', unlike ephemeral novelty singles) thus developed hand in hand. Folk music (and its LP culture) had been building in popularity for several years prior to the arrival of the British bands, but the folk performer Bob Dylan (who had been releasing albums since 1961) entered into mainstream stardom as a performer only in the wake of the Invasion, further complicating accounts of musical change in the period.

The period between1964 and 1968 was characterised by unprecedented and rapid stylistic change for which the British bands are only partly responsible. In fact, it is the intense cross-fertilisation and exchange of ideas between British and American musicians that contributed to the sound of rock as it was being born. Just as black and white musicians in the United States had been in constant creative dialogue for over a century, now United States and United Kingdom sounds were interwoven as well. British skiffle (a kind of rhythmic acoustic folk music popular in the late fifties) was an adaptation of US folk-blues songs whose roots lay back in the British Isles and in Africa; the Merseybeat bands of the early sixties started out playing skiffle and then began re-working US rock'n'roll and rhythm and blues records in live performance settings to create the sound of the British Invasion; folk-rockers like the Byrds performed United States folk songs with British invasion rhythms and arrangements; Bob Dylan's move from acoustic to electric accompaniment, from folk to rock, was in part influenced by the Beatles' and Byrds' innovations; and the middle-period Beatles were heavily influenced by Dylan and the folk-rock sound (listen to 'You've Got to Hide Your Love Away' to hear John Lennon imitate Dylan). Similar transactions were occurring on the blues revival side of the equation, with Chicago-style electric blues being re-imagined as a proto-hard rock by the Rolling Stones and then Cream in the United Kingdom, and by the Blues Project and Paul Butterfield in the United States.

Rock emerged out of the overlapping of several musical cultures, none of which on its own would be considered rock: a teen, Top 40 pop world, no longer rock'n'roll but not yet rock, that was invested in Brill Building professional songwriting, studio production, new sounds and dance rhythms; surf and garage bands in suburbias everywhere; a variety of African–American musical cultures, especially Chicago electric blues and gospel-influenced soul sounds; 'trad jazz', skiffle, folk and blues revivalists in the United Kingdom, and a complex US folk music culture, which included Anglo-Celtic folk, country and blues revivalists, bohemian protest singers and best-selling pop-folkies. Rock did not draw simply on the sounds, styles and techniques of these musical cultures. Perhaps more importantly, rock adopted and adapted aspects of their worldviews, their aesthetic and political sensibilities, and their varied approaches to relations between music, musicians and listeners in a mass mediated, commodity-driven, corporate society. Out of the teen Top 40 came an investment in rapid stylistic turnover, in the exploration of novel sound textures through the technology of the recording studio and a belief that the charts could function as a meritocracy, with the best songs and performers reaching the biggest audiences; from suburban surf and garage bands came an appreciation for passion and spontaneity over technical ability and a musical celebration of primitive aggression; soul music and Chicago electric blues offered performed autobiography as a pinnacle of musical authenticity and provided the technical skills for signifying hard-won truths through vocal and guitar sounds; and, as we shall see in some detail below, the various folk music cultures and their elaborated conceptions of authenticity presented perhaps the richest and most fully articulated source of ideology for what would become rock culture. And it is to the origins and tenets of rock ideology that we now turn.

Folk versus mass society in the USA

While many different musical cultures contributed to the formation of rock, the culture of 'folk' expressed so many ideas that would become central to rock, and in so explicit a fashion, that we must examine this culture more closely. The backdrop against which folk (and ultimately rock) developed in the United States was often called 'mass society'. (Because of post-war austerity, issues around mass society emerge somewhat later and in modified form in the United Kingdom.) This is a term that simultaneously described and critiqued a range of social and cultural developments. Rapid rates of urbanisation and industrialisation were felt to have resulted in a loss of community, tradition and meaning in the lives of ordinary people. More and more of the population in the industrialised West were living anonymous lives in large cities, working at routinised jobs in factories and offices, and seeking escape in the mass-produced fantasies of the culture industries. Massive corporations, institutions and bureaucracies could now affect individual lives to an unprecedented extent. The scale of society had grown so huge that the historical foundations of social interaction were believed to be shifting. As everyday life became increasingly distanced from its traditional, community-based roots, as experiences were more and more mediated or corrupted by technology and commerce, individuals were thought to be becoming more conformist, more susceptible to manipulation, more alienated.

Increasingly, the 'mass' was seen to overwhelm the 'individual' and the 'mass media' were often blamed for a perceived homogenisation and debasement of modern culture. While 'mass society' offered an important critique of the upheavals of industrial capitalism, this was, strictly speaking, neither a populist nor radical perspective. It could equally serve to fuel elitist dismissals of the majority of the population as a kind of ignorant, inhuman and indistinct clay, a shapeless 'mass' that was being moulded and brainwashed by advertising and amusements. From an elitist perspective, the mass culture of comic books, movies and popular music was simultaneously cause and symptom of mass society's failure. This aspect of the critique co-existed with its more progressive side; ultimately 'mass society' articulated a growing anxiety about the unbridled growth of distant, commercial-bureaucratic interests over those of individuals and communities. 'Mass society' signalled the sense of alienation that increasingly accompanied modern, industrialised, urban life.

It is significant that this critical view of mass society was not the exclusive property of marginal folk musicians, nor of an emerging rock culture. It was widely disseminated by influential intellectuals and novelists at the centre of society, and found expression in the 1950s in popular anxieties around 'conformity', 'the rat race' and 'suburbia' in the United States. While these problems have little to do with youth or with rock music, by the 1970s this perspective could be seen to have found its fullest expression in rock music and rock culture. To trace the process by which an emerging rock culture was nourished by the critique of mass society, we must look briefly at the role played by folk music in refashioning many of the elements of this critique.

Folk culture emerged in reaction to the developments of mass society. Folk defined itself in its rejection of mass society and mass culture. It viewed what I am calling the 'mass mainstream' (the Hit Parade of the Top 40 and established commercial popular music) as an enemy emblematic of all that was wrong with modern life: soulless songs and suspect success, manufactured teen idols and manipulated masses. Folk culture saw itself as the serious alternative to the mass mainstream. It was serious because it intertwined social and aesthetic concerns, bringing them together in the folk concept of authenticity. The development of that concept within rock culture will be discussed below. At this point it is important to note that folk authenticity refers to musical experiences that are valued as unalienated and uncorrupted, 'anti-mass' pleasures which were perceived to be musically pure, genuine and organically connected to the community that produced them. By emphasising roots, tradition, the communal and the rural ('folk' was sometimes used as a synonym for what we would now call 'country' music), folk pursued musical authenticity as a bulwark against the alienation of mass society.

The folk music culture that influenced the emergence of rock was, in fact, a folk revival that had been gaining wider interest throughout the 1950s. It attracted educated, urban people who rejected mainstream, mass-produced music as artificial and trivial. In its place, they sought out the musically 'authentic', marginal musical traditions that were associated with rural, pre-industrial and communal music-making, both white and black. Thus they embraced acoustic instruments, orally transmitted songs and vernacular modes of performance. By reviving older styles and songs, folk culture presented an implicit critique of contemporary music. Its emphasis on the blues (in its older and agrarian forms) meant that folk was also a crucial conduit through which African–American musical culture and ideology reached the white middle class.

Folk culture was complex and stratified, and an important wing was more explicitly concerned with music as an engine of social change, embracing folk as a 'people's music'. Protest singers began with traditional styles and songs, adapting lyrics to address contemporary issues. By the early 1960s, however, a great deal of new material in a folk style was being written that presented a polemical view of mass society. Both the explicit polemic of the folk protest singer and the implicit critique of mainstream music by revivalists and college-based pop-folk stars like the Kingston Trio helped shape rock culture's own developing polemic against the mass mainstream.

Since rock emerges in the overlapping of a number musical cultures, however, rock does not simply adopt folk ideology wholesale. Rather, because of crucial differences in the age profiles of their respective audiences and due to diverging attitudes toward success and popularity, rock adapts key aspects of folk ideology to rock's unique situation. Folk culture saw itself as distinct from popular music and was wary of folk performers who crossed over from folk's self-segregated world into the mainstream. The folk polemic had used the issue of authenticity to police the boundaries of folk music against the mainstream of popular music. (Bob Dylan's shift from 'authentic' acoustic instruments to the allegedly 'alienated' and 'artificial' technology of electric guitars c. 1965 was seen by the folk community as a betrayal and a sell-out, a move away from folk and into the mass mainstream.) As well, folk culture was marked by a high degree of inter-generational involvement and included college students, middle-aged bohemians and respected older musicians like Woody Guthrie and Mississippi John Hurt.

Conversely, rock was born *within* the popular mainstream as an *exclusively* youth-oriented music. These differences crucially affected the way rock culture played out its folk-influenced world view, because they allowed rock to emerge in the simultaneous embrace of anti-mass ideology *and* mass commercial success. Raised on Top 40 and unafraid of popular success for select, *authentic* rock performers, the newborn rock culture featured a massive youth audience which saw itself, nonetheless, as opposed to the mass mainstream and all that stood for. This apparent contradiction was fostered by the unique situation of youth in the 1960s.

Youth

From c. 1964–5 on, rock's internal diversity of sound and attitude cohered around the category of 'youth', a more complex term than 'teen'. 'Youth' was not simply a stage of life, although of course the new massive youth population empowered rock's intertwined claims to cultural and marketplace legitimacy. By around 1967, rock had incorporated much of the 25-and-under college audience who, traditionally, had been folk fans. But 'youth' was also an idea and an ideal, and it was during this period that an important cultural shift in the relative valorisation of 'adulthood' and 'youth' was consolidated. Rather than striving for adulthood and its traditional privileges, the desire to stay 'young' for a longer period had become more and more widespread. Rock provided a signal means of affiliating with 'youth'.

Rock culture seemed to have emerged most obviously from the 'teen' side of the adult/teen split institutionalised in the 1950s, and this had important implications for rock's attitude toward success and popularity. The 'teen' was critically shaped by the sensibilities of the Top 40 and the Hit Parade, which did not necessarily consist of one uniform sound or style. Rather, Top 40 could bring together a variety of music, which often shared only the 'fact' of popularity. Rock's stylistic eclecticism and its strong belief that the best music not only had the potential to find a mass audience, but, in fact, *ought* to reach that audience, developed out of this teen Top 40 mentality, and were further amplified by the baby boom's extended buying power. Folk culture, drawing on romanticised – and even invented – agrarian traditions, had often preached populism while practising elitism, suspicious of truly popular taste. Rock's pop-derived 'populism', on the other hand, was born on the terrain of the popular. The continuing sense that sales charts are important indices of the state of rock is a legacy of pre-rock, teen music culture.

So rock retained a symbolic empathy for the 'teen', even as it clandestinely modelled its artistic ambitions on important elements of the 'adult' popular music culture of the 1950s. This is most evident in the way rock stakes its claims to seriousness on the historically 'adult' musical institutions of the album (especially 'theme' or 'concept' albums) and the extended career, rather than on the 45 rpm record and one-hit wonder typical of teen music. (The emphasis, in indie and alternative culture of the 1980s and 1990s, on the independent label 45 was in this regard a contrarian move away from the old rock orthodoxy, even as the rock investment in an ongoing artistic career was maintained.) Like the term 'rock'n'roll', 'teen' wasn't a sufficiently serious label to carry the new weight of 'rock' culture's ambitions. 'Youth' signalled this new seriousness, a maturity that was nonetheless not adult. Like rock, 'youth' exists in tension with both the teen and the adult. Rock culture thus rejected adult easy listening, along with music that was seen as too 'teenage' (such as that of the Monkees).

Teens and youth were not associated with the power and authority of the adult cohort that dominated social institutions. 'Youth' was most crucially defined in opposition to the 'adult', the symbolic representative of mass society. From the 1950s into the 1960s, adult-oriented popular music had dominated films, television, advertising and most importantly, record sales. Adult-oriented LPs (including adult pop, jazz, classical, and folk) accounted for over 60 per cent of dollar sales in the United States in the 1950s, while less than 40 per cent was spent on teen singles. Economically, as well as culturally, the dominant force in popular music was 'adult' music. The economic dominance of adults, like their social power more generally, made it easy for 'adult-ness' to be conflated with the characteristics of mass society in the perspective of an emerging youth culture. Anxieties about mass society's alienation were thus effectively displaced into the category of the 'adult'. If 'youth' was opposed to the 'adult', and the 'adult' was responsible for 'mass society', then 'youth' could understand itself as inherently 'anti-mass', regardless of how many million rock records were sold. Re-reading the 'teen/adult' opposition of 1950s music in terms of a folk-derived – but now youth-articulated – polemic, the 'youth' and the 'adult' became 'two cultures', locked in a taste war that would last long after rock had taken over adult music's position as the dominant segment of the mainstream, and long after the baby boom had left its biological youth behind.

This oppositional conception of 'youth' drew, as well, on a longstanding association of youth with purity and innocence. This link was implicit in the mass society critique, and may be traced to one key influence on that critique: the Romantic movement of the late eighteenth and early nineteenth centuries. In the 1960s, the Hippies, who actually sought to live out rock's Romantic critique of 'straight' society by 'dropping out', signalled their investment in the ideal of 'youth' by calling themselves 'flower children' (even though they tended to be older adolescents and young adults). Hippies embraced an idea of themselves as metaphorical children, and this privileging of a symbolic childhood (e.g. the Beatles' *Yellow Submarine*) became an ongoing feature of rock culture, seen subsequently in the alternative rock community's celebration of the deliberately 'amateur', 'naïve' or 'twee', from Jonathan Richman to Shonen Knife. Stereolab's claim that 'childhood is more authentic' stems from the belief that it is the ultimate realm of innocence and freedom, set apart from the corruption and alienation of the adult world. But this Romantic conception of childhood is, of course, not unique to rock, and it is significant that childhood is privileged more generally by the white middle-class that spawned so much of rock culture. This is further evidence of rock's ongoing reproduction, even in its apparent rebellion, of many of the core values of rock's reviled parent culture.

This emblematic embrace of the child as an extreme 'anti-adult' foregrounds the sense of social subordination and powerlessness associated with the category of youth. As we have seen, the 'adult' served as the repository for all the ills of mass society. Youth could thus see themselves as outsiders, an 'anti-mass' social subgroup with almost subcultural connotations. This sense of difference, of 'otherness', allowed youth to imagine affinities with the cultures of disempowered minorities. Thus, millions of white, middle-class rock fans could appropriate a range of forms of difference, whether these be racial, sexual, class-based or other. This underpins rock culture's continuing fascination with and appropriation of all kinds of marginality and otherness. Whether 'black' music, androgynous style, or working-class rebellion, rock processes each as a surface sign of distinctive difference, to be grafted onto the mass marginality of youth. This is also why so many rock historians have misinterpreted white youth tastes for African–American music, for example, as overt 'political' statements. Instead, white youth tends to adopt this music as a sign of youth's own, privileged difference, expressing above all else their refusal of the mass mainstream.

Rock's constitutive paradox – that it is a massively popular anti-mass music – was fuelled by a demographic anomaly. By the mid-1960s, the segment of the United States and Canadian populations that was aged twenty-five or younger had risen dramatically, approaching nearly 50 per cent of the total population. This meant that a group that had historically been socially marginalised – youth – now possessed an unprecedented social visibility and economic force. Youth formed an economically significant mass market, not only as a result of their numbers, but because this cohort experienced a rapid increase in disposable income in the post-war years. Youth's income tended to be spent almost entirely on leisure. More than any other cultural industry, the music industry was able to offer products that appeared tailor-made for young consumers. This combination of social marginalisation on the one hand, and newly magnified purchasing power (and thereby cultural presence) on the other, contributed to the development of rock's peculiar cultural politics. These contrasting aspects of 'youth' allowed rock simultaneously to revere on a mass scale those phenomena which were perceived as 'anti-mass' – to criticise some performers as sell-outs even as respected rock stars sold in the millions – and to conceive of itself as an underground cult even as rock became the dominant force within the music industry by the 1970s.

Stratification

Rock mythology asserts a creation story whose primal scene is beyond the mainstream: the illicit coupling of marginalised blues and country traditions spawns a bastard wild child, who, after a fleeting, authentic childhood, is captured, co-opted, and corrupted by the music industry. Rock, originating organically outside of mass culture, is thus tamed in the process of its mass distribution (called 'commercialisation'). While this myth tells us a great deal about the structuring principles of rock ideology, it ignores the absolutely central role of an affluent, mass-mediated youth culture in rock's birth in the mid-1960s. The career trajectory of the Beatles, from best-selling teen idols to best-selling rock artists in the space of three years, is emblematic of rock's birth and growth on the terrain of the truly popular. *Circa* 1963–4, the Beatles are not oppositional poet-visionaries, but just a phenomenally successful teen pop group. Still selling millions of records, with a growing percentage of these in album form, the Beatles, by 1967, have come to represent a new stratum of the popular mainstream that is taken to be the very opposite of disposable pop. The Beatles have become serious and significant artists critiquing and contesting the dominant values of Anglo-American society. This contestatory cultural current is carried, nonetheless, by millions of televisions, radios and phonographs, promulgated by mass market magazines, newspapers and cinemas.

The massive youth demographic of the 1960s allowed rock to be born within the mainstream of popular music and, at the same time, to organise itself around an oppositional stance toward mass culture. Arguably the first 'oppositional' form of popular culture to be born within the mainstream, rock grew up and flourished there as well. This is a key element in what makes rock historically and culturally distinctive. Jazz had moved from being a music of marginalised African–Americans, into the mass mainstream with swing, and then out of that mainstream as it became an 'art' music, seeking the deliberate marginality of a more select audience in the 1940s. Folk music struggled against moving into the mainstream, cherishing its relative marginality despite the popular success of a handful of folk songs and performers in the 1950s. While jazz's crossover to a mainstream audience was initially seen as elevating the music, folk's forays into the mainstream were almost always seen to lower that music's cultural prestige.

Unlike jazz and folk, however, rock's history cannot be understood in terms of processes of crossover. At the outset, there is no 'elsewhere' from whence rock is taken and then 'mainstreamed', no 'outside' or place apart from the mainstream that might serve as rock's birthplace. For all of rock's appropriation, modification, or outright theft of African–American, agrarian, or working-class musical cultures, it is not itself a form of crossover, nor a subculture incorporated by the dominant culture, nor a counterculture (the term most associated with rock politics in the 1960s). Rock may wear subcultural clothes, identify with marginalised minorities, promote countercultural political positions, and upset genteel notions of propriety, but from its inception it has been a large-scale, industrially organised, mass-mediated, mainstream phenomenon operating at the very centre of society.

As rock developed over time, it would eventually spawn styles and genres that moved away from mainstream rock and become part of true subcultures, such as hardcore punk or death metal in the 1980s. Elements of these subcultures might subsequently be incorporated into the mainstream, revitalising rock with their subcultural credibility and cachet (the case of grunge is exemplary here). However, these rock-spawned subcultures contribute to a process of internal stratification that rock experiences only *after* it has begun to dominate the mainstream (this internal stratification will be addressed further below). At its very birth, rock is already a component of that mainstream.

The persistent belief that rock somehow emerges outside the mainstream, prior to the involvement of the record industry, mass media, or large audiences, expresses a widespread feeling that, despite its success, rock remains magically untainted by 'the mass'. Rock's mythical, originating 'elsewhere' is neither a time nor a place, though. Instead, it designates the distinctive identity rock carves out of the centre of mass culture. In celebrating authentic individualism via electronic mass media, rock seeks to produce a virtual cultural space outside of consumer capitalism – a space that is, ironically, up for sale. Rock proffers musical shelter from the complexities and contradictions of capitalism and consumerism by conceiving of itself as a 'special case' of mass consumption. Seriousness and self-consciousness serve to distinguish the rock listener's participation in consumer culture from that of the trivialised and unaware 'masses'. This parsing of musical consumption into 'good' and 'bad' spheres is initially manifested as the division of the popular mainstream into 'rock' and 'pop'.

Rock adapted elements of folk's polemic against mass society, and deployed them within (rather than against) the mainstream. The new rock polemic resulted in a stratification of the mainstream, effectively cleaving popular music into two opposing spheres that came to be known as 'rock' versus 'pop'. (In the United Kingdom, the term 'pop' never underwent the sustained critique it did in the United States and Canada, and thus refers in a more neutral fashion to the wider field of popular music.) From the perspective of rock culture, its own sphere consisted of superior, authentic music while the pop sphere contained inferior, alienated music. The significance of this division of the mainstream is that while some previous musical cultures had also sought to distinguish their music from a corrupted mass music, they did so most effectively by segregating themselves from the mainstream, limiting the size of their audiences, and/or moving away from the marketplace entirely. In erecting a new hierarchy on the terrain of the popular, rock broke the pejorative association of mass consumption with degraded and debased art, and abandoned an isolationist struggle against the market system (claiming, in some cases, that it would transform the system from within). However, rock culture retained – and indeed, amplified – many of the core concerns of the mass society critique, most notably its preoccupation with questions of mediation and alienation, authenticity and community, conformity and complicity. Most importantly, perhaps, it maintained the critique's overarching emphasis on distinctive individualism as the key defence against the alienation of mass society.

Thus rock emerges in a stratification that is accomplished through the making of distinctions, within the mainstream, between the 'serious' and the 'trivial', the 'oppositional' and the 'complicit', the 'truthful' and the 'fraudulent', the 'anti-mass' and the 'mass', the 'authentic' and the 'alienated'. The second term of each of these oppositions describes qualities rock ascribes to 'pop'. Like rock itself, pop is not a musical style but a sphere of popular musical culture. From the rock perspective, pop is defined by its obliviousness to the broader social implications of musical production and consumption. 'Pop', of course, is that area of popular music said to be marked by ethical compromise and capitulation. 'Pop' operates as a catch-all category, into which rock dumps adult easy listening, bubblegum teenybop, and sell-outs, frauds and musical trifles more generally. Pop is understood as popular music that isn't (or doesn't have to be, or can't possibly be) 'taken seriously'. Rock, in contrast, is mainstream music that is (or ought to be, or must be) taken seriously.

First-generation rock bands like the Beatles or Rolling Stones were able to move out of teen pop and into youth rock because of their attendance at the birth of rock. With the consolidation of the rock polemic with the expansion of rock magazines and critics in the 1970s, the only movement between the rock and pop spheres will typically be one-way. From the viewpoint of rock, that direction is 'downward' (e.g. Rod Stewart's fall from rock grace to pop pathos). The infrequency with which trivialised pop performers succeed in becoming serious rock artists (e.g. John Cougar becoming John Mellencamp; teen dance queen Alanis becoming Alanis Morisette) proves the rock rule that it's easy to sell out but hard to regain rock respectability.

Rock's displacement of the 'bad' – the negative and corrupt features of mass society – into pop serves to shore up rock's apparent authenticity and autonomy. However, it also obscures rock's own status as mass-mediated, commodity culture. It is interesting that while rock regularly chastises pop for its over-commodification of musical culture (Backstreet Boys lunchboxes, anyone?), rock is less concerned with its own forms of consumption, focusing instead on the conditions of aesthetic and industrial production within rock. (Rock consumers are scrutinised less frequently – and less critically – than are rock musicians and record companies.) Mass commodity *consumption* no longer seems incompatible with rock because rock's critique of the alienation and complicity implicit in that consumption is reworked as a critique of the means of musical *production*.

For example, indie rock's valorisation of non-major label productions, and of the act of purchasing music directly from bands themselves at gigs, misses the fact that indie and mainstream musical consumption are both part of consumer capitalism, different only in the degree of their complicity. Indie rock is defined by its concern for the scale of consumer capitalism, rather than by its radical rejection of an economic system. This concern with reduced scale may also be glimpsed in indie culture's investment in the miniature: in boutique record stores, 45 rpm singles, small runs of home-made cassettes, or the reverent recreation of miniature models of past eras or albums.

To single out seriousness as an overweening value driving so much of rock culture is to challenge the conventional account of rock as a radical and rebellious force actively opposing the dominant values of society. What is truly at stake in rock culture is the differentiation of taste, not an affiliation with forms of cultural action. In simultaneously highlighting, harmonising and hiding the contradictions of consumer capitalism, rock does not in fact contest the system. Instead, rock's oppositionality operates in the service of a different agenda. Rock draws its lifeblood from the systematic stratifications of capitalist consumer society, and it is rock's investment in the idea of seriousness that endows it with oppositionality, rather than the reverse. Seriousness is the key concept here, because rock's distinctiveness from mass pop can be manifested in explicitly non-oppositional ways (for example, the classical ambitions of progressive rock, or the use of innocuous, 'retro' sounds – particularly bygone, mainstream pop styles – by innumerable avant-garde bands, or by U2 launching their 'PopMart' tour in a K-Mart department store). More crucial than overt oppositionality, seriousness is the defining feature of rock, which must always be seen to be engaging with something 'more' than just pleasure or fun. Rebellion, in this sense, is simply the most spectacular 'something more'. Even those bands like the Ramones, who celebrate mindless fun, do so by rebuking pompous and pretentious elements of the dominant rock culture; they distinguish themselves and their fans – who are all 'in' on the critique of 'bad' rock – through an actually quite 'mindful' attitude toward what they see as the mistakes or excesses or trivialities of 'bad', mainstream rock.

('Mindless fun', in this case, is self-consciously elevated into a kind of critical philosophy.)

We should recall that the mass society critique is neither purely radical, purely elitist, nor purely populist. It combines elements of all these, but 'individualism', in one form or another, runs through its various manifestations. The critique can fit easily into the everyday ways in which people cling to their tastes and employ them to differentiate themselves from others. The folk polemic was adopted and used by rock culture, not because of an innate opposition to – or even dissatisfaction with – mass society. (Indeed, one could argue that teenagers in the 1950s and 1960s were the greatest beneficiaries of that society.) Instead, the folk polemic offered a means of distinguishing one segment of the youth audience, with its different, serious attitude toward popular music, from a segment which lacked this attitude. The critique of mass society, central to the folk polemic, was reduced to a critique of mass pop.

In the post-war period, large numbers of teens who grew up in a commodity-saturated world wished to stay intensely involved with the pleasures of commercial popular music well beyond their teen years. Having acquired, via media, marketing and demographic forces, a sense of their own special, distinct identity as a kind of vanguard of modernity, post-war youth had become increasingly wary of the traditional ways in which musical tastes were meant to change with age. Typically, 'maturity' had meant a shift to 'adult' popular music (or classical music, or jazz), and away from those sorts of music which were now, with ageing, meant to seem trivial. Rock culture managed to adopt the dominant culture's value system (with its claims that the serious was better than the trivial), but to find the serious within the realm of mass-produced popular music. To find it there meant that one could continue listening to rock music, and buying it in its various commodity forms, throughout the ageing process, throughout those years in which tastes were to 'mature'.

To take popular music seriously, as something 'more' than mere entertainment or disposable distraction, also meant rejecting those ways of experiencing popular music that cast it as functional – as designed *for* dancing, *for* romancing, or *for* relaxation. In removing musical experience from the realm of trivial or functional diversion, rock listeners were able to engage self-consciously with music as the mark of a distinctive seriousness. They distanced themselves from those fans who didn't take music seriously, setting their own true individualism above and apart from the 'mass'. Rock became the name for this serious stratum of popular music's mainstream. At the same time, authenticity emerged as the over-arching value that brought a unity to rock's various notions of seriousness.

Authenticity

Authenticity can be thought of as the compass that orients rock culture in its navigation of the mainstream. Rock fans, critics and musicians are constantly evaluating the authenticity of popular music, on the lookout for signs of alienation and inauthenticity (including, for example, over-commercialisation, insincerity, manipulation, lack of originality and so on). This preoccupation with 'authenticity' helps rock culture constantly to draw lines of division within the mainstream of popular music – lines which divide rock from pop, and, even within rock culture, divide some versions of rock from others.

'Authentic' designates those music, musicians, and musical experiences seen to be direct and honest, uncorrupted by commerce, trendiness, derivativeness, a lack of inspiration and so on. 'Authentic' is a term affixed to music which offers sincere expressions of genuine feeling, original creativity, or an organic sense of community. Authenticity is not something 'in' the music, though it is frequently experienced as such, believed to be actually audible, and taken to have a material form. Rather, authenticity is a value, a quality we ascribe to perceived relationships between music, socio-industrial practices, and listeners or audiences. Thus, what we feel to be 'really rock' might be 'authentic rock' for us, but not necessarily for everybody, nor for all time. What we might have felt was authentic in our early teens we may now reject as inauthentic; conversely, music we may have deemed 'inauthentic' at the time, (e.g. Kiss, disco, Abba, old-school rap) may now, in retrospect, feel truly authentic. Authenticity is a complex phenomenon, and involves more than personal preferences. It requires a sense of music's external contexts, and a judgement of the 'objective' effect on music of such factors as record company marketing strategies, music-making technologies, or the ongoing history of music's broader stylistic changes.

Much writing on post-war youth music gives the mistaken impression that authenticity is somehow the exclusive property of rock. While notions of authenticity are absolutely central to any account of rock culture, the concept of authenticity has, in fact, been a core value of Western society for centuries. By conspicuously embracing authenticity, rock aligns itself with longstanding and important currents in Western thought. Here, again, rock perpetuates many of the key traditions and values of its parent culture. Because authenticity is such a core cultural value, it generally provides the foundation on which rock's sense of its own seriousness has been built. Rock culture is preoccupied with seriousness, but is forever grappling with the ways in which 'seriousness' may carry negative connotations. Seriousness may be associated with elitist and superior attitudes, or with the exclusivity of 'highbrow', non-mass audiences. Seriousness may also be defined in purely formal terms, divorced from awareness of the social and industrial circumstances under which musical experiences are produced. None of these definitions of 'seriousness' has ever been central to rock culture.

Rock culture asserts its superiority over the 'mass', and this is absolutely crucial to the role it assumes for itself within contemporary societies. However, rock's own mass audience prevents traditionally elitist criteria from holding sway in rock culture. For all of rock culture's polemical concern with rejecting the trivial aspects of mass culture, and with 'correcting' the mistakes of mass taste, rock nonetheless possesses an equally important populism (as in the ideal of the Top 40 as a potential meritocracy). Indeed, it is likely to see mass success as the birthright of those who deserve it. Rock culture embraces authentic success as a validation of artistic quality. For example, while some devout fans of obscure indie or alternative bands might deny their neglected heroes access to a wider audience, the majority would cheer their favourite little band onward and upward, recruiting new listeners, cursing the narrow-mindedness of MTV or BBC radio for ignoring such high-quality music, and then celebrating the band's eventual breakthrough as a kind of 'justice at last'. Though they might turn against the group if it seemed that either the new, mass audience liked them for the 'wrong' reasons (failing truly to appreciate the band as its initial connoisseurs had), or that the band itself appeared to change, losing touch with its core constituency through its pandering to the crowds of the 'big time', most rock fans would want at least some popular success for their favourite performers. Indeed, they would view that success as a vindication of their own, individual, superior taste. Sometimes the mass audience will get it right, sometimes not, but rock culture, having broken the connection between mass popularity and 'bad' music, nonetheless patrols popularity for inauthentic and therefore undeserved success.

Authenticity operates as a criterion of judgement in rock's evaluations of music and musicians. It is a value that coordinates a whole series of calculations of cultural worth, and its foundation is an insistence upon the integrity of the individual self. By focusing most obviously on authenticity as its central value, rock culture can link its emphasis on 'taking popular music seriously' to the dilemma of being an individual in mass society. Rather than simply aping the seriousness of a 'highbrow' culture which might disdain the social dimensions of art, the rock fan's knowledge of the social and industrial contexts of popular musical production, distribution and consumption, together with a self-consciousness about individual musical choices, highlight a commitment to integrating artistic and social criteria in the evaluation of popular music. This means that an ethical dimension is perceived in aesthetic experience, so that 'good' rock music must also be somehow 'just' or 'true'. 'Authenticity' captures this intertwining of judgements. This is, in large part, why the taste preference for rock music can be claimed as 'legitimate', as something 'more' than 'mere' entertainment. Again, rock taste defines itself through more than purely personal preferences or feelings. Authenticity can effectively structure public discussions of the status of popular music because much of the debate is conducted in implicitly ethical terms, organised around apparently 'objective' questions of material success, record industry strategies, and the political economy of mass media. By insisting on a kind of ethical accounting of popular music's involvement in commercial, mass culture, rock culture distinguishes itself from other, supposedly unselfconscious segments of the mainstream.

Through its concern with finding a true self in the midst of corruption and conformity, rock authenticity mingles aesthetic evaluation (is this music beautiful?) with ethical judgements about the degree of music's complicity with the alienating aspects of mass society (is this music compromised?). For example, the common dismissal of music that sounds 'machine-made' involves a complex claim about textual and industrial relations simultaneously. 'Machine-made' music may sound 'slick' or 'formulaic'; but this judgement of composition or arrangement practices is also linked to a concern with the industrial and technological conditions of production. Dismissing music as 'machine-made' equally signals a suspicion that the musical experience in question has been alienated, through the intervention of forces that are interpreted to be somehow anti-individualistic, and thereby inauthentic (synthesisers or samplers, studio musicians, assembly-line songwriting, multi-national record conglomerates, etc.).

Broadly speaking, alienation is the undesirable opposite of authenticity. Authentic musical experiences can serve as bulwarks against the fraudulent and alienating aspects of modern life. The alienation of music and musicians in the twentieth century has largely been understood in terms of mediation, of those things which interfere with an ideal of direct communication between artist and audience. Nevertheless, different segments of rock culture will define 'interference' in very dissimilar ways. For some, the 'machine-made' sounds of industrial music, for example, may actually be the mark of a certain authenticity, of an affinity with the harsh reality of a mechanised, machine-dominated life. A whole range of phenomena may interfere in the link of artist to audience: forms of technological mediation, the involvement of superfluous personnel or industrial procedures, monetary corruption of the performer's motives for performing, an over-investment in sounding 'up-to-date', the repetition of old ideas, or any number of forces which render musical expressions of the self compromised or distorted.

This concern with directness and an absence of mediation may be traced to the origins of the word 'authentic' in ancient Greece, where it referred to the 'self-made'. The 'self-made' can stand against the mass-produced, money-driven, anonymous and alienating aspects of modern life. In this context, rock's search for authenticity underlines a general anxiety about the status of the modern self. Musical experiences considered 'authentic' are thus those which highlight or nourish individual identity, or signal affinities with the smaller communities and subcultures which sustain that identity.

Rock culture's embracing of performers who author their own songs is one key instance of this concern with mediation. Like 'authenticity', the word 'author' is etymologically related to the 'self'. If the rock musician's 'self' is not involved in originating the text she or he performs, rock believes that self is more likely to be corrupted or alienated (and that, in turn, the listener's sense of self may be diminished). Rock is highly suspicious of those singers and musicians who are not also 'authors', involved in the composition of words and music. The singer–songwriter emerged as the ideal of authentic rock in the late 1960s, fostering a sense that the integration of authorship and performance was evidence of ethical integrity. While many popular music cultures are unbothered by a division of musical labour (in which songwriters write songs, arrangers arrange them, sidemen play them, and vocalists sing them), rock culture views it as a potentially distorting and corrupting form of mediation, one that may get in the way of the direct expression of authentic thoughts and feelings. Rock thus favours performers who overcome this division of labour and demonstrate an organic expressivity, through a unity of creation and communication, of origination and performance. In particular, the ideal of the rock band as a self-sufficient and self-contained unit encourages a sense of freedom from mediation, a feeling of autonomy (another word linked to 'self'). This 'self-direction' of the ideal rock band signifies an independence from external interference and control, and, therefore, a greater authenticity. Appearing to be free of any structured organisation of musical creation, the rock band may thus be seen to escape that alienation of musical labour and expression which an involvement in the cultural industries would otherwise imply. (Conversely, well-established rock bands who begin to rely increasingly on outside songwriters, such as Aerosmith, may experience a concomitant decline in their perceived authenticity.)

The recent emphasis on 'unplugged' or acoustic performances by otherwise electrified musicians is another gesture toward this critique of mediation. By removing *some* technology from the communication process, a feeling of directness and intimacy may be achieved (in fact, the Canadian MuchMusic video channel calls its 'unplugged' show – in which the audience may also request songs – *Intimate and Interactive*). However, these must be understood as *symbolic* 'unpluggings' and *virtual* intimacies, since without microphones, video cameras and massive electronic networks these acts of 'direct' communication would not occur. Similarly, the so-called 'lo-fi' movement of the 1990s is yet another symbolic refusal of electronic mediation. In using 'older' (e.g. non-digital) recording equipment (along with a kind of deliberate 'naïvete' in relation to writing and performing), lo-fi bands seek to escape the slick machinery of contemporary sound (re)production. Nevertheless, these bands don't refuse to use electronic recording equipment entirely; they merely scale down its efficiency and reduce its prominence, just as indie and alternative cultures generally underline a commitment to direct communication and authentic performance through their emphasis on the 'miniature' and the scaled-down.

These conceptions of authenticity, autonomy and authorship emerge out of two complementary but distinct historical movements of the eighteenth and nineteenth centuries: Romanticism and Modernism. Both are crucial sources of the mass society critique, and major influences upon rock culture as well. Both Romanticism and Modernism challenged the emergence of industrial, urban capitalism, and both celebrated the author, artist, or musician as a privileged representative of an authentic, individual self. However, they did so in complex and somewhat different ways, and those differences have contributed to rock culture's own complex (and often divergent) formulations and expressions of authenticity.

Authenticity is central to both Romanticism and Modernism. A late eighteenth/early nineteenth-century social and artistic philosophy, Romanticism emerged in response to the social dislocations of the Industrial Revolution. Romantics valued traditional, rural communities, where life could be lived close to nature, and where people's labour was an integral part of their identity, rather than something to be sold for a paycheque. The Romantic artist was seen to be involved in a personal journey of self-discovery and fulfilment, through the direct expression of his or her innermost thoughts and emotions. Developing out of Romanticism in the mid-nineteenth century, Modernism extended and expanded the Romantic notion of the artist as society's conscience, but imagined the artist's political role to be more overtly contestatory. While Romanticism valued nature and the country as genteel escapes from urban blight, Modernism embraced the chaos of the city and the aesthetic possibilities of the machine. Where Romanticism believed in an organic, and even traditional, connection between the artist, the material means of expression and the audience, Modernism encouraged shock effects and radical experimentation, contending that the relationship between artistic materials and meanings was, like power relations in society, ultimately arbitrary and therefore open to change and improvement. Modernism believed that the true artist must break with the past, while Romanticism cherished the pre-industrial past. By rejecting the current state of things in favour of the new, the different and the radical, Modernism produced an implicit political critique of society as it was at that moment. This commitment to radical innovation and experiment is especially evident in the Modernist belief that the true artist must keep moving forward, constantly re-inventing him or herself.

While Romanticism locates authenticity principally in the direct communication between artist and audience, Modernism manifests its concern with authenticity more indirectly, at the aesthetic level, so that the authentic artist is one who is true to the Modernist credos of experimentation, innovation, development, change. Where Romantics see sincere, unmediated expression of inner experience as essential, Modernists believe their first commitment is less to reaching an audience than to being true to their own artistic integrity. This involves rejecting aesthetic complacency and, implicitly, complacency *vis-à-vis* the social world in which the artist lives. Both Romantics and Modernists are anxious to avoid corruption through involvement with commerce and oppose the alienation they see as rooted in industrial capitalism.

These brief characterisations of complex historical and philosophical movements can help us understand and categorise key tendencies and tensions internal to rock culture. Emerging as it does out of the confluence of a number of distinct musical cultures, rock culture is seldom univocal in its beliefs, agendas or practices. Rock's complex genealogy means that there are a number of fault lines running through the centre of rock, and these are perhaps most visible in the competing definitions of authenticity. While rock emerged in a division of the mainstream between rock and pop, it began subsequently to subdivide, stratifying internally into various camps and factions. Although all rock genres emphasise authenticity as their core value, not all understand and express authenticity in an identical fashion. In fact, we can identify two broad families of rock authenticity – what I will call Romantic authenticity and Modernist authenticity. For the purposes of illustration, it may be useful to group together *some* of the key expressions of these two sorts of rock authenticity, while keeping in mind that these are tendencies rather than absolutes:

Romantic authenticity tends to be found more in	*Modernist authenticity tends to be found more in*
tradition and continuity with the past	experimentation and progress
roots	avant gardes
sense of community	status of artist
populism	elitism
belief in a core or essential rock sound	openness regarding rock sounds
folk, blues, country, rock'n'roll styles	classical, art music, soul, pop styles
gradual stylistic change	radical or sudden stylistic change
sincerity, directness	irony, sarcasm, obliqueness
'liveness'	'recorded-ness'
'natural' sounds	'shocking' sounds
hiding musical technology	celebrating technology

These tendencies serve simultaneously to position rock *against* the mass pop mainstream *and* to create and organise internal differences within rock culture. Many rock fans will reject those performers or genres who highlight Modernist authenticity as being somehow 'artificial', while other fans might dismiss Romantic rock as being simplistic or compromised by its populism. Rock's dual versions of authenticity may thus contribute to the formation of diverging scenes, communities, and taste cultures *within* rock. Even as there is a basic, underlying agreement between the various versions of rock that *some* form of authenticity is required to distinguish rock from the corruption of the mainstream, there may be polemical disagreement over what form it should take. Often these distinctions are deployed to divide cultural spaces that are otherwise homogeneous – say, a white, middle-class suburb – so that the minute details over which rock fans argue obsessively may become the only apparent source of individual differences.

We might suspect that fans of, say, Oasis and fans of Blur will both assert that their favourite band is truly authentic, yet each would see that authenticity as being demonstrated differently. Oasis might be valued because they assert a continuity with a Romantic rock tradition from the 1960s, because they emphasise live performance, direct expression, and a sense that they are populists, working-class punters little different from their fans. Blur might be valued because of their Modernist experimentation with various pop styles, because they foreground synthesisers and the recording studio, irony, and a sense that they are part of a rock elite, college-educated and more 'knowing' in their self-conscious playing with sounds and identities.

But, of course, Oasis use the recording studio as expertly as anyone, Blur 'rock out' with noisy, classic 1960s guitars, and both are basically part of the same, vaguely defined rock genre called 'Britpop'. Thus, even though identifying Romantic and Modernist tendencies can help us discern differences between performers or genres, they also can be and often are combined or mixed up in a single genre or performer.

This approach to rock authenticity can help clarify some of the apparent contradictions of rock culture. For example, in the 1970s, punk was seen as the antithesis of rock, a mortal enemy intent on destroying rock culture. But punk was simply fulfilling rock's traditional investment in differentiation and authenticity, distinguishing itself from the rock mainstream. Punk drew on Modernist conceptions of authenticity to attack the dominant Romanticism of 1970s rock. Similarly, while a number of rock critics view artifice as the negation of authenticity, juxtaposing David Bowie's playful obliqueness to Bruce Springsteen's sincere directness, what is at issue is the difference between the two families of authenticity. It is never the artificial alone that is the point of rock artifice. Instead, rock artifice involves a deliberate rejection of the Romantic mode of authenticity, in favour of a complex and nuanced Modernist strategy of authenticity in which the performer's ability to shape imaginary worlds – rather than being shaped by this world – is foregrounded. For example, Prince's flashy androgyny and trickster sexuality highlighted his status as a distinctive artist, operating above mundane norms and conventions of gender and sexuality. In playing with rock artifice, Prince is true to the artist's prerogative to remake himself, employing artifice as ultimate evidence of his Modernist authenticity.

We might think that Romantic authenticity emphasises the rural, while Modernist authenticity values the urban; and yet much so-called 'heartland rock', such as that of Springsteen, celebrates urban backstreets and rooftops even as it is a predominantly Romantic genre. Conversely, we can perceive a kind of pastoral quality in Modernist groups such as the Smiths, who use acoustic or undistorted guitars and Romantic imagery as part of a larger Modernist strategy (that is, playing with the politics of gender and sexuality, heard particularly in Morrissey's subversion of the 'natural' codes of rock singing, even as Johnny Marr's guitar virtuosity works toward Romantic rock's musical 'naturalism').

While most performers or genres will line up on one side or the other of the above table, rock's internal complexity makes it difficult to label individual genres or performers as completely and exclusively 'Romantic' or 'Modernist'. Many will move back and forth across the table. Numerous rock genres or performers work with hybrid versions of authenticity, taking elements of Romanticist authenticity and mingling them with bits of Modernist authenticity (for example, Bob Dylan's mid-60s mix of folk Romanticism in his music and Modernist artistry in his lyrics and

attitude). Rock culture tends to regard as most innovative those rock performers who deploy Romantic and Modernist authenticity more or less
equally, in a productive tension, as with the Sex Pistols in the 1970s or
Suede in the 1990s. Sometimes performers will shift from one form of
authenticity to the other across an extended career. The case of U2 is interesting in this regard; beginning as rock Modernists experimenting with
sound, they very quickly moved into a Romantic phase, which climaxed
with *Rattle and Hum*'s celebration of gritty rock and blues roots traditions
from the United States south. In the 1990s, U2 returned spectacularly to
their formative Modernism on *Achtung Baby*, yet without losing their
Romantic grandeur and epic rock ambitions. The different forms of
authenticity, rubbing up against each other, produce work that is celebrated for its complexity, energy and artistic innovation.

Though we are long accustomed to perceiving these different manifestations of rock as evidence of fundamental disagreements about what constitutes rock, it is clear that they possess an underlying coherence. Rock's
wide range of styles and genres, scenes and communities, are called 'rock'
because they are all invested in the overarching value of authenticity. The
individual gestures of 'making music seriously' may vary, the particular
formulations of authenticity may differ; conflicts between them may drive
rock forward, producing what are often viewed as cataclysmic moments or
musical revolutions. Nonetheless, the key structuring principles of rock
remained relatively stable in the last three decades of the twentieth
century, even as its cultural prominence declined from the 1980s onward.

Conclusion

Rock emerged because one segment of the popular mainstream was associated with a particular demographic anomaly – a huge increase in the
number of affluent youth born in the wake of the Second World War.
Paradoxically, the baby boom's numbers magnified – rather than
'massified' – youth culture. The longstanding sense of youth as marginal
and subordinate allowed this newly dominant culture to continue to
imagine itself as subcultural. (In fact, post-war youth have at times been
mistaken for a subculture as a result of being viewed through the lens of
rock ideology.) Thus, rock was born as a mass phenomenon that retained
its distinctly anti-mass sensibilities. The baby boom's own grand, generational narrative became the story of the epic struggle of outsiders who,
nevertheless, occupied the very centre of society. Their purchasing power
gave legitimacy and significance to teen music, even as that musical culture
was defined by its antipathy to commerce. Rock's sense of entitlement and

legitimacy stemmed largely from the massive generational support accorded it, a support that led rock musicians and fans to believe that they could quite seriously 'revolutionise' the world around them. As the number of teenage baby boomers waned, so too did the rock polemic wane. By the mid-1980s, it was no longer taken for granted that 'rock' represented the most powerful expression of the critique of mass society – it had been so successful, in fact, that it was increasingly just one version among many. As well, the sorts of polemics that had marked rock's rise to cultural prominence were no longer moored in the certainties of a coherent idea of 'youth'.

The result was a decline in the perceived differences between musical cultures, such that many rock fans, regardless of what they may have felt in their hearts, no longer were fearless in their condemnations of putatively 'inferior' or 'alienated' musical tastes. The declining birthrates since *c.* 1960 contributed to what we might call a 'miniaturisation' of rock culture. The fact that a key segment of contemporary rock is called 'alternative' – a term which guilelessly describes a definitive aspect of *all* rock ideology – suggests a capitulation, an abandonment of the ambition and proselytising that marked rock's expansion in the 1960s and 1970s. 'Alternative' implies a loss of rock's originary desire to transform the mainstream, to 'correct' the mistakes of mass taste, and thereby change the world. Instead, the miniaturised contingent of alterna-rock fans are resigned to being just another segment in a fragmented marketplace, adjusting their expectations and their musical experiments to the reduced scale of post-boomer musical culture.

But another reason rock has become just one of many mainstream musical cultures is because it is a victim of its own success in transforming popular conceptions of what popular music can be and do. On the one hand, rock no longer occupies the centre of popular music, no longer commands the singular attention and respect it once did. On the other hand, as rock has become 'miniaturised', the scale of its ambitions and audiences reduced, its cultural values have been dispersed into a range of musical fields. Authenticity, rebellion, oppositionality, artistic legitimacy and seriousness now feature prominently in musical cultures that hitherto lacked or downplayed these features. Worldbeat, dance music, 'new country', and a seemingly infinite variety of other forms now seek and create their own legitimacy by wielding these terms, challenging their historical trivialisation and deploying rock-derived ideas to claim their own value.

Finally, rock's development of an 'anti-mass' culture on a massive scale is arguably the first and certainly most influential example of a broader tendency. The mainstream celebration of oppositional attitudes and the tastes of subcultural or subordinated segments of society is a significant development within contemporary life. Prior to rock, high and low cultures, cultural mainstreams and margins, were seen as clearly distinct. Once rock broke the symbolic link between mass culture and mindless conformity, it became possible to build new distinctions within and upon the terrain of the popular, to express oppositional sensibilities via commercial, mass mediated culture. Rock helped to reorder the relationship between dominant and dominated cultures, producing something that was simultaneously marginal and mainstream, anti-mass and mass, subordinate and dominant. While rock has long served as the most compelling model of what we might call 'subdominant' culture, some of its defining features have begun to appear in other areas of cultural life. Opposition to the 'mass' from within mass, commercial culture is prevalent today, in the bad-boy movie star, the people's princess who breaks with protocol, explicit tabloid talk shows and scatological cartoons on television, or fictional FBI agents who operate beyond the bounds of law, organisation and even rationality. All of these show the dispersion of subdominant cultural impulses far beyond their birthplace in rock.

Further reading

Much of what I've argued here runs counter to dominant versions of rock history, and certainly seeks to challenge the rebellious and countercultural identity that rock ideology affirms for its fans and musicians. Therefore it is difficult to recommend any book-length overviews of rock culture or rock history which take a similar position. Nonetheless, I have drawn heavily on the groundbreaking work of Simon Frith, and would suggest that the interested reader track down two articles in particular: 'Art versus technology: the strange case of popular music' (*Media, Culture and Society* 8(3), 1986, pp. 263–79) and 'The industrialisation of music' in *Music for Pleasure* (Cambridge: Polity, 1988, pp. 11–23). The first piece addresses the indeed strange status of technology within rock ideology, while the second provides a quick overview of key historical shifts in the emergence of rock. Of course, Frith's *Sound Effects* (London: Constable, 1981) and *Performing Rites: On the Value of Popular Music* (Oxford: Oxford University Press, 1996) will also reward the reader interested in the way rock music and culture work, more socially in the case of the former, and more aesthetically in the case of the latter book. For the reader interested in the prehistory of rock, parts one and two of Philip H. Ennis, *The Seventh Stream: The Emergence of Rocknroll in American Popular Music* (Hanover: Wesleyan University Press, 1992) offer a detailed history of the industrial and institutional shifts that led to the rise of rock. The statistics on album versus singles sales in the 1950s can be found in a fascinating 1958 overview of the

United States popular music scene, Richard Shickel's 'The big revolution in records' (*Look*, 15 April 1958, pp. 26–35). If you are interested in swing, Lewis A. Erenberg's *Swingin' the Dream: Big Band Jazz and the Rebirth of American Culture* (Chicago: The University of Chicago Press, 1998) is an important recent account an of the rise of this prototype of rock culture. For a useful discussion of the tensions within the concept of authenticity, see the analysis of the Sex Pistols in Dave Laing's *One Chord Wonders: Power and Meaning in Punk Rock* (Milton Keynes: Open University Press, 1985). For those interested in what became of rock, I highly recommend Gina Arnold, *Route 666: On the Road to Nirvana* (New York: St Martin's, 1993); Arnold's story of the years between punk and grunge is a wonderful, lived account of post-baby-boomer rock. Will Straw's 'Systems of articulation, logics of change: scenes and communities in popular music' (*Cultural Studies* 5(3), 1993, pp. 368–88) is a brilliant analysis of the same era from a more complex theoretical perspective. Finally, the work on taste and the status of art in contemporary society by French sociologist Pierre Bourdieu is absolutely essential to any understanding of what rock does, even though Bourdieu is himself uninterested in rock. A good introduction to his thought can be found in Pierre Bourdieu, 'The field of cultural production, or: the economic world reversed', in *The Field of Cultural Production* (New York: Columbia University Press, 1993, pp. 29–73.)

6 Soul into hip-hop

RUSSELL A. POTTER

Call it soul, call it funk, call it hip-hop; the deep-down core of African–American popular music has been both a centre to which performers and audiences have continually returned, and a centrifuge which has sent its styles and attitudes outwards into the full spectrum of popular music around the world. The pressure – both inward and outward – has often been kept high by an American music industry slow to move beyond the apartheid-like structures of its marketing systems, which, though ostensibly abandoned in the days since the 'race records' era (the 1920s through the 1950s), continue to shadow the industry's practices. However much cross-over there has been between black and white audiences, the continual reiteration of racial and generic boundaries in radio formats, retailing and chart-making has again and again forced black artists and producers to navigate between a vernacular aesthetic (often invoked as 'the street') and what the rapper Guru calls 'mass appeal' – the watering-down of style targeted at an supposedly 'broader' (read: white) audience. So it has been that, within black communities, there has been an ongoing need to name and claim a music whose strategic inward turns refused what was often seen as a 'sell-out' appeal to white listeners, a music that set up shop right in the neighbourhood, via black (later 'urban contemporary') radio, charts, and retailers, and in the untallied vernacular traffic in dubbed tapes, deejay mixes, and bootlegs. The tensions across this divide have been perpetuated, indeed exacerbated by the growing economic distance between whites (and middle-class blacks), whose buying habits have shaped the industry's conception of 'success', and the urban underclass who have been caught on a one-way street of commercialisation, unable to sustain control over the very artforms they themselves created.

In the 1950s, when success came swiftly to labels, such as Memphis's Sun Records, that crossed over this imaginary line in the vinyl, the troubled terminological crossroads between 'rhythm and blues' and 'rock'n'roll' set the tone for things to come. Certainly, many white 'rock'n'roll' artists were originals in their own right, not simply appropriators of someone else's music. The emergence of rock'n'roll onto pop radio created a huge new audience for black music, and eventually displaced altogether the blend of crooners and lightweight swing that had defined pop itself. Yet the recording industry's practice of knocking off cover versions of the songs of successful black artists, such as Pat Boone's relentless series of Little Richard covers, exacerbated existing tensions by siphoning off profits. White cover versions, given heavy rotation on the biggest commercial stations, generated profits for publishers and labels far exceeding the meagre songwriter royalties of their black originators. Thus, even as rhythm and blues gained a larger white audience, its artists did not receive their share of the money being made from the rock 'revolution'. So it was that rhythm and blues, like jazz before it, had to come to terms with its continual appropriation, both economic and artistic, by white musicians, producers and record labels.

Black musicians responded to this appropriation in a variety of ways. Some went for major-label contracts, looking for their own piece of the official pie; others worked around the white recording industry by relying on touring for most of their income and signing contracts with smaller record labels which were more closely cued to black audiences. One result of this situation was that, while 'rock'n'roll' as it appeared on the *Billboard* charts was a relatively homogenous affair, black rhythm and blues remained more heterogeneous, disseminated as it was via black concert venues (the old 'chitlin' circuit') and record labels whose local and regional identities were still highly distinct. Yet at the same time, trends moved freely among this 'grapevine' of localities, as rhythm and blues matured into its own trademark of dance, ballad and vocal styles. The ground was already being prepared in the fifties by artists such as Ray Charles, who brought rich gospel intonations into secular bluesy ballads, and Big Maybelle, whose gospel-rooted shouts shook up the rhythm and blues world.

'Soul' is one name for this music that took rhythm and blues to the next level during the very years – 1955 to 1967 – that rock'n'roll was increasingly dominating the music industry. But what was it? Soul was slower-burning yet hotter, more improvisational, more distinctly flavoured by the vocal character of its performers, and more participatory. If rock'n'roll, along with the faster-paced rhythm and blues styles, were in a sense extroverted, soul was more introverted, implicitly addressed to 'soul' brothers and sisters, an invocative, centripetal force. It took many of its vocal cues from gospel, but its beats were, if anything, more supercharged – even when slower in tempo – than the clap-along rhythm and blues of the mid-fifties. Often recorded by bands, such as James Brown's Famous Flames, which gave hundreds of live performances a year, it was dynamic and rough, angry and reflective, danceable yet unpredictable. For instance, it rarely occurred to white producers or record labels to ask musicians to 'jam' in the studio and just let the tape roll, but soul musicians did it all the time. James Brown, recording in the late 1950s and early 1960s on

Cincinnati's King label, recorded studio jams that bled over onto two, three, or four sides of a vinyl single. Brown was not just a singer, but an exhorter; his trademark screams and yells drove his band and audiences alike to new levels of excitement. Brown's music constituted an ongoing dialogue with his audience, not only via live performances, but also through his incessant re-working of his material, which he would often release in an updated form after he had taken it on the road for a time. This was the kind of dialogue with an audience that was little understood by the executives at major record labels, who relied on radio and sales charts to assess the value of the music they released, and were rarely persuaded to issue the same song twice, unless it was with a different performer.

The majors also relied on the smaller labels to bring artists to their attention, and alert them to trends that they ought to follow. These small labels maintained their own ties with local black radio stations and retailers, and yet also had distribution links to the industry such that a major label could 'pick up' a record if they thought it had 'national' potential. Such was the arrangement at Memphis's Stax, to many, the quintessential label of sixties soul. Stax started back in 1960 in a disused Memphis movie theatre, when a white banker (and former country fiddle player) teamed up with his sister to borrow enough money to buy a single Ampex reel-to-reel tape machine. That theatre, later featuring the legendary neon marquee of the Stax of Wax, eventually housed more talent to the square inch than any recording studio in the country. Some of it was due to fortuitous urban and cultural geography; keyboardist Booker T. Jones was a gangly sixteen-year-old who lived just around the corner; songwriter David Porter worked at the Big Star grocery store across the street; Rufus Thomas hosted a popular show on Memphis's WDIA. But the neighbourhood feel belied the nationwide audience of these artists: at 50,000 watts, WDIA was one of the most powerful black radio stations in the country, with over 1.2 million black Americans in its listening area – over 10 per cent of the black population of the United States at the time. Stax's deal with Atlantic in 1961 connected it with the latter's nationwide distribution and promotion, and guaranteed Stax artists a better royalty rate.

Motown, the yin of Soul beside Stax's yang, was no less successful, but represented the other version of the record industry's uneasy bargain with black musical forms. Motown's Berry Gordy worked his artists hard, sending them on gruelling bus tours to promote the label, and paying as little as a fifth of the standard royalties. Gordy relied on the cross-over appeal to pop music radio and retailers, and generally went for ballads or light-handed dance numbers, each of which was vetted by an in-house 'quality control' team to make sure it fitted smoothly into the Motown style. Instrumentalists received only a basic wage, were almost never given a credit in compositions they helped bring to fruition – and they were strictly prohibited from recording on their own. Stax, on the other hand, sought a distinctly heavier, 'live' sound built around its in-house band, which had an independent career as Booker T. and the MGs, and was generous in giving writing credits when credit was due. And, even though its owner and A&R manager were white, Stax made a stronger commitment to black artists, songwriters, and promotion via black radio. While Motown aimed itself directly at the pop charts – and white consumers – Stax always went for the rhythm and blues audience first, even when, in 1963–5, *Billboard* magazine stopped listing rhythm and blues charts altogether. As Mable John – one of Gordy's first signees – said when defecting to Stax in 1965, 'Motown is not basically a soul company – it's more pop and I'm not a pop singer. Gordy had no soul writers or producers, so I asked for a release.' Still, despite John's discontent, Motown served as the launching-pad for artists, such as Marvin Gaye and Stevie Wonder, who were able to challenge the limits of its house format, and eventually came to be as central to any meaningful definition of 'soul' as Stax giants such as Otis Redding, Sam and Dave, or Carla Thomas.

There were many other regional and local labels which functioned much as did Stax and Motown. Besides Cincinnati's King, there was Chicago's Chess and Vee-Jay, LA's Specialty and Modern, New Orleans's Minit and Josie (home of the Neville Brothers and the Meters), Houston's Peacock, Philadelphia's PIR, Newark's Savoy, and New York's Atlantic (itself a major among minors with its own stable of labels). Together, these smaller companies kept the crucible of soul burning through the sixties, though not without a certain underlying cost. Black artists still only intermittently enjoyed the kind of national distribution and promotion given to comparable white artists, and the large industry players still didn't have a clue as to what black audiences really wanted to hear. These small labels, to an extent, had worked as prosthetic taste buds for the white-controlled music industry. Yet with the dawn of the seventies, the fault lines shifted; Atlantic was gobbled up by Warner's, and its distribution deal with Stax was cancelled; the major labels read their tea leaves and decided it was time to skirt the minors and sign direct contracts with all the black talent they could find, even if they weren't quite sure what to do with it. The results were mixed; some performers found themselves saddled with producers who just couldn't resist a fistful of violins, or A&R departments that had no idea how to get airplay. The major labels were reluctant to issue an album without a 'hit' single, and their definition of 'hit' involved sales figures that newly signed artists could rarely reach, given inept promotion. At the same time, some artists found a golden opportunity; Isaac Hayes's 1970 album *Hot Buttered*

Soul, flushed through the overloaded pipeline that temporarily connected a sinking Stax to CBS records, was an unexpected success, and started a new movement towards a more slinky, sprawling, jazzy brand of Soul.

Others were less fortunate; some, such as the Meters – who, along with the MGs, were the most influential soul instrumental groups of the decade, were stranded on major labels unwilling to release whole albums worth of fine material, even as they released strings of singles by less talented artists in hopes of finding chart success. Their philosophy then – and still now – was to throw it all against the wall and see what stuck. The artists themselves were often further victimised by corrupt managers and promoters, and many of the greats went from stardom to bankruptcy in record time. The result of all this was a serious decline in the range and talent of commercial rhythm and blues recordings, a situation that critic Nelson George has called 'the death of rhythm and blues'. Still, there were already multiple musical developments that augured a coming rebirth: in Harlem the Last Poets were dropping rhymes over funky backup from Kool and the Gang; in the midwest Funkadelic and Parliament were reformulating rhythm and blues and rock into their own brand of funky gasahol; and out in Hollywood, Isaac Hayes, Curtis Mayfield and Willie Hutch were creating a new symphonic soul soundtrack, one that would last long beyond the seventies blaxploitation films for which their songs were written. All three of these forms were primed to come into their own as the seventies progressed, though their arrival was slowed by the music industry's bumbling attempts to pick up the ball.

The first pivotal link between the hard-working beats of sixties rhythm and blues and the more heavily syncopated rhythms of hip-hop and nineties soul, funk is the middle child of black musical forms, always looking for (and getting) plenty of attention. With its roots in the same midwestern industrial cities that had been the destination of the blues a generation before, funk grew up on the cusp of the collapse of heartland industries. Instrumentally, it came directly off the uptempo soul of James Brown, and two of its pre-eminent instrumentalists, Bootsy and Catfish Collins, got their start in Brown's back-up band. Funk's headman and impresario-for-life, George Clinton, rustled up the Collins brothers along with a motley crew of rock and rhythm and blues musicians to form the collectives variously known as Funkadelic, Parliament and (in the nineties) the P-Funk Allstars. Clinton was in many ways the godfather of rap, dropping wisdom with his inimitable pointful wandering, like a late-night deejay with a live band. With such tracks as 'Chocolate City', Clinton brought together the reflective elements of soul's ballad tradition with hefty bass lines and beats from more dance-oriented forms. Funk was slow, not because it couldn't be fast, but because it didn't need to be. Slowness and lowness are its recurring tropes, both verbal and musical, while in the upper registers rhythmic ninth-chords and punctuating horns – the more the better – gave syncopated accents and fills. Funk also, significantly, reclaimed some sonic territory from rock'n'roll, cranking up the fuzz guitars and thumbing its nose with tracks like Funkadelic's 'Who Says a Funk Band Can't Play Rock !?'

Funk had its showier aspects – George Clinton descending from the cosmic Mothership in ten-inch-high rhinestone-studded platform shoes, or Bootsy Collins with his star-shaped glasses and superwide bell-bottom pants, but ultimately it was the music that sustained its audiences. Stadium shows were fine – and in a decade dominated at first by arena rockers, lasers and smoke never hurt – but funk, like the hard-driving rhythm and blues before it, was party music, music whose sonic and psychic universe rotated around social ritual and sexual desire. Many funk bands also gave their own imprint to the soul ballad tradition, adding extra bass and slowing the rhythm to a sensuous grind; groups such as Earth, Wind and Fire played in as many dim-lit bedrooms as they did in crowded stadiums. Funk, ultimately, kept the flame of soul through a time when the music industry, flailing about in search of a trend, hit on disco and worked the music for every sure-fire hit it could find.

If the fumbling of the ball by the major labels in the early seventies was the 'death of rhythm and blues', the commercialisation of disco was the torch for the funeral pyre. Which is not to say that disco was, as its detractors claimed, crassly commercial from the beginning; it evolved directly out of uptempo rhythm and blues and funk, and came of age in the gay club scene in the United States and Europe, both black and white. In terms of its social performance, disco was, at first, a progressive musical force with a strong collective element (though now at the level of consumption rather than production, since disco was by definition 'pre-recorded'). There were tensions in this audience – as much of social class as sexuality – but also a degree of solidarity. Looking at the larger history of dance club music, the recording industry's appropriation of disco can be seen more accurately as a temporary incursion into an established continuum of dance music, which spans from sixties soul into nineties house, techno and jungle. But this time, the commodification of the music was so rapid and thorough that the doppelgangers arrived on chainstores' shelves before the originals, and many latter-day listeners had no means to reference disco within its generic or historical contexts; to them it seemed pre-fabricated from the start, a 'phoney' music forced on an apathetic public.

The central challenge for the recording industry was that disco, to a far greater degree than earlier dance musics, circulated primarily in clubs – that it was, despite having no live performers, the music of a live scene rather than a product for home consumption. As a result, unit sales – of individual records – were low, since deejays were the purchasers as intermediaries with the audience. The industry managed, however, to redirect disco into larger, mass-media phenomena; films such as 1977's *Saturday Night Fever*, consciously or otherwise, worked to shift the connotations of disco away from gayness and blackness, staging it instead as a theatre of class mobility, a place where ordinary, presumptively hetero, working stiffs could go to dress to the nines and dance their troubles away. The sales of singles – disco's primary medium – were channelled back into albums, including soundtracks and concept albums, and sales soon reached astronomical levels. Yet since these records were more the product of the industry, rather than the deejays and crowds that sustained the form, there were few means for big-label disco to grow or respond to its audiences. And, with a bird in its hand, the industry saw no reason to keep searching the bushes; they no longer looked to black radio for new talent and test marketing, and veteran black artists could either get with the trend or get lost. Even well-established performers such as James Brown and Isaac Hayes ended up recording disco imitations of disco's imitations of themselves.

Artists were losers all round, as pre-fab groups were readily assembled by record companies, and new studio techniques enabled vocals and beats to be infinitely substituted. It's worth noting, however, that these new technologies were not inherently uncreative, but rather that the tools were not yet in the hands of the new generation of black artists. It wasn't until 'street' rockers such as Afrika Bambaataa and Davy DMX (named after his favourite drum machine) got their hands on the beat boxes and programmable keyboards in the early eighties that disco regained the funkiness of its rhythm and blues roots, but by then the majors weren't listening. Thus, ironically, it was the industry's rapid-fire cloning of the disco sound that prevented it from being sufficiently in touch with the dance scene to hear the emerging sound of forms such as hip-hop and electro-funk. Long after stacks of overstocked Donna Summer albums were dumped into the bargain bins, dance music was still going strong, though it was now flying well under industry radar.

There was one other important yet (on a mass-market level) barely visible musical innovation of this time, one that predated and was to markedly influence hip-hop. There had always been a talking school of soul; love rappers like Laura Lee and heart-to-heart talks like James Brown's 'King Heroin' were part of a time-honoured tradition that stretched back to 78 rpm-era preacher/singers like the Reverend J. M. Gates. Yet the full range of black verbalism, the toasts, the dozens, or the 'hustler' rhymes spun by the likes of H. 'Rap' Brown and Iceberg Slim, had rarely made it onto recordings. Back in Harlem, though, a new generation of politically conscious young street poets was emerging, improvising rhymes over conga beats and delivering a more militant kind of sermon. Gil Scott-Heron, the angry young man of 'Small Talk at 125th and Lenox', gained national prominence with his anti-apartheid anthem 'Johannesburg', while back in their Harlem loft, the loose collective known as the Last Poets was jamming with percussionist Nilaja. The Poets, though their roots lay in the Black Arts movement and its devotion to Afrocentric jazz, were ready to take on new sounds and new directions; while they started with congas and African drums, by mid-decade they were getting backup from funksters such as Eric Gale and Kool and the Gang. Lead Poet Jalal Nuriddin was no stranger to rhythm and blues, and when he shifted from Jazzoetry to hustler rhymes on 1973's 'Hustler's Convention', he was making a connection that would be made again, though this time by a bunch of street kids whose sharp-edged sensibility would soon make Jalal's hustlers sound like porch-swinging grandfathers.

Much has been written about the emergence of hip-hop in the seemingly arid music landscape of the late seventies. What is often missed is that hip-hop, like previous black musical forms, was not fundamentally new; black kids (and adults) had been signifyin' and trading verbal toasts since slavery days and beyond. What was different was that this hitherto overlooked art, joined to breakbeats lifted from old records (and, later, a 'beat box' or drum synthesiser), made for a combination that had both a novel sound (many of the industry insiders at first derided rap itself as a 'novelty' act) and an intense, danceable beat. There were plenty of precedents – you could argue that Big Maybelle's 1952 'Gabbin Blues', or for that matter Pigmeat Markham's 1929 'Heah come de Judge' were raps – but hip-hop, like soul, was much more than its component parts. Hip-hop's roots were not only deep but wide, drawing on (and influencing) Jamaican toasters such as I-Roy and Big Youth, dub poets Linton Kwesi Johnson and Ranking Anne, and militant jazz verbalists the Last Poets and Gil Scott-Heron. Hip-hop, unlike rhythm and blues before it, was born in a global age, where the space of a few years would see b-boy style spread from New York to Tokyo, from London to Dar-es-Salaam, an age of cultural cross-references and fifteen-second soundbites. Yet it still had an intense sense of locality, with some of its earliest turf wars (such as the Queensbridge/South Bronx rivalry of BDP and the Juice Crew) taking place over a few city blocks. Disdained at first by many of those who belatedly lauded rhythm and blues as a national treasure, perversely pumping out original sounds by (ab)using the techniques of prefabrication, hip-hop was here to stay.

Hip-hop, it's commonplace to say, includes not only rap music but also graffiti and breakdancing. And, while breakdancing has faded from view in the decades since, there is a commonality to these hip-hop arts. They share a sort of scratch aesthetic – a re-valuation of arts that are inscribed upon the decaying infrastructures of city walls, old vinyl records, and cardboard crates. In the same way that a pawnshop guitar and a broken bottle made the blues a vernacular art, the old turntables, jury-rigged faders, and lamp-post electricity of a 1970's 'party in the park' made hip-hop an intrinsically urban, youth art. A black art, certainly, though Puerto Rican and white deejays and breakdancing crews were an intrinsic part of its earliest scenes, and a vernacular art, though never very far from the shadow of mass media (and later, to some, overshadowed by them). And, like other such arts, it was not immediately recognised as anything of great commercial value, even by those who invented it. Grandmaster Flash, one of the first and greatest 'old-school' deejays, used to sell homemade cassette tapes of his work for a dollar a minute, but he wasn't the first one into the studio. He had to undergo the painful initiation of hearing a pre-fab hip-hop crew, the 'Sugarhill Gang', rapping on record before he was able to get his own piece of the action. And even then, it was a while before any rapper – and it happened to be Kurtis Blow – landed a major-label contract, and longer still before Kurtis's protégés Run-DMC proved that hip-hop could top the charts.

Part of this was due to the inevitable time it takes any new musical genre to gain a foothold. But it was also a factor of the industry's reluctance to take on any musical form whose primary appeal was to young black audiences, since those audiences didn't have the pocket-money to drive massive sales. And, throughout its history, hip-hop has been dogged by the same troubled racial dichotomies that pursued rhythm and blues; if an artist addresses him or herself to the aesthetics and concerns of black communities, he or she will not leap up the pop charts, whereas those artists that make their music white-listener-friendly are far more richly rewarded. Inevitably, even the quest for authenticity produces its own weird backlash; white preconceptions about what constitutes authentic 'blackness' mean that a middle-class black rapper who dons a gangsta headrag and baggy pants may well outsell his sister who cuts equally funky rhymes in a flannel shirt and overalls. And, as in previous decades, the major labels' A&R departments are still predominantly white, and persistently clueless as to finding and developing black talent. It's a telling fact that hip-hop's first home was on black-owned labels, huddled survivors of the rhythm and blues era, such as Winley, Sugarhill and Enjoy, though it didn't take as long this time for the major labels to take notice.

In the earliest, 'old school' days (1976–83), hip-hop was primarily dance music, with feel-good call-and-response lyrics ('everybody say hey . . . ho', 'ho-tel, mo-tel, ho-li-day-inn', etc.) and synthesised beats and noises. The deejay art of cutting in and 'scratching' samples of previous recordings, a fundamental part of the music in parks and clubs, didn't carry over substantially onto commercial recordings until later in this period. Grandmaster Flash, in his masterpiece 'Adventures on the Wheels of Steel' (1983), cut up his own records for the most part, and it wasn't until Run-DMC's 'Peter Piper' (1986) that Jam Master Jay became the first to bring actual, scratched-up vinyl (in the form of Bob James's 'Mardi Gras') into a studio recording. But from the start, hip-hop's samples ran the gamut of genres, defying anyone who would delimit hip-hop's palette, and in fact rock samples (Jeff Beck, Def Leppard, Aerosmith) were as common as rhythm and blues ones (James Brown, Bobby Byrd, or the Meters). One curious result of this cross-talk was that when Run-DMC blew up in 1983, it was its collaboration with Aerosmith on 'Walk This Way' that brought hip-hop to rock radio and chart success. For the next few years, in fact, hip-hop was treated by some as a form within rock, and many of the old-school giants (Kurtis Blow, Grandmaster Flash) stumbled on this stylistic speed-bump, since predominantly white rock audiences still reacted negatively to anything that reminded them of disco. It wasn't until the mid-eighties, when hardcore rappers such as LL Cool J and Public Enemy 'brought the noise' back that hip-hop fully secured its spot as an independent genre. By then, scratchy samples were being run out of AKAI digital samplers, and if the record wasn't scratchy you could digitally add some. In much the same way as rock in the wake of the Beatles' *Sergeant Pepper*, rappers exploited the full capabilities of sampling, multi-track recording, distortion, and sound effects.

Public Enemy's *Fear of a Black Planet* (1990) marked the height of this 'scratch aesthetic'; with the aid of the production talents of the 'Bomb Squad', tracks such as 'Welcome to the Terrordome' melded backwards loops, street chants, unrecognisably distorted samples, and deejay Terminator X's ripcord scratches into a dense sonic unit, over which Chuck D's insistent vocals dropped knowledge like a tyre running over hot asphalt. This album also made use of non-music bridging tracks, another hip-hop trademark, which sampled the 'hype' itself: radio talkshow hosts, incensed callers, and commercial voice-overs were sliced and diced and spread out over the music like toppings on a pizza. It was a move that took the hip-hop world by storm, even as it deliberately piqued the anger of those who sought to ban the music altogether. For if the blues, to its detractors, was the devil's music, and jazz the tonality of wanton sensuality, hip-hop was white America's worst nightmare set to music, a sonic uprising in which personal, political, and economic resentment were all merged into one frightening noise.

Yet ironically, even as congressional committees looked into the 'dangers' of rap music, and 'voluntary' parental advisory labels were slapped on just about every hip-hop record, the political momentum stirred by activist artists such as PE, Paris, the Coup, and the Disposable Heroes of Hip-Hopcrisy began to fade, eclipsed by so-called 'gangsta' rap. While it was a label first popularised by its detractors, 'gangsta' had its distinct elements: the beats were slower, and more likely to sample George Clinton than James Brown, and the rhymes, eschewing political commentary, returned to the 'hustler' style of some of the earliest rappers, centring on money, cars and women. It was much more than simple machismo, as many of these new 'gangsta' rappers were women (the Bo$$, Bigga Sistas, the Conscious Daughters, or Heather B); what it seemed to mark was the loss of faith in any sort of a better future enabled via political action of expression. If the Reagan eighties and the decline in aid to cities gave mid-school hip-hop its rage and frustration, the nineties were the ashes of that fire, as rage gave way to despair in many black communities. Hip-hop, like soul before it, reflected the mindset of black youth, and the sensibility of this new generation – young enough to have been born after 'Rapper's Delight' – was one of desperation and hurt pride. The music industry, never one to waste a fire over which its dogs could be roasted, seized on 'gangsta' artists, and released as many as they could find, often regardless of talent. The result has been that the most powerful voices of hip-hop in the late eighties – Chuck D, Paris, even Ice T – have found themselves out in the cold with old-school exiles such as Kool Moe Dee and Whodini.

Yet even as the 'gangsta' style played itself out, hip-hop has continued to branch out in multiple directions across the full range of the musical spectrum. Jazz, once a stranger to the hip-hop scene, found its way in through the offbeat beats and vibraphone loops of 'bohemian' rappers such as A Tribe Called Quest, De La Soul, and the Digable Planets. The rapper Guru, along with his Gang Starr partner deejay Premier, sought out jazz musicians to see if the admiration was mutual, and recruited Donald Byrd, Roy Ayers, and Lonnie Liston Smith to his 'Jazzmatazz' project (1993). Before long, other jazz veterans were trying their hand at hip-hop grooves, among them Ornette Coleman, Herbie Hancock, and Branford Marsalis, while at the same time a new generation of rappers arrived who could plunge far deeper into a jazz groove, such as the Roots. This productive collaboration and cross-influence seems likely to continue, and has the effect of revitalising both musical forms, lending a mellow sophistication to hip-hop and a street credibility to jazz.

There are also regional (and aesthetic) yins and yangs in hip-hop as well. If soul seemed at times to be divided along north–south lines, with Detroit at one end and New Orleans at the other, hip-hop has an east coast/west coast divide, with the bass-heavy, car-speaker funk of California trading barbs and influences with its older, faster, brother in New York. Houston, with a hybrid mix of these tendencies, forms one sort of epicentre, as does Atlanta, a city increasingly pivotal to black culture in the multimedia age. Loosely defined schools within hip-hop have come (and gone), among them the bohemian-hop Native Tongues Posse, the crypto-funky Hieroglyphics crew, and the hardcore Islamic clans who subscribe to the Five Percent Nation. There's even a small school of gospel hip-hop, led by the Washington-based DC Talk, and even the hardcore pair known as the Black Sheep have teamed up with the gospel group Sounds of Blackness to record 'We Shall Not Be Moved'. Wherever hip-hop is headed, there can be little question that it is as vital a force within black music as any of its precursors, and is still a part of them however stark some of its aural contrasts.

Even as hip-hop has moved through an accelerated mid-life crisis, the other scattered children of the interstices of technology and dance continue to multiply. Starting from Afrika Bambaataa's foundational 'Planet Rap', which took its groove from German techno-rockers Kraftwerk, the school of 'electro-funk' has followed its own divergent path. Moving from New York to Detroit in the eighties, it evolved to test the capability of new technology in digital samplers, sequencers, and synthesisers, eventually giving rise to higher beats-per-minute forms such as techno and rave. Techno also experienced a United Kingdom translation not unlike the one rock underwent in the sixties, with spontaneous 'rave' parties springing up in the old abandoned warehouses of Britain's industrial cities. There, encountering the ongoing resonance of reggae, dancehall, and dub, the forms hybridised further, emerging as 'jungle', a dubby, spacey sort of techno that retains something of a Jamaican accent. And, in the outskirts of London and Birmingham, hip-hop, reggae and Bhangra made another unlikely alliance, producing artists such as Apache Indian, whose popularity was as high in India and the United States as it was in the United Kingdom. In France, rapper MC Solaar dropped rhymes in rapid-fire French over sounds taken from the soundtracks to 'spaghetti westerns'; in South Africa, the Prophets of the City took the pulse of their nation after apartheid, and in Japan Scha-dara-parr (translated as 'Tower of

Nonsense') rocked roomfuls of would-be b-boys and b-girls. Hip-hop has become part of a global diasporic mix, and whatever its domestic fortunes, it has formed another link in the rhythmic pathways of postcolonial sound.

Whence rhythm and blues in the hip-hop era? Interestingly enough, hip-hop has actually spurred a rhythm and blues rebirth; after a decade and more of a relatively static 'smooth' soul sound with interchangeable parts, rhythm and blues in the early nineties regained its own footing. Hip-hop has increasingly brought the beat, but it's been more than a rhythmic over-haul; gospel has once again lent a vocal flame, and rock has kicked in a guitar lick or two. Part of this has been due to the idiosyncratic ministry of musicians such as The Artist Formerly Known as Prince, whose Paisley Park studios have brought together rock, funk and hip-hop into a hazy yet uptempo groove, while giving new impetus to the careers of veterans such as Mavis Staples and George Clinton. Yet Paisley Park records, TAFKAP's private demesne, has gone the way of most inside-the-label labels – belly up – and the future of his innovative blends is far from certain. Still there are numerous other threads in rhythm and blues' new coat, ranging from gospel-inflected ensembles such as the Sounds of Blackness and the Sisters of Glory to the husky sonorities of Sade or Me'shell Ndegeocello, both returning to the roots and cultivating new ground. Healthy shots of revival have also come from the United Kingdom, where artists such as Soul II Soul (who took their name from a famous concert in Ghana by US soul musicians) broadcast the beat of 'house', a distinct blend of vocal divas (often brought in by way of a digital sample) and hip-hop or trance deejay beats. And Jamaica, always a sonic funhouse mirror to US black musics, has brought dancehall and reggae beats together with the more ballad-like styles of singers like Beres Hammond (not to mention the rougher stuff of such as Patra, Buju Banton, or Shabba Ranks), giving both rhythm and blues and hip-hop new angles on themselves.

Following along in all of this, as usual, the global music industry (and with Columbia now part of Sony and RCA owned by Bertelsmann, the industry is as multinational as the music it seeks to capitalise upon) has continued to boldly go where black music has already gone, hoping to pick up a hint or two. Yet, just as before, the 'shadow' audience of the black community has been left out of the loop of its own music, while automated services such as Sound Scan automatically tally sales in major retail outlets, bootlegs, mix tapes, and taped radio go uncounted, and at $15 a pop the listeners with the cash are those who will be counted. The modus operandi of the nineties industry, as before, has been to sign young black talent right and left, only to leave artists stranded if their first album sells under

100,000 units. Even among those acts who make it that far, the 'sophomore curse' derives from the fact that album number two is often an unhappy compromise between the label's desire to force artists into the latest trend in order to recoup the label's investment, and the artists' desire to grow and develop in their own way. With the reactionary right and industry critics ready to pounce on anything seen as extreme, a remarkable number of follow-up albums have been cancelled at the last stage, with review copies becoming the only copies. The industry continues to sign expensive deals with established artists, and often uses new acts only as a sort of insurance policy to be sure they don't accidentally miss out on a trend or a come-from-nowhere artist. But, more often than not, the artists who come from nowhere go back there too, and when 100,000 units is considered a failure, the odds aren't good. Hip-hop has always made do with less radio exposure, but ultimately it has a limited number of ways to get around the industry chokehold. Rhythm and blues and hip-hop are still dominated by the major corporate players, and the few independents such as Priority and Profile have never quite mustered the depth of a Stax or Motown. The biggest semi-independent, RUSH Associated Labels (run by old-school impresario Russell Simmons), still has had to rely on outside distribution deals (first with Sony, then with Polygram) to get its product in stores.

Yet ultimately, the record industry's continual drive to catch the next trend in black music has been self-defeating. The old sounds have never gone out of date, and in every new development there are multiple resonances of what has gone before. Hip-hop has always been generous in dishing out the props; the careers of veterans such as James Brown and George Clinton were given new life by their re-appearance as samples and scratches, and in many cases whole songs have been reprised as a backdrop for overlaid raps, such as Naughty By Nature's OPP (which samples the Jackson Five's 'ABC') or the Fugees' cover version of Roberta Flack's 'Killing Me Softly With His Song'. Black music has always been a continuity, has always found renewal in return, and – at least until there are more black-owned labels and A&R managers – will always elude the music industry's craving for predictability. There has been some progress – thanks to Sound Scan, at least it's clear that hip-hop musicians, however they may offend the tastes of 'middle America', can consistently top the sales charts, whereas in the past stores tended to inflate the figures of geriatric rockers that the industry had seen as its bread and butter. Black filmmakers have gained important ground in the nineties, and have brought with them the soundtrack of young black American music, both rhythm and blues and hip-hop. In the wake of corporate acquisitions of large blocs of the commercial radio spectrum, college and community stations have become the new proving ground for young talent, black and white. And, despite the air of machismo that has surrounded hip-hop from the start, many women rappers, among them Queen Latifah, Salt'n'Pepa and MC Lyte, have shown that they are as central to the artform as any men, and no less capable of sustaining success in an area where even getting a third record released makes you a survivor. And on the level of poetry itself, hip-hop constitutes the most vibrant and provocative turn in the history of African–American poetry, and an uptown throwdown to those who think poetry can only be found on a page. Sermon, diatribe, invective, exhortation; dance music, trance music, street music, feet music – hip-hop, in performance poet D-Knowledge's phrase, is 'all that and a bag of words'.

Further reading

For the best further reading on this topic, see Amiri Baraka (LeRoi Jones), *Black Music* (New York: William Morrow, 1967); Nelson George, *The Death of Rhythm and Blues* (New York: Pantheon Books, 1988); Paul Gilroy, *The Black Atlantic: Modernity and Double Consciousness* (Cambridge: Harvard University Press, 1993); Russell Potter, *Spectacular Vernaculars: Hip-Hop and the Politics of Postmodernism* (Albany: State University of New York Press, 1995); Tricia Rose, *Black Noise: Rap Music and Black Culture in Contemporary America* (Hanover: University Press of New England / Wesleyan University Press, 1994); David Toop, *Rap Attack II: African Rap to Global Hip-Hop* (London: Serpent's Tail, 1992).

7 Dance music

WILL STRAW

In 1978, the sociologist Richard Peterson suggested that American popular music was on the verge of its third great revolution of the twentieth century. The first two revolutions, Peterson (1978) claimed, had been ushered in by jazz and rock. The beginnings of the third were to be glimpsed in the rise of disco music, which made dance clubs a powerful force in popularising new records. As Peterson made this prediction, disco records sat atop sales charts in Europe and North America, and the disco film *Saturday Night Fever* was on its way to becoming a major box-office success. Two years later, when much of disco culture appeared to have collapsed, Peterson's prediction would look like an embarrassing miscalculation. It would take twenty more years, shifts in terminology, and a whole set of technological, social and economic developments before his claim of a dance music 'revolution' seemed worth re-considering. In 1997, commemorative books and anniversary dance parties celebrated a decade of frantic dance music activity in Great Britain and Western Europe, amid signs that even white North American youth, long faithful to rock, were migrating towards dance clubs and the sounds of dance music.

Dancing has long occupied an uneasy place within Western popular culture. For centuries, as Ann Wagner's (1997) study of anti-dance campaigns shows, dancing has been the focus of ongoing controversies about 'movement, manners and morals'. Dance remains controversial because it offers us two images of human bodies in motion. In one of these, dance represents the triumph of discipline and restraint. Here, as in the aristocratic world of pre-Revolutionary France, dancing is among the most orderly of social rituals, to be learned along with the rules of dining and courtly conversation. In dancing, individuals submerge their identities within gestures and movements which are not of their own making but, rather, handed down by tradition and authority. Teaching the young to dance is thus an effective way of passing on the rules of comportment and etiquette, of moulding the individual into a good, moral citizen.

In a counter-image, dancing is the very model of social disorder. To dance is to resist the restraints of rules and decorum, yielding to passionate impulses which threaten social stability. To many of those who visited the dance halls of the early twentieth century, dance offered a glimpse of social breakdown, in which desires with no useful purpose or virtuous end were given free rein. From this perspective, dance offers the occasion (and even the excuse) for forms of intimacy and physical expression which would not be tolerated in most other contexts. Dance is no longer about learning the rules of good behaviour, but an occasion for violating those rules. It is this image of dancing which has aroused the ire of moral reformers over several centuries, inspiring repressive laws, cautionary pamphlets and claims that dancing is the devil's work.

In a more modern version of this debate, it is the relationship of dancing to a capitalist economic system which is often in question. Dancing is sometimes seen to embody the worst features of musical culture in a modern, capitalist age. In their attacks on disco music in the 1970s, for example, many writers saw a logical connection between the seemingly mindless hedonism of disco dancing and the formula-driven qualities of disco music itself. Both seemed to prove that aesthetic and moral standards had declined in an age of decadent materialism. Historians of jazz or rock music have often seen dance as a seductive force, luring these musical traditions from the path of artistic seriousness. Dancing is thought to weaken critical faculties by encouraging us to respond to music in ways which involve neither contemplation nor respect. Finally, dance music has been deemed a 'problem' because its own fleeting fads are at odds with the values of tradition and career longevity held high by critics and the music industry alike.

Almost as often, however, dancing will be valued because it seems to run counter to the main tendencies of modern, commercial entertainment. While television, the cinema and concert-going are sometimes accused of making audiences passive, dancing may seem among the most active and creative ways of being entertained. Likewise, while modern media are condemned for isolating individuals in their homes, or within the anonymity of the darkened cinema, dance invites us to interact with large numbers of people in public places. Dancing is sometimes considered a modern remnant of the folk cultures of the past, one of our last links to a world and time in which people gathered together in communal festivities of their own making. Dance will often serve as a focus for new communities, such as those which have taken shape around the gay liberation movement or the subcultures of acid house. Indeed, it is through dancing that music's potential for expressing social solidarity or personal liberation seems to realise itself most fully.

Bodies in movement

In setting out to talk about dance, we confront the lack of a widely agreed-upon vocabulary with which to do so. Scholarly analyses of dance are scattered among a half-dozen disciplines and fields, from anthropology through music history, from the study of high-art choreography through that obscure sub-discipline, the philosophy of dance. The art historian Norman Bryson (1997) has suggested that we study dance as part of a broader investigation of what he calls 'socially structured movement'. Different societies (or groups within societies) organise movement in different ways, from the most minor gestures of courtesy and respect through the parades or other rituals which mark important celebrations. Dancing, Bryson suggests, is a particularly striking example of this 'socially structured movement', but it should not be looked at in isolation.

This sense of a link between dancing and other ways of moving the body has long been noted. Twentieth-century choreography has often tried to break down the barrier between dance and non-dance move-ments, by building dance routines out of most actions of everyday life. (See, for example, many of the dance sequences in a Hollywood film like *On The Town*, from 1949.) In a much less conscious way, fans of popular music often assume that there are connections between an individual's ability to dance and the way that individual moves in other contexts. Such beliefs are at the heart of popular stereotypes about different social, ethnic or racial groups and the degree to which they are at ease with their bodies. These stereotypes include the belief that dancing is at its most sexualised and uninhibited in non-Anglo-Saxon cultures, such as those of Latin–Americans or African–Americans. In fact, as Leopold Senghor once observed, African societies typically disdain physical contact between dancers, and such contact is more common within European social dancing. Likewise, Jacqui Malone (1996) has noted that African–American dancing maintains a constant tension between the discipline of rhythm and personal improvisation upon that rhythm. 'Cutting loose', in the sense of unrestrained sensual abandon, is frowned upon because it lacks the stylisation which is so highly valued within this tradition. Dancing within the white middle class has usually veered between the extremes of elaborate ritual and unbridled individual expression, from the waltz, square dance and other forms popular in the nineteenth century through the free-form abandon of hippy dancing in the late 1960s.

The places of public dancing

The history of popular dancing in the Western world is partly a history of places in which that dancing has occurred. The modern dance club has its roots in the saloons and restaurants of the nineteenth century. Over the last hundred years, dancing has moved out of private balls or social clubs and into these more anonymous spaces in which patrons gather to eat and drink. Whereas, in an earlier time, dancers could presume a familiarity and shared social background with their fellow dancers, the dance venues of the twentieth century, like the cinema and other modern entertainments, would bring together groups of strangers in new places of public amusement. In the dance halls, cabarets and nightclubs which proliferated at the end of the nineteenth century, patrons were more and more likely to mingle with others whose social origin and moral status were unknown. Under these circumstances, dancing would come to be strongly associated with sexual possibility or sexual danger.

These new places of amusement were novel in other ways, as well. The historian Lewis Erenberg (1981) has written of the slow but important shift in notions of entertainment that occurred between the two world wars in North America. In the new dancehalls and nightclubs built to meet a rising demand, the audience itself became the main focus of entertainment, as patrons danced and enjoyed the spectacle of watching others, most of them strangers, dance alongside them. The appeal of a nightclub now depended on the character of its clientele more than the fame or abilities of the professional entertainers it featured. The effects of this shift have remained with us to the present day. In a tradition that extends from the cabarets of the 1920s through the discotheques of the 1970s and beyond, dance venues have become places where one goes to watch a crowd of patrons display their styles of dressing, posing and dancing. While nightclubs are typically thought of as places where people go to find others of similar taste or social background, they are also sites for social tourism. Visiting them, people may venture up or down the social ladder, or explore the margins and subcultures of the modern city.

The dance crazes which have punctuated the history of popular dancing in this century have done much to make dancers themselves the main source of a nightclub's appeal. One goes to nightclubs to watch an audience, usually made up of non-professionals, dance in the latest styles. In the United States, the cakewalk, fox-trot, ragtime and Ballin' the Jack crazes in the first two decades of the twentieth century spurred the expansion of dance floors in restaurants and other establishments. As the tango, Charleston, lindy hop and jitterbug fads which followed made clear, dance crazes have been one of the principal means by which musical styles of African–American or Latin–American origin have crossed over to audiences of white Europeans. (Later, the Twist, Hustle, salsa, Lambada, and dozens of others would function in the same way.)

The nightclubs and ballrooms in which dancing took place are only part of the story, however. The spread of dance styles, from one city to another, and into the living rooms and bedrooms in which dance steps are practised, is closely tied to the development of modern forms of entertainment and communication. The dance crazes of the early twentieth century were popularised through stage shows, which often incorporated these dances into their revue-like formats. Dancing schools, which capitalised on each emerging trend, helped codify the rules for new dances and often sponsored guidebooks or records which pupils could use as they practised at home. The rise of electronic media would speed up the process by which dance styles, and the music which accompanied them, were disseminated across large geographical areas. Musical films, such as the Fred Astaire–Ginger Rogers movies, with their emphasis on solo or 'couple' dancing rather than complex group choreography, proved important in building and sustaining a public for social dancing. Radio was a crucial factor in building audiences for swing music in the United States in the late 1930s, and live broadcasts of big-band music from hotel ballrooms enforced the link between the new music and public dancing. Indeed, as David W. Stowe's (1994) study of swing music in the 1930s suggests, movies, records, radio broadcasts and live performances all interacted to make swing music, and the dancing styles which accompanied it, a genuinely national movement within the United States.

Dancing in the post-war period

In their history of popular dancing in the United States, Jean and Marshall Stearns (1994) suggest that the immediate post-war period was marked by a dance 'black-out', a decline in the popularity of social dancing and the disappearance of many of the venues in which it occurred. Increases in the costs of labour and transportation contributed to the break up of the swing bands, who had combined success on radio and records with live performances in settings where hundreds of people might gather to dance. Ballrooms and dance halls in United States cities closed throughout the late 1940s and 1950s, as migration to the suburbs and a widespread sense that conditions in inner cities were deteriorating lessened the appeal of these venues to the middle classes. New excise taxes on entertainment establishments that featured dancing helped drive popular music towards the non-danceable alternatives of small group jazz and vocal music. In Great Britain, a variety of post-war restrictions on leisure consumption had much the same effect.

Dancing did not disappear entirely, however. It moved into other sorts of venues, into places where music was presented in a variety of new ways. These venues were smaller than the ballrooms of the 1930s, a change that reflected the fragmenting of musical tastes throughout the United States and other Western countries. Philip Ennis (1992) has argued that high school dance 'hops' partially replaced the ballrooms of the swing era as major venues for public dancing, at least in the United States. They did so, however, for a much more exclusively youthful audience than the ballrooms had attracted. In this, the dance 'hops' helped lay the foundations for a new, post-war youth culture in which music and dancing would play an important role. High school dances would be one pathway through which post-war rhythm and blues and early rock'n'roll were popularised as musical styles and as the background for social dancing. The community youth clubs of Great Britain and Western Europe offered spaces in which youth could dance to recordings or locally based musical combos. Jukeboxes, located in bars, restaurants and cafés, allowed youthful patrons to dance to music of their own choosing.

The most important medium popularising post-war musical styles for youth, however, was radio. North American Top 40 Radio, whose programming philosophy involved playing a limited number of songs in rapid rotation, was inspired by the jukebox, which allowed patrons in bars and restaurants to hear their favourite records as often as they wished. As Philip Ennis (1992) has shown, both the jukebox and Top 40 radio were hungry for new records, and this need for an ongoing stream of new product helped spur the creation of dozens of new small record companies. The speed with which records rose and fell in cycles of popularity helped nourish the sense that music was now marked by fads which came and went quickly. 'Rock'n'roll', now seen to have brought about a revolution in twentieth-century popular music, was in many ways little more than another of these fads when it emerged, in the mid-1950s, and it was accompanied by new forms of dancing. The radio disc jockeys who helped popularise this music on the airwaves often took to the road, travelling to local record hops and organising large dances in which a roster of new musical performers might play short sets. As the musical rhythms and group formats of rock'n'roll or rockabilly became standardised, local bands could more easily play this music in such contexts as the high school dance or the youth club. All of these factors encouraged the spread of dancing styles and musical sounds throughout North America and much of the Western world.

In 1957, a local television programme, *Philadelphia Bandstand*, changed its name to *American Bandstand* and began broadcasting nationally. By 1959, over one hundred local stations within the United States were carrying the programme, to an audience of twenty million viewers. *American Bandstand*, along with dozens of other, locally based dance programmes, featured studio audiences of local teenagers dancing to current pop music hits. By making it easy for viewers to learn the steps of new dances, television dance programmes helped fuel the series of dance crazes which unfolded within North America, Western Europe and elsewhere throughout the early 1960s. The best-known of these crazes, which emerged in 1960, was the Twist. Others include the Madison, the Hully-Gully, the Go-Kart, the Frug, the Mashed Potato and the Swim.

As these dance crazes succeeded each other, thoughout the 1960s, they attracted the attention of middle-class adults, and spurred the spread of a new kind of night-life establishment, the discotheque. As Jim Dawson (1995) reminds us, the literal meaning of the term 'discotheque' is 'record library'. In the 1930s, the term would refer to French nightclubs in which patrons might gather to hear the latest imported jazz records from the United States. Clubs of this sort, which featured records rather than live performers, and whose appeal had much to do with the obscure, imported recordings they were able to acquire, continued to open in Western European countries during and after the Second World War. In such venues, we may already glimpse the predecessor of today's dance club disc jockey, an employee whose reputation rests as much on access to new records from faraway or underground sources as on the technical ability to operate equipment and play records in sequence.

In the 1960s, discotheques would open in major cities throughout the West. (Le Club, which opened in Manhattan in 1960, was one of the first in this wave.) During this period, the discotheque came to play the double role which has marked it ever since. On the one hand, discotheques are often havens for devoted fans of obscure kinds of music, offering the chance to hear (and dance to) the latest records and an implicit promise to stay ahead of mainstream tastes and trends. At the same time, however, discotheques are often spectacularly public institutions, attracting a broad range of any given city's night-time society. As such, they may draw together tourists, people working in the fashion and media industries, members of an international jet-set and a range of others whose interest in music itself may be neither deep nor specialised.

Discotheques of the 1960s, which sprang up to accommodate dance styles born in the working class and ethnic districts of large United States cities, confronted the tension between these two roles. The Twist may have begun as a dance style practised by African–Americans and poor whites in inner-city school yards, but within two years it was being danced by social-ites and media celebrities in mid-town discotheques. Marshall and Jean Stearns (1994) suggest that, as middle-class whites took up dancing in large numbers, they gradually eliminated its choreographed, ritualistic qualities in favour of free-form expression. Dances of working-class origin, such as the Madison, with its complicated series of intricate steps, would give way to the frenzied looseness of go-go dancing in the mid-

1960s, or the unstructured self-absorption of hippy dancing by the end of the decade. Discotheques continued to open in large numbers through the mid-1960s, but the appeal of new dance crazes gave way to the promise of a stimulating, multimedia environment. Sarah Thornton (1995) has shown how discotheques during this period, whether in New York, London, or dozens of other cities, came to present themselves as sensory playgrounds. Lighting, decor and overall design became a discotheque's main attractions, but it was necessary that these be changed regularly if a club was not to lose its novelty.

By the late 1960s, one important period in the history of discotheques was over. The sense of an unbroken series of dance crazes, each of which grabbed centre stage for a moment, had come to an end. One reason for this has already been suggested: the dancing of middle-class whites had broken down into a rather formless kind of personal expression, and no longer followed prescribed steps. Just as importantly, however, the development of rock music in the late 1960s took it in the direction of more intricate and extended forms which did not lend themselves easily to dancing. (It was during this period that the idea of the rock 'concert' became dominant.) Dancing in nightclubs was to persist in the late 1960s, but venues would no longer bring together different social classes and racial groups to the same extent as had the dance crazes of the early 1960s. In a pattern that would be repeated many times hereafter, dance clubs retreated into the underground scenes of large cities. In the late 1960s, Hispanic and African–American musical styles, such as Latin soul, funk and boogaloo, were developing into new kinds of dance music which were less and less likely to interact with rock music itself. This music, like rock, was extending the limits of the song and bringing new instruments into the mix, but its long instrumental breaks and increasing emphasis on percussion and bass made it much more suitable for the new dance clubs being built in deserted warehouses or other large spaces.

In New York City, a number of new dance clubs opened in 1969 and 1970, partly in response to the new-found sense of community within gay culture following the so-called Stonewall Riots of 1969. (A major feature of these riots was the demand by gays to be able to congregate in bars and clubs without police harassment.) These clubs included Salvation, the Sanctuary and Haven, and many of their features anticipated the disco culture which flowered in the mid and late 1970s. Clubs were now just as likely to open in vacated industrial sections of large cities as in the fashionable centres of commerce and entertainment, a shift which added to the sense that nightlife involved a journey into an urban underground marked by a sense of danger. Increasingly, the disc jockeys in these clubs were becoming celebrities of a new kind, known for their ability to create and sustain a mood over several hours, and acknowledged by record companies for their influence on the musical tastes of their patrons.

Disco and the 1970s

The disco boom of the 1970s may be said to have begun in 1974, when two singles which had received their original public exposure in dance clubs rose to the top of industry sales charts in the United States and each sold two million copies. These records were 'Rock The Boat', by the Hues Corporation and 'Rock Your Baby' by George McCrae. 'Disco' would come to mean a distinctive sound, marked by a 4/4 beat and the use of instruments (such as strings, woodwinds and brass) more typical of classical music than of rock. Originally, however, it referred simply to records designed to 'cross over' from discotheques to the broader audience for pop music. In the strategic thinking of record companies, dance clubs were a medium in which an initial audience for songs could be built, spurring the addition of records to radio playlists and the eventual sale of albums on which a song appeared. If record companies turned to dance clubs to 'break' records in the mid 1970s, it was partly because radio stations, in North America at least, had grown more conservative in adding new songs to their playlists. Dance clubs offered a venue in which the appeal of records could be tested before radio stations made the decision to include them in their programming.

At one level, the emergence of disco was a slow affair, as the sorts of dance clubs which had begun appearing in the late 1960s grew in number and were copied throughout the Western world. The musical styles associated with these clubs likewise took shape gradually, shaped by the ornate production styles of Philadelphia soul or large-ensemble funk in the first half of the 1970s. Nevertheless, disco music seemed suddenly to burst into popular culture in 1974–5, in part because record companies rushed to capitalise on the new ways of promoting records which discotheques seemed to offer. At the same time, like the cabaret owners in the early decades of the twentieth century, who found that dance floors were an effective inducement to drinking and eating, restaurant and hotel managers throughout the world moved to add dance floors and nightclubs to their facilities in the mid-1970s. The explosion of disco music would see 10,000 discotheques operating in the United States by 1976, many of them integrated within hotel chains or run as franchise operations. In 1979, Andrew Stein, chair of the borough of Manhattan, credited discos with helping to revitalise the economies of cities like New York, during a decade in which these cities faced fiscal crises and desertion by the white middle classes. In such disco capitals as New York or Montreal, local television programmes set in discotheques combined instruction on the latest dance steps with gossipy coverage of urban nightlife and a revitalised downtown celebrity culture.

Widely varying interpretations of the disco phenomenon were put forth in the 1970s. From one perspective, discos represented a conservative return to older, even pre-war traditions of nightlife. With their emphasis on glamorous dress, couples dancing to prescribed steps (such as 'The Hustle') and lushly orchestrated sounds which bore little resemblance to the textures of rock music, discotheques evoked the supper clubs and cabarets of the 1930s and 1940s. Just as often, however, disco culture was perceived as one step on a long road of cultural decline, joining the hedonistic excesses of rock culture (such as drugs and promiscuous sexuality) to the shallow, conspicuous consumption associated with an upwardly mobile urban middle class. In fact, the success of discotheques had much to do with the degree to which they brought together patrons of very different social backgrounds and lifestyles, from suburban heterosexuals seeking a night's diversion to those who lived in inner city gay communities, from members of the white working classes to young black urban professionals.

Remixes and extended singles

In 1975, large numbers of dance club deejays received a promotional item from RCA Records, a twelve-inch record on which one song was extended over an entire side. The record was 'Dance, Dance, Dance', by the group Calhoun, and it represented the introduction of a record format with enormous effects on the future development of dance music. Extended singles were one response to a problem which deejays had faced for a half-decade or more. Improvements in nightclub audio systems since the 1960s allowed for a wider sonic range than had earlier been possible, but the 45 rpm, seven-inch singles on which dance records normally circulated could not carry this range. The new twelve-inch single allowed for wider grooves, so that bass and percussion sounds were deeper and overall tones were richer. It also allowed the length of a song to be extended, so that instrumental breaks at beginning and end were now possible. Records could be blended by overlapping these transitional breaks at the end of one record with those at the beginning of another, and by slightly manipulating the speed of turntables so that the rhythms of both records were synchronised. The twelve-inch extended single was instantly popular with deejays, and, in 1976, companies began making them available for sale to the general public. (The record '10 Percent' by the group Double Exposure, on the Salsoul label, was the first twelve-inch single to receive a commercial release.)

One of the ironies of dance music history is that, while the twelve-inch single was intended to help promote dance records to a mass audience, by encouraging deejays to play them within dance clubs, its long-term effect has been to help isolate dance music from the rest of musical culture. For many observers, the introduction of 12-inch singles hastened the collapse of disco music as a commercial force, by giving dedicated disco fans something to buy other than the album on which record companies had placed their hopes. (The problem of 12-inch singles 'cannibalising' the sales of albums would be noted regularly throughout the late 1970s.) More importantly, perhaps, the twelve-inch dance single would stimulate the production of new forms of music which were no longer simply modifications of the 'real' versions of songs. This new format would cease being merely a professional tool, and become a distinctive cultural form in its own right.

Since the early 1970s, deejays in dance clubs had become important sources of information for record companies. They reported to such companies on the success or failure of records among nightclub patrons and offered useful feedback on emerging trends and the sorts of production techniques which worked well in clubs. By 1975, deejays in most major cities had joined together in 'pools', associations which coordinated the delivery of new records from record companies to deejays and gathered the 'response sheets' which deejays completed as a way of letting record companies know how records had fared in their clubs. Soon, record companies began hiring deejays to remix dance songs for their twelve-inch dance-club versions.

All of these changes set in place a process by which the dance club deejay came to be at the centre of dance music, rather than simply one more intermediary, like the radio station programming director, to be won over by record company promotion personnel. Deejays who began as remixers often realised they might almost as easily produce their own tracks, particularly since many disco 'groups' had no existence or recognisable public presence outside the recording studio. The sense that a twelve-inch single consisted of a conventional 3–4 minute song with a few additional elements slowly withered. Rather, the twelve-inch single offered a new way of conceiving music, by providing a format in which new kinds of rhythmic structures and sonic effects might be tried out. By the beginning of the 1980s, records which existed only in the twelve-inch vinyl single format were being produced in large numbers. Around them had taken shape a complex set of institutions and circuits of information through which these records, and news about them, could circulate. Independent dance music stores, distribution and importation companies, tip sheets for deejays, deejay pools and specialty magazines reviewing twelve-inch singles were all in place by the end of the 1970s.

All of these developments began the ten-year process which would help make dance music a globally underground phenomenon, rooted in a world of independent labels and small-scale production teams even as it became the most popular music for youth in many parts of the world. In the late 1970s, these changes were one among many factors which made it more and more difficult for major record companies to market disco music successfully. From the beginning of the disco explosion, the record industry had worried that disco music changed too rapidly for large companies to exploit its commercial potential efficiently. The life cycle of dance records is notoriously short-lived, as deejays and club patrons tire of them and demand novelty. To market a dance record successfully, then, requires responding quickly to feedback from the club scene, ensuring that enough copies are in record shops to meet demand without spending money needlessly to press, distribute and promote records which are destined to fail. Small record companies have typically been more skilled at responding quickly to the marketplace than have major, multinational companies.

More importantly, in an industry that came to see singles as promotional vehicles of little commercial value, the problem of translating a song's popularity in dance clubs into large-scale sales for albums containing that song were acute. Most albums of disco music were seen by the public to contain a hit song and much filler, and fans of the song were too often content to buy the single in its seven-inch or twelve-inch forms. As the orchestration and production of disco records did not lend themselves easily to being reproduced in live concerts, the promotional value of tours was limited. To make matters worse, the record industry had come to realise, by 1979, that a large percentage of disco fans treated the music as an ongoing soundtrack to urban life rather than a series of separate songs to be identified as such and sought out in record stores. This 'soundtrack' was easily available from the radio stations which offered continuous disco mixes, or on the compilation records which brought together a dozen recent hits.

Dance music after disco

It is commonplace, in recent histories of popular music, to claim that disco 'died' in 1979, because record companies had saturated the market with low quality, standardised product in a reckless desire to capitalise on a passing fashion. It is true that many of the specific musical styles associated with disco withered or evolved, in the years 1979–80, and that the clientele for dance clubs split into a variety of specialised taste groups. Nevertheless, the infrastructures of dance club culture, the specialty record stores, small record labels, and dance clubs themselves, continued to grow throughout the 1980s and beyond, allying themselves with a variety of new musical styles. The Hi-NRG sound of gay dance clubs was at its most popular in the early 1980s, and electro-funk, British synth-pop, Eurodisco, rap and many other styles flourished in dance clubs during the same period.

At the beginning of the 1980s, the most important question facing dance music might have seemed to many to be its relationship to rock. Rock fans of the 1970s typically disdained disco music, but by 1980 music industry trade magazines were already speaking of the popularity of something they called 'Dance-Oriented Rock', as dance clubs added records by post-punk groups such as Blondie or Talking Heads to their play-lists. The increased production of rock records intended for dance clubs was spurred by two developments within Anglo-American musical culture. One of these was the move by discotheques themselves to embrace rock-based sounds, in order to capture a new audience and survive as the disco market splintered and shrank. Disco's rising popularity in the late 1970s had resulted in discotheques opening in suburbs, on college campuses and in other locations where the pool of potential patrons was likely to be dominated by rock fans. Less obviously, danceable rock was one response to the question (posed by punk musicians and critics) of how punk would develop and resist becoming stagnant after the dramatic gestures of 1976 and 1977. Punk splintered into dozens of new styles and movements, and several of these (such as synthesiser pop and the revival of ska music) embraced dancing and dance clubs. The history of post-punk music over the next decade would be marked by a range of more-or-less danceable musical styles, from the militant funk of the Gang of Four or Scritti Politti, through the white-boy soul of Spandau Ballet or Dexy's Midnight Runners, the gothic rock of Siouxsie and the Banshees or the Cure, the quirky, danceable pop of the B-52s or Yello, and the stark industrial electronics of such groups as Cabaret Voltaire or Test Department.

The clubs in which this music was played, in the first half of the 1980s, differed from the discotheques of the 1970s in several important ways. Their clientele, particularly in North America, was more likely to be almost exclusively white, as the audiences for post-punk rock music and new forms of African–American music seemed to diverge significantly. At the same time, the highly ritualised and couple-oriented nature of most disco dancing in the 1970s gave way, within rock dance clubs, to styles of dancing marked by more restrained movements and an unspoken prohibition on physical contact between dancers. Finally, while the discotheques of the 1970s had attracted people from a broad range of ages, with young adults in their twenties and thirties as a core, post-punk dance clubs, like the raves and house clubs which followed, drew a much more uniformly youthful clientele.

At regular intervals, during the 1980s, rock criticism announced the appearance of new hybrids of rock and dance music, embracing each as the sign of a new unity within youth culture. This was the case in the early 1980s, when dancing to rock records in newly vibrant club scenes seemed to suggest that the antagonism between rock and dance audiences had withered away. Similar claims about a rock–dance synthesis were popular in 1989, with the emergence of a wave of British bands (such as the Happy Mondays and Stone Roses) whose tastes had been shaped in the raves and acid house culture of the mid-and-late 1980s. In 1997, the music press spoke once again of the coming together of dance and rock, as such dance acts as the Prodigy or the Chemical Brothers offered a rough dance sound in which guitars and other rock instruments were common, and as samples from heavy metal bands turned up in more and more records directed at dance clubs.

In fact, the fate of dance music in the 1980s and 1990s has had very little to do with the ways in which it has blended with rock. The popularity of these hybrids has almost always remained internal to the musical culture of young whites, with few effects on the production of black dance music. More importantly, it seems clear that the most significant event in the history of dance music since 1980 has been the rise of house music, whose style and development have had very little to do with rock music itself. As a new musical fashion, house captured the attention of dance music fans in the mid 1980s, and helped lay the basis for the massive dance explosion which followed. The house sound, born in the clubs and warehouse parties of Chicago in the early 1980s, gave dance music a new rhythmic foundation which would remain dominant for a decade and remain a central feature of dance music all through the 1990s. The 'four-on-the-floor rhythms' of house offered a structure over which a seemingly unlimited number of other musical and non-musical elements could be laid. The ability of house to incorporate other sounds, and adapt to shifting tempos or new influences, is a major reason for its success. At one level, house was merely the latest in a series of dance music crazes. Like disco before it, the introduction of house music saw a flurry of records which exploited the new fashion: old songs redone with a house beat, medleys of older tunes set to a house rhythm, and the remixing of new pop songs so as make them compatible with the rhythms of house-dominated dance clubs.

The effects of house extend far beyond its distinctive rhythmic structure, however. House intensified the process by which dance club music detached itself from other sorts of popular music. By offering a consistent rhythm, from one record to another, house music changed the nature of deejay work. More and more, the idea of songs gave way to the notion of 'tracks', records lasting from four to ten minutes in which the important things going on had to do with the relationship between a consistent rhythm and the wide variety of things which might be mixed over the top of it. A deejay might use bits of one record to offer a house rhythm; over the top of that rhythm, fragments from other records, or sounds played live on electronic instruments might be added. While the practice of assembling music out of bits of other records was not new, it had been a key element of rap music since the late 1970s. House music lent itself more easily to creating long stretches of unbroken music, often lasting several hours, as records and sounds were interwoven by deejays in a process that might be considered one of live composition.

House music has developed in innumerable directions since the mid 1980s. Styles have ranged from the busy, cluttered sound of 'sample house' through the deep, soulful styles of garage, from the manic, synthesiser-based jubilation of hardcore through the pastoral soundscapes of ambient house. House has momentarily merged with pre-existing musical styles, like rap and Hi-NRG, and been interwoven with other styles, such as techno, trance and big beat, which have flourished alongside it. Whereas there was once a sense that these various styles might replace each other, the growth and fragmentation of dance music culture has meant that almost all of them now continue to develop, each with its specialised clubs and record labels, and each allotted a review section in the dozens of magazines which have emerged to catalogue and evaluate new dance records.

Rave culture and the trans-Atlantic divide

The explosion of dance music culture has not been uniform throughout the Western world, however. By the late 1990s, this boom had made Great Britain the international centre for dance club music production, and a laboratory for the cross-fertilisation of dance music styles, but it would widen the gulf between the musical tastes and buying habits of Europe and those of North America. There are many possible reasons for this gulf, and the relative weight of each is difficult to assess. Some trace the underdevelopment of dance club culture in the United States and Canada to a continued musical segregation of audiences along the lines of race. They point to a well-entrenched split between white rock culture and an African–American music dominated, since the mid-1980s, by hip-hop or more pop-like strains of rhythm and blues (such as so-called 'swingbeat'). Others trace these differences to the relatively small geographical size of Great Britain, and the presence of a lively and influential music press, factors which allow for a quicker spread of fads and a constant generation of excitement around new sounds and new records. The tighter population densities of Great Britain, and of Europe in a broader sense, have nourished the popularity of dance club tourism, which takes club-goers and deejays from one city or vacation resort to another for marathons of dancing often stretching over several days. As well, dance music has a much greater presence on radio in Great Britain and Europe than in North America, a possible effect of dance music's greater popularity which may, over time, have become one of its causes.

In the mythologies which surround the new dance culture, North America and Great Britain each figure differently. Until the emergence of drum and bass and trip-hop, in the mid 1990s, the major styles of dance music could each be traced to a United States birthplace: house to Chicago, techno music to Detroit, the garage sound to New Jersey and New York City. These musical scenes have all remained the stuff of legend, even when the most important developments of these styles have clearly taken place elsewhere. Great Britain's place within dance music mythologies is bound up with the ways in which the rave, as an event, has given dance culture the features of a genuinely revolutionary subculture. Sarah Thornton (1995) and others (e.g. Benson 1997) have described the emergence of the rave out of reggae sound systems and the warehouse dance parties which became common in Great Britain in the early 1980s, when rising costs of real estate and a backlash against the elitism of big-city nightclubs led promoters to hold dance events in abandoned warehouses. Harassment by local police forces limited the spread of warehouse parties, and promoters began seeking other places, less susceptible to police intervention, in which dance events could be held. New kinds of events, called raves, were held in wide-open spaces, such as fields or parking lots. The locations of these events, which might attract 5,000 people or more, were frequently kept secret until shortly before they began.

Since 1995, a number of books, almost all of them British, have documented the history of raves, and offered claims about their revolutionary impact. The rave helped to spread the notion that dancing might take place at spectacular events, rather than at clubs whose decor and musical styles remained unchanged from night to night. In this respect, dance culture has taken on some of the features of the rock concert, just as raves and outdoor dance parties have come to stand as modern equivalents of the rock festival. While vast numbers of people continue to dance to Top 40 music at local discotheques, raves enshrined the idea that dancing and dance music might be both mass phenomena *and* the central focus of new undergrounds. The fact that new kinds of sensory environments (music, lighting, decor, and so on) have gone hand in hand with newly popular drugs, such as Ecstasy, has allowed rave culture to define itself as the basis of a new counter-culture, if not of a broader mutation of knowledge and experience – and not merely a passing trend in youth leisure. Raves help popularise the notion that patrons come to dance over several hours, organising their weekends and their consumption of beverages and drugs accordingly, rather than simply spending a couple of hours in a club between other night-time activities. As a result of the legal and judicial opposition they have confronted, dance culture and the rave have helped shift the focus of popular music's politics, away from the age-old controversies over authenticity and commercialism common in discussions of rock, and towards more concrete battles over the right to occupy public or quasi-public spaces and congregate in large numbers.

The importance of raves in Great Britain further solidified the differences between Britain and North America. Raves remained uncommon in North America until 1992 or 1993, and then encountered a number of developments which have limited their growth. One such development has been the opening of new, more conventional night clubs to capitalise on the rising interest in dance music among North American youth. Another is the growth in North American tours by celebrity deejays, large numbers of them from Great Britain, who perform in large events which resemble raves in scale and format but are more likely to be above ground and legal. In 1997, it appeared that alternative rock, which had been hugely popular among white North American youth since the early 1990s, was losing its appeal, as audiences turned towards the sorts of dance music which had been popular in Great Britain for a decade. While North America may, indeed, be at the beginning of its own dance 'explosion', the movement of dance music styles to the heart of North American rock music culture has often involved a disavowal of the sense that the appropriate place to hear such styles is in the dance club. The term 'electronica', introduced to describe the electronically based club music newly popular among North American youth, seems more and more like a label for music designed for quiet contemplation or concert-like performances.

The stable fragility of dance club culture

In his history of swing music, David Stowe (1994) wrote about the tendency of swing fans in the 1930s to become connoisseurs of big-band music, comparing solos and musicians with almost as much fervour as they would master new dance steps. Even as they appear to be losing themselves in physical abandon, dance music fans are often notoriously judgemental, quick to announce the passing of a style and denounce the growing commercialisation of dance music culture overall. Dance clubs have survived and mutated over the past forty years, despite the claims, which have come in regular intervals, that dance music is dying, the victim of too much hype or of an invasion by club-goers who are drawn to the fashion rather than the music. As thousands of dance clubs and hundreds of small dance record companies come and go, and as dance music styles themselves are made obsolete or fragment into a dozen variations, the fragility of dance music culture often seems all too obvious. In fact, it might be argued, venues for live rock performances and radio formats for broadcasting popular music have undergone just as many changes over the past four decades. From the twist clubs of the early 1960s through the 'speed garage' scene of the late 1990s, dancing in public places, to records played by a deejay, has been a consistent and vital feature of youth culture.

Further reading

Writing on dance is scattered across a range of fields and academic disciplines, but three important strands in this writing are worth noting. One consists of historical studies of particular dances, such as Jim Dawson's *The Twist: The Story of the Song and Dance That Changed the World* (London: Faber, 1995), Marshall and Jean Stearns' *Jazz Dance: The Story of American Popular Dance* (New York: Da Capo, 1995), and Marta E. Savigliano's *Tango and the Political Economy of Passion* (Boulder: Westview Press, 1995). A second strand consists of work, much of it very recent, in the field of dance studies. The anthology edited by Jane C. Desmond, *Meaning in Motion: New Cultural Studies of Dance* (Durham and London: Duke University Press, 1997) is perhaps the best of these collections. Finally, the last few years have seen an explosion of writing on rave and house music culture, mostly in the United Kingdom, best exemplified by such books as Hillegonda C. Rietveld's *This Is Our House* (Aldershot: Ashgate, 1998) and Jeremy Gilbert and Ewan Pearson, *Discographies: Dance Music, Culture and the Politics of Sound* (London: Routledge, 1999).

8 World music

JOCELYNE GUILBAULT

Attempts to define the label 'world music' – or those categories to which it is linked, such as worldbeat, ethnopop, New Age, *sono mondiale*, and *musique métisse* (hybrid music) – have long been marked by contradiction and controversy. It may be noted, for example, that the geographical reference to 'the world' which the label suggests has been defined in the narrowest of terms. World musics are taken to be those musics which come from outside the 'normal' Anglo-American (including Canadian and Australian) sources, and mainly from tropical countries. And because the attraction of world music is seen to lie in its use of rhythm, so essential to the aesthetics of African music, the term has usually been associated with musics from Africa and the African diaspora. With time, however, the umbrella covering world music has become more inclusive. It now covers American, Asian and European musics, albeit those of minority groups within these geographical areas. We may conclude, then, that world music is the product of aggrieved populations, either from third world countries (Africa and the African diasporas), or from disadvantaged population groups in a general sense. Given all this, it is both appalling and revealing to note that, within the global economy of popular music offered on MTV, the United States' main music video service, world music is taken to represent a tiny subculture.

By looking at the ways in which world music has been talked about in promotional and academic contexts, I want to show how world music cannot escape being seen in terms of the power relations of today's music industries. I will then offer a contrasting account of world music, drawing on ethnographic studies of calypso and soca, with particular attention to the musical practices of the superstars associated with this music. As this study will argue, world music should not be seen as simply oppositional or emancipatory. Neither, however, should world music be viewed as merely the result of cultural imperialism or economic domination. To understand world music fully, we must look at its place within the complex and constantly changing dynamics of a world which is historically, socially and spatially interconnected.

The selling of world music

In strictly musical terms, world music is usually described as the blending of modern and traditional musics. These are usually associated with, respectively, the musics of the first and third worlds. In graphic terms, as scholar Tony Mitchell (1993) has noted, this fusion of the modern and the traditional is often symbolised in the design of record jackets. One side of the record sleeve will offer a Western look, showing the artist wearing clothes of the first world. The other side will offer a more exotic view, usually by showing the artist in non-Western clothes, often surrounded by mystical symbols or landscapes typically associated with faraway lands. This type of record sleeve design recalls claims made by scholars of post-coloniality, who have noted the ambivalence inherent in stereotypes of the Other. One finds, in these graphic elements, a simultaneous sense of identification with, and estrangement from racial and geographical Otherness.

At the linguistic level, world music is habitually taken to mean 'not in English', with translations of lyrics frequently included in the liner notes of recordings. In advertisements, world music is often referred to as dance music, as a thrilling source of unusual and original sensations. Read, for example, how 'A Beginner's Guide to Worldbeat Music' published in a Canadian daily newspaper speaks of calypso: 'Carnival music from Trinidad provokes the Caribbean's dirtiest dancing. Sweaty, ecstatic fans jam and wine and wave towels in the air' (Feist 1994). At other times, the reader is even invited to experience such dances: 'Yes, it's time to boogie to a new beat; not rap, rock, reggae, or disco. Try gyrating those hips to soukous, rai, juju, or zouk. But be forewarned, these global sounds are seductive and addictive . . .' (Wentz 1991). In record stores and music magazines, 'world music' has displaced the older label 'international music', as the category under which musics from third world countries are classified. At the same time, 'world music' is seen as the outgrowth of an evolutionary process which has enriched non-European musical styles.

Writings on world music have grappled with the difficulties of defining this new category. Everyone seems to agree that world music cannot be defined in clear and consistent terms, and that it remains elusive as a genre or category. Nevertheless, it has been constructed as a genre. It has its own sections in record stores, and is the focus of its own magazines, recording labels and advertisements, its own festivals, radio and televison programs, and so on. World music, we may conclude, has been institutionalised within the music and media industries.

It is instructive to look at the ways in which the category of world music has been used to include and exclude some population groups. If world music is associated with non-Anglo-American sources, and, more specifically, with tropical countries and cultural minorities, does this mean that world music is the exclusive product of certain territories and spaces, of specific racial and ethnic groups, of particular classes of people? What becomes clear is that the use of this new category tells us little about what it is meant to 'contain', and much more about the perspectives of the people employing the category. These perspectives are informed by a Euro-American, postcolonial vision. The various ways in which world music is marketed in the west – as exotica, quality art-rock, dance crazes, musical for mystical mind-expansion, scholarly folklore – all presume an Other with rather specific characteristics. That Other is not from here (that is, not marked by Northwestern Euro-American origins or influences), exotic (in the sense of unusual), sensual (in its connections with dance), mystical (in its philosophical dimension), and attractive.

On the whole, one may conclude that the label 'world music' presumes a number of things: (a) a sense of geographical space as consisting of stable, bounded territories; (b) a corresponding sense of cultures as homogeneous and belonging to particular locales; (c) a notion of race which sees it in terms of fixed biological and musical characteristics; and (d) the sense that all those participating in this phenomenon must be disadvantaged – socially, economically, or otherwise – whether they be Africans, members of the African diaspora, or minorities of Europe and the Americas.

Controversies over world music

Of the many issues which arise within the production, marketing, distribution and consumption of world music, one of the most controversial concerns the ways in which local, national and racial identities are being defined through musical fusion. From one perspective, world music may contribute to a loss of identity on the part of the people it is meant to define through musical fusion. By causing musicians to abandon forms of music rooted in longstanding cultural traditions, in the interests of commercial profit, the global music industry is seen as a force for cultural imperialism, bringing about the homogenisation of musical cultures throughout the world. From another perspective, however, world music is regarded as an opportunity for musicians to offer resistance to the dominant Anglo-American culture and its institutions. Through its fusion of forms within new, eclectic combinations of musical elements from around the globe, world music is seen as defying the limits of national boundaries and the exigencies of the music industries.

The key concept in these controversies is that of appropriation. This term, which refers more often than not to the appropriation of third world musics by people working in the first world, implicitly pits the people of the first and third world countries against each other, and raises a series of ethical and moral issues. These issues include the use of cheap labour in the hiring of musicians without due payment for their talents; the exploitation of human and artistic resources without proper acknowledgement and the appropriate payment of royalties; and the censorship of elements seen by the creators of music as essential to the meanings or identities of the songs in question. Typically, instances of musical appropriation are seen as rooted in a lack of personal ethics on the part of musicians and others. As has often been pointed out, however, media imperialism is not perpetuated by musicians on their own, but is part of the cultural hegemony of the West built into the structures of the global music industry.

In the actual production of music, musicians associated with world music often run into obstacles in attempting to obtain the sort of mix required by their music, both in the recording studio and at live performances. These obstacles may be described in terms of the ways distinct musical sensibilities compete with each other. In the mixing of mainstream music, the tendency to highlight certain sounds or specific instrumental lines often takes precedence over other ways of thinking about sounds. In other cases, non-Western music is recorded with less attention to processes of mixing and arrangement, in response to the belief that the perceived authenticity of such music constitutes one of its main attractions for Westerners.

The new combinations of sound and practices which one finds in world musics, and the fusion of musical elements that often result, have led to important debates over the new aesthetics at work here. To what extent, it is asked, are developments in world music judged according to their compatibility with Western definitions of music? Might the aesthetics of world music be better evaluated using such concepts as that of pastiche, which acknowledge the loss of referentiality in a postmodern, global culture? Does the process of mixing various elements together in new musical contexts challenge the epistemological limits of those once-dominant aesthetic theories inspired by classical, European models?

While so many views of world music focus on the processes of loss and disorientation which are seen to mark it, or on the cooptation, deception, or confrontation which surround it, world music is also seen by some as a context in which musicians may mount a resistance to Anglocentric musical hegemony. It is sometimes claimed, for example, that when musicians working within world music use new, eclectic combinations of musical elements from around the world, they are defying the constraints of national boundaries and the exigencies of the mainstream music industry. Similarly, the appropriation of new technologies by musicians from third world countries is seen as giving them greater independence from the recording studios of first world countries, and an enhanced capacity to experiment musically. For some observers, musicians working within world music may even have the capacity to turn national, minority cultures into global majorities with significant economic, political and social potential.

In this respect, the transnational and transcultural interactions which mark world music are seen as having a positive effect on local cultures. They are said to have contributed, for example, to the revitalisation of certain local genres, and to the emergence of a new breed of entrepreneurs who are able to take advantage of the growing popularity of world music. At the same time, world music in a general sense is seen as having made possible new sorts of alliances, both through its aesthetics and through the various practices which surround it. The production, marketing, distribution and consumption of world music may all be interpreted as evidence of openness to the Other, as part of processes by which racism and intolerance will be discredited and musical sectarianism attenuated. In this respect, many musicians involved in world music present themselves and are perceived as social and political activists, a role which they fulfil as a function of their activity as musicians and may also, on occasion, adopt as an explicit personal objective.

It is not the intention of this chapter to choose between the pessimistic and optimistic accounts of world music offered here. What is clear, however, is that these issues continue to be formulated in terms of power relations and territorial divisions. World music is seen as involving both first and third world countries, and these in turn are perceived as distinct entities. They are physically distant from each other, and opposed to each other within relations of inequality, relations which mirror the broader pattern of inequalities between North and South.

World music in practice

The issues which surround world music cannot be considered in isolation from the world system of which this music is a part. In this section, I propose to look closely, not at local but at localised practices of musical production and consumption. More specifically, I will look at calypso and soca superstars of the English Caribbean, and at the ideologies, lifestyles, activities and networks that circulate between their countries of origin and their host countries. Caribbean superstars, and the musical practices associated with them, will be examined from an explicitly transnational perspective. Indeed, most superstars of the Caribbean move so frequently and with such familiarity between their society of origin and such places as Toronto, London or New York, that it becomes difficult to identify where they belong. Regardless of where their permanent homes might be, their lives are stretched across geographical, cultural and political borders. Within this context, it can be argued, Caribbean superstars live as transnationals.

To speak of Caribbean superstars as transnationals is to emphasise that their subjectivities and their identities, their actions and their commitments, are embedded in relationships that connect them simultaneously to two or more nation-states. These artists must be seen in terms of the increasing internationalisation of capital, the restructuring of production processes and the resulting disruption of local economies. Most importantly, this leads us to consider the ways in which Caribbean superstars, as transnationals, are changed by the transnational nature of their activities, just as these activities themselves will alter both the artists' original nation-states and those nation-states in which they might now live.

The term 'transnational' is not new. In his book *Transnational Diasporic Citizenship* (1997) anthropologist Michel Laguerre notes that it was first used in 1916, with reference to what was then called 'transnational America'. The term was meant to signal that immigrants in the United States were not the only ones transformed by the process of migration. Their countries of origin, and not simply the host countries which received them, were transformed as well. The term transnational is used here, not in reference to musical practices which are the same everywhere, but to designate those practices which cross the borders of nations, nation-states, or other traditionally circumscribed spaces. The term is meant to suggest that ideas about world music which are built upon the rigid dichotomy of first and third world countries – themselves thought of as occupying different locations, distant from and in opposition to each other – are not adequate to account for the complexity of all those population groups and musical practices dubbed 'world music'.

The present-day transnational character of Caribbean artists must be seen in terms of the specific historical circumstances from which these artists have emerged. These artists are part of a tradition of migration, one which has been woven into Caribbean lives for over a century and a half. In the case of Trinidad, for example, the colonisation period, followed by decolonisation in the 1960s, the restructuring of the local economy, and the ongoing attempt to redress things since the fall in oil prices in the 1980s, have all provided a context in which many Trinidadians, including artists, have emigrated. This emigration may be seen as both response and resistance to their marginal positioning within the global economy and, in the case of musicians, within the global music industry. Transnational practices, however, have not been nurtured solely because of affective ties, cultural practices or lingering political attachments which join emigrants to their countries of origin. Racial discrimination, as well as the dominant emphasis on ethnic identification in those countries where Caribbean diasporas have tended to settle (as reinforced through policies of multiculturalism, for example) have provided serious incentives for maintaining ties with home.

Within this context, Caribbean superstars have developed complex networks of transnational relations and activities. These are articulated as much through the production of their music in recorded form as through the distribution, marketing, live performance and consumption of this music. In this respect, the production of a typical album by the calypsonian Arrow offers a telling example. Arrow is a calypsonian from Montserrat, who does most of his recordings in New York City, often at the recording studio owned by Charles Dougherty, a musician originally from Jamaica. For each track, Arrow often uses two arrangers who do not necessarily originate from the same country – one for the brass parts and another for the rhythm and bass arrangements. Regularly, Arrow asks Trinidadian Leston Paul, one of the most sought-after arrangers in the English Caribbean, to fly to New York to write and direct the horn parts for his songs. Arrow always uses a mix of musicians from the United States and the Caribbean to produce a special sound in the horn section. As Leston Paul explained to me,

> [Arrow] always uses an American horn section, especially with the trumpets and trombones (expensive! you know), and on sax, you could always use a West Indian . . . but for that punch there, that, sometimes what we do, we use an American for the first [trumpet], a West Indian for second trumpet, and an American trombone . . . We're looking for that high pitched sound. And also, we need to lock into the soca groove. Because the music is also a groove, you know. Sometimes, if we would use all Americans in that horn section, it would sound a little too funky over the rhythm and it would sound a little alienated. We need to get that swing feel that we still do, a kind of dance feel. So we mix [the musicians].

The fully developed transnational practice represented in the production of Arrow's recordings, as described above, is not unusual. The production of Caribbean recordings typically involves musicians from different nationalities and territories, and various stages of the recordings often take place in different locales. The recording of the rhythm section may be done in one studio in Trinidad, and, while the horn section and final mixing may both take place in New York, they may be done in different recording studios.

The transnational practices of superstars of the English Caribbean are not limited to North–South axes. In fact, polylateral exchanges among third world countries in the new world, as well as those occurring among southern third world countries and the nations of Asia have helped create a growing commercial market. Among the eighty artists with whom Leston Paul works annually, we find a Japanese group for whom he wrote arrangements. Kenny Philips, an equally famous musician from Trinidad, has written arrangements for calypsonians from St Kitts, Antigua, Dominica, St Lucia, Barbados and Grenada.

We can conclude from all this that Caribbean superstars follow agendas which are explicitly transnational, and which both shape and are shaped by the global music industry. Artists strive to increase their options and revenues and to enhance their social status, both locally and internationally. At the same time, they draw on their pool of relationships to increase their knowledge of the international scene, so that they can respond to – and resist – the demands of the global music industry.

By facilitating the flow of ideas and products across the boundaries of nation-states, the transnational practices of Caribbean superstars have played a key role in reinforcing ties between emigrants and those who remain in their countries of origin. In 1995 alone, the five-time calypso Monarch Leroy Calliste, known as 'Black Stalin', did over one hundred shows, spread over the Caribbean islands, Canada and the United States. A better idea of what this entailed can be gleaned from Black Stalin's own description, in 1995, of the shows taking place between February and early September of that year:

> Immediately after Carnival in February, I went to Antigua for a concert organised by the Ministry of Education; a few days later, to Barbados, for the Spektakula yearly show which features 'the cream of the Trinidad carnival calypso'; in April, back to Antigua for the Spektakula second anniversary show. This show in Antigua was on Saturday night and then I played the Sunday night in Brooklyn for Isaac MacLeod's birthday, the guy that organises the shows at the Madison Square Garden; then I went back to Trinidad and, at the end of April, I went back to New York for a Chutney show with Sundar. We did that on Saturday night and the Sunday, I went back to Trinidad and did the celebration show in San Fernando for Black Stalin Victory [Black Stalin won the calypso Monarch competition that year]; then I went to St Lucia for one night, which was Sandal's hotel

[ownership] first anniversary – a private show that night. Then I went back to Trinidad for the sixth of May and did the Chutney final in San Fernando. Then, I went back to New York for Mother's day [third week of May]; for that, we try to bring artists from all the Caribbean islands . . . So not everybody fall on the same night. [In connection with that], this year, I did three shows in all, one in Madison Square Garden and two in Brooklyn. After Mother's Day, I stayed in New York and did two concerts in Atlanta for the Peach Tree Carnival in the last weekend in May; well, I miss out something, you know . . . The show, the end of April at the SOB [Samba of Brooklyn] one night; I did that the day before the New Orleans show; then I went back to Trinidad and then another show in Barbados for a private organiser; then in Toronto for a one-night show for an independent organiser mid-June – a show which we usually do the eve of Confederation Day on the first of July. Then I went to St Thomas with Sparrow for a one-night show, on a Friday; and then on Saturday, for a beauty parlor in Miami at a yearly show organised by a friend of mine. After that, I went back to Trinidad, and around the 6th of July, I went to St Vincent for a celebration of Becket's twentieth anniversary [as a calypsonian]; then on the 16th of July, there was the Central Park concert, a summer stage concert; then I had one Family Day show organised by the Police Department in San Fernando, and one show organised by the government for Emancipation Day on the lst of August at Laborie [in Trinidad]. And then two nights for Caribana in Toronto in the first week of August; after that I am flying to New York where the 13th August I have two shows to do, one for Labor Day Festival Committee and another one at a high school in Brooklyn; then on the 25th of August, I am working in Houston for a pre-carnival something they have with the Carnival committee; the 28th of August, I work with Sparrow for the last summer show that the city gives; then later on, I am playing on the 31st for the Soca Chutney show at the Brooklyn Museum; then on Friday night, I am going to do a Chutney jam in Calypso City [in Queens] with Sundar; on Saturday night, I am working for Spektakula at the Rose Bowl in Manhattan for two nights; and on Labor Day, I work at three o'clock in the evening and then that morning I fly to Atlanta for a Family evening show.

Black Stalin sees his touring as 'servicing' the Caribbean communities, wherever they are. As he explains further, '[a] show is like a roti, it feeds people. It is a piece from home. It stays with the people for weeks, for months.' In the process, Black Stalin and other transnational artists like him could be said, over the years, to have contributed to a large extent to the development of pan-Caribbean identity, and also to have given voice to an identity that reflects the transnatonal experience shared by the artists and migrant populations.

For this to happen, though, the key element is 'circulation'. For Caribbean artists to circulate, they must be connected to the entertainment industry on which they are dependent. By facilitating exchange between various nation-states in and outside the Caribbean, the entertainment industry creates a transnational field for both migrants and Caribbean artists. For instance, the artists hired by Trinidadian-owned Spektakula Promotions have greatly benefitted in recent years from the shows it has organised, not only in Trinidad, but also in Barbados, Antigua, Toronto and, since 1995, in New York. By enabling calypsonians and other musical entertainers to circulate among these various locations with the same hit tunes, Spektakula Promotions and other organisations like it can be said to have helped significantly in mapping the experiences of Caribbean communities marked by physical distance from each other. On a large scale, the numerous Caribbean carnival organisations around the world (especially in England, Sweden, Canada, the United States and several Caribbean islands) have been key in furthering the circulation of commonly appreciated cultural phenomena by providing top calypsonians with performing venues.

From the same perspective, those Caribbean music organisations which have taken on transnational dimensions, and on which Caribbean superstars have come to depend on many levels, such as Caribana and the Labor Day festival, may also be seen as important contexts in which the collective identities of Caribbean artists and diasporic populations have been defined, mediated and contested. Through the transnational performances these organisations have promoted, they have effectively contributed to a reconfiguring of social and political spaces. With respect to the Labor Day festival, for example, the authors of *Nations Unbound* remark,

> These public expressions of West Indian collective identity are also the statements of a group making claims to political space in the ethnicised structure of New York politics. Within this milieu . . . eating a Jamaican pattie on the Eastern Parkway assumes a symbolic significance it never had in Jamaica. The annual outpouring of tens of thousands of West Indians on Labor Day, claiming the Eastern Parkway in Brooklyn for their strut in full carnival regalia, is a further staking of political ground. Their ownership of this day has become so complete that now even New York City's mayor and national political leaders like Jesse Jackson take their place at the head of the parade. (Basch et al. 1994: 74–5)

The transnational fields in which Caribbean superstars operate, which encompass many different nation-states, are the contexts in which these superstars construct, contest and reformulate their own identities and strategies, interacting with the hegemonic processes operative in the various locations in which they live. The transnational experiences of Caribbean superstars are evident in the artistic decisions they make in creating their music as much as in the subjectivities and identities which result from the networks of relationships through which they are connected simultaneously to many nation-states. Their transnational experiences shape their musical creation, not only with respect to the choice of topics for their songs – which must take into account the political, economic, social, etc., experiences of the various population groups with which they interact – but also their choice of sounds, tempi and musical instrumentations. These become coterminous with the various soundscapes and ideoscapes which weigh upon them as artists and lead them to make certain decisions and take particular actions.

The following musical examples are offered to show how musicians participate in the global industry and in particular, how calypsonians respond to and resist some of the tendencies within that industry. They are also meant to demonstrate how the music of these calypsonians is marked by the influence of, and interaction with, a wide variety of musics, not all of which come from the so-called mainstream.

The first song, 'The Doctor Daughter', was released in December 1995 for Carnival 1996 by Lord Kitchener, a legendary and most revered figure, a pillar of the calypso artform on a par with Mighty Sparrow, who is now seventy years old and still active in the music scene (Lord Kitchener, 'The Doctor Daughter', *Incredible Kitch,* JW Productions, 1996). The song illustrates how the use of global music industry's latest 'sound' on the veteran calypsonian's last album has not prevented him from remaining faithful to the traditional format of calypso song. In 'The Doctor Daughter', the audible use of the drum machine, synthesisers and, more generally, of particular timbres in fashion in recent years, is combined with the characteristic verse/refrain and sensually oriented subject matter of calypso lyrics. The call-and-response arrangement is distributed in typical fashion among the various parts of the brass section and between the song-leader (Kitchener in this case) and his choir of responders.

The second example, 'Out de Fire', is also by a veteran calypsonian, Roaring Lion who, after being away from the limelight for several years, has re-emerged with outstanding success over the past four years with remixes of his old calypsos (Roaring Lion, 'Out de Fire' on *Carnival Special '96: Ringbang,* Ice Records 1996). 'Out de Fire' shows how calypso arrangers are influenced by some of the musical genres most prominent within both the global and local Trinidadian musical soundscapes of the 1990s – genres which, we shall see, do not necessarily come from the usual Euro-American musical centres. Released on a 1996 Carnival Special compilation, the new version of the 'Out de Fire' mixes the singing of Roaring Fire with an arrangement which could be said to be influenced by 'dub' – the internationally acclaimed musical genre (also called dancehall) from

Jamaica, a so-called third world country but recognised world musical centre. The dub influence is evident in an ensemble of characteristics, including the slow tempo at which the song is performed, the use of a prominent bass line, and the sparse and carefully distributed instrumentation in which the rhythmic section is emphasised.

The third example is intended to show how, in their lyrics, calypsonians integrate their own transnational experience and that of a great many members of the Caribbean population. In 'Iron Band Jam', released in the summer of 1995 (*Black Stalin: Message to Sundar,* Ice Records,1995), calypsonian Black Stalin recounts how Trinidadians belong to several worlds, celebrating their carnival and going to hear the 'engine room', that is, the rhythm section of the steelbands in Brooklyn, New York, as well as in Point Fortin, one of the southernmost villages in Trinidad: 'Jean she went back to Brooklyn last year and hear how she boasting, How Trini Carnival she really had a bachanal, Joyce she went with the steelband, May she went with the brass-band, She went Point Fortin for Jouvert, just to hear the engine room play.'

The fourth example features a soca song played at an extremely fast tempo – a tendency in Trinidad throughout the 1990s. Instead of being played, as in former years, at the usual tempo of ♩110 or ♩120, this song – 'Bounce', by Superblue, which won the Road March competition in Carnival 1996 – is here played at ♩144 (*Carnival Special '96: Ringbang,* Ice Records, 1996). The explanations given by West Indians for the fast speed of soca songs in the 1990s are worth recounting, in order to demonstrate how musics outside the Euro-American mainstream may influence each other. The 1990s move towards faster tempi in Trinidadian soca songs is said to have been influenced by soca bands such as Burning Flames, from Antigua, who have been using fast tempi since at least the mid 1980s. In turn, these bands from Antigua are said by musicians from both Guadeloupe and Dominica to have developed their fast speed through the influence of zouk music from Martinique and Guadeloupe. The fast pace of zouk from Martinique and Guadeloupe, in turn, is said to have been influenced by soukous from French Africa, via the close collaboration of zouk and soukous musicians in Paris.

The fifth and final example shows how some of the decisions and actions taken by certain superstars may willingly go against what appear to be dominant trends, through the creation of songs which might be read as resistance or challenges to the demands of the global music industry. Black Stalin's 'Man Out For Change', released in 1995, seems to be doing just that. In contrast with the usual instrumentation, which typically includes a brass section, rhythmic and solo guitars, synthesisers, bass, drum kit, cowbell and conga, Black Stalin is accompanied solely by an acoustic guitar and a drum beat produced by a drum machine, and he sings, at an unhurried pace (♩76), a text which seems to be produced more for listening than for dancing. This kind of calypso song is rare in the 1990s.

From these examples, we could say that, as a whole – and with few notable exceptions – the musical styles and cultural tastes developed by and reflected in calypso and soca recordings by Caribbean superstars articulate a transnational social, musical and political field that spans and bounds the experiences and attitudes of Caribbean people living in Caribbean nation-states and elsewhere.

World music in strife

What is missing from the ethnographic account offered so far is consideration of the various struggles at the heart of the transnational practices of Caribbean superstars, and the double-edged implications these practices may have, both at home and in the various nation-states in which these artists are active.

In many ways, the transnational practices of Caribbean superstars could be said to help reinforce the very system which forced them to adopt these transnational practices in the first place. Through their transnational activities and their numerous concerts, calypsonian artists give the impression of a far healthier Caribbean music industry than is actually the case. (Most Caribbean musicians must still hold down a day job to earn their living.) As a result, these artists do not lead the people living in the home societies to reckon with the needs of musicians on a local level – through, for example, the enforcement of copyright laws, or through the institution of regulations governing artists' working conditions (in terms of salary or adequate working spaces). As a result, musicians continue to be forced to live as transnationals in order to make a living. Moreover, as mentioned above, in the process of doing so they contribute to reinforcing the hegemonic cultural and economic practices of those nation-states whose domination has forced people to emigrate or become transnationals. They do this, for example, through the rental of their facilities.

At the same time, while transnational musical practices have allowed the calypsonian superstars to resist subjugation in their host and home societies, these practices, in a sense, perpetuate this subjugation and the resulting need to live as transnationals. Because they allow musicians to move between host and home societies in emotional, cultural and material terms when the conditions in either place become intolerable, transnational musical practices diminish the likelihood that calypsonians will collectively challenge either system.

At another level, Caribbean superstars, as transnationals, are dependent upon Caribbean diasporic populations and organisations for their living, particularly insofar as record sales and concerts are concerned. Apart from the affective, cultural and political ties that bind them to many members of these diasporic populations, calypsonian artists need to maintain their social relationships with many of these people in order to continue their transnational practices. This means, for example, regular phone calls and other forms of interaction. At the same time, these artists help to perpetuate that longstanding protectionist system through which, in order to receive recognition, an artist must win (or at least participate in) a calypso competition in the home societies. Thus, a migrant artist who is relatively successful in a nation-state other than the home countries, and who may be appreciated for the moral and economic support he or she may provide to Caribbean artists from home during their transnational performances, is not extended the same opportunities to perform at home. This system is reinforced within diasporic populations, meaning that Caribbean transnational organisations usually invite only calypsonian superstars from 'home' to perform in their concerts.

While Caribbean artists have, on occasion, made strides in helping to reorder social and political spaces – for example, during the aforementioned Caribbean carnival on Labor Day in New York – they have not always been successful in their efforts to be heard, taken seriously, and respected. More often than not, they have been engaged in an ongoing struggle against some of the longstanding stereotypes about Caribbean communities and individuals. Ethnomusicologist Anne-Marie Gallaugher (1995) has observed that the mainstream press in Toronto, Canada, reports on calypso and Caribana in ways that prevent the history and identities of people involved in these practices from getting through to mainstream culture. Caribbean cultural forms are often reduced to tourist commodities, talked about in terms of the millions of dollars which Caribana has injected into the city's economy.

In this section, we have offered concrete examples of the ways in which the transnational practices of calypsonian superstars, in such contexts as New York, might be seen as emancipatory. These practices have helped claim political spaces, and reinforced collective identities in the face of such forces as racial discrimination and ethnic ghettoisation. At the same time, we have observed how transnational artists may also contribute to the reinforcement of hegemonic structures and practices, both in the society of origin and in those nation-states in which these artists operate.

Consciously or not, artists may contribute to the enforcement of protectionist measures, or to the perpetuation of an exploitative system. These tensions are symptomatic of the dilemmas facing transnational musicians in a world marked by clear inequalities and by a complex set of relationships between musical production at the local level and the global music industries.

World music in perspective

It should be clear that the label 'world music' cannot be interpreted solely through the reductionist lens of a Marxist perspective, and that the politics of world music may not be celebrated unconditionally. A Marxist approach will prove inadequate because its basic premises presume a world neatly divided on the basis of clearly bounded categories, a world of homogeneous groups which divide neatly into the dominant or the dominated, of spaces designated as either central or peripheral, of cultures defined as either first world or third world. These premises are now being challenged. There are third world spaces in the United States and Canada, just as there are world centres for music in cultures often considered part of the periphery, as, for example, in Jamaica. Furthermore, those spaces traditionally thought of as centres are being displaced, as the global music industry undergoes a restructuring. It is no longer the case that the best studios are located in London, Paris and New York, exclusively. In the same vein, as we noted above, the usual definition of the international market in singular terms (referring, most of the time, to North/South relations) is no longer valid. Those people considered dominated are not the passive recipients of goods and styles they were once assumed to be.

Having said that, it must be acknowledged that the label 'world music', and the people and products it purportedly embraces, cannot be celebrated unconditionally as the sign of liberatory politics. There are still, within the world music industry, many musicians who are denied opportunities on account of race, audiences who are manipulated to cultivate orientalist attitudes, and musical practices which are appropriated to accomplish ends opposed to those for which they were intended. The use of reggae music in Coca Cola advertisements is a clear example.

The notion of world music stars as transnationals may become a key to our understanding of the socio-political, economic and cultural constraints and opportunities which these stars are confronting at a local and global level. This notion helps us better to appreciate the interconnectedness of people and practices on which the global music industry is built. More precisely, it helps us to grasp how musicians participate in this global industry, by changing it and, at the same time, complying with many of its characteristics. In concrete terms, it leads us to observe how artists, like the superstars we have examined, develop intimate links between diasporic populations, and explains how they may benefit from such links. Through an examination of all these features, we can see how the intentions of artists and the global structures of mediation interact to inform the transnational practices of world music and the fields in which this music circulates.

World music, we could conclude, is most certainly not about a specific repertoire and a specific group of people, but rather about the positioning of particular musical practices in relation to the mainstream. As a label, its appellation may be quite appropriate in referring to the transnational movements of musics and artists and the new alliances, both social and musical, these continually permit. In fact, it may be the label which evokes best the unfixable, by including musics which arise from the meeting of different times and places, from necessity as well as pleasure. While it may offer and invite a wide range of musical experiences, the label 'world music' in and by itself is a reminder of the hierarchy the dominant music industries impose on the music markets they control: by using the indescribable appellation 'world music', they keep at bay any music – and by extension its artists and fans – which falls outside the so-called mainstream.

Further reading

In 'Global imaginings', Gage Averill provides a critical and an incisive analysis of the relation between products with local specificity (such as worldbeat recordings) and global culture industries (in *Making and Selling Culture*, edited by Richard Ohmann, Hanover, NH: Wesleyan University Press, 1996, pp. 203–23). Veit Erlmann's *Music, Modernity, and the Global Imagination* (New York: Oxford University Press, 1999) is a great example of so-called 'world musics' in historical perspective. In this study, Erlmann skilfully highlights how the multi-faceted experiences with the international music industry by several key artistic figures from South Africa articulates not only the profound entanglement of South Africa and the West, but also the legacies of the colonial and postcolonial world. Steven Feld's 'A sweet lullaby for "world music"' (in *Public Culture*, Globalisation Issue, edited by Arjun Appadurai, Millennial Quartet, volume 2, January 2000) forcefully addresses some of the most common problems experienced by the music-makers of so-called 'world music', most particularly in regard to copyright and ownership issues. In *Dangerous Crossroads: Popular Music, Postmodernism, and the Poetics of Place* (New York: Verso,

1994), George Lipsitz offers invaluable insights in a series of essays that addresses in theory and in practice the complex positioning of several non-mainstream popular musics at the cultural, socio-political and economic levels on both the local and international scenes.

Star profiles II

BOB MARLEY, DAVID BOWIE, ABBA, MADONNA,
NIRVANA, PUBLIC ENEMY, DERRICK MAY, THE SPICE
GIRLS

Rock emerged in the 1960s as a way of putting new audiences together, pursuing new cultural dreams, putting music centre stage in people's lives in new ways. It was utopian – which is why sixties pop stars are still regarded so nostalgically; and it was Anglo-American. Since then popular music has been routinised both commercially and aesthetically; new music markets, new music worlds, have been niche markets, with the most significant artists defining themselves against the mainstream. And yet superstars have still appeared, still surprised; sounds still travel around corporate networks in unexpected ways. Bob Marley didn't just help make Jamaican reggae music a normal part of the Western pop diet, he also prefigured the third to first to third world circuit that was eventually christened 'world music'. Abba weren't just Sweden's biggest export they also helped define a new sort of European dance pop culture that was to have unexpected repercussions on both sides of the Atlantic. At the same time, the very transparency of rock commerce fired new sorts of artistic ambition. The importance of, first, David Bowie, and then Madonna, was not so much that they placed themselves in the worlds of art and fashion (though they did do that) than that they made the selling process itself – the making of brand and image – an aspect of their art. Their influence is obvious on pop phenomena of the late 1990s, the Spice Girls, who combined the most old-fashioned glee of the girl group and boy band with the most sophisticated, self-conscious and controlled approach to marketing.

It was against such upfront commercialism that indie rock of all sorts continued to define itself, most confrontationally as punk, most determinedly as heavy metal, most poignantly in the music of Nirvana, and most importantly as rap, the latest form of African–American vocal music which became the most successful musical genre of the 1980s and 1990s, spreading round the new global music circuits in ways which were both dependent on and defiant of corporate ideology. The politics, art and confusions of rap were best voiced by Public Enemy. And meanwhile, under the urban noise of rap another musical revolution was happening: new kinds of dance music meant new cross-cultural alliances; new technologies of production meant a new kind of music maker – musician as engineer, mixer,

deejay; a new dance floor aesthetic celebrated records that were anonymous, wordless. Derrick May is thus the least-known name here but his
music shows the circle turning once more in the ongoing musical trade that
defines pop and rock, between Europe and the United States, art and commerce, machines and emotion.

Bob Marley

Bob Marley was the first star of what came to be called 'world music'. He
was born in Jamaica in 1945. His mother, who brought him up, was black;
his father, whom he hardly knew, was white. Marley grew up in the
extraordinary Jamaican musical culture of the 1950s, to the sounds of
African drumming, Protestant Revivalist hymns, European ballroom
dance, Caribbean calypso and rumba, US rhythm and blues. Hooked into
the networks that linked Jamaican families to diasporic communities in
England and North America (Marley's mother moved to Wilmington,
Delaware, in 1964), part of a local inter-island club and hotel circuit, for
Jamaican popular musicians the local was already the global.

Seventeen-year-old Bob Marley cut his first records (as a singer) in
1962, and formed a vocal group, the Wailers, in 1963. Inspired by contemporary American soul acts like Curtis Mayfield's Impressions, the Wailers
were used by their producer, Coxsone Dodd, as an in-house group to front
whatever was currently fashionable on the local dance floor: cover versions
of international soul and pop hits, ska, rocksteady. Between 1963 and 1966
the Wailers released around eighty singles with enough hits to establish the
group as Jamaica's most successful. In 1966 the group was reduced to a
vocal trio (Marley, his childhood friend, Bunny Livingstone, and Peter
Tosh). The stripped-down Wailers were committed to Rastafarianism and
began working with producer Lee Perry, who added a rhythm section
(Aston and Carlton Barrett on bass and drums) and encouraged the group
to develop their own material and sound.

The Wailers' records from this period helped define reggae and if, initially, this was a Jamaican music (Bob Marley even spent the summer of
1969 living with his mother in Delaware and working for Chrysler) it soon
began to make its mark on British pop too. Chris Blackwell, a Jamaican
musical entrepreneur, who was involved both in supplying reggae records
to the British Jamaican community (through the Trojan label) and developing new rock acts (on his Island label), heard the new Wailers sound and
realised that his two markets needn't be separate. The Wailers were a
reggae act which could be sold to rock fans.

Marley's first Island album, *Catch a Fire* (1973), remains a blueprint for

Figure 8 Bob Marley
© Redferns. Photo: Keith Morris

world music marketing. There could be no denying the Wailers' difference, not simply in the complexity and verve of reggae as against rock rhythms, but in the exoticism of Rastafarianism itself – the locks, the language, the spliffs. But, at the same time, the Wailers' music was made familiar – in the production values, the uplifted guitars, the sweetness of Marley's voice (compare the Island and Lee Perry versions of the same songs). As both a recording and performing artist Bob Marley became immediately popular, his rock status confirmed by Eric Clapton's hit cover version of his 'I Shot the Sheriff' in 1974. As a vocal trio the Wailers soon broke up (Bunny Livingstone and Peter Tosh pursuing solo careers), but between 1974 and 1981 (when he died of cancer) Bob Marley became a global superstar.

His status as a world music figure remains unique. His vocal tenderness, his stage charisma and his skill as a songwriter gave him a rockstar-like personal appeal (Island tried, unsuccessfully, to repeat the process with the African musician, King Sunny Ade). But what made his career special was that he never ceased to be a third world musician. Marley's Rastafarianism meant both that his origins in the poorest part of Jamaican society were never forgotten and that his global appeal wasn't simply as an entertainer – for the Zimbabwean independence movement, for the aboriginal people in Australia, even for white punks in Europe, reggae in the 1970s became the musical form with which to voice protest. Not surprisingly, then, Marley's popularity and influence survived his death. By the end of the twentieth century sales of Wailers' records were greater than ever.

David Bowie

David Bowie's career makes better sense looking backwards than forward. Moment by moment his changes of sound and image seemed opportunist and/or wilful. In retrospect the steps that led from the nervy ersatz-cockney pop singer of the mid-1960s to the suave artist/entrepreneur floating himself (or, rather, his back catalogue) on the New York Stock Exchange in 1997 were quite logical. Bowie is often said to be the musician who most successfully brought arguments and attitudes from the high art world to the low world of commercial pop, but many of his peers were pop artists in this sense (the Who, Velvet Underground, Roxy Music). David Bowie was special for another reason: he was the first musician to appreciate the pop importance of artist as brand, and he understood early on that brand identity (and brand loyalty) did not mean musical consistency: Bowie's dramatic changes of musical style became one mark of his 'Bowieness' and in career terms one can see that his film/acting roles have been as carefully chosen as his stage personae (he is one of the few rock stars with credible acting credits).

As member/singer of various aspiring suburban sixties beat groups Bowie was not obviously marked out for stardom (his 1973 album, *Pin Ups*, is a wry tribute to the bands who did then make it) but he did develop two interests that were to mark his music. First, he became interested in

Figure 9 David Bowie
  © Redferns. Photo: Debbie Doss

narrative/character songs. He explicitly admired Anthony Newley but, in the end, he was less influenced by the British music hall or variety tradition than by the European traditions of chanson and German cabaret (he was to cover songs by both Jacques Brel and Brecht/Weill). Story songs – 'Space Oddity'(1969), for example, Bowie's first big hit – need staging, and this meant Bowie's second, unexpected, interest: performance art. Although it became commonplace later, Bowie was one of the first rock stars to treat a concert as a show, to choreograph each song, and by the beginning of the 1970s he clearly had a different ambition from most of his London peers: he saw rock stardom as an artistic project, and placed himself in the con- temporary American/European art worlds (so that Andy Warhol was as much an inspiration as Bob Dylan, Joseph Beuys as much as Kraftwerk).

Over the next decade Bowie moved from glam rock (*Hunky Dory, Ziggy Stardust, Aladdin Sane, Diamond Dogs*) to white soul (*Young Americans, Station to Station*) to Euro electronica (*Low* and *Heroes*) before settling for a kind of intelligently playful eclecticism (*Scary Monsters (And Super Creeps)*). The 1970s were undoubtedly Bowie's decade, not so much in terms of sales (his 1970s releases have probably sold better as repackages) than as an influence on audiences (the 'Bowie Boys' who haunted British provincial streets in the mid-1970s were the precursors of punk) and artists (as producer and performer Bowie has worked with a remarkable variety of musicians).

While other acts have become icons despite themselves, David Bowie took on the role of 'rock star' deliberately, scripting a part for himself that he could (and sometimes did) equally script for other people. His skill, from this perspective, is as an actor/image manager; he did for himself the work undertaken by other artists' managers, producers and public rela- tions teams. But he could only do this successfully because of his grasp of both pop and technological detail. His most remarkable gift was to capture a cultural moment in a three-minute pop song ('Rebel Rebel', 'Boys Keep Swinging', 'Let's Dance'). And if since those days he's become rather grand, David Bowie remains one of the few ageing rock stars who could still do something surprising.

Abba

The Swedish quartet, Abba, are the most successful ever Europop group. Europop is music made in Europe for general European consumption. It can be contrasted to European music made for particular national consumers (Dutch speakers, say) and to music made in Europe for the Anglo-American market. Europop hits contain traces of their national

Figure 10 Abba
© Redferns. Photo: Richie Aaron

origins and, as a genre, Europop has had international significance, via the dance floor, but, in general, the label is attached to music that denies linguistic and cultural borders in Europe without crossing the Atlantic or reaching American ears. Abba were much less successful in the United States market (where 'Dancing Queen' was their only hit) than anywhere else.

The first Europop hit is generally taken to be Los Bravos's 'Black is Black', a million seller in 1966. Los Bravos were a Spanish group with a German lead singer and a British producer. Their success was a model for both cross-European collaboration and commercial opportunism. Ideal Europop adapts the latest fashionable sound or rhythm to Euroglot lyrics (which can be followed by everyone with a classroom foreign language) and a chorus line (which can be sung in every continental disco and holiday resort). Other early successes in the genre were Middle of the Road's 'Chirpy Chirpy Cheep Cheep', which sold ten million copies in 1971, and Chicory Tip's 1972 hit, 'Son of My Father', the English version of a German/Italian song which had originally been recorded by one of its writers, Giorgio Moroder. But Abba's only serious rival in the 1970s was Boney M, a foursome from the Caribbean (via Britain and Holland), brought together by German producer Frank Farian, who sold 50 million records in 1975–8.

Abba had eighteen consecutive European top ten hits following the victory of 'Waterloo' in the 1974 Eurovision Song Contest; by the end of the decade they were said to be an even bigger foreign earner for Sweden than Volvo. Abba, like Boney M, appealed (particularly through television) to listeners older and younger than the usual club and disco crowd, combining child friendly chorus lines with slick choreography and a tacky erotic glamour that gave them a camp appeal that was a major influence on late 1970s gay music culture. The most successful British pop production team of the 1980s, Stock, Aitken, Waterman, was clearly influenced by Abba and by the promotion processes that supported it. Pete Waterman's 1990s project, Steps, were, in effect, Abba clones.

Abba broke up at the beginning of the 1980s but by the mid-1990s it was clear that their music had a second life. The Australian film, *Muriel's Wedding*, about an obsessive Abba fan, was a global box office hit. The Abba tribute band, Bjorn Again, became one of the biggest draws on the live circuit. *Mama Mia*, a musical of Abba songs, became a long-running London West End show. The continued appeal of Abba's songs isn't simply nostalgic but a measure too of their pop quality, and in this respect Abba clearly transcended the limits of the Europop genre. The group came together for emotional rather than commercial reasons (they were married to each other) and although their producer, Stig Anderson, was important for their success the group wrote all their own songs. Before Abba they were already experienced and successful entertainers – Anni-Frid Lyngstrad (who was actually Norwegian) and Agnetha Faltskog as solo singers, Benny Andersson in the Hep Stars, Bjorn Ulvaeus as a Hootenanny Singer. Their most Swedish characteristic was undoubtedly folk and if Abba followed Euroglot conventions lyrically 'Mama Mia', 'SOS', 'Ring Ring', 'Fernando' – their melodies had a charm, their harmonies a freshness, their arrangements a sheen that was unusual in Europop. As the group became successful they used the banality of the Europop genre to articulate something of the banality of new European affluence. 'The Day Before You Came' remains a classic of middle-class pop.

Madonna

Madonna Ciccone was the biggest pop star of the 1980s and early 1990s, a star who became so well known globally that she is likely to command media interest and record sales for the rest of her life. She was, with Michael Jackson, the first pop star to understand and exploit the video clip as a means of promotion and to ally herself with a global sponsor, Pepsi-

Figure 11 Madonna
© Redferns. Photo: Michel Linsen

Cola. Of all pop and rock acts she has most successfully integrated sound
and image (as a film star and model as well as a musician), and she was the
first post-feminist female icon: there has never been any doubt that she is
in control of her own destiny and rarely any suggestion that she hasn't
loved every moment of her fame.

Madonna's genius was a matter of taste, not technique, and undoubtedly involved an element of luck. Following stage/dance/performance

classes, she arrived in New York from Detroit at exactly the right time. She became a pop diva in the wash of Debbie Harry, who had pioneered the craft of marketing thrift-store sex appeal as performance art, playing out the fantasies of the knowing big sister and the wannabe little sister simultaneously. She became a disco diva at the moment when New York's dance scene was at the height of its glorious ride along the cusp of the mechanical and the soulful, with old rhythm and blues conventions of vocal dirt and desire being deployed by a new generation of engineers who layered the dance floor's background noise with a new percussive subtlety.

One source of Madonna's success, then, was the way she traded off the disposable anonymity of her singles – dance tracks designed to grasp the fashionable moment on the dance floor – with the rococo semiotics of her videos (the most academically over-analysed example of pop culture ever). If, in disco terms, Madonna's voice is a thin instrument – there's not much body in it; her vocal chords don't, in themselves, make enough noise to defy a rhythm track – she has been shrewd in her choice of producers and co-writers. Her hit songs were designed for the dance floor but lyrically captured something more resonant. 'Everybody', 'Holiday', 'Like a Virgin', 'Material Girl', 'Into the Groove', 'Papa Don't Preach': Madonna sang the chorus lines of big city single girl hedonism (the narrative was left to the videos). Her adroitness in writing lyrical lines that changed their rhythmic structures as they unfolded gave her voice the necessary physical momentum while her deftness in constructing melodic units out of conversational stress-points let certain words and phrases float free and, in the end, it was this sense of spontaneity (rather than her elaborately orchestrated videos) that gave Madonna her fan appeal. Add to this the sheer pleasure she took in stardom and it is not surprising that she became an icon. As Robert Christgau wrote of her greatest hits albums, 'their corny, cool postfeminist confidence, pleasure-centred electronic pulse, and knowing tightrope dance along the cusp of the acceptable capture a sensibility as well as an age'.

Nirvana

When Nirvana's writer/singer/guitarist Kurt Cobain killed himself in 1994 he gave the Nirvana story such a dramatic ending that it was difficult not to read it as a new telling of an old rock'n'roll myth. A trio of teenage losers with nothing else going for them defy years of schoolyard mockery by forming a band. The intensity of their determination to be heard gives them a fanatical following first locally (in and around Seattle) and then,

Figure 12 Nirvana's Kurt Cobain
  © Redferns. Photo: Mick Hutson

after signing to the SubPop label, on the national indie circuit. SubPop do a distribution and promotion deal with a major label, Geffen; 'Smells Like Teen Spirit' becomes an MTV phenomenon, and *Nevermind* the album of a generation (netting $80 million dollars for Geffen Records alone). A second Geffen album, *In Utero*, and two years of tours and festivals make Nirvana global rock stars too. Living a life now in which every hedonistic fantasy can come true, Cobain commits suicide, a suicide which gives his anguished lyrics a new frisson (and guarantees that the commercial exploitation of his music will be even more systematic after his death than before).

Before accepting this myth there are two points to consider. First, Cobain didn't kill himself because he was a rock star; rather, stardom was a new kind of pressure – if rock had once been the escape from everyday problems it was now the everyday problem itself. (And from a fan's point of view it was obvious that Cobain's drug problem wasn't a rich star's indulgence but a poor man's despair.) Cobain was the one grunge kid for whom Nirvana couldn't be a site of rock utopianism. He knew how much labour and corporate capital Nirvana's success took. Grunge music as defined by Nirvana asserted the power of noise – whether rhythms pumped up to exploding point, guitar thrash-din, or simply massed chorus lines – over anxiety, over fractured lyrics, hesitant melodies, vocal breaks (in Nirvana's case this often meant Cobain's voice being lost in the rock charge he was himself leading). This could be a description of the indie rock aesthetic generally: exhilaration with a discordant undertow, escape down musical dead ends; the sound of people hopelessly defying circumstance. Nobody in the 1990s captured this sense of adolescent frustration as brilliantly as Nirvana; no group was more loved by its fans.

And this leads to the second point. Nirvana was indeed dependent on the corporate clout of Geffen and MTV for its ultimate success, but it was equally dependent on the cultural community it had built up before anyone was sharp enough to spot their mainstream potential. This network of shops and radio stations and magazines and clubs was essential to Nirvana's sense of themselves as a group (hence the local friends and idols used in their MTV Unplugged session), and if the band came to stand for indie music in the middle of the 1990s, forty years after the origins of rock'n'roll and at a time when everything had become grist to the marketing mill, it was not because of the introspective and/or anarchic nature of their songs (nor, indeed, because of Cobain's suicide – a private matter), but because of their unwavering sociability, the indie sociability that was to take full advantage of changing technology, from home taping to MP3, from fanzine to web site.

Public Enemy

Rap is the popular form which can best claim some affinity with blues. In both cases we find a basically (but not exclusively) African–American music which is initially dismissed by the commercial pop establishment as artistically primitive and socially crude, then exploited by it as a cheap-to-make novelty, and finally essential to it as a genre which is endlessly flexible (on film and commercial soundtracks, for example) and mobile – by the end of the 1990s there were rap acts, usually using their own language (if with Americanisms thrown in) all over the globe. Within a decade of moving from clubs and streets and meeting rooms to radio, television and cinema, rap had become a world-wide way for minority groups to voice their identity. And all this without ever really getting the approval of the American cultural establishment. The virulence of attacks on rap acts, on their politics, violence and misogyny, far exceed anything that has been thrown at rock'n'roll.

Public Enemy were the group who more than any other defined the possibilities – and problems – of rap as a music that is both mass entertainment and minority protest, which uses new technology to articulate long-standing grievances at the racialised nature of the American power structure. Just as recording technology was what enabled the blues to flourish as popular form – people could now hear the unique vocal and instrumental qualities of a particular blues performance; so sampling and digital mixing enabled rap acts to use the sounds of the streets and the media as their performing site. Rap foregrounds words but its art is in the background, in the organisation of the sounds against which the rappers have to make themselves heard, in the insistence of the pulse which drives the rappers on, riding the moment, nervy like graffiti artists, wild style. And even as Public Enemy were giving aesthetic shape to the sheer din of black youth they were also suggesting a politics: black youth as public enemy, the stance which was both simplified and glamorised by the MTV's *Yo, MTV Raps!* and gangsta rap.

Race relations lie at the centre of the history of twentieth-century popular music, and Public Enemy addressed the implications with unusual force, whether in terms of the possibility (or impossibility) of musical separatism or by reference to the old blues dilemma: what does it mean or matter that black rage and suffering are the source of white folks entertainment? But what Public Enemy's records show most of all is that rap is art and not just sociology, craft and not just a spontaneous communal outpouring. Public Enemy itself was formed at Adelphi University on Long Island in 1982: Chuck D and Hank Shocklee mixed shows for the

Figure 13 Public Enemy
© Redferns. Photo: David Redfern

college radio station (where they were joined by Flavor Flav), ran a mobile deejay service and a live rap venue. In 1987 the group was signed to Rick Rubin's Def Jam label, adding Professor Griff as ideologue and Terminator X as deejay. From *Yo! Bum Rush the Show* (1987) to *It Takes a Nation of Millions To Hold Us Back* (1988) to *Fear of a Black Planet* (1990), Public Enemy provided the best samples and slogans, the smartest sense of black cultural sounds and history, the clearest blueprint for rap as the most important popular music of the late twentieth century.

Derrick May

'I want my music to sound like computers talking to each other', Derrick May once told a journalist. 'I don't want it to sound like a "real" band. I want it to sound as if a technician made it. That's what I am: a technician with human feelings.' May was one of a group of technicians from in and around Detroit who in the 1980s developed the dance music that was, appropriately, called techno. This was urban music which didn't so much reflect the ruined industrial landscape of post-Fordist, post-riot Detroit than see through it to a utopian future in which the relics of heavy industry were transformed electronically into a weightless magic motion.

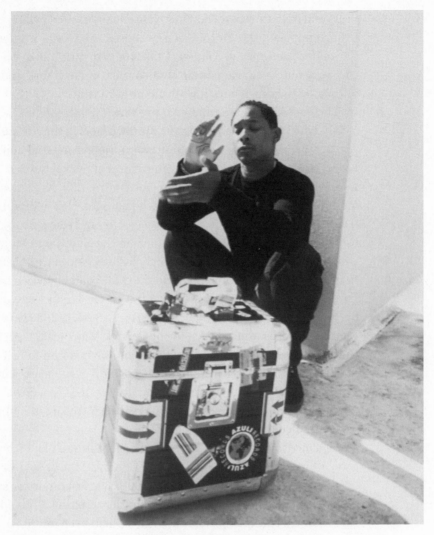

Figure 14 Derrick May
© Graham Proudlove. Photo: Graham Proudlove

New York garage, Detroit techno and Chicago house music transformed the sound of the European dance floor in the late 1980s and helped
shift the centre of gravity of the British music scene, as dance clubs and
clubbers became the focus of youth groups and independent entrepreneurs who had previously been primarily interested in rock. But then
techno in particular was, from the start, a music which defied accepted
genre wisdom. Derrick May and his friends – Aaron Atkins, Juan Atkins,
Kevin Sanderson – got their musical education from a local radio deejay,
the Electrifyin' Mojo, whose shows denied all musical boundaries. They
took their world view from Alvin Toffler's vision of a cyber future, *The
Third Wave.* They made their first musical experiments on cheap synthe-

sisers and cassette recorders. They were equally excited by European electronic pop – Giorgio Moroder, Gary Numan, above all, Kraftwerk – and
the odder examples of George Clinton's futuristic funk. They started
checking out the various new club sounds in New York and Chicago,
putting on their own 'progressive' nights in Detroit.

The contrast between these young musical entrepreneurs and Berry
Gordy, who had founded the Tamla Motown label in the city almost thirty
years earlier is striking. Motown drew on the live musical culture of the
gospel church and black family entertainment; its key session musicians
were jazzmen, part of Detroit's jazz club community; its market was built
up on radio play and touring Motown packages. House producers made
records for themselves – to play as deejays, to cart from club to club. They
were neither musicians nor performers in the traditional Motown sense
and their community existed only in their clubs. And yet, ironically, techno
flourished because it could travel on the trade routes between Detroit and
Europe that Motown had helped establish, not just in its 1960s pop heyday
but also in the 1970s, as an aspect of Northern Soul. In 1988 Northern Soul
veteran Neil Rushton heard some of Derrick May's local Detroit releases
(under the name Rhythim is Rhythim) and invited him to Britain; liking
May's unreleased tracks even more, Rushton went back with him to
Detroit to put together a compilation: *Techno! The New Dance Sound of
Detroit*. One track, Kevin Sanderson's 'Big Fun' (recorded by Inner City)
was an immediate British top ten hit.

As dance music's best British chronicler, Matthew Collin, has written,
garage, house and techno music shared a premise: the use of technology to
heighten perception and pleasure. In late 1980s Britain drugs, specifically
Ecstasy, were used to the same end, and the resulting Acid House scene
broke down cultural boundaries which had been in place since the
rock/pop split of the early 1970s. A new generation of indie bands – the
Shamen, Primal Scream, Happy Mondays, Prodigy – were inspired equally
by techno and rock'n'roll, and rave culture emerged as a remarkable synthesis of the various subcultural politics of pleasure – hippie, punk, dance.
One track always cut through the confusion: Rhythim is Rhythim's
'Strings of Life', Derrick May's instrumental classic which is, despite itself,
as soulful as anything that has come out of Motown.

The Spice Girls

The Spice Girls were Britain's biggest pop phenomenon of the 1990s and,
more surprisingly, the most successful British teenpop act ever in the
United States, rapidly topping both singles and albums charts there in

Figure 15 The Spice Girls
© Redferns. Photo: Mick Hutson 9619

1997 with their debut releases, 'Wannabe' and *Spice*. Like most overnight successes, the Spice Girls had actually followed a long and winding road to the top. Victoria Adams, Melanie Brown, Emma Bunton, Melanie Chisholm and Geraldine Halliwell (known in a piece of inspired marketing as Posh, Scary, Baby, Sporty and Ginger Spice) met while scuffling mostly unsuccessfully at the bottom end of show business. They got together to write songs and work out stage routines as a group in 1993; their career took off when they hooked up with a manager, Simon Fuller, who got them a deal with Virgin records and put them in touch with some of London's leading session musicians. By the time they were launched publicly, in June 1996, they weren't just another pop group, they were an ideological package: Girl Power!

In many respects the Spice Girls' story is familiar. They were marketed by Virgin like a boy band (in a tradition going back through Take That and Bros to Wham! and the Bay City Rollers); their songs drew on the even older tradition of the sassy, conversational girl group. The Spice Girls were unusual (though not unprecedented – Madonna was their obvious model) in their cross-gender appeal, and they managed the difficult trick of retaining an individual personality while lightly touching all the bases of contemporary pop and dance music. Their own long considered role in the making of the Spice Girls' sound and image was important here, just as their lasting success confirmed that they were not just some Svengali's puppets – their break with Simon Fuller at the end of 1997 had little effect on their fortunes.

What made the Spice Girls something new in pop terms was their grasp of the now limitless scope of the pop world itself. The scale of their success marked the triumph of the *Fame* approach to stardom; they were followed in Britain at least by a stream of stage school pop acts. And its speed reflected the remarkable pace now of the circulation of stardom across different media – singles on the radio, videos on television, interviews and photo-shoots in magazines, scandals in the tabloids. By the end of the 1990s each of the Spice Girls was famous in her own right, and their solo records seemed more designed to promote their individual names as names than to advance any kind of musical career. And whereas this would once have marked them clearly off from the world of rock (the Monkees weren't the Beatles) now, thanks to dance music, media superstardom seemed quite compatible with club culture. At a time when the most uncompromising of rap stars were routinely courted by Hollywood, and the hippest of Ibiza deejay tracks could reach the general public via the soundtrack of a television commercial, it became possible for the Spice Girls to be an old-fashioned showbiz act and contemporary trend-setters simultaneously. And if, after *Spice*, their music lacked much character and was made only to keep them in the public eye, then couldn't much the same be said of the Rolling Stones?

PART III

Debates

9 Pop, rock and interpretation

RICHARD MIDDLETON

Everyone with an interest in pop has opinions about it – about its meanings, value, effects and significance. But some opinions – those of critics and academics, for example – claim more attention than others, largely because they have access to the public ear; and, actually, surprisingly little is known about ordinary fans' interpretations. Does this matter? Articulate description of musical responses is always rare; but more is at stake here than the familiar 'mystery' of music.

The announcement of the 1994 Mercury Music Award, by a panel chaired by noted pop music scholar Simon Frith, led trade magazine *Music Week* (6 August 1994) to bemoan the involvement of 'egghead academics and journalists who think too much for their own good'. Thirteen years earlier, the first international conference of the recently formed International Association for the Study of Popular Music was greeted with mocking incredulity in a London *Times* feature (16 June 1981), as was the first issue of the Cambridge University Press journal *Popular Music*. There seemed, evidently, to be an obvious incongruity here – high-value educational capital invested in the study of worthless music, rationality applied to the obstinately irrational, articulate discourse to the wantonly dumb; and this incongruity runs deep through the academy's involvement with pop. There are often suspicions that pop is being used. Thus male leftists, with the radical political commitments of the '1968 generation', largely drive the shape of the early waves of scholarship, 'rockist', 'masculinist' and anti-establishment as it is. More recently, 'postmodernist' intellectuals find in 'knowing' post-punk pop a seemingly ready accomplice in their search for a politics of 'identity'. The 'populist' alternative – 'let the fans speak for themselves' – loses its simple appeal once its inversionary logic becomes apparent. For conflicts and intersections of involvement and reflection, pleasure and theory, 'people' and 'intelligentsia', create the very conditions of existence for all interpretations of vernacular music culture.

Mass culture critique and the search for authenticity

A persistent question, both in the academy and on the street, has been whether pop – product of a highly capitalist industry – can nevertheless find ways of expressing real feelings; even if it is made by them, can it stand for us?

The music originates at a time when capitalist society was being significantly re-structured, and much of the earliest writing on pop bears the marks of its roots in 1960s re-configurations of cultural fields and educational institutions which resulted from this re-structuring. Despite the appeals to cultural and political change, however, there is at the same time a debt to older positions, notably those associated with the early twentieth-century critiques of mass culture. In Britain, the influence of the literary critic F. R. Leavis; in the United States, the work of the sociologists of mass society; in Europe, the critical Marxism of the Frankfurt School: all these distinct but complementary bodies of theory lie behind the search for a popular music, and an interpretation of it, that could be seen as escaping the baleful embrace of commercial exploitation.

In post-war Britain, Leavis's defence of 'minority culture' validated by 'truth to experience' and grounded in 'organic community' offered a powerful paradigm. Richard Hoggart drew upon it in order to argue the superiority of the 'traditional' music culture of the working men's club over the 'shiny barbarity' of rock'n'roll. But by the mid-sixties the marker of discrimination had begun to shift, so that 'serious' work, with a capacity for 'inner growth', was now seen by some commentators as possible within pop. Though approved sources – jazz, blues, folk – were still favoured over their adaptations in commercial pop, the way was opened to a politics of authenticity in rock studies, together with a search for musical expressions of community, centred on the new social category of 'youth' (see Hall and Whannel 1964; Hughes 1964).

American writers, while drawing on partly different traditions, arrived at similar positions. Greil Marcus (1977) searches for a music of 'risk' and 'freedom' where 'each individual attempt implies an ideal community'; his account of Elvis's notorious passage from heroic youth to flabby music industry plaything is organised around, not anything so crude as 'selling out' (the vulgar version of this position), but loss of faith. It is this perspective which energised the countercultural rock magazines – *Rolling Stone*, *Creem* – just as the assumptions of 'Left-Leavisism' seeped pervasively into the British pop music press (not to mention some of the early academic musicology of pop).

Against the background of an emergent New Left, the late 1960s myth of rock authenticity shifted its colouring from liberal towards marxisant; Marcuse crossed with the American Beats formed the matrix within which a 'college aesthetic' (in Britain, specifically an art-school aesthetic) developed, moulding musical practice, vernacular theory and academic discourse alike. In a parallel (and inter-linked) move, British cultural studies, centred on Stuart Hall's Centre for Contemporary Cultural Studies at Birmingham, was crossing semiotics and poststructuralism with the theory of hegemony associated with the Italian Marxist Antonio Gramsci to create what became known as subcultural theory.

Despite subcultural theory's new conceptual trappings, the debt to older mass culture critique is clear enough: Leavis's 'folk', classic marxism's proletariat, Marcuse's bohemians and outcasts, are replaced by youth subcultures: teds, mods, rockers, hippies, punks, as subjects of revolution – or at least resistance. The theoretical advance is the use of Gramsci to develop an account of pop styles as neither simply 'imposed' nor simply self-generated but as a form of 'negotiation' over constantly shifting cultural terrain. This was coupled with an interpretation of musical consumption as an aspect of meaning-production: style-elements, mass-produced as they are in their origins, are 're-articulated' to the expressive needs and social contexts of the subculture. The approach stands or falls with the concept of homology (structural 'fit'). But few subcultural studies demonstrate the music's fit, rather than assuming it; those which attempt to often fall into analytical generalisation, vagueness or inaccuracy, a deficiency which is a symptom of the deeper-level problem that, in cultures marked by fluidity and multiple mediations, it is difficult to protect social ownership of cultural forms (see Willis 1978; Hebdige 1979). Punk was the watershed. As the internal contradictions of both music and cultural style burst it apart, so images of socio-musical homology lost credibility (Laing 1985).

In recent years, 'authenticity' as such has also struggled for intellectual credibility, contaminated as it is by romantic wish-fulfilment and political exploitation. Yet models built on a distinction between 'art' and 'trash' or 'mainstream' and 'underground' (and indeed 'pop' and 'rock') still figure strongly in popular discourse. But the authenticity here has lost focus; it marks distinctions but without clear reference to social subjectivity. Arguably, to rehabilitate the concept would require that more attention be paid to 'articulation', less to 'homology', so that the fluidity of subjectivity and social positioning can be acknowledged, and the music's role theorised within rather than beyond the circuits of commercial media processes.

Sarah Thornton's study of dance music 'club cultures' suggests that it is possible to do this. Against the Birmingham approach, she insists that subcultures are constructed through the media, not in spite of them, and are not separable from commercial logics. Retreating from analytical depth, she claims that 'authenticity is ultimately an effect of the discourses which surround popular music . . . [and hence] subcultures are best defined as social groups that have been labelled as such'. As vehicles of 'subcultural capital', they simply mark distinctions, assert hierarchy, claim exclusivity, transferring differentiating mechanisms typical of bourgeois society into youth culture itself. This persuasive picture reveals, though, how thin the concept of authenticity has become. Moreover, something of an older circularity remains – 'As a deep-seated taste dependent on [social] background, music preference is therefore a reasonably reliable indicator of social affinity' – and both the broader determinants of 'social background' and the part played by musical sounds themselves remain relatively obscure (Thornton 1995: 66, 162, 112–13). Thornton's language – 'consumers', 'brands', 'labels', 'niche markets', and so on – suggests something of an alignment between dance music subcultures, and her own ethnographic methodology, on the one hand, and the wider ideology of new-right consumerism, on the other. She is well aware that 'difference' is potentially repressive as well as liberating; yet she seems to shrink from any attempt to connect the new cultural segmentation to broader social forces.

That subcultural theorists have often ignored, or under-estimated the power of such forces is now easy to see, and it also helps to explain the neglect of the most imposing of the mass culture theorists, T. W. Adorno (1990), usually dismissed as simply an elitist snob. True, Adorno's message, at its most sweeping, would reduce popular music studies to nothing more than affirmations of the music's status as commodity-fetish. He re-writes formula (a potentially productive ground for creativity) as standardisation of musical form. He over-reads monopoly, to a point which empirical studies of both industry and consumption show to be unjustified. And he aligns music history to a uni-linear Marxist–Hegelian project of human emancipation which reduces the species anthropology 'upwards' into the perspective of a declining (Middle-European, bourgeois) class. Yet who could deny that the tendential strategies of the entertainment conglomerates and their 'gatekeepers' often approximate to the Adornian nightmare? Any cultural theory of pop's meanings must work with fully open eyes within this horizon, but few have done so.

Grasping the musical text

What do listeners hear when they listen to pop? How do they construe the inter-relationships and meanings of the sounds? The discipline of musicology is the one that should be able to answer these questions. Yet its established methods have not always proved suitable for the task. One of the problems with Adorno is his musicology, which in its method is simply transferred from its classical home and applied (or misapplied) to a repertory with arguably different requirements. This is not uncommon in the early attempts at a musicology of pop – though not always in such an unqualified form (see Mellers 1973). Indeed, a dominant theme in the work of the younger generations of pop musicologists who appeared from the 1970s on, and who were influenced by emergent cultural studies, is precisely the issue of analytical method: how is the pop text to be grasped? – a question sometimes reduced to an attack on the received musicological paradigm tout court (Tagg 1982; McClary and Walser 1990; Shepherd 1991).

Pop is different in many respects from classical music. So there is a need to hear harmony in new ways, to develop new models for rhythmic analysis, to pay attention to nuances of timbre and pitch inflection, to grasp textures and forms in ways that relate to generic and social function, to escape from what Tagg calls 'notational centricity' (that is, the tendency to focus on a score rather than the sounds). Just as important, though, is that at a second level, the methodological problems arise from deeper, conceptual contradictions within the musicological paradigm. To locate music's meaning in its objectively constituted sound-patterns, regardless of its cultural contexts, social and emotional effects, and the bodily movements which accompany and perhaps generate it, is part of a broader tendency within post-Enlightenment bourgeois aesthetics. The trans-historical 'autonomy' of the work; the demand for 'disinterested' listening; the separation of a 'spiritual' from a lower physical sphere of expression; the reification of the 'composition': all fit together to form an ontology which would seem quite to exclude the secular life-processes of the pop song. To listen that way (as traditional analytic method implies we should) expropriates practice for 'art'.

Simon Frith (1996) has argued that 'musicology produces popular music for people who want to compose or play it'; its text is constructed around the interests of production – rather than listening. For anyone who believes (as I do) that this need not be so – that the 'musicologist' should also masquerade as the 'critic', who in turn tries to impersonate the 'fan' – the challenge is to show that analysis can produce an account of responses grounded both in intuition and scientific knowledge.

But if analysts are also fans, they are fans of an atypical sort. The question, 'who, in an act of textual analysis, is the listener?', might prompt as one response an excursion into ethnomusicology, where the problem of how to relate 'etic' (outsider) and 'emic' (insider) perspectives is a familiar one. The issue is that of pertinence (of interpretive code, of analytic paradigm). Often, large-scale contrasts are drawn between Western classical music on the one hand, African–American and pop musics on the other. The former is said to focus on *syntax* ('embodied meaning', 'extensional development'), the latter on *process* ('engendered feeling', 'intensional development') (Keil 1966; Chester 1990). There is a good deal in this – but care is required. Such either/or distinctions are usually suspect, and probably all musical styles mix both approaches in varied proportion. Moreover, the same piece can be heard in different ways: even if a song seems to the analyst (an 'outsider' trying to get 'inside') to fall into a particular category, this does not of itself tell us whether all listeners would agree; and thus we are still left wondering where exactly 'inside' is (or indeed whether it has a single location at all).

Most textual analysis of pop has looked not to ethnomusicology but to semiology – the 'science of signs' – for inspiration, fired by a belief that 'social meaning' is crucial here. Listeners, it would seem, find songs meaningful. The question is, how the music produces this effect. The work that has been done varies in focus and in degree of methodological eclecticism. Certain issues constantly reappear, however: which musical features are the most important; how the features and parts of a song divide up and inter-relate; what exactly is the musical 'text' (a song, a style, a performer's repertory) and how it relates to 'contexts' of various sorts; whether meanings are 'coded' into particular sound-features, or attributed to them more flexibly by listeners; how far the interpretive process is a product of our experience, how far it constructs experience. Philip Tagg's well-known method relies more than most on empirical testing. Tagg reads meaning by, first, substituting discrete elements (a pitch, a rhythm, etc.) in the music to find how this changes the effect, and second, by 'inter-objective comparison' with other pieces in the same or similar repertories; in both cases, a body of respondents is consulted. This works well for dramatically characterised styles, especially those connected with visual images (film music, television themes) – though it can be criticised for apparently pinning down meanings too precisely, with little allowance for effects of context and disputed interpretation. It works perhaps less well for the more predictable and repetitive processes of typical chart pop or dance records, when there are fewer clear 'sound-images' to pick out.

In later work Tagg (1992) has placed more emphasis on larger-scale pointers to meaning: 'style indicators' (norms of the style in question) and 'genre synechdoches' (part-for-whole references to other styles), both of which bring clusters of associations with them. In a not dissimilar move, I myself, drawing on Mikhail Bakhtin's theory of dialogic meaning, have tried to construe musical textures and processes as dialogues of style-elements and their associations, through which a multiplicity of 'voices' speak (Middleton 1995). This is to situate meaning not 'in' the text but at the conjuncture of intersecting (and often contesting) discourses. Interestingly, two of the most accomplished recent interpretive studies, by Robert Walser (1993) and David Brackett (1995), work with methods that stress the importance of discursive contexts. But, as Walser argues, music itself also functions as discourse – just as texts create contexts in addition to being defined by them. Similarly, as analysis starts to accept its proper place, telling one story among many that attach to the music, so music – musical practice – emerges more clearly as itself one branch of theory, implicitly commenting on its surroundings, musical and non-musical.

It is in this sense that dance music might be said to theorise the much-touted 'end of rock'. And in doing so, it may dramatise the possibility that, even though music is certainly everywhere wreathed in meanings, the idea of *musical representation* – the musical text designed to express some pre-existent reality – ties the semiotic perspective no less than the rock aesthetic to a specific form of meaning–production which may now be in decline. If dance textures do tend to evacuate the representational *mise-en-scène* formerly guaranteed above all in pop by expressive sung words, what seems to expand into this space is the gesturing body.

The pop body

Perhaps, though, this body was never really absent. The *physicality* of pop – 'the galvanising, primal joy of rock'n'roll itself' (Carson 1990: 448) – has been obsessively thematised since the very beginnings of the music. The sense that pop brings together, in specific ways, *feeling* and *movement* is often regarded as finding a focus in the performer, especially the star, whose person seems to embody the feelings the music expresses, and whose gestures both incite and stand for the corporeal responses of fans, through dance and in other ways. Paradoxically, however, there has been little serious study of star behaviour from this point of view, or of performance in general; and while the rush of work following the prominence of pop video brought the benefits of film theory to visual analysis, it often tends to miss links to the music (for example, to the 'gestures' structured into the movements of the sounds) and to older forms of (live) performance choreography.

Singing has an importance beyond 'expression' here, since in singing, after all, the body's pulsations are protruded on to a stream of breath. Arguably, though, the body's input extends throughout the music – and in a fashion, according to some, which bypasses the mediations of 'expression' altogether. To Peter Wicke – who rejects the apparatus of semiology and elevates 'sound' above form – it is a question of 'the *collective* presentation of emotions, postures and gestures'; 'the most important thing here are "structures full of movement" . . . [the music] is not a sign of something beyond itself but stands for something by itself, it is the mimic presentation of movements, patterns of movement, scenes of movement' (Wicke

1990: 19; my emphasis). Similarly, Walser (1993: 45) describes moments when 'the music is felt within as much as without, and the body is seemingly hailed directly'. But if, as John Shepherd (1993) argues, the movements of sound as such constitute a site of exchange between interior and exterior, where the material sociality of subjects and their bodies is negotiated, the problem becomes that of specifying what is distinctive about pop – and this in turn asks questions about how 'direct' the body's 'presentations' can be, if the mediatory codes inscribed in particular cultural instances are taken into account. This demands, surely, a theory of musical gesture grounded both in the spectrum of 'natural' rhythms which are all around and within us (including body-rhythms), and in the culturally mediated practices of specific musical traditions.

Such a theory – which translates the musicians' vernacular of 'groove' into a broader notion of rhythm permeating all aspects of musical texture – suggests a 'hidden' semiology, its meanings untranslatable but, precisely, *grasped*. This notion might remind us of Roland Barthes' 'figures of the body', or 'somathemes' – the body's gestures as they work in the music. Barthes' study of musical 'grain', though it says nothing about pop, quickly became canonic within pop studies, no doubt because it seems to offer a way of theorising intuitions of the music's gestural stratum. 'Grain' marks 'the body in the voice as it sings ... the limb as it performs' (Barthes 1990: 188). It is the *surplus* in the interplay of signifiers, moving on the level of what Barthes calls *signifiance*, and opening to the listener the possibility of *jouissance* (the 'bliss' of self-loss – as opposed to the confirmation of identity associated with *plaisir* and effected by *signification* of culturally inscribed meanings). Pop listeners who have been 'lost in music' will know what Barthes is pointing towards.

Unfortunately, Barthes' influence on pop writing has by and large been at the level of generality: vague appeals to 'grain' (often reduced, mistakenly, to timbre); romanticising of 'bliss'. All too often, his limitations have transferred too: the social construction of the body and its signifying practices tend to be neglected, the variable interplay of *plaisir* and *jouissance* is reduced to an opposition, while 'bliss' seems to inhabit not so much the psychoanalytic sphere of the Imaginary as a strangely neutral pleasure-zone free of cultural marks. To challenge Barthes' elitist freedom to locate *signifiance* where he will (usually in modernist, avant-garde texts, while *signification* ('meaning') is left for the 'adjectival realism' of mass-culture products) requires the acknowledgement of an *encultured* body.

This means, above all, a *gendered* body. The analysis of gender codings in pop is an increasingly powerful stream. However, it is one thing to note the social conventions governing male and female roles in pop, another (more difficult) thing to find ways of discussing how modes of 'masculinity' and 'femininity' are constructed in the music itself. Can we connect specific musical styles or techniques to gendered values? Susan McClary (1991), diagnosing patriarchy in Western music as asserting itself through linear narrative and tonal closure (the Law of the Father, rationality triumphant), has explored the ways in which Madonna subverts it: through irony, rejection of linearity, refusal of cadence and 'phallic backbeat'. Robert Walser (1993) connects driving beat and high volume in heavy metal, together with the power guitars and controlled virtuosity, with machismo, but again finds some scope for modulation of this masculine image, especially in androgynous glam-metal. In *The Sex Revolts*, Simon Reynolds and Joy Press (1995) extend a similar reading to the whole of macho 'rebel rock', but they also construct an alternative, in the oceanic, pre-oedipal, 'womb-badelic' bliss of ambient, dream-pop and psychedelia. For Richard Dyer (1990), the contrast with the 'thrusting' 'phallic' beat of rock is to be found in the more poly-rhythmic, whole-body (and hence liberating) eroticism which he finds in disco.

All these writers would, justifiably, refuse the label of essentialism. Yet an implicit binary divide ('dominant masculinity' in its relationship to something 'other') maps their readings to pre-conceived gender positions. Thus, for Dyer, 'even when performed by women, rock remains indelibly phallocentric'. Is such an approach capable of situating the full range of pop textures and structures, and their gender readings – from, say, 'girl groups' to rap? This question is a symptom of a wider problem which eases once gender codings are defined not by a binary 'cut' but as mutually constitutive, giving rise to discursive interplay, multiple gender histories and varied possibilities for musico-erotic pleasure. The idea of Mick Jagger as the embodiment of phallocentric macho desire, of androgynous camp, or of a pseudo-adolescent narcissism, all find equally plausible support from the Rolling Stones' music itself.

Genre, discourse, identity

For any discovery of meaning in music to take place requires first that 'conditions of audibility' are met – that is, that the events in question are classed as 'music', then, as a familiar sort of music, and finally, as a sort whose procedures and values are understood. This is akin to Franco Fabbri's (1982) definition of musical genre: 'a set of musical events (real or possible) whose course is governed by a definite set of socially accepted rules'. For Fabbri, such rules are formal and technical, as one would expect, but also semiotic, behavioural, social, ideological, economic and juridical. It is within this matrix – dense, powerful yet mutable – that understandings of

rock ballad, Britpop, trip-hop, etc. are generated, not to mention the over-
arching symbiotic tension of 'rock' and 'pop' itself. But these categories are
never stable. Musicians, marketing labels and taste publics do not always
map the boundaries in identical ways; and besides, 'a continuous
definitional struggle is going on among the interpretive communities'
(Fornas 1995). This means that rock is best pictured not as a single life-
history, but as the multivalent subject of a permanent dialogue, now (and
to some) appearing as a struggle between alternative genealogies, now
(and to others) as a centre (male, white, rebellious, subcultural) defined
through relationships to a range of Others. Always, though, we can say that
'through its generic organisation . . . music offers people . . . access to a
social world, a part in some sort of social narrative' (Frith 1996) – or in
other words, an identity.

The 'discursive turn' evident here – and in much recent work – has had
several effects. Among them is a renewed privileging of the 'local' – specific
musical scenes and the 'social narratives' embodied not only in their
musical practices but also the ways in which they construct themselves and
are described. This perspective may be seen both as a re-writing of longstanding interests in youth consumption practices, and as a reponse to
postmodern narratives of fragmentation and globalisation. There is a
danger that the moment of consumption is torn from the longer circuits of
music circulation, bracketing both processes and effects of production,
and larger patterns of dissemination. Will Straw's (1991) influential study
of 'communities' and 'scenes', though it pays little attention to the musical
dimensions of genre, does situate local musical spaces within cosmopolitan networks of taste. The old idea of self-authenticating musical subcultures gives way to 'scenes' marked by mobile 'alliances' of musical
categories whose legitimacy is governed by the logics of specific discursive
and institutional practices. The idea that 'particular social differences . . .
are articulated within the building of audiences around particular coali-
tions of musical form' fits many of the patterns of contemporary musical
flow – even if it also seems to evacuate any broader political interpretation
of cultural power.

This shrinking of perspective is hard to avoid for local studies. Barry
Shank's (1994) rich ethnography of the music scene of Austin, Texas
focuses on how a succession of musical styles all cohere round what he sees
as the master discursive figure of the local club scene, 'sincerity'. Similarly,
Tricia Rose (1994) locates New York rap where traditions of 'black cultural
expressivity' meet 'cultural fractures produced by postindustrial oppression'. In both cases, the wider musical world, including the 'mainstream'
(within the location as well as beyond), is present in the story but as audience rather than actor. 'Belonging' is secured through selectivity, and

rather at the expense of the historical dialogues inscribed in the development of the musical styles. When, in the 1980s, Austin 'sells out' to a
growing music industry presence, Shank, committed to 'sincerity', falls
back on the banal explanation of 'commercial corruption'. Rose, taking on
critics of rap's 'repetitions' and 'noise' with appeals to black difference,
reduces two of pop's great tropes to ethnic exclusivity, rather than locating
them within the larger dialogues of modern culture as a whole.

Admittedly, finding the right connecting mechanism between local
and global is not easy. Lawrence Grossberg (1992) offers 'affective
alliances'. These are articulations of 'cultural formations', such as the 'rock
formation', to particular social contexts. The concept is close to Straw's;
but Grossberg's swerve away from *meaning*, his insistence on *effects*, their
'positivities' and 'lines of force', empties the field of agency, and the music
of specificity: 'there are . . . no musical limits on what can or cannot be
rock'. But, arguably, musical identity is always *connected* to the definitions
of genre and choices of historical narrative that people make. Music
history can be construed as a *dialogue*, in which popular memory,
grounded in real distinctions, plays its part. If, for most commentators,
rock'n'roll coheres around such figures as Elvis Presley, Chuck Berry and
Little Richard, things may look different to Los Angeles Chicanos, whose
rock'n'roll hero, as George Lipsitz (1990) points out, was Richie Valens; yet
Valens learned from African–American and country as well as Latin
musics, and his hybrid style produced international best-sellers.

Thus, once within the pop field, all musics, however local in origin,
come under the sway of a particular long-lived discursive formation.
Simon Frith (1996) contrasts 'folk', 'art' and 'commercial' discourses,
which are focused around ideas of 'authenticity', 'originality' and 'popularity', respectively. These operate across all musical categories in modern
societies, forever trying to make musical distinctions. Frith's sociologism –
musical effects are always placed by their discursive and social contexts – is
qualified by his constructionism – music makes available possible identities, constructs audiences, rather than representing pre-existing social
facts; yet the need, consequently, to account for music's specificity, leads
him not only into some surprisingly conventional areas (bourgeois music
aesthetics, for example) but also into textual exegesis of his own. This
rather expert 'musicology' (illuminating interpretations of songs, singing
styles, performance techniques, etc.) jars a little with the vernacularist
thrust of the theory, resulting in a somewhat problematic connection
between 'music' and 'discourse'. This connection is the nub. If music is
always mediated by discourse and institutional placing, these in turn are
mediated by distinct patterns of musico-productive practice. As Georgina
Born (1993) makes clear, in her authoritative critique of 'consumptionism',

to grasp the 'cultural object' that is at issue here as 'a complex constellation of mediations' requires the full reinstatement into theory of aesthetic agency, institutional power and creative strategies.

Modernism/postmodernism

Pop values are caught within the over-arching discursive dialectic of High and Low, which runs the musical field as a whole. (For anyone who doubts that this is still the case, the 1996 'Handel House affair' is instructive. A proposal to establish a museum dedicated to Handel in the London house where he lived was followed by consternation in the classical music world when it was pointed out that Jimi Hendrix had lived in the same house; perhaps he should be commemorated with a plaque as well!) 'Art', 'folk' and 'commercial' discourses all refract and at the same time play into this dialectic, and all originate in that same late eighteenth-century moment when the formulations of cultural hierarchy characteristic of late-modern society began to emerge. But now, according to some, a blurring of the high/low boundary can be seen, symptom of a broader emergent post-modern formation, marked by acceptance of commodity form, valorisation of local, fragmented identities, celebration of ironic surface. Such blurring is certainly apparent on the aesthetic level: compare minimalism and rave, for example; or try to categorise Brian Eno, Orbital, Psychic TV or Glenn Branca – or Freddie Mercury and Montserrat Caballé duetting on the 'operatic pop' of 'Barcelona'; it is also evident to some extent within aspects of production, partly in uses of electronic technology, partly as a result of more thorough commodification of classical music.

There is debate over the exact moment of the 'break' – the end of punk? the beginning of 'dance'? More important, as just remarked, on the sociological and discursive levels, the old hierarchy does still have force. Thus, despite certain stylistic and ideological links across boundaries (between various avant-gardes, for example), classical and pop musics by and large still circulate in different economies, have different uses, target different audiences. Perhaps there is a way to start to bridge the social/aesthetic disjunction, though. Born (1993) has explored the appeal of musical investments in 'culturally imagined community', both global (the pleasures of mass popularity) and local (the pleasures of 'alterity'). Frith's (1996) argument ends up in a not dissimilar place, with an eloquent description of music's power to offer 'alternative modes of social interaction', at once ideal and acted out. Jacques Attali (1985) has described music as a practice capable of pre-figuring changes in political economy. Less excitedly, Antoine Hennion (1990) insists that for pop theorists a sociology of music is less useful than a 'musicology of society'. To the extent that music's socially constructive power is now accepted in cultural theory, the remnants of modernism in Born's vision may be no less important than the reformulation of a debate – between the 'musical' and the 'social' – that has been central to pop music study since its beginnings. It remains, then, to tackle the reconnection of the 'imaginary' and the 'real', if the political promise located from the start in pop, by fans and academics alike, is ever to be redeemed.

Further readings

On Record: Rock, Pop and the Written Word, ed. by Simon Frith and Andrew Goodwin (London: Routledge, 1990) contains a representative selection of pieces in the mass culture critique and cultural studies traditions, including several subcultural theory classics. It also offers a range of more musicological studies, and anti-musicological essays by Hennion and Barthes. *Reading Pop: Approaches to Textual Analysis in Popular Music*, ed. by Richard Middleton (Oxford: Oxford University Press, 2000) brings together a collection of interpretative studies. *Key Terms in Popular Music and Culture*, ed. by Bruce Horner and Thomas Swiss (Oxford: Blackwell, 1999) contains several essays relevant to the subject of this chapter. Simon Frith's *Performing Rites: On the Value of Popular Music* (Oxford: Oxford University Press, 1996) is the most accomplished monograph on popular music aesthetics. Richard Middleton's *Studying Popular Music* (Milton Keynes: Open University Press, 1990) develops many of the arguments outlined in this chapter at greater length. The best single-author interpretative books on pop are Robert Walser's *Running with the Devil: Power, Gender and Madness in Heavy Metal Music* (Hanover, NH: Wesleyan University Press, 1993), David Brackett's *Interpreting Popular Music* (Cambridge: Cambridge University Press, 1995) and Dave Laing's *One Chord Wonders: Power and Meaning in Punk Rock* (Milton Keynes: Open University Press, 1985). Jason Toynbee's *Making Popular Music: Musicians, Creativity and Institutions* (London: Arnold, 2000) is an important attempt to re-validate the significance of creative agency through a notion of 'social authorship'.

10 Popular music, gender and sexuality

SARA COHEN

On a cold winter evening in the mid-1990s a three-piece indie rock band named Kyzer Sozer performed at Liverpool's Lomax venue. There were around twenty or so people in the audience and most of them stood far back from the stage, clustering around the bar with pint glasses in hand and leaving the area in front of the stage quiet and deserted. This did not appear to bother the members of Kyzer Sozer and they launched energetically into a song entitled 'Girls'. The band were well-rehearsed and 'tight' and the song revolved around a strong melody and dynamic variations in volume and pace, beginning with a softly strummed electric guitar accompanied by the deep throbbing beat of a Fender bass and bass drum, and then shifting to a slightly distorted riff-driven guitar sound that built up to a crescendo for the finale. Darren altered his powerful and resonant singing voice accordingly, varying its pitch and timbre. He had a shaved head and wore a feather boa and silver trousers which accentuated the twists of his body as he played the guitar and stretched towards the microphone. Chris stood beside him in training shoes, black jeans and a leather jacket that swung open to reveal a scarlet bra and bare stomach. Her hair flopped over one side of her face and shone as she accompanied her basslines with nods of her head. Sam sat at the back of the stage in a black shirt and purple velvet trousers that were largely obscured from view by his drum kit. There were some claps and a few cheers at the end of the song and when the performance was over the band left the stage and joined the audience to watch the next band. They were neither pleased nor disappointed with their performance or with the event as a whole.

In this chapter I want to consider how a performance such as this one might relate to gender. Rock and pop music are closely associated with gender – with patterns or conventions of male and female behaviour and with ideas about how men and women should or shouldn't behave. (They are also closely associated with sexuality – with men and women as sexual beings who have feelings and identities related to bodily pleasures and desires.) Gender can be studied in relation to all aspects of rock and pop culture, from representations of masculinity in rap lyrics to differences in the activities and tastes of male and female fans of country and western music, but the chapter will focus on live music performance and on so-called 'indie' rock (by which I mean white, guitar-based, post punk bands), using illustrative material on Darren from Kyzer Sozer in order to attempt a more detailed understanding and explanation. Drawing on ethnographic research conducted in Liverpool, the chapter dismisses the suggestion that there might be any natural or essential connection between the performance of indie rock and the biological sex of its producers and consumers. Nor does it suggest that indie rock music reflects pre-existing cultural conventions concerning gender. Instead the chapter examines the way that gender is constructed through indie rock performance. It argues that attempts to explain this process need to take into account not just the performance styles and texts involved but also the relations, events and contexts that shape their form and meaning. Furthermore, whilst rock and pop music have always provided an arena through which issues of gender and also sexuality have been explored, this chapter will nevertheless emphasise how the construction of gender through rock and pop is at the same time constrained.

Gender, performance practice and ideology

Kyzer Sozer's performance at the Lomax can be used to illustrate how the music, image and performance styles of rock and pop musicians may be linked with particular gendered practices and ideologies, and how gender is constructed, performed and embodied through rock and pop music.

Darren, the lead singer and guitarist with Kyzer Sozer, was twenty-six years old and had been performing in indie rock bands since the age of eleven. Since he was sixteen years of age he had also worked on a part-time and largely unpaid basis as a sound engineer in a Liverpool-based recording studio. He and Sam (nineteen years old) used to perform in an all-male indie rock band called Fuzzy Models which had a traditional line-up of two guitars, drums and bass guitar. The band broke up just as they were about to sign a contract with a major London-based company. Darren eventually signed the contract as an individual songwriter and he and Sam decided to form a new band which they named Kyzer Sozer. At the same time Sam also regularly played drums with a local 'cover' band that performed or covered songs that had been made famous by other bands, and he taught drumming in local schools. Darren and Sam recruited Chris (twenty-four years old) to join them as bass player for Kyzer Sozer. Darren had worked with Chris several years earlier when she had spent some time on a work experience placement at his studio whilst completing a university degree course in Band Musicianship. With their manager, Carl, and with other friends and colleagues, Darren and Sam had debated Chris's suitability for the band at great length. She was a guitarist and had never played bass before, but she and Darren got on well and it was thought that they would look good together on stage, and that as a woman and a lesbian Chris would help to create a new and distinctive image for the band. Chris was rather nervous about joining the others just when they had a new publishing deal, and she lacked confidence as a performer and particularly as a bass player, but she was keen to be involved. She, Darren and Sam got on extremely well, with Darren describing the 'bonding' between them as 'tight and telepathic', leading to a 'group consciousness' and to corresponding changes in the band's music and visual image.

Darren's previous band, Fuzzy Models, had been musically proficient and well-rehearsed, performing song-based material that was of medium/slow tempo, melodic and harmonic. Darren and Les formed the core of the band and both played guitar and sang lead vocals. They had been close friends for many years, socialising together on a regular basis. Les had been an electrician for Camel Laird shipyards until he was made redundant in 1995. Darren wrote most of the band's songs, taking the lyrics and basic melody to Les for approval before working on them with the rest of the band. Darren had once taken Les some ideas for a song entitled 'Boys R Us' which he had written after watching a television documentary about transsexuals in India. The lyrics of the song were based around a few sexual terms and phrases that fascinated Darren (including 'fag hags' and 'lipstick femmes'), and around the chorus line 'Boys R Us and I have no need to judge'. Darren was at that time thinking about his own sexuality and about his relationships with women and he found music and lyrics to be the best way of exploring and expressing these concerns. However, Les made fun of the lyrics in what Darren described as 'a slightly homophobic and judgemental' manner, and he said that he couldn't understand why Darren wanted to write such a song.

When he formed Kyzer Sozer Darren began to write new songs and to experiment with different vocal and guitar sounds and production techniques. The sound became, as Darren descirbed it, more 'stripped down' and 'drier', moving away from the bigger and more resonant drum sounds and complex sound production of Fuzzy Models which, Darren now thought, had 'diluted' their songs. The new sound, said Darren, reflected a new honesty in his music-making, an honesty about his feelings and relationships: 'if you are putting your soul on the line and singing with honesty you need to lay yourself bare and not hide anything'. With Kyzer Sozer, he said, 'we all convey the song and are subservient to it'. His favourite singers were those who sang about things with conviction. He wanted to believe them and he wanted others to believe him.

'Girls' was a song Darren wrote to express his love of women and to address the way that his relationships with women, and his attitudes towards them, had changed as he had grown older. The lyrics to the song's chorus were:

> yes these girls are good, these girls are fine
> it's the very thing to make you mine
> from the moment you arrived
> it's the young inexperienced kind for me

The first line of the chorus was accompanied by major chords and a processed string synth that gave it a dated sixties feel and reminded Darren of a James Bond theme tune. He had used these sounds to indicate beauty and voluptuousness. When Darren sang the next line of the chorus his voice became more hoarse. This was accompanied by a shift from major to minor chords and the sound became more raucous and distorted (or 'bollocky' as Darren put it). During the third and fourth lines, however, Darren's voice sounded slightly more wistful and at the end of the fourth line the guitar chords moved from a major tonic to a subdominant major seventh producing a sound that Darren described as 'little boy lost'. The chorus ended with a guitar riff that had a raunchy, punky, seventies feel to it, a sound that Darren described as much more 'powerful' than the preceding sounds, and as indicating 'rock angst'. In one chorus alone Darren had thus used a range of musical sounds and vocal timbres which he had chosen to convey different images of masculinity and to help him explore the kind of man he was or felt he could or should be, and the way he felt about both men and women. He saw the sounds as linking together fragments of himself and his life.

Darren also explored different masculine types through Kyzer Sozer's visual performance style. When he was young he used to put on shows for his family, wearing different costumes and impersonating his hero Elvis Presley, but he said that when he performed with Fuzzy Models, who dressed on and off stage in a casual, sporty, 'lads-off-the-street' style, he could never have dressed up like that. However, when performing with Chris in Kyzer Sozer Darren said that he felt freer to express,

> the feminine side of myself . . . because I don't always feel male, even off stage
> . . . I'm quite female as a heterosexual male and Chris is quite male as a
> female . . . and I haven't got Les from Litherland looking over my shoulder . . .
> it's an honesty thing. It felt right.

Darren thus perceived people as being made up of masculine and feminine selves. As part of Kyzer Sozer he adopted a more feminine and androgynous stage personae in relation to Chris's rather 'masculine' style of dress and posture. He bought a rubber shirt and silver trousers to wear on stage and he considered the pros and cons of wearing make-up. He also began to focus more on Kyzer Sozer's stage gestures and movement and sought advice on them from his brother who was an actor. Later on he encouraged Chris also to change her stage image and become more 'glam', hence the leather jacket and scarlet bra she wore for the Lomax gig. However, it was important to Darren that Sam remained 'the archetypal very heterosexual young lad'. It was as though from Darren's perspective Sam balanced things out so that the band and Darren himself wouldn't appear too feminine or homosexual, and the heterosexuality of he and Sam was reinforced by the way that together with Chris they talked about and ogled women as a band.

The behaviour and interaction of the members of Kyzer Sozer thus shows gender to be a relational category. The on stage masculinity of one male musician, Darren, is constructed in relation to the masculinity of his fellow male and female musicians, Chris and Sam, and also in relation to the masculinity of his previous band as well as to his own off stage masculinity. Male and female images of masculinity and femininity are thus continually constructed in relation to each other, as are images of homosexuality and heterosexuality. Gender is thus a category that embodies social difference and it is constructed through relations and distinctions between men and women, men and other men, women and other women. Darren's comments on the musical sounds and images of Kyzer Sozer also illustrate how gender exists as a set of ideas about men and women and about male and female behaviour. These ideas were explored through the way in which Darren talked about his music-making, through music performance these ideas were also enacted. And through the way in which he stood, moved, dressed and so on, Darren also physically embodied such ideas. Some scholars have found it useful to describe this as a 'performance' of gender that takes place not only on but also off stage (e.g. Butler 1990), meaning by this that in our everyday lives we are continually putting ideas about gender into practice. Gender and sexuality thus appear as part of the many different roles that musicians enact or perform in their lives.

This brief description of Kyzer Sozer and Fuzzy Models shows how gender is a social construct. One of feminism's main aims has been to question assumptions about the natural basis of sexual differentiation. Feminists have been concerned to emphasise that biology doesn't determine the ways in which women and men act and think, and they have used gender as social construction as opposed to the biological categories of genes and sex. They have pointed to the ways in which we are socialised into male and female ways of acting in and experiencing the world. Darren's notions of masculine women and feminine men highlight a difference between men and masculinity, women and femininity, and the different meanings attached to terms such as 'man' and 'woman', 'masculine' and 'feminine', 'male' and 'female' emphasise the fact that these are not biological but social categories, one of the many ways in which people and their bodies and behaviour are classified. There is therefore no natural connection between rock and pop music and the biological sex of the musicians and audiences involved (Frith and McRobbie (1990) produced an early and seminal critique of such assumptions).

In addition, Darren's musical performance did not simply reflect or express a pre-existing male culture. Rather, Darren actively 'constructed' masculinity by producing, through his songs and performance styles, images of and ideas about men and how they should behave (Frith 1990; Taylor and Laing 1979; Negus 1996; Walser 1993). Gender roles and ideologies do not exist prior to music to be expressed or suppressed by it. Rather, music contributes to the process through which patterns of male and female behaviour, and the ways in which we think about men and women and how they should or shouldn't behave, are established. Rock music is not male in any fixed or essential way but actively made as male through social practice and ideology, part of a continual process through which a variety of masculine roles and categories are defined, contested and transformed. In order further to understand and explain this process, however, the following sections will briefly examine some of the contexts and events through which Kyzer Sozer's music was produced.

Gender, genre and scene

The construction or performance of gender through rock and pop music is influenced by, and also influences, specific social and cultural contexts. This can be illustrated by focusing on the particular music genre and scene that Kyzer Sozer were connected with.

As Tagg (1990) and Shepherd (1991) have shown, certain musical sounds and structures and certain vocal registers have become codified as male or female within particular social and cultural contexts so that they signify, to those familiar with those codes, familiar male and female images or stereotypes. Likewise, musical instruments and music technologies have also become codified as male or female (Bayton 1997; Walser 1993; Gabbard 1995; Green 1997; Théberge 1997; Keightley 1996). Within Euro-American cultures there has tended to be a popular assumption that rock music is male culture comprising activities and styles that have come to symbolise male sexuality, dominance and prestige (Leonard 2000;

Gottlieb and Wald 1994). Women have been associated with a marginal, decorative or less creative role within rock culture, hence the popular stereotypes of glamorous women who act as backing singers for male groups or feature on their videos and other merchandise, and girls as adoring fans who scream at male performers. Journalistic and academic accounts of rock and pop have often ignored or belittled the activities of women musicians. Women's authorship and creativity have been denied, they have been judged on their appearance rather than their musicianship, and their music has been wrongly assumed to be naturally different from that composed by men and devalued because they are women. Creativity and control, and the production of music, have largely been associated with men. Music styles and genres are thus seen as gendered and have their own particular conventions concerning male and female behaviour.

Robert Walser (1993), for example, has highlighted the existence of several masculine types within heavy metal. There are bands like AC/DC who create musical fantasy worlds without women; bands like Guns N'Roses who express misogynist attitudes towards women; bands like Bon Jovi who appear as romantic heroes; and bands like Poison who adopt more androgynous and 'glam', 'feminine' or 'camp' styles of performance and dress. These styles express different types of control over women but they don't necessarily reflect any real power on the part of the men involved in making or listening to the music. Rather, they present a spectacle of male power and offer a musical means through which men can demonstrate their manhood. Thus heavy metal, according to Walser, does not simply reflect a pre-existing male culture but actually plays a role in creating that culture through a deliberate 'forging' of masculinity. Metal sounds, lyrics, and visual performance symbolise, through use of familiar codes and conventions, collective images, ideas and meanings concerning masculinity within Euro-American cultures. The electric guitar, for example, as well as black leather or denim stage clothes, and a rasping, throaty singing voice, are all recognisable images and stereotypes of male power drawn upon by many metal performers.

Indie rock culture is also male dominated. In terms of its performers it is probably slightly less male dominated than heavy metal, but during the mid 1990s the vast majority of indie rock musicians in Liverpool were men and most of the several hundred or so bands were all-male. Of the minority of women musicians involved, most were singers and there were perhaps only one or two all-women bands. Audiences for local indie bands who hadn't yet achieved commercial success tended to be predominantly male, and the overwhelming majority of those working in the local music industry were men (Cohen 1991b). The masculine types promoted through indie rock were different from those within heavy metal, with less emphasis on male power and aggression, on blatant misogyny or on heroism and glamour, and more emphasis on 'the lads' and on male angst and vulnerability. Indie rock in Liverpool also featured a strong emphasis on song and melody rather than on rhythm and discord or on power chords and feedback, and the male vocals were generally not deep or rasping but relatively high-pitched and thin, reedy or nasal in tone.

According to Darren, men like himself probably got involved with rock music-making because they wanted to express their femininity and rock allowed them a publicly acceptable means of doing so. Darren had tried to move away from the typical 'laddish' indie rock image that he had adopted in his previous band Fuzzy Models, but in his experiments with new images he still drew upon pretty conventional gender types within indie rock and within rock in general. Rock performers like David Bowie and Marc Bolan have, for example, used theatrical camp and androgynous imagery in their performance styles, images and lyrics, and female performers such as Annie Lennox, Madonna and kd lang have generated much discussion and debate by incorporating a variety of masculine and androgynous images into their performances (and occasionally lesbian and homosexual ones as well). In most cases of such so-called 'gender-bending' in rock and pop a clear distinction has been made between the real and performed selves of such artists, although this distinction has sometimes been deliberately or unintentionally blurred (Leonard and Cohen, forthcoming). Rock and pop performers such as these have sometimes managed to highlight gender conventions and ideologies that were previously taken-for-granted as the norm. Many female punk and indie rock musicians have done likewise through aspects of their music and performances, including their ironic use of stereotypically feminine styles of dress, such as the ripped fishnet stockings of the female punks and the baby-doll dresses of so-called 'riot grrrl' performers. Chris's new 'glam' image within Kyzer Sozer could, particularly in view of her lesbianism and her unusual position as a female instrumentalist within a male dominated local music scene, be interpreted as a similar performance strategy and as a contribution to the politics of gender and sexuality within rock and pop music.

In many ways, however, indie rock culture in Liverpool involved an active celebration of masculinity, and it was often described by those involved with it as a culture characterised by male aggression and competition and fragile male egos. For men like Darren, being in a rock band was an attractive alternative to unemployment or a monotonous, unfulfilling job, and although Darren didn't as yet earn an income from his band, his involvement with it offered a seductive potential route to rock stardom and wealth. Being in a band also provided Darren with a set of friends and a social life, and it gave him an identity outside of his domestic sphere and a sense of confidence and purpose, as well as a set of dreams and aspirations. The recording studio where Darren worked and where Kyzer Sozer rehearsed and recorded was, like many of the institutions central to Liverpool rock culture (including music instrument shops and live music venues), a predominantly male space from which many women (as well as some men) felt excluded. The studio was frequented largely by men and situated at the centre of a social network through which men regularly circulated and exchanged information, advice and gossip; instruments, technical support and additional services; music recordings, journals and other products. Together they shared the jokes, jibes, hype and bravado that commonly surrounded rock bands, and they exchanged band-related stories that reinforced male comradeship and collectivity. Their conversation was often sexist, with women treated as objects of sexual desire, conquest or derision.

The masculinity of Liverpool rock culture was in many ways constructed in relation to ideas about women and notions of femininity. For some men involvement with rock bands offered close and intense male comradeship and interaction free from the pressures of relating to women; for some music promised success, status and the possibility of attracting women; for others music represented an escape or retreat from women and a way out of domestic obligations (Cohen 1991a). Like many other local indie musicians Darren used his music-making as a means to think through and explore his relationships with women. Most of the lyrics he wrote were about love, betrayal, broken relationships and 'the way that my paths cross with women'. He never discussed such issues directly with family or friends, so through his music he expressed ideas and sentiments in a manner that was generally discouraged in other public settings. Some Liverpool indie rock musicians said that when they were younger they were labelled a 'cissy' by their male peers if they indulged in music-making in or out of school. Music-making was associated with femininity because it was regarded as a leisure pursuit that was 'soft', unlike most competitive sports, and perhaps because of its links with the emotions and with the body. Such attitudes might have encouraged some indie rock musicians to exclude women from music-making in order to distance themselves from such associations and enhance their masculinity.

Darren and many of the musicians he had worked with came from white, working-class Liverpool families which were often, as with the families of Darren and Les, of Irish descent. Within such families there were marked differences in male and female interests and activities and single-sex leisure activities were commonplace. Liverpool is a port city and the port used to be a major employer in the region, recruiting a casual and unskilled labour force (Darren's uncles and grandfather had all worked on the docks). Music-making was popular with many men who were away at sea or were resting at home in-between jobs because it was a way of passing the time or a means of earning extra income. Meanwhile the female relatives of such men were typically linked with the home, even if they earned a wage outside of it, and were largely in control of the day-to-day running of the family, household and domestic economy. Many local musicians, including Darren, emphasised the support (financial and other) and encouragement that they had received for their music-making from their girlfriends, wives and female relatives (Cohen and McManus 1991). Liverpool's port activity has declined over recent decades and the rate of local unemployment is high, but the port promoted male and female roles and images that still have considerable influence on the city's social and cultural life.

The families of musicians like Darren, Les and Sam held relatively fixed and conservative ideas about men and women and how they should or shouldn't behave, with intolerance often expressed towards those who transgressed the boundaries. Darren explained Les's homophobic response to his lyrics for 'Boys R Us' by describing Les as a 'swaggering wide boy with a cheeky grin who still had that male stereotype thing of an honest day's work', and he attributed such attitudes to the continuing influence of the port within certain geographical areas of Liverpool. Some local rock musicians regarded such intolerance as characteristic of the city in general. Well-known Liverpool rock musicians like Pete Burns from Dead or Alive and Holly Johnson from Frankie Goes to Hollywood, have described in interviews the hostility they encountered in Liverpool for their flamboyant appearance and sexuality, and other local musicians have told of being thrown out of Liverpool clubs and pubs or attacked verbally and physically in the streets for adopting even a slightly hippy or punk style of dress.

Gender, events and interpretation

Kyzer Sozer's musical construction or performance of gender was thus influenced by gender conventions within rock culture in general and within Liverpool indie rock culture more specifically. This process did vary, however, according to the particular performance event involved.

This chapter began with Kyzer Sozer's performance at the Lomax. Typically for a relatively unknown local band, their gig attracted only a small audience that consisted largely of local male musicians, including those due to perform next on stage, as well as Kyzer Sozer's manager, Carl, and a few of his colleagues and associates, some of the band's friends and relatives, such as Darren's father and brother who attended nearly all of his performances, and the owner of the Lomax venue and his bar staff. Kyzer Sozer had not yet released a record so their audiences were restricted to their live shows and they were heavily dependent upon relatives and peers for critical approval of their performances and their musical creativity. Significantly absent from the audience at the Lomax were the record company representatives from London (commonly referred to as 'A&R men') who had promised to attend the gig and whose attention and appreciation the band and their manager so desperately sought, although the band weren't aware of this absence until their onstage performance was over.

Most of the Kyzer Sozer's gigs took place in Liverpool, but shortly after the gig at the Lomax Kyzer Sozer performed at a gay club in Manchester and as a support act for another Liverpool band who were engaged in a United Kingdom tour to promote their new album. These performances were different kinds of events with their own specific conventions of male and female behaviour. At the Lomax the audience members were predominantly male, casually dressed and generally serious and contemplative. They engaged in little interaction with the band and they did not dance. Audiences on the tour were quite different. The band that Kyzer Sozer were supporting had been enjoying chart success and the attention of the national media. Their tour therefore attracted sizeable and responsive audiences that included large numbers of young women who were generally out to have a good time and to be entertained. These women crowded around the front of the stage and danced, screamed and sang along to Kyzer Sozer's music, and some of them engaged in verbal dialogue with Darren during the band's performance. Meanwhile the audience for Kyzer Sozer's performance at the gay club in Manchester consisted largely of homosexual men, many of whom wore flamboyant and glamorous styles of dress and behaved in a rather boisterous, noisy manner. Some directed humorous comments at the band members.

Each of these performance events presented Kyzer Sozer with a different set of relationships and concerns, and the band slightly tailored their set of songs, and the manner and order in which they performed them, to suit each event and the audiences involved. The band's performance at the Lomax was one of their first Liverpool gigs as Kyzer Sozer and Darren had thought a great deal about how the audience and venue management might respond to his new image. He was well aware of the masculinist and heterosexist nature of local rock culture and he had anticipated a strong reaction of some sort or at least some teasing. The band's first performance at a gay club was also problematic for Darren but in a different way. He worried that the audience might find his dress and demeanour patronising and wondered whether to ditch the feather boa, and he had to pacify Sam who had never been exposed to gay culture and felt uncomfortable and insecure about the show. Kyzer Sozer's performances for the tour were much more enjoyable for the band's members because of their camaraderie with the headlining band and because of the enthusiastic response of their audience, particularly that of some of its female members.

When he talked about his music Darren expressed the concern that the band's audiences should listen to and understand his lyrics and the meanings, experiences and sentiments that he intended to convey through them and through the accompanying music. He said that he had tried to write and perform 'Girls' in a way that would make them do so, persuading his listeners through his 'passion and control' and through the skill and force of his performance. Musical meaning is not fixed, however, but open to interpretation. Darren may have included familiar gender codes in his music, image and performance style in order to convey particular meanings, but he was unable to determine the impact of such performances on his audiences. Musical meaning is not located solely within musical texts but is created through the interaction of listeners with such texts and influenced by the specific listening practices, events and contexts involved. Songs like 'Boys R Us' and 'Girls' could thus take on a range of alternative meanings for Kyzer Sozer's audiences.

According to Walser (1993), male fans of 'harder' styles of heavy metal have often denounced glam metal with its fusion of male and female images and its suggestions of homosexuality, pointing out that 'real men don't wear make up', whilst female fans have defended glam performers by praising their musical abilities, emphasising the intensity of the experience they provide, or by simply admiring their 'guts'. Walser also highlights differences between gay and straight readings of metal musicians and songs. It cannot be assumed, however, that the audiences of Kyzer Sozer were quite so homogenous with regard to their interpretation of the band's music, with men and women, gays and straights sharing collective interpretations. Even the members of Kyzer Sozer and their close network of creative collaborators interpreted the songs 'Girls' and 'Boys R Us' in quite different ways. Les, for example, had made fun of 'Boys R Us' perhaps partly because he was worried by the idea of having to perform such a song in public and how this might affect his image. Chris knew what the song 'Girls' was about and what it meant to Darren, but when asked what it meant to her she simply described it as 'a great song to play'. Darren linked the 'little boy lost' sound in 'Girls' with the sound of Prefab Sprout, but the A&R person from the publishing company that Darren was signed to likened the song to the music of Cat Stevens, whilst his colleague likened it to the music produced by John Lennon during his career as a solo artist. Whilst it is common practice to describe the music of one artist by comparing or contrasting it with the music of other artists, it is also typical for A&R personnel to do so in order to relate music to familiar, pre-existing product types and marketing categories. People thus hear and interpret music in different ways and it may thus be the case that gender is only one of several common 'interpretive moves' (Feld 1994b) that Kyzer Sozer's audiences made when they listened to the band's music. Even if the music was connected with gender in some way the range of potential meanings was still pretty broad.

Gender, performance and constraint

Examining performance contexts and events can highlight ways in which musical constructions and interpretations of gender are enabled but also constrained by the specific circumstances involved. Throughout the history of rock and pop musicians and audiences have used music performance to explore gender and sexual behaviours, images and identities, and in doing so they have often challenged or subverted more established or acceptable conventions and ideologies. Some scholars have celebrated this process, describing those involved as active agents engaging in symbolic acts of resistance and empowerment. Rock music certainly offered Darren a space in which he could explore his behaviour and identity as a man and express alternative male identities, and the sensual and specific nature of music as performance may well have heightened this sense of possibility. It is possible, however, to over-emphasise and over-celebrate the elements of freedom and resistance involved. Darren operated within a music scene in which behavioural conventions and ideas concerning gender tended to be rather fixed and ingrained, and whilst this encouraged him to try to challenge such conventions and explore alternatives through music performance, it also restricted his performance of masculinity.

In addition, like many other Liverpool rock bands Kyzer Sozer were desperate to sign a recording contract and their music was produced accordingly, hence 'Girls' represented a deliberate attempt by Darren to write 'a really commercial song'. At their London-based publishing company Kyzer Sozer's sound and image were the subject of detailed debate, largely between Darren and Steve, the band's representative from the company's A&R division. Steve had his own strong ideas about how

Kyzer Sozer should look and sound and he and the band had to compromise over several issues, although because of Steve's position at the publishing company and Kyzer Sozer's position as a relatively unknown act, it was the corporate priorities, strategies and budget considerations of the publishing company that took precedence. Steve wanted to market Darren as 'the Elvis Costello of the 1990s' and initially he wasn't too keen on 'the female bass player thing', although he did become more enthusiastic and supported Darren's aim to develop Chris's stage image into something more glamorous. Discussions on such matters between Darren and Steve were guided by their knowledge of popular music trends within the commercial marketplace, and of the national and international indie rock world with its own set of media, institutions and ideologies, and its own established conventions of male and female performance. Kyzer Sozer's sound, image and identity were thus shaped in relation to established indie rock bands and styles which meant that they were encouraged to be 'different' but at the same time to conform to familiar gender types, recognisable niche-markets and tried and tested promotional strategies.

It is thus important to relate gender to issues of power and constraint, a point that can also be illustrated in relation to Chris from Kyzer Sozer who had been the subject of so much discussion regarding her performance image and style. Despite the absence and exclusion of women from indie rock culture in Liverpool, women like Chris nevertheless managed to play an active and visible role in local rock music-making, although many of them complained that they were not taken as seriously as male musicians (Cohen 1991a, 1991b; Bayton 1998). Chris's position as a woman and a lesbian presented her with a set of problems or constraints that were different from those experienced by Darren and Sam. Darren and others discussed what she should wear on stage but she wasn't consulted for her views on their appearance. She also felt that their preferences regarding her stage appearance reflected male heterosexual notions of female glamour which were quite different to those of her lesbian friends. Meanwhile Steve from Kyzer Sozer's publishing company introduced Darren to his colleagues but ignored Chris and Sam, and when Kyzer Sozer performed on tour with the commercially successful local band it was Darren and Sam whom the young women backstage were waiting to see rather than Chris. In addition, although Chris was close to Darren and Sam she sometimes found their behaviour too 'laddish and heterosexual'. She was happy to become 'one of the lads' to a certain degree, but she worried about 'where to draw the line' and she remained unsure of her musical abilities and contributions within the band and felt like an outsider or newcomer to Liverpool's rock scene. She said that she was anxious not to be, 'like other girl bass players in indie rock who just stand there', but her musical performance was often interpreted and valued according to the fact that she was a woman whereas the performances of Darren and Sam were not linked to issues of sex and gender in quite the same way. Gender is thus a category embodying not just difference but also inequality.

Conclusion

The illustrative case material presented in this chapter has been rather brief and sketchy but I have tried to use it to make several key points about how pop and rock music relate to gender. By focusing on the live music performances of one particular indie rock band the chapter has highlighted the way that gender is practised and embodied as well as thought about, and the way that gender involves a process of becoming rather than being a fixed or essential identity that people are born into. It has thus been emphasised that there is no natural or simple connection between rock and pop music and gender; rather, rock and pop offer both musicians and audiences a means of musically constructing and performing gender. Gender has been shown to be musically constructed not only through performance texts, images and styles but also through the relations, events and contexts that shape their form and meaning. Kyzer Sozer's musical performance of gender was constructed through relationships between the band's members and between the band and their audiences, colleagues, peers and associates within Liverpool rock culture and within rock culture and the music industry more generally. These relationships were shaped by particular gender conventions, and they inspired and enabled but also restricted the band's performance, showing how through rock and pop gender is both created but also constrained.

Further reading

There are several key readings on rock and pop music, gender and sexuality. In 1978 Simon Frith and Angela McRobbie wrote a seminal article entitled 'Rock and Sexuality' which, despite its title, is actually about gender and presents a sociological argument for the maleness of rock. A useful critique of the article appeared in *Screen Education* 31 (1979) written by Dave Laing and Jenny Taylor, and the article was reprinted in Simon Frith and Andrew Goodwin's (eds) *On Record: Rock, Pop and the Written Word* (London: Routledge, 1990) along with Frith's 'Afterthoughts' on it. *On Record* also includes some other important articles on popular music, gender and sexuality. Mavis Bayton, for example, writes about how women become rock musicians, Barbara Bradby analyses the music of girl-groups,

Richard Dyer discusses sexuality in relation to disco music, whilst Sue Wise relates sexuality to her own personal experience of being an Elvis Presley fan and Sheryl Garratt discusses gender in relation to her experience of being a young Bay City Rollers fan. Apart from *On Record*, some of the major theoretical debates concerning popular music, gender and sexuality are also reviewed by Keith Negus in a chapter of his book *Popular Music in Theory* (Cambridge: Polity Press, 1996).

In addition to the above more wide-ranging sources, there are some key books that are entirely devoted to the study of rock and pop music, gender and sexuality. They include a collection of articles addressing a broad and diverse range of relevant issues entitled *Sexing the Groove* (edited by Sheila Whiteley, London: Routledge, 1997), *The Sex Revolts: Gender, Rebellion and Rock'n'Roll* by Simon Reynolds and Joy Press (London: Serpent's Tail, 1995) which incorporates a psychoanalytic approach to the study of masculinity and femininity in rock and pop, and Lucy Green's study of *Music, Gender, Education* (Cambridge: Cambridge University Press, 1997) which, like Susan McClary's *Feminine Endings* (Minneapolis: University of Minnesota Press, 1991) focuses on classical music as well as on rock and pop and discusses gendered discourses on music and how they relate to music teaching in schools. Meanwhile, a particularly useful publication devoted to the study of rock and pop music and masculinity is Robert Walser's sophisticated analysis of heavy metal music entitled *Running with the Devil: Power, Gender and Madness in Heavy Metal Music* (Hanover, NH: Wesleyan University Press, 1993) which adopts an interdisciplinary approach that draws mainly on musicology and cultural studies.

There are also a few monographs that focus on women in pop or rock, including *Frock Rock* by Mavis Bayton which is based on extensive sociological research on women rock musicians (Oxford: Oxford University Press, 1998), and a collection of books written in a more popular, descriptive and less analytical style. The latter include *Signed, Sealed and Delivered* by Sue Steward and Sheryl Garratt (London: Pluto Press, 1985) which features interview material with women working in the music business; *Women, Sex and Rock'n'Roll: in their Own Words* by Liz Evans (London: Pandora, 1994); *She's A Rebel: The History of Women in Rock and Roll* by Gillian Gaar (London: Blandford, 1993); *She Bop: The Definitive History of Women in Rock, Pop and Soul* by Lucy O'Brien (London: Penguin, 1995); *Never Mind the Bollocks: Women Rewrite Rock* by Amy Raphael (London: Virago, 1995); *Sweethearts of Rhythm: The Story of Australia's All-Girl Bands and Orchestras to the End of the Second World War* by Kay Dreyfus (New South Wales: Currency Press, 1999) and *Will You Still Love Me Tomorrow?* by Charlotte Grieg (London: Virago, 1989).

Finally, there are some useful books on popular music and gay or lesbian culture, including *Queering the Pitch: The New Gay and Lesbian Musicology* edited by P. Brett, E. Wood and G. Thomas (London: Routledge, 1994); John Gill's *Queer Noises: Male and Female Homosexuality in Twentieth-Century Music* (London: Cassell, 1995), and Richard Smith's *Seduced and Abandoned: Essays on Gay Men and Popular Music* (London: Cassell, 1995).

11 Rock, pop and politics

JOHN STREET

Some of the strongest claims for the political importance of popular music have been made by its greatest enemies. Its most radical effects have been identified by those who most despise the pleasures of rock and pop. From the earliest days of rock'n'roll, priests, parents and politicians have warned of the dangers inherent in the rhythms, the voices, the words and the images of the music. And each new wave in pop history has been greeted by the outcry of those who fear for its consequences. In the West, the political right has been terrified that it will undermine capitalism, family life and traditional values. Racists have seen it as a threat to 'white purity'. Communists have seen it as subverting the socialist dream. These enemies have warned of its extraordinary power to influence the way people think and act. Their fears have not just prompted outbursts of indignation, but have actually resulted in policies and practices that directly affect the production and consumption of pop. Censorship has been a constant feature of the music's history. Under communism and capitalism, in the name of apartheid and Islam, pop music has been banned and musicians punished.

In 1995, Bob Dole led a campaign in the United States Senate against the conglomerate Time-Warner. He attacked the company for its promotion of rap artists like Snoop Doggy Dogg, who were signed to a Time-Warner subsidiary and who, said Dole, were promoting attitudes and behaviour that were an affront to the American people. Dole's campaign succeeded, and Time-Warner severed its links with its subsidiary. At the same time in Britain, the government introduced the Criminal Justice Act which, among other things, outlawed particular forms of musical performance. A decade earlier, the Parents' Music Resource Centre, led by the so-called 'Washington Wives' (including Tipper Gore, wife of Al Gore), persuaded record companies to introduce a system of labelling to identify music that might cause offence. Before this, in the 1960s, records by the Beatles were ritually incinerated in the American south; in the 1970s, the British Broadcasting Corporation refused to play a song about Northern Ireland by Paul McCartney. Such censorship was a way of life in the Soviet Union and Eastern Europe; just as it was under apartheid in South Africa. It continues today in China, Afghanistan and Algeria, among other places. In their diverse reactions and for their diverse reasons, these enemies of pop and rock have achieved one thing: they have made popular music into a political issue, and they have invested it with the potential to endanger and disrupt the established order.

Strangely perhaps, those who have defended and delighted in popular music have never been quite so sure about the music's politics. There have been times, of course, when the rhetoric of revolution was accompanied by a 4/4 beat. In the late 1960s, there was much talk of revolution: at festivals, at happenings; in the songs and sounds of the Beatles, Bob Dylan, Country Joe and the Fish, Jefferson Airplane and many more. The revolution was even available, according to the endorsement on the record sleeve, on a budget-priced sampler from CBS. But the difference here was that no one – certainly not at the Columbia corporation – thought of it as a revolution in the traditional sense; there were no vanguard parties or cadres, no manifestos or five-year plans; no sweeping political reforms. This revolution was experienced as a collective dream; it did not have policies and programmes. It owed more to aesthetics than to ideologies, and its politics were acted out *within* the industries that produced it.

The 1970 Isle of Wight Festival – starring the Doors, Jimi Hendrix, the Who and Joni Mitchell – was a microcosm of pop's politics. The stars played along with the radical rhetoric, but haggled over their fees backstage. Activists from France and Britain pulled down the fences, while the organisers pleaded with them to stop and for the fans to pay, all in the name of a utopian communal ideal. The entrepreneurs, like the musicians, were caught between political idealism and commercial reality, between belief and the bottom line. Arguably, it is this tension which actually generates pop's finest moments and its truest politics. Utopian fantasies tend to issue in bland sounds, and self-righteous polemics in dull tunes. The politics of popular music are best animated by the attempt to combine commercial logic with romantic ideals.

Were the music not so commercially successful, its obscenities would be of little concern to its enemies. Or alternatively, were it commercially unsuccessful, but the beneficiary of state subsidy, only then would the political right be concerned. Equally, if it were not for the music's ability to inspire passion in its fans, and to capture their dreams, it would not justify the extravagant rhetoric that cloaks its commercial routines and which prompts its populist politics.

Any attempt to make sense of the politics of pop and rock must, therefore, try to understand the ways in which these conflicting and contradictory needs are negotiated; it must navigate between the fears of the outsiders and the opportunism of the insiders, between utopian rhetoric and authoritarian disgust. It must, ultimately, recognise the different views taken of pop's power. On the one side stand those who see music as a way of representing political ideas and promoting political causes, who see it as a form of political expression. From this point of view, music has symbolic force, it deploys the power of language to create visions, articulate ideals and to form bonds. On the other side stand those who fear for music's effects, for whom the politics lie in its ability to exercise power over its listeners, to shape and influence thoughts and actions. These two dimensions of pop's power – the power to represent and the power to effect – establish the broad boundaries of pop's politics. This chapter explores both, arguing in the end that they are intimately linked.

Marking time

In a now familiar proclamation, Raymond Williams declared that 'culture is ordinary'. This 'ordinariness' is not, however, mundane. Culture is part of, and derived from, the circumstances of people's lives. It does not just reflect daily existence, though, it both orders it and looks to better ways of living. 'A culture has two aspects', he wrote (Williams 1989), 'the known meanings and directions, which its members are trained to; the new observations and meanings, which are offered and tested.' Culture is lived. It embodies the hopes and rules which form people's existence. And to the extent that their lives are patterned by political struggle, then their culture too is inscribed with political experience.

This insight leads to the stories told about pop music's past. Pop becomes a form of social history (an aural history); every record collection becomes a memoir, and the histories of peoples and societies are told in popular song. Such thinking inspires the use of pop music on film, documentary or advertisement soundtracks; the music acts as an easy shorthand for an era. Scenes of the Paris events of 1968 are accompanied by the Stones' 'Street Fighting Man'; scenes of hippies are enlivened by the Beatles 'All You Need is Love'. Pop becomes the expression of its political and social context. The history of black music in the United States is sometimes told like this, as a chronicle of the changing political awareness of African-Americans. So the gospel hopefulness of the Impressions' 'People Get Ready' becomes the more assertive, impatient demands of Aretha Franklin's 'Respect'; which is followed by the disillusion and militancy of Nina Simone's 'Revolution'. And this view – music as social realism and political education – persists in accounts of rap which glory in accounts of ghetto life in the Bronx or Los Angeles.

The idea that pop is part of its time is reinforced by the emphasis put upon release dates and playlists, both of which lock the music into a moment and consign the immediate past to oblivion. But there is a danger of reading too much social significance into this process. Record releases, and the fashions which accompany them, may organise the passage of time and the operations of the market, but they do not necessarily mark social and political change. (One summer recently, I watched three men dressed as nuns miming to 'Respect' in a French campsite. There was little sign of its associations with civil rights and women's emancipation.)

To view pop's politics in this way, to see it as the direct product of political history, is too simplistic. There is no straightforward causal relationship between the times and their sounds (and in the era of the remastered and re-released CD collection, the connection becomes ever more confused – what are we to make of previously unheard tracks by the Beatles, recorded in 1963, but released in the 1990s?). Music's politics cannot be read straight from its context because music-making is not just journalism with a backbeat. The music is the result of the interplay of commercial, aesthetic, institutional and political processes.

The same is true for the consumption of music. Musical pleasure is not just (or even) a consequence of political experience. There is no simple connection between the times and the sounds that were 'popular'. It is not enough to assume that, because the music was bought, it therefore reflected people's experience. Newspapers constantly represent themselves as speaking for the people. In editorials and articles, there are direct or implied references to what ordinary people think. But such claims owe as much to rhetoric as reality. There are, after all, no direct conduits through which popular views (if indeed such things exist) can be transmitted to editorial conferences or newsrooms. The same is true for music. Even where artists claim to be expressing the authentic voice of 'the street', this is more a matter of argument and credibility than actuality. It certainly cannot be treated at face value, because to do so would be to hear only the rhetoric of marketing departments and music journalists, and to ignore the interests of the institutions that mediate and manage the production of popular music. There can be no determinist connection in which particular political experiences find expression in particular sounds, and no reason why these experiences must sound like Diana Ross or like Aretha Franklin. Rock journalists may have insisted that the 'authentic' sound of black politics was Stax not Tamla, but such claims were *part* of pop's politics, not a description of them.

To the extent that the politics of popular music derive from the politics of their context, it makes as much sense to see the music as *shaping the times*, rather than reflecting them. In his account of punk music in Britain, the writer Jon Savage (1991) provides a running commentary on the social and political changes that shaped the 1970s. But the strength of Savage's story is not in the connection that leads from the social history to the music, but rather in the one that goes in the opposite direction. Savage includes many extracts from his personal diary of the time, and it becomes increasingly clear that it is the experience of punk that is patterning his view of the world. The Sex Pistols frame and interpret the times. Punk gives a structure to the feelings of change and decay.

This perspective on the link between music and society is, in many ways, truer to Williams' original vision of culture as ordinary. The music establishes a context through which politics is viewed and judged. But in seeing the relationship like this, attention inevitably shifts from the social to the musical – to the sounds, images and words. It locates the politics in the text rather than the context. Here pop's symbolic power becomes most explicit.

Textual politics

Musicians from the left and the right have used popular music as a vehicle for their politics, translating their views into blank verse or rhyming couplets, and setting them against the thump of the bass drum. Many performers have made their politics a defining part of their art and their careers: Bob Dylan, Merle Haggard, Curtis Mayfield, Joan Baez, the Clash, John Lennon, Victor Jara, Bob Marley, Peter Gabriel, Public Enemy, Tracy Chapman, Sting, Thomas Mapfumo, Midnight Oil, the Gang of Four, Crass, the Dead Kennedys, Billy Bragg, Christy Moore, Rage Against the Machine and so on.

That music should be used like this is a consequence of its history as an accessible and flexible platform for political sentiment. It has the advantage for those living under authoritarian regimes that songs (like poems) can disguise their politics in metaphor and gesture, enabling their performers to avoid systems of censorship organised around the literal and the visual. The use of pop and rock as political platforms has also been greatly aided by the relative accessibility of the form itself and the permeability of the institutions that organise it. Despite its commercialisation and industrialisation, pop music has been less dependent on the barriers created by training, technology and capital that apply to other forms of popular culture. And because of its commercialisation and industrialisation, it has not been subject to the same scrutiny that has been applied to the subsidised arts (like theatre) or high cost commercial products (like film).

Partly as a consequence of its accessibility and the limits to regulation, popular music has given voice to many different political ideas. Music can claim to be the most democratic and the most politically radical mass popular form. Similar politics may, it is true, be found within fringe theatre, but the latter's reach is very limited (as is the case with radical newspapers). And while television may reach further with its politically charged dramas and documentaries, it is highly constrained, formally and informally, by the conventions of constitutional politics and commercial interests (such as advertisers). Even the most telling of television satires would hesitate to give vent to the political anger of Public Enemy.

But in drawing attention to the political reputations of performers and the political content of the lyrics, there is a danger of making these the defining feature of the music's politics. It would be a mistake, though, to see the words, at least as they appear on the sleeve, as conveying the (political) meaning of the song. Not only are they heard in the context of the other aspects of the song (the beat, the production, etc.), they are also heard through the tone of voice and inflections of the singer. A song is more than its words. The same song can change in different performances. Compare, for example, two versions of Elvis Costello's 'Shipbuilding', a song about war and the conflicting feelings it generates – a hope of work, a fear of death. One version is by Robert Wyatt, the other by Suede; one is understated and hesitant, the other melodramatic and wayward. In each case the singers sing the same words, but their effect, the emotions they convey are quite distinct.

Words are not just ways of representing experience, but of expressing it; they are the material through which singers register emotion by letting their voice explore the sound of the syllables. They may produce a political meaning, but it may not be the one that the written text suggests. Vocal inflection and style can, in fact, work against the ostensible meaning of the lyrics. Tammy Wynette's 'Stand By Your Man' becomes less a plea for domestic subservience than its words seem to represent, when you pay attention to the regret in her voice. ' "Sometimes it's *hard* to be a woman", Tammy Wynette begins, and you can hear that it's hard and that Tammy Wynette knows why – her voice is a collective one' (Frith and McRobbie 1990). Similarly subversive subtexts can be heard in rock. The rock rebel pose – from Mick Jagger to Jim Morrison to John Lydon to Kurt Cobain – may seem to be a celebration of freedom, but it is equally the sound of a desperate flight from commitment and intimacy. The music tells another story, one which belies the words and the images. Even wordless songs can convey a wealth of meaning. Liz Fraser of the Cocteau Twins has been described as singing 'a garbled phoneme soup (imagine Welsh sung backwards, through a sieve) that's mostly indecipherable but always sounds rich in wholly private, non-verbalisable meaning' (Reynolds and Press 1995). Analysing music's meaning like this suggests a very different approach to its politics. The politics lies in the sounds and their structures, in the way they refuse or embrace musical orthodoxies, in the way they follow and disturb expectations. The message can be in the mix.

The other side to such arguments is that explicitly 'political' songs, ones in which the words address a specific issue or cause directly, may turn out to lack any actual political resonance. Words that observe a formal concern with political ideology may fail *as lyrics* because they do not acknowledge the constraints (and opportunities) of their medium or genre. The political analysis may be correct but unless the listener is moved, unless the song works as a song (as melody and rhythm), then its politics may become irrelevant.

If the political meaning of songs – as texts – is more opaque than might at first appear, this suggests that we should either attempt a more fine-grained reading of them, or that we should abandon this approach altogether. Ultimately, the latter may be the only recourse. Although we may indeed reveal more about the political nuances within a song by the first route, my suspicion is that these readings will serve as no more than *readings*, which tell us as much about the reader as the text. Instead, I would argue that a more productive route lies in seeing how particular songs or performances engage with particular political moments and issues. This is not to return to the music as the expression of a time or era, but rather to its role in shaping and focusing experience.

Saving lives with a song

Music's ability to do this can actually be measured. We can count the cash that has been raised by Live Aid, Farm Aid or War Child. We can note changes in awareness that result from Rock Against Racism or Rock the Vote, or concerts for Nelson Mandela or Amnesty International.

These are cases of pop engaging with politics. The form of engagement, and the accompanying ideology, may be different in each instance, but there is no disguising the fact that pop can make a political difference. Soon after the success of Band Aid, Bob Geldof met Mrs Thatcher, then Britain's Prime Minister. He records in his autobiography, 'I knew I would only get a couple of seconds with her, so I had to be blunt' (Geldof 1986). There followed a sharp exchange on European Union food surpluses. 'Every time I said something', Geldof remarks, 'she came back. By now I was getting the icy stare.' Geldof may have failed to change the PM's mind, but he was able to function as a legitimate political representative. He visited the White House, negotiated with the Ethiopian government, and stalked the corridors of Whitehall. And all of his authority was the product of a pop success.

His achievement was to organise and shape a sense of compassion for a cause. Geldof and his fellow musicians forged a way of seeing a problem and responding to it. They used their skills to fashion our concern. Our (the audience's) feelings were constructed through pop's various musical, visual and other devices. In this process of constituting concern, the political potential of the music was revealed. It became part of the process by which we think and feel and act. This process is not, however, a simple, determinist one. The politics of compassion can assume many guises.

Take, for example, the different judgements made of Live Aid. For some, it promoted a bland, universal humanism, no different from (and little better than) the mass marketing of a commercial product like Coke. For others, Live Aid provided a site from within which it was possible to challenge the (a)moralistic hegemony of Thatcherism. New Right individualism was confronted by a collective compassion. Take, too, the arguments about the Amnesty tour led by Sting, Peter Gabriel and Bruce Springsteen. While, from one perspective, this represented an attempt to spread the cause of freedom and to challenge oppression; from another, it provided the basis for a form of colonial moralism, in which Western interests and values usurped local ones.

In these arguments, familiar political debates about imperialism and modernisation were overlaid with aesthetic ones about the music – its meanings and its effects. It is not just a matter of supporting one cause or another, or about the reasons behind such a stance. It was about how you support it aesthetically. The British Rock Against Racism campaign adopted a different musical strategy to that adopted by its United States equivalent. Where British RAR defined itself against disco and allied itself with reggae and rock, its American counterpart, wary of the 'disco sucks' rhetoric adopted by the British, built upon a more inclusive strategy which deliberately sought to involve all forms of music.

This combination of the aesthetic and the conventionally political is brought into sharpest relief when assessing the success of these various ventures. Not every cause adopted by rock and pop stars gathers the same support. It is apparent, for example, that some causes fare better than others. The reasons for this are never wholly aesthetic ('if only they had a better song/singer . . .') or political ('if only they had analysed the problem like this . . .'). It is about how music and politics actually interact, about how political and aesthetic responses are connected.

Sound theories

Here the politics of music become linked to competing social theories and the relationship between cultural and social action. The ability to use pop symbolically rests upon claims about people's relationship to their cultural practices. This is a question which, like much else in the study of popular music, begins with Theodor Adorno.

Adorno's claims about standardisation and pseudo-individualisation within popular music, and the corporate sources of both, would seem to support the view of those who see such things as Live Aid as sustaining the dominant order. There is little reason to suppose that music can do anything more than reinforce pre-existing sympathies and trends. Against this stands those who want to present popular music as a weapon and as a source of group identity. For them, audiences are actively involved in the consumption of their music; and they can use it as a means of articulating an alternative vision. Consumption is imbued with political significance – more than that, it is a form of political practice. It is not a merely utilitarian, commercial transaction, but a statement of collective identity. And as such, it establishes an alternative to the prevailing order. Popular culture comes to be as important, politically, as the workplace and the state. It becomes the political expression and resource of the marginalised and dispossessed.

The danger here is of an uncritical populism, one which overlooks the material conditions of consumption. In making grand political claims for the music, the populist is actually shifting attention from the sounds to the way they are consumed, and to the interests and aspirations of the consumer. The music acquires its political importance from the way it is used. But it does not explain why and how the music comes to work like this. The populist reading of music depends more upon the sociology of the subculture than the aesthetics of the music. Little attempt is made to discover how, or in what sense, the music actually constitutes a political response.

This problem has elicited two reactions. First, there have been those who have argued that the cultural populism of 'resistance' offers a bland relativism, in which everything is what you make it. It simply celebrates anything that is popular, finding signs of resistance everywhere. What is needed, instead, is the exercise of judgement to discriminate between texts which articulate different political dispositions and which serve more or less effectively as works of art. This means tracing more closely the ways in which political meanings are derived from cultural consumption, to see how memories and myths are contained within popular music, and how each tells a different version of the imagined communities which animate people's lives.

One of the important implications of these revised approaches is that the politics of the music are not pre-given. It cannot be assumed that music serves to undermine or to question the prevailing order. Indeed, it is perfectly conceivable that they serve to confirm it. The conservatism of country music may reveal a radical heart, just as Springsteen's radicalism may prove to be deeply conservative. But even where the music is not conservative, it remains important not to treat the content at face value. We have to understand the processes by which people come to hear and have access to the music, both as performers and listeners. Music is neither freely made nor freely consumed. Fans are organised into consumption practices, just as musicians are organised into (or out of) the production process.

If this is the case, then the politics of popular music cannot be confined to its symbolic role, its ability to represent ideas and articulate identities. To identify the politics of popular music, we need to move from concern with the power *of* music, to concern with power *over* music.

Sound practices and policies

So far pop's politics has been identified with its capacity to articulate states of mind and feeling, to represent social experience, to promote political ideas and causes. But one dimension of the politics of music may get lost in this approach. This is, perversely, the most conventionally political dimension: the impact of policy and the role played by the state. Popular music is the product of political processes, as well as commercial and aesthetic ones.

The failure to take seriously these formal political practices has led to an uncritical acceptance of the logic and the fact of globalisation. It has been assumed that intermediary institutions (especially national governments) can make no substantial difference to the form and character of a globalised culture. And yet there is considerable evidence to the contrary to show that states can deflect or re-shape global pressures.

We cannot afford to ignore the political economy of popular music. As much recent scholarship has indicated this is a key site in the determination of the character of pop and rock, and hence crucial to understanding its politics. It is not enough just to read the music ideologically. Attention has to be paid to its political economy, to the ways in which economic and policy considerations etch out the music's contours. We can neither understand the form of the music, nor the way it is received, without reference to the process by which it is delivered and the forms of access that are thereby organised into popular culture.

This process was most obvious under Soviet communism. Popular music may have been targeted less frequently than some other cultural forms (the printed word, for instance), but it was nonetheless subject to considerable state censorship and control. Musicians were imprisoned and exiled. They were, however, also fêted and promoted by the state.

Censorship was often accompanied by sponsorship. These practices are still evident in repressive states, but they can also be detected in 'liberal' regimes. Censorship has been practised by broadcasters. Sometimes this has been explicit, sometimes it has been the result of routines of selection and legitimation through the use of devices like the chart and the playlist.

These same states are also implicated in the promotion of music – in judgements about the allocation of radio frequencies, in the regulation of festivals and venues, and in the system of arts subsidy. In these ways, the state shapes the sounds of, and the access to, popular music. But what makes this a political relationship is not the mere fact of state involvement. It is the fact that it requires political judgements to be made about music. In Britain, the decision to legislate for raves in the Criminal Justice Act constituted a judgement about the music (and 'the repetitive beats' specified in the legislation), about its effects and significance. In a similar way, the British state has made judgements about the extent to which pop music should occupy the airwaves. Equivalent judgements were also implicated in decisions about the content of the national curriculum for schools – to what extent were children to encounter pop music (and if so, in what form), and how were they to learn about it – as performers or as audiences? These political decisions have their parallel in those of countries who impose quotas on 'foreign' music. They are also part of a general practice, in which the local and national state establish rules and regulations that govern the consumption and performing of music. They can lie in decisions to fund particular types of music or to cater for particular audiences.

These policy issues, attempts to exercise power over popular music, are not so much concerned with the ability to act symbolically, to provide an expression of certain views or feelings. Rather, their concern is with the effects of music, with its ability to change things, to subvert or sustain existing practices, traditions and identities.

Conclusion

In emphasising the politics of power over popular music, and worries about its effects, it would be wrong to suggest that we are dealing with starkly alternate ways of reading pop's politics – either as symbol or as effect. The point is that they are intimately linked, and that it is impossible to separate them. This connection has implications that are too often overlooked. The symbolic politics of music are constituted in part by institutional practices, and policy can alter the ways in which music matters. How this happens can perhaps best be illustrated by the ways in which states respond to the so-called globalisation of popular music.

Two options are typically on offer: to protect indigenous/national musical forms; or to remove all barriers to outside influences. These options form themselves around a debate about 'cultural imperialism' and the perceived threat of global homogenisation. The debate engages with arguments about the cultural formation of identity and the political formation of culture. The sides in the debate seem to emerge in disputes about local culture versus global culture, about protectionism versus deregulation. But this is to ignore the way in which musical forms may represent political positions. The crude 'cultural imperialist' debate ignores the different ways in which (global) culture is incorporated into local contexts. Different types of relation can be established with this culture, and in this difference political statements can be made. Put another way: adherence to traditional forms need not be radical or authentic, but actually conservative or reactionary; and as a corollary of this, the use of 'foreign' styles may be more radical. Non-traditional styles can represent a political challenge to a dominant order. This politics is not merely a struggle over symbolic meaning, it is also the politics of policy and institutional formation.

To focus on the organisation of popular music is to emphasise the ways in which 'content' and 'effect' are themselves the product of prior political processes, and that neither can be seen as defining pop's politics. At the same time, to draw attention to the ways in which policy decisions affect music is not to be committed to a form of political engineering. Observing the role of policy is not the same as endorsing it. It is, though, to take the view that music does not exist autonomously of other social, economic and political institutions. Music may still be able to change the world as well as reflecting it, but, when we talk of music's politics, we are not just talking of the way in which it articulates ideas and emotion. We are also talking of the politics that shape it.

Further reading

The journal that tirelessly monitors censorship across the world, *Index on Censorship*, devoted an entire issue to music, thoughtfully including a CD of the offending tunes (*Smashed Hits: The Book of Banned Music*, Index on Censorship, 6, 1998). For a more detailed study of the censorship of music, I would recommend Martin Cloonan's *Banned! Censorship of Popular Music in Britain 1967–1992* (Aldershot: Arena, 1996). The use of popular music to promote political causes is well surveyed in Reebee Garofalo's edited collection, *Rockin' the Boat: Mass Music and Mass Movements* (Boston: South End Press, 1992). This phenomenon is given an intriguing and sophisticated analytical twist by Ron Eyerman and Andrew Jamison in

Music and Social Movements: Mobilizing Traditions in the Twentieth Century (Cambridge: Cambridge University Press, 1998). One of the best attempts to identify the politics of dance culture is the wonderfully titled *Senseless Acts of Beauty: Cultures of Resistance since the Sixties* (London: Verso, 1996) by George McKay. The politics of corporate and state involvement in music gets several different takes in Tony Bennett, Simon Frith, Lawrence Grossberg, John Shepherd and Graeme Turner (eds.) *Rock and Popular Music: Politics, Policies, Institutions* (London: Routledge, 1993). Simon Reynolds and Joy Press' *Sex Revolts: Gender, Rebellion and Rock'n'Roll* (London: Serpent's Tail, 1995) provides a splendidly iconoclastic re-reading of the politics of pop's key figures. For an insight into the life of the contemporary political pop performer, see Andrew Collins' *Still Suitable for Miners. Billy Bragg: The Official Biography* (London: Virgin, 1998). And finally, one of the best books which I have read that links all these and other themes is Robin Kelley's collection of essays *Yo' mama's disfunktional! Fighting the Cultural Wars in Urban America* (Boston: Beacon Press, 1997).

12   From Rice to Ice: the face of race in rock and pop

BARRY SHANK

There should be no argument that the transformations in popular music that we associate with the rise and development of rock were the result of white fascination with black music. During the 1950s, increasing numbers of white teenagers tuned into radio stations that were programming music for black audiences, began to request recordings by black musicians at their local record stores, and tentatively ventured into nightclubs in black neighbourhoods in order to hear black performers. Rhythm and blues music seemed to promise some young white listeners a different relationship between the pleasures of the body and the dominant social formation of modern industrialised America. Whether racist primitivism or liberal cross-cultural identification, this white fascination with black music was nothing new (see McClary and Walser 1994).

In 1828, Thomas D. Rice, an itinerant musician, watched an older African–American with rheumatism perform a strange twisted dance while singing, 'Weel about and turn about and do jus so; Every time I weel about, I jump Jim Crow.' Rice was an experienced performer who was looking for gimmicks to add to his act. He learned this song and dance, wrote new verses and used burnt cork to make himself up to look like his source for this material. The act created a public sensation and toured major entertainment centres, including New York and London. Not surprisingly, this interpretation of African–American culture was a misinterpretation. The melody to 'Jim Crow' had been a familiar English tune and the words – neither unusual nor especially clever – were mostly Rice's creation. The key to Rice's popularity was the social tension his act was able to address. 'Jump Jim Crow' was the first international popular music sensation based on a white interpretation of black culture. This inter-cultural performance style – blackface minstrelsy – firmly placed race as one of the central issues in popular music.

The story of T. D. Rice and 'Jump Jim Crow' complicates traditional understandings of the effects played by race in popular music. Rice was not simply 'ripping off' black music for the economically dominant white audience, but rather he was using music to figure racial difference and racial identity according to the needs of his white audience. The nineteenth-century cauldron of racial formation (including the beginnings of industrialisation and wage labour, the debate over slavery and the sectional crisis leading up to the American Civil War) was the world within which T. D. Rice, Dan Emmett, Stephen Foster and many others created blackface minstrelsy and inserted America's fascination with racial difference into the heart of its popular music. Eric Lott, David Roedigger, and other scholars have demonstrated the contradictory contribution to the construction of whiteness played by white fascination with black culture (Lott 1993; Roediger 1991; Saxton 1990; Radano 1996). The audience for blackface minstrelsy in the early nineteenth century relied on white depictions of black culture in order to mark simultaneously a longing for pre-industrial life (coded racially as 'blackness') as well as the increasingly modernised condition of the white working class. Since the middle of the nineteenth century, then, popular music in the United States and in Britain has been a primary site for the continual negotiation and re-definition of both blackness and whiteness as racial formations (see Gilroy 1987).

In all forms of popular music since minstrelsy, racial identity has been asserted, defended, negotiated and denied. The musical signatures of racial identity undergo constant transformation as the dialogic re-negotiation of racial difference stimulates the production of new forms. The history of racial segregation in the United States shaped the creation of the music industry and left us with a fractured soundscape of racially distinguished musical traditions. Continuing racially based social inequality increases the intensity with which racial meanings in rock and pop are scrutinised, analysed, internalised or rejected. While some scholars have argued against the validity of terms like 'black music', 'African–American music', or 'white music', insisting that all current popular musical traditions share traits derived from both Europe and Africa, there can be no denying that the interrogation of race and racial difference – whiteness as well as blackness – lies at the core of rock and pop. Focusing on the history of the racial dialectic in rock and pop and limiting its scope to the conditions that shaped this history in the United States, this chapter does not attempt to deal with either the racial formation of musical cultures in other English speaking nations nor does it deal with newer racialised constructions of Asian–American music or the multiple musical cultures of Latino/a peoples. In this limited space, I hope to be able to narrate a specific history, while exploring a more general point. The key to unlocking the racial significance in music lies not in specific musical traits but in the social uses to which any popular music is put (Tagg 1989).

For some members of the black community, the authenticity of black music provides a necessary set of cultural functions, drawn from the history of slavery and segregation, centred on the promotion of group cohesion. For others, the mainstream success of black music represents a step towards cultural and social integration. For some whites, black music becomes a means to interrogate their own racial identity, perhaps providing a potential resource for resisting some of the worst aspects of an inherited ideology of white supremacy; in the words of George Lipsitz (1994), black music can become the material through which some whites can stake out a 'strategic anti-essentialism'. While for other whites, black music serves only to confirm already existing racist beliefs.

The explicit display of whiteness in certain forms of music – from the fiddles and banjos of bluegrass and country to the stunted syncopation of big band jazz to the blistering guitar runs of heavy metal to the screaming minimalism of hardcore – links musical whiteness to European-derived understandings of social organisation and the 'progress' of modernity in different ways. Those forms of country and bluegrass that self-consciously emphasise their roots in the Scots–Irish ballad and lyric song tradition stand back from rising technology and managerial organisation, suggesting an anti-modern racial identity nostalgically linked to independent agriculture (Malone 1985; Sharpe 1917). Heavy metal and big band jazz, on the other hand, seem to celebrate the rise of technological and bureaucratic modernity, while punk spits on its collapsing hulk. In every case, within every popular musical genre, crossover exceptions to the typical racial identification exist; for in the very vibrations of its being, music doesn't know race.

Race is a cultural construct that was invented in order to explain the social phenomenon of racism. The concept of race attained its status as a scientific term in the nineteenth century, almost three hundred years after English traders visiting Africa reported their initial perceptions of what only later would be termed racial difference. As Winthrop Jordan (1974), Edmund Morgan (1975), Barbara Fields (1982), and others have suggested, the scientific concept of race became necessary only when English and American elites had to explain the contradictions between their asserted ideals of democracy and equality and their lived experience in an imperialist or slave-holding society. When that need arose, the concept of race developed as an attempt to justify social inequality – colonialism and slavery – by virtue of assumed biological differences. I say 'assumed differences' because recent genetics has shown that these differences largely do not exist. In other words, race – the concept that links social and cultural difference to biological difference – is a lie.

But as the philosopher Anthony Appiah (1985) has argued, 'To establish that race is relatively unimportant in explaining biological differences between people . . . is not yet to show that race is unimportant in explaining cultural difference.' For cultural constructs are funny things: their effects do not disappear just because someone has shown them to be false concepts. Cultural constructs build up historical residue which then gives shape and form to lived experience. The belief in white supremacy, in tandem with the historical experience of colonialism and slavery, has over time created the lived reality of racialised difference. The experience of racial difference, the living of a racial formation, the ongoing cultural effects of race, are shaped and determined by its historical roots in colonialism and slavery (Omi and Winant 1986: Keil 1994).

Race, then, enters the analysis of rock and pop as a bundle of contradictions which have been mobilised both politically and musically. The perception of race in rock and pop can take the form of recognisable musical sounds – certain rhythms, timbres, song styles and pitch structures; or it can be seen in the racial identifications of the performers or the audiences for the music; or it can be traced through the racially targeted branches of the music industry; or it can be acknowledged retrospectively as contributing to a certain racialised musical tradition. At each such moment when race does enter the perception of rock and pop, a renegotiation of the meanings of blackness and whiteness takes place, a renegotiation which is both musical and political.

Reebee Garofalo (1993) has discussed some of the ironies that occur when the discussion of race in rock and pop focuses on the racial identifications of either the performer of or the audience for the music. As he points out, to highlight the racial identification of the performer is to essentialise and dehistoricise the concept of race and, in the end, to remove the music itself from the discussion. In reality, some white-skinned performers can make black music, and some black-skinned performers can sound very white. To focus on the intended audience merely reifies the organisational marketing structure of the recording industry – a structure that developed historically in accordance with the cultural values of a segregated society. In fact, to focus on the phenomenon of crossover might seem to reaffirm *prima facie* the validity of separate musical traditions before discussing the different purposes to which different groups put their music. In order to avoid these traps, and in order to provide a 'cultural working definition of black or white . . . music', I want to provide quick discussions of the historical development of the American music industry and the musical encoding of race.

History, segregation, and the recording industry

Before 1954, racial segregation was not illegal in the United States. The music industry developed separate and unequal branches to cater to racially segregated markets. While the mainstream pop audience was served by a relatively coherent and organised network of retailers, jobbers, and distributors, the 'specialty' markets (the industry's term before the Second World War for the race and hillbilly audiences) relied on a catch-as-catch-can system of mail order and retail sales in barber shops and furniture stores. *Billboard* magazine developed charts to track the success of recordings during the 1940s, and by 1947 had developed separate charts to track the success of 'pop' and 'race' recordings. From the 1920s through the 1940s, the recording industry operated under the (probably accurate) assumption that the mainstream of the demographically larger white audience would more eagerly purchase music played by white musicians. Before the 1950s, whenever a new form of African–American popular music would attain growing commercial popularity, greater economic rewards would go to the white performers who had adopted the broad outlines of the current musical style and who had better access to the channels of the music industry that catered to the larger white audiences. At that point in the historical process, however, the social connotations of the sounds that defined that particular musical form, and which musically encoded race, would change: what had been 'black', became 'white'.

By virtue of the organisation of the music industry, therefore, 'popular' music, the music that hit the 'pop' charts in the trade magazines, meant 'white' music – the music that was distributed in white neighbourhoods. Racialised assumptions built into the industry's structure reproduced racialised categories of cultural and economic dominance (Jones 1963).

At the same time that the recording industry created 'race' music and 'race' records, it also created 'hillbilly' music. Hillbilly music was developed in order to market recordings to southern whites. Like race music, hillbilly music was targeted towards another 'specialty' market also figured as different from the mainstream 'popular' audience. But rather than marked directly by race, their taste was overtly marked by geographic region – the South. This geographic region was also directly associated with an alternative position on the relations between work and pleasure. Southern whites were believed to be culturally distinguished from the mainstream white 'popular' audience by virtue of their anti-modernism, their nostalgia for the 'Old South', and their resistance to the cultural consequences of the development of urban industrial America. The South's position on modernity was crucial to the region's self-image. The anti-modernism of the South was linked to a nostalgia for the antebellum world, a society built upon a pre-industrial economy – that is, cash-crop agriculture dependent on racialised slave labour.

The first deliberate attempt by a major recording company to service the specialty market of southern whites came about when Ralph Peer signed Fiddler John Carson for Okeh in 1923. Before he recorded 'Little

Old Log Cabin in the Lane', Carson was famous in Atlanta for winning the 'Georgia Old-Time Fiddlers' Championships' several years running. Held annually since 1913, these 'old-timey' contests were key sites for the musical construction of southern whiteness. Combining a nostalgia for the old South with a certain set of musical sounds, these contests associated the timbres of fiddles and banjos along with a certain squeezed vocal tonality with a longing for a pre-industrial world and, in so doing, articulated a core component of the whiteness of hillbilly music. As Bill Malone has pointed out, however, it is important to remember that the banjo is a descendant of an African instrument sometimes referred to as the 'banjar'. Before the Civil War, furthermore, many of the most highly acclaimed fiddlers in the South were African–American. It was only in the late nineteenth and early twentieth centuries that the sounds produced with these instruments were coded as white. Thus the whiteness of hillbilly music was not an inherent quality of particular sounds, nor was it simply derived from an explicit expression of white supremacy, but it was produced through a specific musical practice that associated the whiteness of hillbilly music with a critique of modern industrial labour through a nostalgic link with the southern past (of racialised slave labour). Bluegrass and country and western, the forms that derived from hillbilly music, inherited much of this articulated conception of whiteness (Malone 1985).

The structure of the music industry at the rise of rock'n'roll then, was reflected in a mainstream 'Hot 100' chart and two charts marked off from that mainstream – 'Rhythm and Blues' and 'Country and Western' (changed from 'Race' and 'Hillbilly' in the late forties). Each of the sub-branches carried a specific racial coding; although the specific musical sounds that distinguished these genres were subject to change, each was marketed to racially segregated audiences. Although individual whites had been buying black blues and jazz for decades, rock'n'roll began at the historical moment when it became possible for performers working within racially distinguished musical traditions to crossover the barriers of a segregated society and reach the 'pop' mainstream (Riesman 1990).

The musical encoding of blackness

In his autobiography, *Upside Your Head*, Johnny Otis (1993) defines African–American musical artistry as a 'critical balance between sophistication and heart', and argues that, 'when there are Black people in the audience, African–American performers get a special lift . . . With a Black audience the crowd becomes part of the performance in a very unique way.

Much as in the Black church, a call and response often develops, and Black magic fills the air.' Otis was the son of a Greek immigrant who grew up in a racially mixed neighbourhood. His career demonstrates that it is possible for white musicians to become 'black by persuasion', but it also demonstrates the key test that must be passed. For music to be functionally black, it must bring the black audience and the musicians together into an embodied group performance of cohesion and unity.

The importance of black music in the construction of black identity is deeply rooted in African–American history. For Samuel Floyd (1995), as for Sterling Stuckey (1987), the slave practice of the 'ring shout' provided the cultural rituals and performative context within which 'the musical practices of the slaves converged in the Negro spiritual and other African–American musical forms and genres'. Much as old-timey fiddlin' contests functioned for hillbilly music, the ring shout provided the cultural matrix within which the core meanings of black music developed. Floyd's masterful text, *The Power of Black Music*, includes an exhaustive list of characteristic African–American musical elements – 'calls, cries and hollers; call-and-response devices; additive rhythms and polyrhythms; heterophony; pendular thirds, blue notes, bent notes, and elisions; hums, moans, grunts, covables, and other rhythmic-oral declamations, interjections, and punctuations; off-beat melodic phrasings and parallel intervals and chords; constant repetition of rhythmic and melodic figures and phrases (from which riffs and vamps would be derived); timbral distortions of various kinds; musical individuality within collectivity; game rivalry; hand clapping, foot patting, and approximations thereof; part-playing; and the metronomic pulse that underlies all African–American music'. Each of these traits can function as a 'signifyin(g)' trope capable of conjuring up the 'cultural memory' that links the history of African–Americans with the contemporary (American) experience of blackness. At times, however, each and every one of these techniques has been used in a musical form that cannot be considered black music, which is why Floyd relies on the concept of 'cultural memory' to anchor these signifyin(g) traits.

Portia Maultsby (1985; 1990), on the other hand, refuses to rely on a key set of sounds or a discrete list of specifically black musical traits. She argues instead that the blackness of black music must be found in its distinctive conceptual approach. Floyd's position seems closer to Maultsby's when he insists that the musical 'interpretative strategies of African–Americans are the same as those that underlie the music of the African homeland ... and that they continue to inform the continuity and elaboration of African–American music' (Floyd 1995: 6). Floyd's notion of interpretative strategy holds much in common with Maultsby's distinctive conceptual approach. Both concepts are means of discriminating authentic contributions to black musical traditions.

But perhaps the key defining characteristic of black music for both Maultsby and Floyd is the cultural function that it inherited from West African societies: 'The fundamental concept that governs music performance in African and African-derived cultures is that music-making is a participatory group activity that serves to unite black people into a cohesive group for a common purpose' (Maultsby 1990: 187). The need for cultural activities that organise and promote intra-group cohesion was reinforced by the severe conditions of the middle passage and life under slavery; this was the social and political context within which the ring shout preserved certain African musical traits.

But rather than focusing on specific traits, which have often shifted their racial connotations, it might be more useful to focus on the cultural function of black music as its key defining characteristic. Both before and after the Civil War, 'Black musicians serve[d] as spokesmen, counselors, politicians, historians, entertainers, and role models for the black community. Through their songs, they [addressed and continue to] address concerns, problems and social issues that pervade the black community' (Maultsby 1985: 46). Thus, black music became a crucial site for the articulation of blackness – that is, for negotiating the meaning of belonging to the black community. The crucial defining characteristic of black music remains its ability to perform this function. Therefore if a musician with white skin could use music to articulate blackness and to bring together a group of people concerned with the problems and issues of the black community, then that musician, like Johnny Otis, would be performing black music. On the other hand, if the musician has simply learned techniques or African-derived musical traits from the black musical tradition without carrying on the cultural tradition of the black musician, then the *very same sounds* would no longer be functioning as black music *per se*.

If we apply this cultural definition within the arenas of rock and pop, then we have an understanding of black music that allows us to avoid a reliance on either market categories or the skin colour of the performer. We might classify Johnny Otis's music as black, but not necessarily M C Hammer's. When Whitney Houston sings the gospel music of her roots, she could be considered to be performing black music, but singing 'I Will Always Love You' in the movie, *The Bodyguard*, probably would not meet the requirements of this definition. The rap group Third Base could possibly qualify, while House of Pain might not. The actual job of making these judgements is the role and function of critics and audiences, who, in the process of discrimination, are always responding to extra-musical social and political considerations as well as the music 'itself'.

The musical encoding of whiteness

If we hold blackness in music to the social standard of creating and reinforcing group cohesion, what constitutes musical whiteness? Are whites
constructed as whites through the social practice of listening to racially
encoded musical forms like heavy metal or bluegrass? In Austin, Texas, in
the middle 1970s, whiteness was musically constructed through the development and promotion of progressive country music. Relying on a combination of instrumental timbres from traditional country and western and
post-sixties rock, progressive country melded the punch of loud electric
guitars with the whine of fiddles and the sweet singing of pedal steel
guitars. The sounds of the pedal steel and especially the fiddle linked progressive country to the history of country and western music, particularly
to its point of inception at old-timey fiddlin' contests. More often than
not, progressive country's rhythmic base was locked into the common
rock 2/4, but occasionally a country shuffle or honky-tonk 'sock' rhythm
could be heard. Dominated by male singers like Willie Nelson, Waylon
Jennings, Jerry Jeff Walker, and Michael Murphey, the vocal signatures of
progressive country ranged throughout the gruff to nasal tonalities of the
southern country music tradition, evoking the memories of singers like
Jimmie Rodgers, Roy Acuff, Ernest Tubb, Hank Williams and Lefty
Frizzell.

During the height of progressive country, Joe Gracey was one of
Austin's most listened-to deejays. In an interview conducted a few years
after the commercial peak of this form, Gracey made clear its racialised
meaning.

> Country music is relatively mild-mannered; it's pretty, you can dance non-
> aggressive dances to it. It is music created to have fun with. There is nothing
> ominous about it ... There was the added fact that country music is
> essentially indigenous to Texas and people here were rediscovering their ...
> roots ... Just like the Chicanos, just like the blacks, we realised that we were
> about to lose our roots, and everybody said, 'Just wait a damn minute. I'm
> from Texas, I love Texas, it's a great place to live. I love the way we eat, I love
> the way we dress, I love our habits and our customs, and I love the way I talk.
> I love everything about this state – and why wouldn't I? It's a great place!'
>
> (quoted in Shank 1994: 58)

The cultural power of progressive country music derived from its ability to
delineate the differences between 'Chicanos', 'blacks', and 'Texans'; it was
clearly a musical construction of whiteness.

Perhaps the most successful progressive country synthesis was created
in Jerry Jeff Walker's version of the Guy Clark song, 'Desperados Waiting
for a Train'. The recorded version of the song emphasises the musical

history of the progressive country genre, starting with a fiddle and guitar arrangement evocative of hillbilly music and old-timey fiddlin' contests, then moving on through the honky-tonk style of sock rhythms and solid snare beats, and ending up with the distorted guitars and driving rhythm section of a rock song. The lyrics describe an emotional connection between white men across generational divides, a connection only made possible by the continuity of white Texan cultural tradition.

'Desperados Waiting for a Train', along with the entire progressive country genre, represented a specific re-articulation of whiteness within a local culture divided by the Civil Rights movement, the Vietnam war, and drug use. This combination of musical sounds and lyrical themes reinvigorated the musical whiteness of the anti-modern southern-based tradition of country music, and then relied on this core racialised identity to re-link successfully the culture of post-sixties 'Anglo'-Texan youth with the dominant cultural traditions of the previous generations.

And yet, the musical characteristics of country music are not the sole property of individuals with white skin. Charley Pride won the 1971 performer of the year from the Country Music Association and still performs to standing room only crowds at the Grand Ole Opry. DeFord Bailey was the black harmonica player in the original Grand Ole Opry house band, performing throughout the twenties and thirties. In white traditions as in black traditions, neither the musical sounds, the skin colour of the performers, nor the racially defined market for a musical genre guarantees anything about the racial meaning of popular music. Such meaning comes from the social uses and purposes to which any set of musical sounds is put.

Crossover and contradiction

As Charles Hamm (1981) has pointed out, the rise of rock'n'roll in the 1950s marked the first and the last time that a single recording could top all three of the music industry's culturally (that is, racially) distinguished charts. Elvis Presley, the Everly Brothers, Johnny Horton, and Jerry Lee Lewis each found their recordings listed on all three charts during that decade. Since that time, many recording artists have been able to crossover from one specialised market to the mainstream pop audience. Artists identified as country and western, from Charlie Rich to Garth Brooks, have achieved 'pop' chart success. Countless rhythm and blues, soul, and rap musicians – from Sam Cooke to the Four Tops to Marvin Gaye to Coolio – have seen their recordings top the 'Hot 100'. Since the fifties, however, it has not happened that any artist has been able to claim all three markets. Public understanding of racialised musical difference obviously continues to fracture the soundscape of popular music, reinforcing racial stereotypes and shaping the contradictory significance of the phenomenon of crossover.

The two most prominent positions on the crossover of black musicians to white audiences were laid out by Steve Perry (1988) and Nelson George (1988). Perry saw the phenomenon of black artists topping the 'Hot 100' as akin to integration and, in his eyes, positive in its implications for cross-racial harmony. George interpreted crossover as a dilution of black social and cultural power, arguing that black artists who aimed at the mainstream were forsaking the black musical tradition. In a wonderfully deft article, Reebee Garofalo (1993) pointed out the strengths and the weaknesses of each of these positions, suggesting that the final chapter in the crossover debate has yet to be written. None of these articles, however, discussed the intriguing crossover of black rock.

In the mid nineteen-eighties, the Black Rock Coalition, co-founded by musician Vernon Reid and journalist Greg Tate, staked out a public position on this phenomenon, supporting and advocating the performance by black musicians of musical styles publicly associated with whiteness – hard rock, heavy metal and thrash. The black hardcore band from District Heights, Maryland, Bad Brains, might be said to have initiated this converse crossover in the late seventies. In the words of Greg Tate (1992), Bad Brains did not 'transmute their white rock shit into a ridimically sensuous black rock idiom: . . . they play[ed hardcore] just like the white boy – only harder'. Tate found this ironic for all the obvious reasons. 'The Brains are black; hardcore is white . . . and who would've ever thought that one day some bloods would go to the white boy looking for spirit?' Bad Brains did blend some reggae stylings into their thrash; they failed, however, to perform functionally black music. Their audiences remained 95 per cent white. The Black Rock Coalition was formed in 1985 not only to reaffirm the black origins of what had become white rock (pointing not only to rhythm and blues pioneers but also and specifically to black rock artists like Chuck Berry and Jimi Hendrix) and to combat racial stereotyping in music, but also to work to re-establish rock forms as functionally black music and as further proof of black music's power to make innovative leaps.

Featuring the guitar work and songwriting skills of Vernon Reid, Living Color was the band most closely tied to the Black Rock Coalition. Avoiding the overtly Africanist rhythms associated with rap music, the beats heard on their first album, *Vivid*, owed more to the drum style of John Bonham than Clyde Stubblefield. Likewise, Reid's guitar playing made references to the entire lineage of metal from Jimmy Page to Eddie Van Halen, and

Corey Glover's vocals could be mistaken on first hearing for Sammy Hagar. Yet the lyrics to songs such as 'Open Letter (to a Landlord)' made direct references to the conditions of life for inner-city black Americans. 'Which Way to America' contrasted two visions of the nation – the prosperous and happy middle-class families seen on television with the depressed conditions the song's narrator could see out his window. Although the distinction between the two Americas was not explicitly racialised, that implication was reinforced through the distinction between 'your America' which is 'doing well' and 'my America' which is 'catching hell'. The pronouns suggest a white audience and this suggestion is reinforced by one line in the song that pinpointed the problematic politics and economics of crossover, 'Don't want to crossover / But how do I keep from going under?' 'Funny Vibe' was an attempt to contextualise Living Color's hard rock both lyrically and musically. Also addressed to an assumed white audience, the lyrics assert, 'No, I'm not gonna rob you . . . beat you . . . rape you / So why you wanna give me that funny vibe?' After a few bars of standard hard rock riffing that introduce the song, the band breaks into an almost funky bass-driven groove for the verse. Then, as if this musical suggestion of blackness were not enough, a middle break follows featuring Chuck D. and Flavor Flav of Public Enemy. This break lasts only long enough for Flav to shout 'Hey Chuck, we got some non-believers out there', and for Chuck to reply, 'Yeah, Flav, I'm tired of them dissin' the brothers in the media out there. We gotta do somethin' about this. Know what I'm sayin'?' The sound mix introduces some brief scratching and some of the explosive percussive sounds common to Public Enemy's recordings. Yet Living Color continues playing their own funk throughout the quick break. The effect of this brief section of 'Funny Vibe' is to situate Living Color's relation to black music. On this track, the band seemed to want to be heard as participating in the tradition of black music, as linked to it socially and politically (that is, culturally), and capable of playing with and within the tradition (that is, of signifyin(g) on it); yet it is equally clear that they are speaking to and playing for an audience that includes and, in some cases, foregrounds, whites. Living Color maintained this two-way stance throughout their entire career. They took advantage of the possibilities of strategic anti-essentialism not only to disrupt racial stereotyping in music but also to extend the possibilities of black music, recognising that, on occasion, racialised others (that is, whites) need to be addressed in the conversation. Rather than solely uniting blacks into a cohesive group, then, the music of Living Color embodied the potential of responsible crossover, of communicating black issues beyond the black community.

The year that *Vivid* was released, 1988, was also the year that NWA released *Straight Outta Compton*, the most explosive gangsta rap album recorded to that date. Although *Straight Outta Compton* emphasised the most black-oriented elements of rap music and seemed to exclude white listeners both musically and lyrically, many whites bought this album, demonstrating the crossover sales potential of 'ghetto-centricity'. Gangsta rap grew increasingly popular throughout the early 1990s, reinvigorating debates about the social impact of music, emphasising the paradoxical double responsibility of black music in the age of crossover. In order to maintain their position of authenticity, musicians working within street-oriented rap must continue to push the edges of their sound, both lyrically and musically; they are forced to create ever more startling images of the disruption of urban life. The resulting representations of violence and misogyny can appear, however, to reinforce the worst stereotypes of a racist culture, suggesting that the problems of inner-city life are not the result of a public policy that fears its cities and its minorities, but of a 'pathological' black culture. At this point, the ability of gangsta rap to perform the internal social function of black music runs up against the recognition that the potential audience for all forms of popular music can exceed the initial intended listeners and, furthermore, that that other audience can shift the meaning of the music simply by the use to which they put it.

An example of this potential transformation of meaning can be found in the controversy that surrounded 'Cop Killer', a song released in the spring of 1992 by Ice-T's 'all black hardcore band' Body Count. Body Count followed the musical path laid out by Living Color and Bad Brains. Musically and lyrically, they addressed a white audience, relying on rigid yet driving 2/4 rhythms pushed to hardcore speeds and blistering distorted guitar runs. The lyrics of 'Cop Killer', however, drew from the violent images and confrontational styles of gangsta rap. The song, therefore, seemed a promiscuous blend of contrasting traditions, musically evoking whiteness while lyrically conjuring blackness.

That spring of 1992 also saw the not-guilty verdict brought by the jury in the Rodney King beating case and the resulting days of violent upheaval and street protest in Los Angeles. By the summer months, those days of violence had become central signifiers in the 1992 campaign for the Presidency of the United States. Also that summer, a campaign arose to force Warner Brothers Records to remove 'Cop Killer' from Body Count's album. Throughout the public debate in press conferences, newspapers and television appearances, 'Cop Killer' was referred to as a rap song. Its mulatto identity – both 'white' metal and 'black' rap – was ignored and it was declared to be 'black' almost as if by the 'one-drop' rule. The effort to label 'Cop Killer' a rap song and then censor it can only be understood in the context of the intensified public debate over the meaning of and the explanation for the Los Angeles rebellion. Represented as a rap song capable of inciting its listeners to violence, the attack on 'Cop Killer' stood in for an indictment of black culture itself. Where Ice-T and Body Count had meant for the song to communicate the experience of inner-city black rage to white listeners – using musical forms coded as white to express lyrics coded as black – the song was used by police organisations, conservative commentators, and candidates for national office as an example of the black culture that they were holding up as responsible for the rebellion in Los Angeles (Shank 1996).

The social tensions addressed by 'Cop Killer' only illustrate the ongoing power and complexity of race in rock and pop. In a society still distorted by racialised social inequality, the evocation of blackness, whiteness, or even the undeniably mulatto character of contemporary American life can produce powerful musical statements that will draw conflicting and contradictory responses from different audiences. The racial meaning of a song can never be discussed in the abstract, but must always be considered in terms of the musical and lyrical traditions out of which it comes as well as the social uses to which it is put. From blackface minstrelsy to progressive country to black rock, popular music clearly illustrates Stuart Hall's (1988) assertion that, 'the central issues of race always appear historically in articulation, in a formation, with other categories and divisions'.

For all of its social power and all of its contradictions and complexities, one can never talk simply and solely about race. Popular music in the age of rock and pop provides a necessary cultural forum wherein the social tensions that orbit around the axis of race can be performed, heard, analysed, critiqued, and danced to, in all their embodied complexity.

Further reading

A wealth of material exists on the representations of race in popular music and on the history of racialised divisions that both gave birth to and are explored through the performance and enjoyment of rock and pop. The debates about the precise racial meanings of rock and pop often founder, however, on essentialist notions of race. The fallacies that torment essentialist theories of race are detailed in Philip Tagg, 'Open Letter: "Black Music", "Afro-American Music" and "European Music"' (*Popular Music* 8(3), 1989, pp. 285–98) and Charles Keil, '"Ethnic" Music Traditions in the USA (Black music; Country music; others; all)', (*Popular Music* 13(2), 1994, pp. 175–8). In order to escape that problem, many scholars have begun to conceptualise the ways in which popular music has been used in the social processes of racialisation. This work builds upon anti-essentialist theories of race and ethnicity that argue that race is not a biological condition but a social category that is used to support systems of inequality. The undeniable fact is that popular music has been both a means of crossing racial boundaries and of reinforcing them.

Early works that specify the black contributions to rock, pop and soul include LeRoi Jones, *Blues People: The Negro Experience in White America and the Music that Developed From It* (New York: William Morrow and Company, 1963), Charles Keil, *Urban Blues* (Chicago: University of Chicago Press, 1966), Paul Oliver, *The Story of the Blues* (2nd edition) (Boston: Northeastern University Press, 1997) and Robert Palmer, *Deep Blues: A Musical and Cultural History of the Mississippi Delta* (New York: Penguin Books, 1981). Of the large synthetic works that attempt to detail the specific contributions of black diasporic peoples to the production of rock and pop, among the the most ambitious are Samuel Floyd's *The Power of Black Music: Interpreting its History from Africa to the United States* (New York: Oxford University Press, 1995) and Paul Gilroy, *There Ain't No Black in the Union Jack: The Cultural Politics of Race and Nation* (London: Hutchinson Press, 1987). Books that explore the larger contributions of black culture include Sterling Stuckey, *Going Through the Storm: The Influence of African American Art in History* (New York: Oxford University Press, 1994) and Lawrence Levine, *Black Culture and Black Consciousness: Afro-American Folk Thought from Slavery to Freedom* (New York: Oxford University Press, 1977). Work that attempts to uncover the roots of white fascination with black music generally begins by analysing the historical traditions of blackface minstrelsy. Among the most important books here are Eric Lott, *Love and Theft: Blackface Minstrelsy and the American Working Class* (New York: Oxford University Press, 1993), Dale Cockrell, *Demons of Disorder: Early Blackface Minstrels and their World* (New York: Cambridge University Press, 1997) and W. T. Lhamon Jr, *Raising Cain: Blackface Performance from Jim Crow to Hip Hop* (Cambridge, MA: Harvard University Press,1998). Works that discuss the social meanings of whiteness in music include George Lipsitz, *The Possessive Investment in Whiteness: How White People Profit from Identity Politics* (Philadelphia: Temple University Press, 1998) and Barry Shank, 'Fears of the white unconscious: music, race, and identification in the censorship of "Cop Killer"', *Radical History Review* 66, Fall, 1996, pp. 124–45. Jeffrey Melnick focuses on cross-racial collaboration in *A Right to Sing the Blues: African Americans, Jews and American Popular Song* (Cambridge, MA: Harvard University Press, 1999).

While most work on race and popular music develops out of a black/white dichotomous conceptualisation of race, recent theories of racialisation acknowledge the multiple ongoing processes that continually produce new racial formations. Among the most important of these works is Michael Omi and G. Howard Winant's *Racial Formation in the United States: From the 1960s to the 1990s* (New York: Routledge, 1994). Crucial to understanding the new developments in Asian–American cultural studies are Lisa Lowe's groundbreaking *Immigrant Acts: On Asian American Cultural Politics* (Durham, NC: Duke University Press, 1996), and David Palumbo-Liu's *Asian/American: Historical Crossings of a Racial Frontier* (Stanford, CA: Stanford University Press, 1999). Analysts of Latino/a culture using border theory highlighting the cultural construction of new racial divisions include Jose David Saldivar's *Border Matters: Remapping American Cultural Studies* (Berkeley: University of California Press, 1997) and Carl Gutierrez-Jones' *Rethinking the Borderlands* (Berkeley: University of California Press, 1995). The impact of this new work on race is only now making itself felt in the study of rock and pop. But it is sure to become a growing influence.

13 The 'local' and 'global' in popular music

JAN FAIRLEY

The relationship of the 'local' and the 'global' in popular music is one of the most complex, controversial and significant issues of the new millennium. Scholars have been drawn into the debate from across disciplines and with reference to work on musics from around the world. Arguments are not just academic; they are emotional and political, and concern the personal and the political, the micro and macro. Indeed, in straightforward analytic terms, as descriptions of networks and power relations, 'global' and 'local' are ill-defined terms, offering multiple vantage points. Whatever else, though, they have become vital for re-assessing questions of cultural imperialism, and that is what I am interested in here. I want to consider the creative and commercial relationships of the 'local' and 'global' in terms of 'world' music: how were these categories established, upon what terms; how are they maintained, to whose advantage (or disadvantage)? For most musicians, the creation and performance of music means involvement in a *process*: relationships produce music, relationships between musicians, relationships between musicians and their publics. It is in relationships that communication happens, and meanings are produced and felt. The question that interests me, then, is the nature of the local and global networks which motivate and propel the 'world' music scene and the relationship processes involved.

First, though, what do we mean by 'local' and 'global'? By 'local' do we mean musicians performing in a community space, be it home, tavern or pub, to a local audience? Or do we mean 'local' musicians like the Taraf de Haidouks, a village band from Romania, having their music made available throughout Europe and beyond, wherever it can be distributed, by a small independent French company, Mélodie? Or do we mean like Cesaria Evora, a barefoot diva from the Cape Verde islands, whose regular performance space was a local piano bar until she recorded also for Mélodie and became the toast of Paris, Europe and beyond? Do we mean Chilean musician, Mauricio Venegas, founder of the group Quimantú, based in Essex in England, recording with Indian and English musicians, financing his own CDs in association with Tumi music, selling them at gigs, as well as through Tumi's distribution circuits? Or do we mean by 'local', multinationals investing in local talent so as to thoroughly exploit 'local' markets? By global do we mean the constant expansion of the major leisure corporations into markets around the world, selling 'transnational' product from Phil Collins to U2? Or a company like EMI's Hemisphere signing Québecoise group La Bottine Souriante and marketing discs like *Rock and Reel* and *La Mistrine* (originally recorded by them on their own label, Millepattes) worldwide? Or do we mean a 'global' approach, as global companies take over national companies in order to use their expertise and control their markets? Is 'global' music, music which gets global media attention, like the recent recording of Cuban musicians, the Buena Vista Social Club? Or music which flows through the new digital communications networks, through the web and the Internet, as with bands now selling their songs to www.people.sound.com?

The point I'm making here is that global and local aren't simply contrasting descriptive terms. They suggest, rather, different perspectives of the same process. From one perspective the term globalisation is used to describe the process in which local musicians may be seen to lose their local identities as they begin to employ musical elements from the global soundscape, from 'transnational' musical forms (like rock). From another it is used to describe the way in which global musicians adopt local sounds, and may appropriate local 'traditional' copyrights. In both cases arguments are about motives as well as effects. Many musical cases do not fit into either of these perspectives. Do local musicians in the Caribbean, for example, adopt 'Euro-American scales and tunings, harmony, electronic instruments now seen as standard, accessible dance rhythms, and a Euro-American based intonation' (Guilbault quoted in Lipsitz 1994: 62) because of their musical interest or because they want to reach an international market (and earn an international income)? Do global rock stars like Peter Gabriel adapt African musical forms because of their musical value or their commercial effectiveness? The answer in both cases is probably both. Many musicians have all their lives had to struggle to earn a living from their craft; the tension between making your own music and finding an audience has always affected choice of repertoire, arrangement and style.

In this sense the dynamics of globalisation (and by implication cultural imperialism) are hardly new. Musicians have always tried to keep up with the times, not just to please their audiences but also to rejuvenate their own playing, to experiment and out of curiosity. The complexity of the reasons for musical change are brought out in recent research by Carlos Nuñez, who is re-discovering and re-arranging old Galician music (*A Irmandade das Estrelas*, BMG Ariola). Nuñez's introduction of what now sound like 'new' playing styles rests on his perception that bagpipe tunings in Galicia changed in the twentieth century from the modal tunings still used for much Scottish bagpipe music, and that piping then lost its technical detail and nuanced playing style. This happened not because of the pressure of transnational tastes or media but rather through pipers' need to adapt to survive, to change their repertoire during the 1930s and the subsequent Franco period in Spain, when their professional status was diminished. They introduced what was then a 'new' repertoire, much of it in fact drawn from the music of the Galician diaspora, from Galicians who had migrated to Cuba and the Americas and brought back to Spain different tunes and new ways of playing them.

World music

Within much Western writing on so-called 'world music' a clear contrast can be drawn between pessimists and optimists. As Peter Jowers suggests, the pessimistic definition could be summed up as 'Western pop stars appropriating non-Western sounds, as third world musicians using Western rock and pop, or as Western consumption of non-Western folk music'. His contrasting, optimistic suggestion is that

> a uniquely new type of music is in the making. It is hybrid in the sense that those from one musical tradition are incorporating elements from other traditions without lapsing into mere eclecticism. On this view involvement in such music becomes a deepening affair in which a hermeneutic 'fusion of horizons' grows and develops from which interest in music broadens out into exploration of an area's history and its wider culture. In turn this brings critical attention to contemporary political and economic issues and the role of the West in sustaining exploitation . . . Further, as this type of involvement grows, the need for an overarching label of 'world music' becomes increasingly redundant and banal, although it has served a useful mediating role in gaining media attention and respectability . . . it may have temporarily attracted the fickle followers of musical fashions . . . but it has established an audience of its own which has now stabilised and will probably expand, if very slowly.   (Jowers 1993: 69–71)

Jowers is challenging here the cynical journalistic suggestion (once offered by *Melody Maker*'s Paul Oldfield and Simon Reynolds) that, in fact, 'world' music devotees like Peter Gabriel, Paul Simon or David Byrne scarcely discover anything unfamiliar in the other cultures. Instead they've created this 'world' to staunch the crisis of faith in British and North American pop and have grafted their own very Western, very eighties pre-occupations onto it. Identifying two groups who enjoy world music – non-Western musicians, Western fans – Oldfield and Reynolds suggest that each group is attracted to the other because they are both disillusioned with their own societies in crisis and project onto the other culture a 'vicarious sense of belonging, of community, *wherever* it is to be found' (quoted in Jowers 1993). There is a postmodern point here about the forging of non-geographical, non-spatial, imaginary societies, but there is also a straightforward question: is 'disillusion' a motivating force? Was this really – empirically – the dynamic of the 1990s world music scene? As Jocelyne Guilbault argues in this book, 'World music should not be seen as simply oppositional or emancipatory . . . (nor) as the result of cultural imperialism or economic domination. To fully understand world music, we must look at its place within the complex and constantly changing dynamic of a world which is historically, socially and spatially interconnected.'

All this is to suggest that many of the arguments about world music, pessimistic and optimistic, lack the backing of ethnographic evidence, of empirical analysis of how local/global musical communication actually works. The issue here, even in commercial terms, is not just which music is released on which labels, but the entire set of power relations through which acts get signed, tracks recorded, releases playlisted, concerts booked, and so forth. (I'm sometimes struck by the irony that, while not wishing to ignore macro economic power relations, the most pessimistic readings of world music in terms of cultural imperialism tend to be the most culturally ethnocentric, showing the least understanding of the motives of either the musicians or entrepreneurs involved.)

Importance of networks

In Europe the main role in world music marketing is played by small independent companies not global corporations, and what is most apparent is the significance of networks. Jowers, focusing on WOMAD (The British based World of Music, Arts and Dance organisation) as a pivotal point for the 'world music movement' in the United Kingdom (bearing in mind that WOMAD also organises festivals in continental Europe and other parts of the world), identifies networks as the crucial world music characteristic, meaning 'network structure as predicted by new social movement theory' (Jowers 1993). Whether WOMAD, international festival organiser and record company, with links to Peter Gabriel's Real World company and recording studios, is the pivot, or the magazine *Folk Roots*, run by musician and record producer, Ian Anderson, or an individual like Ben Mandelson, musician, record producer and director of Globestyle, the world music 'scene' in Britain is clearly the network which links up all these people and their contacts in a variety of recording, performing, distributing and broadcasting projects. As Jowers writes in his study of WOMAD,

> Networks are non-hierarchical, display multiple leadership, and entail
> temporary ad hoc organisational structures founded upon variable
> individual commitments. Any organisations which emerge alter according
> to the learning process of their acting members. Each node of a network
> (individual, group, organisation) makes its own decisions, and

communication flows from node to node in any direction. Densities of
interaction make key areas of networks more central ... the network as a
whole monitors performance ... friendships, trusted contacts, implicit rules,
and understandings, legitimacy founded on past performance all emerge.

(Jowers 1993: 71)

I want to examine this argument with reference to two case studies – the
United Kingdom world music scene and the European world music
charts – before coming back to consider paradigms of collaborative
local/global music making.

Networks and world music in Britain

The British part of the 'world music movement' originated in a group of
interested music industry people who came together after various ad hoc
conversations in London in 1987 (see Anderson 2000). They met at 7 p.m.
at a pub called the Empress of Russia, St John Street, Islington, on 29 June,
13 July, and 27 July, following formal invitations from Roger Armstrong
and Ben Mandelson of Ace/GlobeStyle Records to attend an 'International
Pop Label Meeting'. Full minutes of meetings were taken and circulated to
those present, those who had been invited but could not attend, and others
it was thought might be interested (these are now available on the *Folk
Roots* website, see Anderson 2000). Those attending were people running
small record companies, journalists and promoters. The problem they met
to discuss was how to sell 'our kind of material' 'how to broaden the appeal
of our repertoire'. Points for discussion included identifying the target
audience, how to reach them, how to deal with this at the retail level and
crucially 'adoption of a campaign/media title'. Six sales devices were discussed: (i) browser cards with a 'World Music' heading and individual
logos of the companies involved; (ii) a *New Musical Express* 'World Music'
cassette to which each company would contribute material; (iii) a *Music
Week* advertorial (*Music Week* is the British music industry trade paper,
aimed primarily at retailers); (iv) shop counter leaflets/joint cata-
logues/posters; (v) collectively hiring a PR company; (vi) a World Music
Chart.

   In the event, October 1987 was designated world music month. Eleven
independent record companies invested in a promotional fund according
to the size of their catalogue (the largest contribution to the £3,500 raised,
£1,100, came from Globestyle/Ace Records; the other companies paid
between £100 and £400 into the specially opened account). Browser cards
were designed and manufactured for distribution to shops; Sterns African
Music Shop distributed co-operative starter boxes of 25/50 records, on a

sale or return basis, to accompany the browser cards and to encourage rack space to be given to the campaign. Freelance press officer Suzanne Parks was hired on a short contract, press releases and information packs were written and distributed. Ben Mandelson assembled a compilation cassette for promotion and sale through the *NME* who distributed 1,500 cassettes, called *The World At One* (the cassette title was a punning reference to the BBC's lunchtime radio news service). Tracks were selected and provided by each participating record company; one side of the cassette was 'danceable', one side 'listenable'. The accompanying press release stated the campaign's intentions quite clearly:

> The demand for recordings of non-Western artists is surely growing. This is where problems can start for the potential buyer of WORLD MUSIC albums – the High Street record shop hasn't got the particular record, or even an identifiable section to browse through, it doesn't show on any of the published charts, and at this point all but the most tenacious give up – and who can blame them?
>
> In response representatives from most of the main independent record labels dealing with international/ roots music met and agreed to launch a concentrated WORLD MUSIC campaign throughout October. Practically this means that the term world music will be used to make it easier to find that Malian kora record, the music of Bulgaria, Zairean zoukous or Indian Ghazals – the new WORLD MUSIC section will be the first place to look in the record store . . . the NME WORLD MUSIC CASSETTE with a stupendous compilation of tracks from all eleven labels . . . release date October.

Record promotion was backed up by live music, by the Crossing Border Festival at the Town and Country Club (John Martin from Crossing Border/11th Hour having attended the various meetings).

Those attending the first meeting were Chris Popham; Ben Mandelson, Roger Armstrong and Ted Carroll from Globestyle/Ace; Jonathan Rudnick from Crammed US; Amanda Jones, Thomas Brooman and Steve Hadrell from WOMAD; Charlie Gillett from Oval; Mark Kidel from Channel 4; Ian Anderson and Lisa Warburton from *Folk Roots*/Rogue Records; Anne Hunt, Mary Farquharson and Nick Gold from Arts Worldwide/World Circuit; Scott Lund and Iain Scott from Sterns/Triple Earth; Joe Boyd from Hannibal and writer Chris Stapleton. More people attended subsequent meetings (Anderson 2000: 37). According to Anderson

> it was the first bunch who you can blame for 'World Music' as the genre that now exists . . . The logic set out by Roger Armstrong was that an established, unified generic name would give retailers a place where they could confidently rack otherwise unstockable releases, and where customers might both search out items they'd heard on the radio (not knowing how to spell a

mis-pronounced or mis-remembered name or title) and browse through a wider catalogue. Various titles were discussed including 'Worldbeat' (left out anything with drums), 'Tropical' (bye bye Bulgarians), 'Ethnic' (boring and academic), 'International Pop' (the death-by-Johnny-and-Nana-syndrome) and 'Roots' (left out Johnny and Nana). 'World Music' seemed to include the most and omit the least, and got it on a show of hands. Nobody thought of defining it or pretending there was such a beast: it was just to be a box, like jazz, classical or rock … (Anderson 2000: 37)

The eleven United Kingdom labels eventually involved in this sales drive were Cooking Vinyl, Earthworks, Globestyle, Hannibal, Oval, Rogue, Sterns, Triple Earth, Topic, WOMAD, and World Circuit. As their press release explained,

Whilst not all of these labels are devoted exclusively to world music, they have united in giving recognition to the many diverse forms of music as yet unclassifiable in Western terms. Trying to reach a definition of 'WORLD MUSIC' provoked much lengthy discussion and finally it was agreed that it means practically any music that isn't, at present, catered for by its own category e.g. reggae, jazz, blues, folk. Perhaps the most common factor unifying all these WORLD MUSIC labels is the passionate commitment of all the individuals to the music itself. (Anderson 2000: 37)

This commitment, and the essentially subjective aesthetic of those involved (however tempered by colonial and post-colonial relationships and personal connections and journeys) is summed up in a comment from Ben Mandelson of Globestyle: 'The music is only chosen by us if we dig it personally.' And the idiosyncratic basis of recording and licensing decisions was a significant characteristic of the world music movement in its initial phase. Obviously such decisions were informed by cultural background, education, contacts, linguistic abilities and other more indefinable musical affinities, but they weren't based on market knowledge, on an attempt to 'give the people what they want', nor were they driven by competition for market share. In September 1987, Ian Anderson, of *Folk Roots*, suggested in an editorial on the availability of folk records that 'the only glimmer of hope in all this is the lesson that could be learned from the way that world music labels have co-operated to campaign jointly, share trade information and bang the heads of their various distributors together. Perhaps the folk/roots labels should do the same; it only took an amicable evening's meeting in a London hostelry to get that admirable co-operation under way' (*Folk Roots*, 51, 1987: 4). (Anderson later called the initial world music marketing budget: 'The best £2,500 (*sic*) spent in the entire history of the media and music business.' (Personal communication, 14 May 1995))

The British world music scene was later criticised for its croneyism, its metropolitan London centricity, for leaving people (and the provinces) out, and eventually for its racism. But this is the essence of networking. The Empress of Russia meetings were between people who had already helped each other get established; the idea was to 'keep it to a manageable number of known enthusiasts' (Anderson, personal communication, 14 May 1995). When journalist Rick Glanville called the campaign 'mistaken at best, exploitative at worst', Anderson replied that

> Glanville simply cannot understand the enthusiast who will do something, be it put out a record, organise tours or concerts for artists, play music on their radio programmes or whatever, entirely because they want more people to share in something they have discovered . . . thus the enthusiast who goes all out to bring said music to mass attention is seen as enemy, and all kinds of half-baked socio-political arguments are used to destroy their credibility. (*Folk Roots*, 64, 1988: 4)

Glanville went on to spell out his reaction in the London based *City Limits* in an article entitled 'Bullshit detector', levelling paternalism and white middle-classdom at the participants. In a sense Anderson and Glanville's positions, 'write large' what Steven Feld sees as narratives of 'anxiety' and 'celebration' (Feld 2000), a post-Marxian explanation of motive.

There were a number of other events which marked out 1987 as something of a key moment for 'world music' in the United Kingdom. It was the year of Paul Simon's *Graceland* tour; Peter Gabriel and Youssou N'Dour staged British concerts together. The BBC's classical music station, Radio 3, held their influential 'Music of the Royal Courts' Festival in London's Barbican, concerts of a great variety of world musics were transmitted live on air each night for two weeks. And it is to the role of radio for world music to which I will now turn.

Radio: the world music charts Europe

One essential means of the diffusion of 'world music' in Europe is through radio, despite the fact that in many European countries there is only one (perhaps even only one hour) world music programme a week. At the same time, most of these programmes are compiled by freelance journalists who, whatever their personal knowledge and resources, have limited institutional support. Two things have followed from this. First, it makes sense for world music deejays to network like world music record companies (in the deejay case through the European Broadcasting Union's World Music Workshop). Second, in considering the difference between what music is actually available (the totality of global record releases) and what is actually played (for all their idiosyncrasies world music deejays tend to have records in common on their playlists, largely influenced by the distribution of records to the group during the same period) we need to understand how the deejay and record company networks are connected.

My argument here is that 'world music' in Europe centrally consists of musical output from a small number of independent, one-person production companies, some run on the lines of a cottage industry, with that one person's aesthetic serving as the *raison d'être* for company policy/direction (examples would include Globestyle, London: Ben Mandelson; Piranha, Berlin: Christoph Borkowsky Akbar; Triple Earth, London: Iain Scott; World Circuit, London: Nick Gold) . Sales of music are variable, but distribution to possible radio outlets is highly efficient, through the servicing of the members of the EBU World Music Workshop (which in the 1990s also had links with Sean Barlow, the producer of Afro-Pop Worldwide, aired on National Public Radio in the United States). What is striking is that these relationships are focused (just as in the mainstream European music market) through the use of charts.

The World Music Charts Europe (WMCE) were launched by a Berlin deejay, Johannes Theurer, in May 1991. Theurer had support from the EBU for his initiative, and a print outlet, the Berlin daily newspaper, *Berliner Morgenpost.* Although charts had been on the agenda of the Empress of Russia meeting, nothing had come of that discussion and Theurer (who knew no one in the London network) had the idea independently, approaching the EBU for support at its World Music Workshop meeting in Berlin in autumn 1990. He found sponsorship for the charts (which he owns) from various Berlin radio stations. The Charts are compiled from the monthly votes of producers and deejays (who must have a weekly world music programme on a radio station which is an EBU member). These Charts are not based on record sales but on deejay tastes and playlists; they are distributed to a wide range of interested parties: journalists, music magazines, shops, newspapers, etc. Each deejay faxes or emails their monthly list of ten titles on the same date each month to Berlin (by November 1998 the thirty-nine deejays involved came from seventeen countries: Austria, Belgium, Czech Republic, Finland, France, Germany, Hungary, Italy, Netherlands, Norway, Poland, Russia, Slovenia, Sweden, Switzerland, Turkey and the United Kingdom; in November 1999, forty-six deejays were listed from twenty countries). Votes are allocated to albums from which tracks were played on the deejays' weekly programmes; and to the albums deejays have most played from the previous month's releases (the number one title on a list gets ten points, number two nine points and so on). The selection of records is open and subjective within the bounds of the records each person has received and sought. Record suppliers (who also get the Chart) are encouraged to distribute their new releases to every contributing deejay simultaneously, so as to maximise the exposure of the deejays to the same artists and discs in the same period. Small, independent companies tend to benefit most from this system which does not suit the normal multinationals' territory-by-territory release policy. BMG, for example, released Carlos Nunez's *Irhmandade das estrellas [Brotherhood of Stars]* in Spain in 1996 but not in the United Kingdom until 1998. Despite selling 150,000 copies in Spain, the record never entered the WMCE.

These Charts are, then, an unusual musical map. On the one hand, they rest on each contributor's cultural and personal aesthetic bias, the character of their programme, and their freedom of choice (most European world music shows are presenter produced and not subject to overt control or censorship, although there may be playlist guidance in the programme brief). Indeed, the unusual nature of these programmes in contrast to their stations' usual mainstream pop and rock output leads in many cases to a distinctly idiosyncratic approach, with deejays moving deliberately between more accessible and more unusual sounds, between say Senegalese mbalax artist Youssou N'Dour and Mongolian throat singing from Huun-Huur-Tu. But for all this ideological individualism, the Charts are also about bringing some agreed shape to world music radio in Europe and in this respect, a quick Chart glance suggests that 'transnational' music released by multinational companies does not pre-dominate. WMCE's annual reports, which summarise the year's posi-tions, confirm this – in this Chart, at least, big and small companies compete on equal terms. There are recurring patterns nonetheless (partly reflecting the programmes involved, the descriptions of which vary from traditional/folk to dance/tropical). Certainly there are many recordings from musicians who by no means could be described as either 'exotic' or a European 'other'. The largest percentage of records are certainly, in music-ological terms, African, although in the second half of the 1990s more European titles entered the Chart, and more Cuban music (a response to changes in its licensing and distribution arrangements). In other words, even if the WMCE may not much affect the sales of records (and there is little evidence that they do immediately, although for the smaller compa-nies, in particular, radio play may be the only way to alert the potential market to a new release), it does help construct the framework in which some records (but not others) are heard as 'world music' in the first place. And this leads me to a second way in which radio programmes become central to the world music network, by creating their own 'listening communities'.

Veit Erlmann (1993: 12) suggests that 'many of the styles more conventionally associated with the term "world music" become demarcators of community through the forging of affective links between dispersed places. At a deeper level of significance, however, the re-configured time–space relationship in "world music" does away with time and place altogether.' Certainly, in my own experience of presenter/producing Earthbeat, a weekly, one-hour world music programme for four years for BBC Radio Scotland, 'world music' radio listeners do commonly record their programmes on cassette to circulate amongst networks of friends (an activity which at least in the early 1990s, before the web provided online shopping possibilities to those living away from urban centres, was partly an effect of the difficulty of finding/hearing such sounds and small budgets for purchasing them). 'Listening habits', as Erlmann (1993: 12) suggests, may 'register different musical traditions as simultaneously fragments of a completely different type of cultural space than the one represented by the earlier notion of an organic totality.' And while we need more research on radio listening before we can confidently make such claims about it, it is the case that many world music radio programmes work precisely (if implicitly) with such simultaneous fragments. World music deejays juxtapose music from different artists, countries and continents without any 'localised' contextualisation at all. In short, the world to which all these musics belong is shaped by networks that no longer have much to do with geography. In November 1998, for example, the WMCE was topped by *Vihma*, the latest album from the Finnish group Värttinä which was also top of the United States college radio charts. The other records in the WMCE top ten involved artists from South Africa, Madagascar, Brazil, Senegal, Ecuador, Cuba, Tuva, Spain and (generally) from Europe and the United States (contributing to a double CD of Euro-American klezmer music). It is to two of the free-ranging musician networks and musical 'friendships' that occur from time to time in these charts that I will now turn.

Music making paradigms

What I want to describe are two possible paradigms for transnational, 'local/global' musical relationships. These accentuate the whole notion of the process of music making. I will take Ry Cooder and Paul Simon to represent, rather clearly, contrasting approaches to working with musicians from different musical cultures and other parts of the world. This is not to suggest that these are exclusive or exemplary paradigms, or the only means of musical collaboration: other musicians one might consider are Peter Gabriel (and his record label Real World); David Byrne (and his record label Luaka Bop); Henry Kaiser, David Lindley, Mickey Hart, to name a number of those most well known (see also Feld 2000). Rather, I want to use Cooder's and Simon's world musical activities as a useful way into the questions about the local, the global and cultural imperialism raised earlier. On the one hand, they exemplify how 'first' world musicians may work alongside 'third' world musicians; on the other hand, they show how international stars, signed to major record companies, may be promoted globally. They provide us with narratives with their own attendant mythologies in which we can situate all musicians taking part in such processes. Who is 'local' and who 'global' in these cases is less obvious than it may first appear. What can be said immediately is that both Simon's and Cooder's world music records had a tremendous impact. Paul Simon's *Graceland* sold seven million copies in the 1980s (and introduced African musical styles to listeners who had never previously heard them). The record on which Ry Cooder worked, *Buena Vista Social Club,* had sold three million copies at the beginning of 2000 (inspiring the Academy Award nominated Wim Wenders 'documentary' film of the same name).

The Cooder paradigm

This paradigm can be described as an encounter between a musician with a global reputation and 'local' musicians, that is musicians only known heretofore within their own geographically defined market. In this encounter the musicians come together and engage in music making with a publicly released outcome to the satisfaction of all those taking part. It is a narrative of co-operation and respect. Through the mediation of the global musician all the participants are brought to the attention of a global audience.

Ry Cooder's work with Cuban musicians on the recording *Buena Vista Social Club* took place early in 1997, under the executive direction of the British-based world music label, Nick Gold's World Circuit. Cooder participated on all tracks, playing various guitars and other instruments, such as the African mbira, with contributions from his son Joachim Cooder. He has a production credit on the subsequent World Circuit CD.

Accounts of Cooder's part in this project suggest that he followed the pattern he had established when working with Malian guitarist, Ali Farka Toure, on *Talking Timbuktu* (World Circuit). Here Cooder clearly gave Toure and his Malian repertoire centre stage. While his presence makes this a different recording than it would have been without him, he acts primarily as a bridge, bringing Toure's established style to a wider, possibly larger audience. (*Talking Timbuktu* won a United States Grammy award in 1995. It was rare then for non-North American musicians to have such an impact on the United States market.) Even earlier, in 1992, Cooder worked with a North Indian classical musician from Jaipur, Vishwa Mohan Bhatt, their collaboration resulting in *A Meeting By The River* (Water Lily Acoustics). Jelaluddin Rumi, who played a part in organising this encounter, provides a narrative account of the recording process:

> With no planning whatsoever, and no preparation, the musicians soon established a dialogue through which they could probe each other so as to know where the bends in the river were going to be, how deep, or how swift the waters . . . two streams merged to form a river. The rhythm of this river was Sukhvinder's tabla, and the *dumbek* played by Joachim, Ry's fourteen-year-old son . . . this recording was unplanned and unrehearsed.
>
> (*A Meeting By The River* sleeve notes)

In drawing attention to the musical and instrumental affinities between Bhatt and Cooder, Rumi is describing a pattern set by previous Cooder collaborations with Flaco Jimenez and others. Cooder's approach is to hear the essence of a music and work with it. On his 1976 album, *Chicken Skin Music,* for example, he was equally at ease with gospel, Tex-Mex and Hawaiian forms, and throughout his career his approach to music he likes has been the same: meet up with musicians, set up a musical dialogue and after a few obvious preliminaries record in as short a time as possible.

Cooder's contribution to the Buena Vista Social Club was just as subtle as his previous collaborations, and just as unproblematic. (Even though its origins were somewhat fraught. The original plan had been to have Cooder record in Cuba with a number of guitarists, including some from Africa. This had to be cancelled, and the Buena Vista project, which had been mooted but not developed, was put together in a few days, on the back of the Afro-Cuban All Stars, a project already in the Egrem studio being recorded by World Circuit.) As Cooder explains:

> This album is blessed with some of the finest musicians in Cuba today – their dedication to the music and rapport with each other is unique in my experience. Working on this project was a joy and a great privilege. This music is alive in Cuba, not some remnant in a museum that we stumbled on. I felt that I had trained all my life for this and yet making this record was not what I expected in the 1990s. Music is a treasure hunt. You dig and dig and sometimes you find something. In Cuba the music flows like a river. It takes care of you and rebuilds you from the inside out. My deepest thanks to everyone who participated in this record.
>
> (Introduction to booklet accompanying the CD)

Cooder takes production credits on *Buena Vista Social Club* but all music is credited to the musicians concerned.

The Simon paradigm

This paradigm refers to the 1986 Paul Simon album, *Graceland*, recorded for Warner Brothers. As Simon's own initiative, this is different from Cooder's project in various ways, including the fact that Simon worked with more than one group of musicians from more than one country. In this paradigm, then, one musician invites others to record with him or her. They do so (on what some see as unequal terms dictated by the employing musician) with an outcome which is only partly satisfactory to those taking part (some are quite satisfied, some rather less so). On the song, 'All Around the World', for example, words and music are credited to Paul Simon while the end credit reads 'with Los Lobos'. The various African collaborators (members of Ladysmith Black Mambazo, for example) get co-songwriting credits for the tracks to which they contributed; the CD sleeve makes clear, though, that all songs on the album are 'copyright 1986 Paul Simon'.

At the time of its release, arguments about *Graceland* focused on the problems of dealing with apartheid South Africa – was Simon right to break the UN ban on cultural contacts? But the contrasting relations he had with his collaborators were also telling. The Los Angeles Chicano group, Los Lobos, accused him of treating them badly: recording them, and then taking the credit for their tunes. Ladysmith Black Mambazo, by contrast, recorded an album, *Shaka Zulu*, with Simon as producer, which won the 1988 Grammy for best world music recording and went on to sell 100,000 copies. Undoubtedly many of the third world musicians involved in *Graceland* thought themselves lucky to be recording with a world-class artist. Ladysmith indeed have gone on to be very happy with the enormous gains they have achieved from the worldwide exposure *Graceland* has given them and their music: for example going on to become household names and playing to very broadly based popular audiences as well as more specialist world music/African music fans in the United Kingdom, through the use of one of their songs in a Heinz Baked Beans television advertisement. Ladysmith see their popularity as having been gained without any musical compromise whatsover (interview Joseph Shabalala, 17 March, 2000)

What rankled with *Graceland*, nonetheless, for many commentators were the power relations involved: Simon did the whole thing on his own terms, taking musical credit even when his role was clearly as arranger rather than originator of material. Unlike Ry Cooder, Simon became the focus for questions about appropriation and power. As Steve Feld writes

> Scrutinising his role in terms of overall ownership of the product (Simon's name above the title, 'Produced by Paul Simon,' 'All Songs Copyright . . . Paul Simon') . . . [one can see] . . . how this ownership maintains a particular distance between his [Simon's] elite pop star status and the status of the musicians with whom he worked . . . It seems to draw the boundary line between participation and collaboration at ownership. Whose music? Paul Simon's music . . . Recent recordings by other international pop stars, for example, Peter Gabriel's *So* or Talking Heads' *Naked,* could also be approached through this kind of archaeological stylistic stratigraphy, revealing layers and varieties of appropriation, circulation, and traffic in musical grooves, and concomitant embeddings and solidifications of musical ownership.   (Feld 1994a: 241–2).

While there may be questions of limitations of copyright for black South African musicians at that time, and private deals may have been done, what is clear is that the relationship between Simon and the other musicians involved in *Graceland* was in many ways unequal. This may have been a watershed album, with huge world wide impact, but it leaves an uncomfortable trail of suspicion behind it. To quote Feld again,

> It is clear . . . that the flow of products and the nature of ownership is differentiated by market valuation factors . . . the revitalising cycle of Africanisation/ Afroamericanisation in world beat comes to be increasingly entangled with issues of power and control because of the nature of record companies and their cultivation of an international pop music elite with the power to sell enormous numbers of recordings. These forces tend to draw upon and incorporate African and African–American materials, products, and ideas but stabilise them at the levels of labor, talent, or 'influences,' levels at which they can be continually manipulated for export and recirculation in made-over forms. The politicised aesthetic of a record like *Graceland* then looks more and more like an ink-blot test whose projection is a much too literal map of the black and white of world music.   (Feld 1994a: 246)

Conclusion

If we return to the dynamics of the local and global with which this chapter began, it is clear that world music (for many an utopic all-embracing term like jazz or classical, for others a restrictive ghettoisation) offers a rich field of debate for popular music studies. This debate concerns not only definitions, processes and practice as well as musical product, but also a 'category' around which many contentious issues surrounding critiques of cultural imperialism and post-colonialist and post-modernist practices cluster. Whatever disagreements people have with 'world music' as a term, it has played a part in getting much music that was not being heard launched on the world market, raising its profile considerably. However, rather than this fitting easily into arguments concerning the master strategy of multi-national record companies or the work of aesthetically bankrupt western musicians, attention has been drawn to the complex ways in which various independent networks of individuals working with this music have played a part. Indeed I would like to stress the significant power of these informal networks of record companies, festivals and media outlets. How the activities of such networks fit into or impact upon macroeconomic moves and shifts of international capital and the ways this has affected markets have yet to be fully assessed. What is certain is that it is not possible to reduce such networks and their activities to easy generalisations about cultural imperialism or post-colonialism, due to the complexity of the relationships – between musicians and entrepreneurs, small businesses and enthusiasts, cultural curators and administrators and the media. Attention has been drawn to the complex sets of power relations and the notion of music making not as an end in itself but as a process within which meanings through experiences are generated. The implications of such relationships are at times both ethical and moral, particularly when questions of representation, copyright and ownership are moot (Feld 2000). World music is part of a larger industrial world full of economic inequalities. As I said at the very beginning, ultimately the processes involved define the advantages and disadvantages for different groups of musicians: the mechanics and articulations, the economic, legal and political relationships within the music making practice, are under scrutiny. What is interesting is the way that various key musicians have been brought into the ethical and moral arguments which 'world music' relationships have raised (Reed 1999). What is needed is ethnographic research and case study work to explore the basis of both practical and theoretical positions being taken. In the context of this book it seems world music is significant not just as a narrative about people in different places creating, hearing and using different sounds, but also in the ways it raises new questions, approaches and challenges for popular music studies.

Further reading

For a participant's account of the United Kingdom world music scene, read 'World Wars' by Ian Anderson, the editor of *Folk Roots* and proprietor of Rogue Records (*Folk Roots*, No. 201, March 2000, pp. 36–9). Anderson was stimulated by an article in the *New York Times* by musician David Byrne (who runs the Luaka Bop label). For another musician and label owner's view, see 'Peter Gabriel in conversation with Lou Reed' (*Real World Notes*, no. 8., Summer 1999, Real World Holdings Ltd, pp. 4–6). It is a rather tame account of Real World Records, which offers few insights but does reveal a number of facts about the label. Anderson gives critical mention to Rick Glanville whose 'World music mining, the international trade in new music', in F. Hanly and T. May (eds.), *Rhythms of the World* (London: BBC Books, 1989), was one of the first to raise many of the issues concerning the implications of first/third world musical relationships, albeit on a journalistic level. Louise Meintjes' excellent 'Paul Simon's *Graceland*, South Africa and the mediation of musical meaning' (*Ethnomusicology* 34(1), 1990, pp. 37–73) offers a pluralistic account of approaches to leading musician Paul Simon's controversial work with South African artists at a time when apartheid still held force in South Africa. Steven Feld's 'A sweet lullaby for world music' (in *Public Culture* 12 (1), April 2000, pp. 147–71) sets out what might be viewed as a post-Marxian binary, a discourse of the trophes of 'anxiety' and 'celebration' surrounding world music, focusing in part on questions of copyright, ownership and monies/royalties gained from recordings. The second part is a detailed account of controversy surrounding the recent 'sampling' by Deep Forest of 'Rorogwela', a field recording of Afunakwa from the Baegu Community, without full permission, the melody later used inadvertently by Jan Garbarek, a situation which has raised many as yet unsolved issues about globalisation and power. Hugo Zemp's 'The/an ethnomusicologist and the record business (*Yearbook for Traditional Music* 28, 1996, pp. 36–57) charts the beginning of the controversy.

Peter Jowers' 'Beating new tracks: WOMAD and the British world music movement' (in Simon Miller (ed.) *The Last Post, Music After Modernism*, Manchester University Press, 1993, pp. 52–8) is a very interesting account of the role of networks in the world music scene, from an academic who in another life worked for WOMAD. Both Jocelyne Guilbault, in 'On redefining the "local" through world music (*The World of Music* 35(2), 1993, pp. 33–47) and Debbie Pacini Hernandez, in 'A view from the south: Spanish Caribbean perspectives on world beat' (*The World of Music* 35(2), 1993, pp. 48–69), offer strong accounts, revealing rather different North American viewpoints on the questions surrounding 'world beat', the American term for 'world music', describing the same phenomenon but a slightly different animal. Veit Erlmann sheds theoretical light in 'The politics and aesthetics of transnational musics' (*The World of Music* 35(2), 1993, pp. 3–15), while Reebee Garofalo's 'Whose world, what beat: the transnational music industry, identity and cultural imperialism' offers a thought-provoking approach (*The World of Music* 35(2), 1993, pp. 16–31). Garofolo's edited collection, *Rockin' The Boat: Mass*

Music and Mass Movements (Boston: South End Press, 1992), makes excellent background reading. The problematic 'cultural imperialism' debate surrounding world music which came in early on as part of re-thinking in a post-Marxist intellectual climate, can be traced through key articles by Andrew Goodwin and Jo Gore 'World beat and the cultural imperialism debate' (*Socialist Review* 20(3), July–September 1990, pp. 63–80) and Dave Laing's 'The music industry and the 'cultural imperialism' thesis (*Media Culture and Society* 8(3), 1986, pp. 331–41). David Hesmondhalgh's 'Globalisation and cultural imperialism: a case study of the music industry' (in R. Kiely and P. Marfleet (eds.), *Globalisation and the Third World*, London: Routledge, 1998, pp. 163–83) continues the theme. Roy Shuker's *Understanding Popular Music* (London: Routledge, 1994) is well worth a read. Steven Feld's thoughtful pieces are always good, particularly 'Notes of world beat' (*Public Culture Bulletin* 1(1), 1988, pp. 31–7), reprinted in *Music Grooves*, Feld's book with Charles Keil (University of Chicago Press, 1994, pp. 238–46). Line Grenier and Jocelyne Guilbault's 'Créolité and francophonie in music: socio-musical repositioning where it matters' (*Cultural Studies* 11 (2) 1997, pp. 207–34) is a seminal article which explores social relations, networks and alliances with respect to narratives of zouk and the Québecoise mainstream.

References

Adorno, T. W. (1990) 'On popular music', in S. Frith and A. Goodwin (eds.) *On Record: Rock, Pop and the Written Word*, New York/London: Pantheon/Routledge, pp. 301–14

Anderson, I. (2000) 'World wars', *Folk Roots Magazine* 201, pp. 36–9

Appiah, A. (1985) 'The uncompleted argument: DuBois and the illusion of race', *Critical Inquiry* 12(1), Autumn, pp. 21–37

Attali, J. (1985) *Noise: The Political Economy of Music*, Manchester: Manchester University Press

Aubert, L. (1992) 'The world dances to a new beat: an invitation to the "Great Pluralistic Jamboree"', *World Press Review* 39, pp. 24–5

Barthes, R. (1990) 'The grain of the voice', in S. Frith and A. Goodwin (eds.) *On Record: Rock, Pop and the Written Word*, New York/London: Pantheon/Routledge, pp. 293–300. (Also: Barthes, R. (1972) 'Le grain de la voix', *Musique en jeu* 9, pp. 57–63)

Basch, L. et al. (1994) *Nations Unbound: Transnational Projects, Postcolonial Predicaments and Deterritorialized Nation-States*, London: Gordon and Breach

Bayles, M. (1994) *Hole in Our Soul: The Loss of Beauty and Meaning in American Popular Music*, New York: The Free Press

Bayton, M. (1990) 'How women become musicians', in S. Frith and A. Goodwin (eds.) *On Record: Rock, Pop, and the Written Word*, New York/London: Pantheon/Routledge, pp. 238–57

    (1997) 'Women and the Electric Guitar', in S. Whiteley (ed.) *Sexing the Groove: Popular Music and Gender*, London: Routledge, pp. 37–49

    (1998) *Frock Rock*, Oxford: Oxford University Press

Beatty, S. and Hymowitz, C. (2000) 'How MTV Stays Tuned to Teens', *The Wall Street Journal*, 21 March, p. B1

Bennett, T., Frith, S., Grossberg, L. Shepherd, J. and Turner, G. (eds.) (1993) *Rock Music: Politics, Policies and Institutions*, London: Routledge

Benson, R. (1997) *Nightfever: Club Writing in the Face 1980–1997*, London: Boxtree

Bissoondath, N. (1994) *Selling Illusions: The Cult of Multiculturalism in Canada*, Toronto: Penguin

Blacking, J. (1977) 'Some problems of theory and method in the study of musical change', *Yearbook of the International Folk Music Council* 9, pp. 1–26

Born, G. (1987) 'Modern music culture: on shock, pop and synthesis', *New Formations* 1(2), pp. 51–78

    (1993) 'Afterword: music policy, aesthetic and social difference', in T. Bennett, S. Frith, L. Grossberg, J. Shepherd and G. Turner (eds.) *Rock and Popular Music: Politics, Policies, Institutions*, London: Routledge, pp. 266–92

Borzillo, C. (1992) 'Afropop program is spreading the world on world music', *Billboard* 104, 66, 13 June

Brackett, D. (1995) *Interpreting Popular Music*, Cambridge: Cambridge University Press

Bradby, B. (1990) 'Do-talk and don't-talk: the division of the subject in girl-group music', in S. Frith and A. Goodwin (eds.) *On Record: Rock, Pop and the Written Word*, New York/London: Pantheon/Routledge, pp. 341–68

(1993) 'Sampling sexuality: gender, technology and the body in dance music', *Popular Music* 12(2), pp. 155–76

Bryson, N. (1997) 'Cultural studies and dance history', in J. C. Desmond (ed.) *Meaning in Motion: New Cultural Studies of Dance*, Durham and London: Duke University Press, pp. 55–77

Butler, J. (1990) *Gender Trouble: Feminism and the Subversion of Identity*, London: Routledge

Carson, T. (1990) 'Rocket to Russia', in S. Frith and A. Goodwin (eds.) *On Record: Rock, Pop and the Written Word*, New York/London: Pantheon/Routledge, pp. 441–9

Chester, A.(1990) 'Second thoughts on a rock aesthetic: The Band', in S. Frith and A. Goodwin (eds.) *On Record: Rock, Pop and the Written Word*, New York/London: Pantheon/Routledge, pp. 325–19

Cheyney, T. (1993) 'Artists in Southern Calif. march to a world beat', *Billboard*, 2 October, 1, p. 88

(1991) 'The importance of planet beat: myriad influences make world of difference', *Billboard* 103, 52, p. 56

Clarke, G. (1990) 'Defending ski-jumpers: a critique of theories of youth subcultures', in S. Frith and A. Goodwin (eds.) *On Record: Rock, Pop and the Written Word*, New York/London: Pantheon/Routledge, pp. 81–96

Cloonan, M. (1996) *Banned! Censorship of Popular Music in Britain 1967–92*, Aldershot: Arena

Cohen, S. (1991a) *Rock Culture in Liverpool: Popular Music in the Making*, Oxford: Oxford University Press

(1991b) 'Survey of the music industries on Merseyside', *Music City Report*, Liverpool: Ark Consultants

(1991c) 'Popular music and urban regeneration: the music industries of Merseyside', *Cultural Studies* 5(3), pp. 332–46

(1995) 'Popular music in 20th-century Liverpool: a case study', *Popular Music Perspectives* 3, Berlin: Humboldt University

(1997) 'Men making a scene: rock music and the production of gender', in S. Whiteley (ed.) *Sexing the Groove*, London: Routledge, pp. 17–36

Cohen, S. and McManus, K. (1991) *Harmonious Relations: Popular Music and Family Life on Merseyside*, Liverpool: National Galleries and Museums on Merseyside, pp. 1–59

Collin, M. (1997) *Altered State: The Story of Ecstasy Culture and Acid House*, London: Serpent's Tail

Cross, B. (1993) *It's not about a Salary . . . Rap, Race and Resistance in Los Angeles*, London: Verso

Cushman, T. (1991) 'Rich rastas and communist rockers: a comparative study of the origin, diffusion and defusion of revolutionary musical codes', *Journal of Popular Culture* 25, pp. 17–61

Dawson, J. (1995) *The Twist: The Story of the Song and Dance That Changed the World*, Boston and London: Faber and Faber

Dixon, R. (1980) 'Suggested scales for the measurement of musical involvement and genre tastes', *Popular Music and Society* 7 (4), pp. 223–44

Duffy, T. (1992) 'Pop goes the global music scene as MIDEM provides a stage for the universal language', *Billboard* 104, 10, 8 February

du Gay, P., Hall, S., Janes, L., Mackay, H. and Negus, K. (1997) *Doing Cultural Studies*, London: Sage

Durant, A. (1984) *Conditions of Music*, London: Macmillan

Dyer, R. (1990) 'In defence of disco', in S. Frith and A. Goodwin (eds.) *On Record: Rock, Pop and the Written Word*, New York/London: Pantheon/Routledge, pp. 410–18

Ellison, M. (1989) *Lyrical Protest: Black Music's Struggle Against Discrimination*, New York: Praeger

Ennis, P. H. (1992) *The Seventh Stream: The Emergence of RocknRoll in American Popular Music*, Hanover, NH: Wesleyan University Press

Eno, B. (1983) 'The studio as compositional tool – part I and II', *Down Beat* 50 (7 and 8), July and August, pp. 56–7, 50–3

Erenberg, L. A. (1981) *Steppin' Out: New York Nightlife and the Transformation of American Culture, 1890–1930*, Chicago: University of Chicago Press

Erlmann, V. (1993) 'The politics and aesthetics of transnational musics', *The World of Music* 35 (2), pp. 3–16

    (1994) 'Africa civilised, Africa uncivilised: local culture, world system and South African music', *Journal of Southern African Studies* 20, pp. 165–79

Fabbri, F. (1982) 'A theory of musical genres: two applications', in D. Horn and P. Tagg (eds.) *Popular Music Perspectives*, Gothenburg and Exeter, pp. 52–81

Feist, D. (1994) 'A beginner's guide to worldbeat music', Special Supplement, *The Gazette*, 12 November

Feld, S. (1994a) 'Notes on "world beat"', in C. Keil and S. Feld, *Music Grooves*, University of Chicago Press, pp. 238–46

    (1994b) 'From schizophonia to schismogenesis: on the discourses and commodification practices of "world music" and "world beat"', in C. Keil and S. Feld (eds.) *Music Grooves*, Chicago: University of Chicago Press, pp. 257–89

    (2000) 'A sweet lullaby for world music', *Public Culture* 12 (1), pp. 145–71

Fields, B. (1982) 'Ideology and race in American history', in J. M. Kousser and J. McPherson (eds.) *Region, Race and Reconstruction: Essays in Honor of C. Vann Woodward*, New York: Oxford University Press, pp. 143–78

Fleming, T. (1999): 'Awfully affecting. The development of a sentimental text in the lyric of British and American popular song', PhD thesis, Department of English Studies, University of Strathclyde

Floyd, S. (1995) *The Power of Black Music: Interpreting its History from Africa to the United States*, New York: Oxford University Press

Fornas, J. (1995) 'The future of rock: discourses that struggle to define a genre', *Popular Music* 14(1), pp. 111–25

Foucault, M. (1991) 'Politics and the study of discourse', in G. Burchell et al. (eds.) *The Foucault Effect: Studies in Governmentality*, University of Chicago Press, pp. 53–72

Fox, T. (1986) *In the Groove: The People Behind the Music*, New York: St Martin's Press

Frith, S. (1981) *Sound Effects: Youth, Leisure, and the Politics of Rock'n'Roll*, New York/London: Pantheon/Constable

(1986) 'Art versus technology: the strange case of popular music', *Media, Culture and Society* 8(3), pp. 263–79

(1988) *Music for Pleasure: Essays in the Sociology of Pop*, Cambridge: Polity

(1990) 'Afterthoughts', in S. Frith and A. Goodwin (eds.) *On Record: Rock, Pop and the Written Word*, New York/London: Pantheon/Routledge, pp. 419–24

(1992) 'The cultural study of popular music', in L.Grossberg, C. Nelson and P. A.Treichler (eds.) *Cultural Studies*, New York and London: Routledge, pp. 174–86

(ed.) (1993) *Music and Copyright*. Edinburgh: Edinburgh University Press

(1996) *Performing Rites: On the Value of Popular Music*, Oxford: Oxford University Press

Frith, S. and Horne, H. (1987) *Art into Pop*, London: Methuen

Frith, S. and McRobbie, A. (1990) 'Rock and Sexuality', in S. Frith and A. Goodwin (eds.) *On Record: Rock, Pop and the Written Word*, New York/London: Pantheon/Routledge, pp. 371–89

Frith, S., Goodwin, A. and Grossberg, L. (eds.) (1993) *Sound and Vision: The Music Video Reader*, New York and London: Routledge

Gabbard, K. (ed.) (1995) *Representing Jazz*, London: Duke University Press

Gallaugher, A. (1995) 'Constructing Caribbean culture in Toronto: the representation of Caribana', in A. Ruprecht and C. Taiana (eds.) *The Reordering of Culture: Latin America, the Caribbean and Canada in the Hood*, Ottawa: Carleton University Press, pp. 397–408

Gardinier, A. (1991) ' "World music" or sounds of the times', *The UNESCO Courier*, March, pp. 37–9

Garofalo, R. (1991) 'Review of Simon Frith's *World Music, Politics and Social Change*', *Popular Music* 10(2), pp. 255–7

(1993) 'Black popular music: crossing over or going under', in T. Bennett, S. Frith, L. Grossberg, J. Shepherd and G. Turner (eds.) *Rock and Popular Music: Politics, Policies, Institutions*, London and New York: Routledge, pp. 231–48

Gehr, R. (1993) 'World beat: world music library', *Spin* 9, November, pp. 130–1

Geldof, B. (1986) *Is That It?* London: Sidgwick and Jackson

Gendron, B.(1986) 'Theodor Adorno meets the Cadillacs', in T. Modleski (ed.) *Studies in Entertainment: Critical Approaches to Mass Culture*, Bloomington: Indiana University Press, pp. 18–36

George, N. (1988) *The Death of Rhythm and Blues*, London: Omnibus

Gilroy, P. (1987) *There Ain't No Black in the Union Jack: The Cultural Politics of Race and Nation*, London: Hutchinson

(1992) 'Cultural studies and ethnic absolutism', in L. Grossberg et al. (eds.) *Cultural Studies*, New York and London: Routledge, pp. 187–98

(1993) *Small Acts: Thoughts on the Politics of Black Cultures*, London: Serpent's Tail

Glanville, R. (1989) 'World music mining, the international trade in new music' in F. Hanly and T. May (eds.) *Rhythms of the World*, London: BBC Books, pp. 58–68

Goodwin, A. (1992) 'Rationalization and democratization in the new technologies of popular music', in J. Lull (ed.) *Popular Music and Communication* (2nd edn). Newbury Park, CA: Sage, pp. 75–100

—— (1993) *Dancing in the Distraction Factory: Music Television and Popular Culture*, London: Routledge

Goodwin, A. and Gore, J. (1990) 'World beat and the cultural imperialism debate', *Socialist Review* 20, pp. 63–80

Gottlieb, J. and Wald, G.(1994) 'Smells like teen spirit: riot grrrls, revolution and women in independent rock', in A. Ross and T. Rose (eds.) *Microphone Fiends: Youth Music and Youth Culture*, London: Routledge, pp. 250–74

Green, L. (1997) *Music, Gender, Education*, Cambridge: Cambridge University Press

Grenier, L. and Guilbault, J. (1997) 'Créolité and francophonie in music: socio-musical repositioning where it matters', *Cultural Studies* 11(2), pp. 207–34

Grossberg, L. (1992) *We Gotta Get Out of this Place: Popular Conservatism and Postmodern Culture*, London: Routledge

Guilbault, J. (1993a) 'On redefining the "local" through world music', *The World of Music* 35(2), pp. 33–47

—— (1993b) *Zouk: World Music in the West Indies*, Chicago: University of Chicago Press

Hall, S. (1988) 'New ethnicities', in K. Mercer (ed.) *Black Film, British Cinema*, London: BFI/ICA, pp. 27–31

Hall, S. and Jefferson, T. (eds.) (1976) *Resistance Through Rituals: Youth Subcultures in Postwar Britain*, London: Hutchinson

Hall, S. and Whannel, P. (1964) *The Popular Arts*, London: Hutchinson

Hamm, C. (1981) 'The Fourth Audience', *Popular Music* 1, Cambridge: Cambridge University Press, pp. 123–41

Haralambos, M. (1974) *Right On: From Blues to Soul in Black America*, London: Eddison Press

Harley, R. (1993) 'Beat in the system', in T. Bennett, S. Frith, L. Grossberg, J. Shepherd and G. Turner (eds.) *Rock and Popular Music: Politics, Policies, Institutions*, London: Routledge, pp. 210–30

Harvey, S. and Bates, P. (1993) 'Behind the groove', *DJ*, 'Disco Supplement' 84, 11–24 March, pp. 4–9

Hebdige, D. (1979) *Subculture: The Meaning of Style*, London: Methuen

—— (1987) *Cut 'n' Mix*. London: Comedia/Methuen

—— (1988) *Hiding in the Light*, London: Routledge

Hennion, A. (1989) 'An intermediary between production and consumption: the producer of popular music', *Science, Technology, and Human Values* 14 (4), pp. 400–24

—— (1990) 'The production of success: an antimusicology of the pop song', in S. Frith and A. Goodwin (eds.) *On Record: Rock, Pop and the Written Word*, New York/London: Pantheon/Routledge, pp. 185–206

Hirsch, P. M. (1972) 'Processing fads and fashions: an organization set analysis of cultural industry systems', *American Journal of Sociology* 77, pp. 639–59

Hoggart, R. (1957) *The Uses of Literacy*, London: Chatto and Windus

Hosokawa, S. (1984) 'The Walkman Effect', *Popular Music* 4, pp. 165–80

Hughes, D. (1964) 'Pop music', in D. Thompson (ed.) *Discrimination and Popular Culture*, Harmondsworth: Penguin

Johnson, J. H. (1995) *Listening in Paris: A Cultural History*, Berkeley: University of California Press

Jones, L. (1963) *Blues People: The Negro Experience in White America and the Music that Developed From It*, New York: Morrow Quill

Jones, M. (1998) 'Organising pop – why so few pop acts make pop music', PhD thesis, Institute of Popular Music, Liverpool University

Jones, S. (1992) *Rock Formation: Music, Technology, and Mass Communication*, Newbury Park, CA: Sage

Jordan, W. (1974) *The White Man's Burden: Historical Origins of Racism in the United States*, New York: Oxford University Press

Jowers, P. (1993) 'Beating new tracks: WOMAD and the British world music movement', in S. Miller (ed.) *The Last Post, Music After Modernism*, Manchester: Manchester University Press, pp. 52–87

Kealy, E. R. (1979) 'From craft to art: the case of sound mixers and popular music', *Sociology of Work and Occupations* 6(1), pp. 3–29

Keightley, K. (1996) ' "Turn it down!" she shrieked: gender, domestic space, and high fidelity, 1948–59', *Popular Music* 15(2), pp. 149–77

Keil, C.(1966) 'Motion and feeling through music', *Journal of Aesthetics and Art Criticism* 24, pp. 337–49

(1984) 'Music mediated and live in Japan', *Ethnomusicology* 28(1), pp. 91–6

(1994) ' "Ethnic" music traditions in the USA (black music; country music; others; all)', *Popular Music* 13(2), pp. 175–8

(1995) 'Transnational citizenship', a keynote address delivered at the annual meeting of the Sociology of Education Association, Monterey, California, February

Laguerre, M. (1997) *Transnational Diasporic Citizenship*, Berkeley: Institute of Governmental Studies, University of California

Laing, D. (1969) *The Sound of Our Time*, London: Head and Ward

(1985) *One Chord Wonders: Power and Meaning in Punk Rock*, Milton Keynes: Open University Press

(1994) '*Scrutiny* to subcultures: notes on literary criticism and popular music', *Popular Music* 13(2), pp. 179–90

Leonard, M. (1997) 'Rebel girl, you are the queen of my world: feminism, "subculture" and grrrl power', in S. Whiteley (ed.) *Sexing the Groove*, London: Routledge, pp. 230–55

(2000) 'Gender and the Music Industry: an analysis of the production and mediation of indie rock', PhD thesis, University of Liverpool

Leonard, M. and Cohen, S. forthcoming, 'Gender and sexuality', *Encyclopaedia of Popular Music of the World*, London: Cassell

Leppert, R. (1993) *The Sight of Sound: Music, Representation and the History of the Body*, Berkeley, Calif.: The University of California Press

Lipsitz, G. (1990) *Time Passages: Collective Memory and American Popular Culture*, Minneapolis: University of Minnesota Press

(1994) *Dangerous Crossroads: Popular Music, Postmodernism and the Poetics of Place*, London: Verso

Lott, E. (1993) *Love and Theft: Blackface Minstrelsy and the American Working Class*, New York: Oxford University Press

Malm, K. and Wallis, R. (1993) *Media Policy and Music Activity*, London: Routledge

Malone, B. (1985) *Country Music, U.S.A.* revd edn, Austin: University of Texas Press

Malone, J. (1996) *Steppin' On The Blues: The Visible Rhythms of African American Dance*, Urbana and Chicago: The University of Illinois Press

Manuel, P. (1993) *Cassette Culture: Popular Music and Technology in North India*, Chicago: University of Chicago Press

Marcus, G. (1977) *Mystery Train: Images of America in Rock'n'Roll Music*, New York: E. P. Dutton

Marsh, D. (1985) *The First Rock and Roll Confidential Report*, New York: Pantheon

Martin, L. and Segrave, K. (1993) *Anti-Rock: The Opposition to Rock'n'Roll*, New York: Da Capo

Maultsby, P. (1985) 'West African influences and retentions in US black music: a sociocultural study', in Irene Jackson (ed.) *More than Dancing: Essays on Afro-American Music and Musicians* (prepared under the auspices of the Center of Ethnic Music, Howard University) Westport, CT: Greenwood Press, pp. 25–58

(1990) 'Africanisms in African American music', in Joseph Holloway (ed.) *Africanisms in American Culture*, Bloomington: Indiana University Press, pp. 185–210

McClary, S. (1991) *Feminine Endings: Music, Gender and Sexuality*, Minneapolis: University of Minnesota Press

McClary, S. and Walser, R. (1990) 'Start making sense! Musicology wrestles with rock', in S. Frith and A. Goodwin (eds.) *On Record: Rock, Pop and the Written Word*, New York/London: Pantheon/Routledge, pp. 277–92

(1994) 'Theorizing the Body in African-American Music', *Black Music Research Journal* 14(1), Spring, pp. 75–84

McLuhan, E. and F. Zingrone (eds.) (1995) *Essential McLuhan*, Concord, Ontario: Anansi Press

Meintjes, L. (1990) 'Paul Simon's *Graceland*, South Africa, and the mediation of musical meaning', *Ethnomusicology* 34, pp. 37–73

Mellers, W. (1973) *Twilight of the Gods: The Beatles in Retrospect*, London: Faber

Middleton, R. (1990) *Studying Popular Music*, Buckingham: Open University Press

(1995) 'Authorship, gender and the construction of meaning in the Eurythmics' hit recordings', *Cultural Studies* 9(3), pp. 465–85

(ed.) (2000) *Reading Pop: Approaches to Textual Analysis in Popular Music*, Oxford: Oxford University Press

Mitchell, T. (1993) 'World music and the popular music industry: an Australian view', *Ethnomusicology* 37, pp. 309–37

Moore, A. (1993) *Rock: The Primary Text*, Milton Keynes: Open University Press

Morgan, E. (1975) *American Slavery, American Freedom: The Ordeal of Colonial Virginia*, New York: Norton

National Research Council (2000) *The Digital Dilemma: Intellectual Property in the Information Age*, Washington, DC: National Academy Press

Negus, K. (1992) *Producing Pop*, London: Edward Arnold

(1996) *Popular Music in Theory*, Cambridge: Polity

(1999) *Music Genres and Corporate Cultures*, London: Routledge

Nettleford, R. (1993) 'Introduction', in *Inward Stretch Outward Reach: A Voice from the Caribbean*, London: Macmillan Caribbean, ppvi–xiv

Omi, M. and Winant, G. H. (1986) *Racial Formation in the United States: From the 1960s to the 1980s* New York: Routledge and Kegan Paul

Opie, P. and I. (1985) *The Singing Game*, Oxford: Oxford University Press

Otis, J. (1993) *Upside Your Head: Rhythm and Blues on Central Avenue*, Hanover: Wesleyan and University Press of New England

Pacini, D. H. (1992) 'Bachata: from the margins to the mainstream', *Popular Music* 11(3), pp. 359–64

(1993) 'A view from the south: Spanish Caribbean perspectives on world beat', *The World of Music* 35(2), pp. 48–69

Pareles, J. (1987) 'Record-it-yourself music on cassette', *The New York Times*, 11 May, C13

Park, R. (1996) 'The city: suggestions for the investigation of human behaviour', in K. Gelder and S. Thornton (eds.) *The Subcultures Reader*, London: Routledge, pp. 16–27

Peatman, J. G. (1942–3) 'Radio and popular music', in P. F. Lazersfeld and F. Stanton (eds.), *Radio Research*, New York: Duell, Sloan and Pearce

Perry, S. (1988) 'Ain't no mountain high enough: the politics of crossover', in S. Frith (ed.) *Facing the Music*, New York: Pantheon Books, pp. 51–87

Peterson, R. A. (1978) 'Prof compares disco to jazz and rock eras', *Billboard*, 22 July, p. 61

(1997) *Creating Country Music: Fabricating Authenticity*, Chicago: University of Chicago Press

Pratt, R. (1990) *Rhythm and Resistance: Explorations in the Political Uses of Popular Music*, New York: Praeger

Radano, R. (1996) 'Denoting difference: the writing of the slave spirituals', *Critical Inquiry* 22(3), Spring, pp. 506–44

Reed, L. (1999) 'Peter Gabriel in conversation with Lou Reed', *Real World Notes* 8, Summer, Real World Holdings Ltd, pp. 4–6

Regev, M. (1986) 'The soundscape as a contest area: "oriental music" and Israeli popular music', *Media, Culture and Society* 8(3), pp. 343–55

Regis, H. A. (1988) 'Calypso, reggae and cultural imperialism by reexploration', *Popular Music and Society* 12, pp. 63–73

Reynolds, S. (1990) *Blissed Out: The Raptures of Rock*, London: Serpent's Tail

Reynolds, S. and Press, J. (1995) *The Sex Revolts: Gender, Rebellion and Rock'n'Roll*, London: Serpent's Tail

RIAA (Recording Industry Association of America) (2000) 'The recording industry association of America's 1999 consumer profile', web address: http//www.riaa.com

Riesman, D. (1990) 'Listening to popular music', in S. Frith and A. Goodwin (eds.) *On Record: Rock, Pop, and the Written Word*, New York/London: Pantheon/Routledge, pp. 5–13

Roediger, D. (1991) *The Wages of Whiteness: Race and the Making of the American Working Class*, New York: Verso

Rose, T. (1994) *Black Noise: Rap Music and Black Culture in Contemporary America*, Hanover, NH: Wesleyan University Press

Savage, J. (1991) *England's Dreaming*, London: Faber

Saxton, A. (1990) *The Rise and Fall of the White Republic: Class Politics and Mass Culture in Nineteenth-Century America*, New York: Verso

Schlemm, W. (1982) 'On the position of the 'Tonmeister' (sound recordist) in the musical communication process', in Kurt Blaukopf (ed.) *The Phonogram in Cultural Communication*, Vienna: Springer-Verlag

Schneider, A. (1991) 'Traditional music, pop and the problem of copyright protection', in M. P. Bauman (ed.) 'Music in the dialogue of cultures: traditional music and cultural policy', *International Music Studies* 2, Berlin: International Institute for Comparative Music Studies and Documentation, pp. 302–16

Shank, B. (1994) *Dissonant Identities: The Rock'n'Roll Scene in Austin, Texas*, Hanover, NH: Wesleyan University Press

　(1996) 'Fears of the white unconscious: music, race, and identification in the censorship of "Cop Killer"', *Radical History Review*, Fall, pp. 124–45

Sharpe, C. (1917) *Folk Songs from the Southern Appalachians*, London: Oxford University Press

Shepherd, J. (1982) 'A theoretical model for the socio-musicological analysis of popular musics', *Popular Music* 2, pp. 145–77

　(1991) *Music as Social Text*, Cambridge: Polity

　(1993) 'Music as cultural text', in J. Paynter et al. (eds.) *A Companion to Contemporary Musical Thought*, London: Routledge, pp. 128–55

Sheridan, M. (1993) 'Jamaica Brings Copyright Law in Step with Globe', *Billboard*, 11 September, 9, p. 80

Sievert, J. (1978) 'Les Paul', in J. Ferguson (ed.) *The Guitar Player Book*, New York: Grove

Simosko, V. (1990) 'World Music Appreciation: 1990', *The Bulletin of Canadian Folk Music*, 24, pp. 8–10

Sinclair, D. (1992) 'World music fests flourish in UK: WOMAD throwing 7 events this year', *Billboard* 104, p. 12 and p. 31

Starr, F. (1983) *Red and Hot: The Fate of Jazz in the Soviet Union*, Oxford: Oxford University Press

Stearns, M. and J. (1994) *Jazz Dance: The Story of American Popular Dance*, New York: Da Capo

Stibal, M. E. (1977) 'Disco: birth of a new marketing system', *Journal of Marketing*, October, pp. 82–8

Stowe, D. W. (1994) *Swing Changes: Big-Band Jazz in New Deal America*, Cambridge, Mass.: Harvard University Press

Strauss, D. (1999) 'I have seen the future of rock, and its . . . a shrubbery!', *The New York Observer*, 25 January, p. 42

Straw, W. (1991) 'Systems of articulation, logics of change: communities and scenes in popular music', *Cultural Studies* 5(3), pp. 368–88

　(1993) 'The booth, the floor and the wall: dance music and the fear of falling', *Public* 8, pp. 169–82

Street, J. (1986) *Rebel Rock: The Politics of Popular Music*, Oxford: Blackwell

Stuckey, S. (1987) *Slave Culture: Nationalist Theory and the Foundations of Black America*, New York: Oxford University Press

Tagg, P. (1982) 'Analysing popular music: theory, method and practice', *Popular Music* 2, pp. 37–67

(1989) 'Open letter: "black music", "Afro-American music" and "European music"', *Popular Music* 8(3), pp. 285–98

(1990), 'An anthropology of stereotypes in TV music?', *Svensk Tidskrift fur Musikforshning*, pp. 19–42

(1992) 'Towards a sign typology of music', in R. Dalmonte and M. Baroni (eds.) *Studi e Testi 1, Secondo Convegno Europeo di Analisi Musicale*, Trento, pp. 369–78

(1994) 'From refrain to rave: the decline of figure and the rise of ground', *Popular Music* 13(2), pp. 209–22

Tankel, J. D. (1990) 'The practice of recording music: remixing as recoding', *Journal of Communication* 40(3), Summer, pp. 34–46

Tate, G. (1992) 'Hardcore of darkness: Bad Brains', in *Flyboy in the Buttermilk: Essays on Contemporary America*, New York: Simon and Schuster, pp. 20–4

Taylor, C. (1996) 'Modern rock fans surprisingly affluent, study says', *Billboard*, 12 March, p. 72

Taylor, J. and Laing, D. (1979) 'Disco-pleasure-discourse: on rock and sexuality', *Screen Education* 31, pp. 43–8

Théberge, P. (1989) 'The "sound" of music: technological rationalization and the production of popular music', *New Formations* 8, Summer, pp. 99–111

(1997) *Any Sound You Can Imagine: Making Music/Consuming Technology*, Hanover, NH: Wesleyan University Press

Thornton, S. (1995) *Club Cultures: Music, Media and Subcultural Capital*, Cambridge: Polity Press

Wagner, A. (1997) *Adversaries of Dance: From the Puritans to the Present*, Urbana and Chicago: University of Illinois Press

Wallis, R. and Malm, K. (1984) *Big Sounds from Small Peoples*, New York/London: Pendragon/Constable

Walser, R. (1993) *Running with the Devil: Power, Gender, and Madness in Heavy Metal Music*, Hanover, NH: Wesleyan University Press

Wentz, B. (1991) 'It's a global village out there', *Downbeat* 58(4), p. 22

Wicke, P. (1985) 'Aesthetic aspects of rock music', paper presented to the Third International Conference of IASPM, Montreal

(1990) *Rock Music: Culture, Aesthetics and Sociology*, Cambridge: Cambridge University Press

Widgery, D. (1986) *Beating Time: Riot'n'Race'n'Rock'n'Roll*, London: Chatto and Windus

Williams, R. (1989) 'Culture is ordinary', in *Resources of Hope*, London: Verso, pp. 3–18

Willis, P. (1978) *Profane Culture*, London: Routledge and Kegan

Index